APPRECIATIVE INQUIRY
Handbook

The First in a Series of AI
Workbooks for
Leaders of Change

APPRECIATIVE INQUIRY
Handbook

The First in a Series of AI
Workbooks for
Leaders of Change

David L. Cooperrider, Ph.D.
Case Western Reserve University
Weatherhead School of Management

Diana Whitney, Ph.D.
Corporation for Positive Change
and Saybrook Graduate School and Research Center

Jacqueline M. Stavros, EDM
Lawrence Technological University
Graduate College of Management

Foreword by Ronald Fry

Crown Custom Publishing, Inc.
Brunswick, OH

BERRETT-KOEHLER PUBLISHERS, INC.
San Francisco

Co-published by Crown Custom Publishing, Inc. and
Berrett-Koehler Publishers, Inc.

Crown Custom Publishing, Inc.
1656 Pearl Road
Brunswick, Ohio 44212
(330) 273-4900
(877) 225-8820
www.crowncustompublishing.com

Berrett-Koehler Publishers, Inc.
235 Montgomery Street, Suite 650
San Francisco, CA 94104-2916
(415) 288-0260 Fax: (415) 362-2512
Toll-free orders: (800) 929-2929
www.bkconnection.com

Ordering Information

Individual sales: This book can be ordered direct from either Crown Custom
Publishing, Inc., or Berrett-Koehler Publishers at the addresses above.

Quantity sales: Special discounts are available on quantity purchases by corporations, associations, and others. For details, contact either Crown Custom
Publishing, Inc., or Berrett-Koehler Publishers at the addresses above.

Orders for college textbook/course adoption use: Please contact Crown Custom
Publishing, Inc. at (877) 225-8820.

Orders by U.S. trade bookstores and wholesalers: Please contact Publishers
Group West, 1700 Fourth Street, Berkeley, CA 94710. Tel: (510) 528-1444;
Fax: (510) 528-3444.

ISBN 1-57675-269-0
Printed in the United States of America

Library of Congress Cataloging-in-Publication Data
First Edition   10 9 8 7 6 5 4 3 2 1

Production Coordinator: Carl L. Wirick
Copyediting: Marianne Miller
Proofreading: Sue Henderson
Cover design: James Fedor
Interior design/production: Tia Andrako, LA graphics, Ltd.

Books in the Appreciative Inquiry Workbook Series

Mission Statement

This book is the first in a series of workbooks intended for practitioners of planned change. In its most practical construction, Appreciative Inquiry is a form of organizational study that selectively seeks to locate, highlight, and illuminate the "life-giving" forces of an organization's existence. The Appreciative Inquiry Workbook series provides a practical foundation and tools for such planned change.

This book, of course, is the foundational piece of the series. While broad in scope and inclusive of theoretical underpinnings of the field, it also seeks to provide pragmatic tools in Parts II and III that can be used to conduct an Appreciative Inquiry intervention. Other entries in the series will be designed to build upon the book in two distinct ways:

1. Add in-depth examinations of and worksheets for each separate component of the fully implemented Appreciative Inquiry process, including:
   - Discovery: asking the "positive question" (see *Encyclopedia of Positive Questions*, Vol. One, 2002)
   - Dream: the visioning process
   - Design: steps to create the ideal system for the organization
   - Destiny: sustaining an appreciative environment
   - The AI Summit: using the Appreciative Inquiry process for large-scale organization transformation.

2. Illustrate applications of Appreciative Inquiry to different organizational types and different organizational or cultural settings:
   - Large corporations
   - NGOs—Non-government organizations
   - Global organizations
     (see Gibbs-Mahé, *Birth of a Global Community: Appreciative Inquiry in Action*, 2003)
   - Educational institutions
   - Governmental organizations

The hallmark of each of these series entries will be that they are: a) applied and experiential; and b) rich in forms, surveys, and other tools likely to be of assistance to those who "want to know how."; c) brief, cogent, and terse in their delivery (i.e., under 350 pages).

These brief books are written for life-long leaders and learners of change. These books are written by Appreciative Inquiry theorists and practitioners interested in sharing their models, approaches, programs, resources, and tools to facilitate Appreciative Inquiry initiatives.

David L. Cooperrider, Ph.D.
Diana Whitney, Ph.D.
Jacqueline M. Stavros, EDM
Ronald Fry, Ph.D.
Amanda Trosten-Bloom

Contents

PART 1 **Essential Elements of Appreciative Inquiry**

PART 2 **Application of the 4-D Cycle of Appreciative Inquiry**

PART 3 **Learning Applications and Resources**

Detailed Contents

PART 2   Application of the 4-D Cycle of Appreciative Inquiry

Chapter 4: Discovery: *What Gives Life?*

Chapter 5: Dream: *What Might Be?*

Chapter 6: Design: *How Can It Be?*

List of Tables, Figures, and Exhibits

Foreword

"Be the change you want to see in the world."
—Gandhi

As I was sitting among five hundred participants in the First International Conference on Appreciative Inquiry in October, 2001, in Baltimore, I was witnessing a real turning point, a peak moment in my decade of involvement with the development and application of a theory now known as Appreciative Inquiry (AI). What I remember most vividly was the contagious sense of energy and shared aspiration in that large ballroom to "be the future we most hope and pray for." Coming so soon after the September 11 events in the United States, the opportunity to have healthy conversations about the possibility of business-as-an-agent-for-world-benefit was not only sane-making, it resulted in what felt like a quantum leap in momentum toward a collective wish to make a positive difference in the world with the help of the AI approach.

Now, with the publication of this book, I am experiencing another high point in this adventure with AI which I fondly refer to as "Magnifying the Momentum." I have borrowed this phrase from the MBA students at the Weatherhead School of Management. They used it to summarize their highest hopes for a schoolwide strategic planning process, a process they were launching with an "AI summit" to discover the best of our school's past and core principles to preserve as input to a strategic planning process involving all stakeholder groups. My deep hope and confident assertion is that the resources provided in this volume can only magnify that momentum toward positive change for business and society that I felt in Baltimore that October to involve more and more people—(practical scholars and scholarly practitioners, servant leaders and innovative followers, change agents and stewards, protagonists and antagonists) in being with each other to bring about positive change to make our boldest dreams of individual, organizational, and global well-being become reality.

The resources brought forth in this book are truly a bounty. I expect you, the reader, no matter your prior experience with AI ideas and processes, will want to reference it again and again as you uncover the wealth of guidance and information offered here. From multiple design agendas to introduce AI to detailed stories about AI interventions, from abstract principles underlying AI to actual worksheets used in different settings, from lecture notes to practical tips and guidelines, and from interview guides to actual overheads and slides you can adapt, the authors have amassed in one place, for the first time, all of the foundation concepts, examples, and aids necessary to engage yourself and others in AI.

The fact that David, Diana, and Jackie have produced this volume is noteworthy on several fronts. First, as they make clear in the early pages, this is the work of many voices. The spirit of inclusion and the centrifugal pattern of ever-expanding involvement of voices in an AI process are mirrored in the recognition of the contributors. This book brings as much as possible from what has been tried and learned about AI over the past decade into the "commons," thereby creating learning opportunities for even more voices from here on. Related to this is my strong sense that the publication of this volume asserts another important value embedded in AI, that of generosity. The authors here, in the name of a host of additional contributors, have generously given us a wealth of information, artfully assembled for accessibility and application, that in most other settings or disciplines would be accessible only through the legal minefields of patents, trademarks, and proprietary debates. What I am trying to express is that there is a wholeheartedness to this publication that accompanies the technical matter. Generosity is praised in all spiritual traditions around the globe. In Tibetan Buddhism, for example, it is one of the six perfections—a practice for the benefit of others in order to attain enlightenment. I see the giving of this book as a similar gesture. We all gain in our personal and professional endeavors by the unconditional sharing of that which we most value and believe can benefit others. The author team also merits my recognition and gratitude. As a former student and long-time friend and colleague, David models the consistent "be-ing" of AI like no other. As many of us can attest, being in his presence is inspiring—always. Diana is my "champion for change." Her passion for being (versus doing) AI and her unrelenting courage to try out new things result in a unique sense of "compelling grace" I experience when working with her. In Jackie, David and Diana have found the "glue" to bring everything together. She brings the crucial element of continuity to the team and to the text. From assembled pages of varying form, she has been invaluable in writing and creating linkages and bridges so the reader can absorb both the breadth and depth of this material. In this case, she is the link between theory and practice.

Finally, I will risk to speak for all the voices represented in the words and works included in this book by saying there is absolute agreement that AI is not a fixed method or "tool kit" as the term "book" might imply. Let the contents of this book be a palate of colors from which you create your painting. Take the 4-D model for instance. Our colleagues, Jane Watkins and Bernard Mohr, add a "definition" phase to make it five Ds. Another colleague, Mac O'Dell added, "dancing and drumming" after his experiences using AI with women in Nepalese villages. Embrace this book as a reference guide to provide the confidence and platform for you to experiment and discover what factors, designs, questions, interview guides, and so on, "give life" to the very best in human connection and positive social transformations. To return to the message in Gandhi's quote, the practice of Appreciative Inquiry is much more about a way of being—a holistic posture of standing in front of a situation (of engaging with others) with the will and curiosity to look into what there is to be valued in order to imagine most boldly what is possible for the future. The will to look for the best of what is will be reciprocated in mutual recognition and positive human connections. The curiosity will reveal new ideas and exciting experiments. These are the true gifts of AI and the generous offering of this book.

Ronald Fry
Weatherhead School of Management
Case Western Reserve University
Cleveland, Ohio
Spring 2003

Preface

Appreciative Inquiry: A Powerful Positive Revolution in Change

This book is an invitation to an imaginative and fresh perception of organizations and the process through which they change. Its "metacognitive" stance is choicefully affirmative. Its central thesis—as an extension of the Lewinian premise that human action depends on the world as constructed rather than the world as it is—is pragmatic and hopeful. It teaches how to build and sustain an organization from the positive core. It offers a fresh approach to using the contributions of any and all stakeholders to design and redesign the systems within organizations for a more effective and sustainable future.

In its most practical construction, Appreciative Inquiry (also referred to as AI) is a form of transformational inquiry that selectively seeks to locate, highlight, and illuminate the "life-giving" forces of an organization's existence. It is based on the belief that human systems are made and imagined by those who live and work within them. AI leads these systems to move toward the creative images that reside in the positive core of an organization. This approach is based on solid proven principles for enabling creativity, knowledge, and spirit in the workplace. These principles call people to work towards a common vision and a higher purpose.

AI seeks out the best of "what is" to help ignite the collective imagination of "what might be." The aim is to generate new knowledge that expands the "realm of the possible" and helps members of an organization envision a collectively desired future. Furthermore, it helps to implement vision in ways that successfully translate images of possibilities into reality and belief into practice. The methodology results in a win-win situation.

This book provides a comprehensive presentation, the theory and the practical application of AI methods. Theories and activities in this book have been developed from the work of small and large corporations and international organizations working on issues of sustainable development. Research on AI has been conducted in organizations in over one hundred countries around the world.

Material in this book is designed to facilitate theoretical understanding and the effective use of AI by organization leaders, managers, members, and consultants. This book is the first volume in an ongoing series. It contains everything needed to plan, design, and lead an AI initiative. We invite readers to adapt it to their needs, in accordance with the copyright guidelines.

As Goethe reminds us, "Whatever you can do or dream you can, begin it. Boldness has genius, power and magic in it." What are you waiting for? Go for it!

David L. Cooperrider, Diana Whitney and Jacqueline M. Stavros
February 2003

Acknowledgments

We would like to thank the following people who have contributed to the creation and content of this first Appreciative Inquiry Book. From the Appreciative Inquiry Consulting Founders Alliance are Frank Barrett, Steve Cato, David Chandler, Joep de Jong, Marsha George, Mette Jacobsgaard, Jackie Kelm, Ralph Kelly, Jim Lord, Jim Ludema, Ada Jo Mann, Adrian McLean, Bernard Mohr, Ravi Pradhan, Anne Radford, Diane Robbins, Judy Rodgers, Marge Schiller, Barbara Sloan, and Jane Watkins.

Other colleagues and friends who contributed resources to this book include Stan Baran, Gervase Bush, Diane Ruiz Cairns, John Carter, Dawn Cooperrider Dole, Ronald Fry, Pamela Johnson, Ed and Martha Kimball, Jason Kirk, Anne Kohnke Meda, Claudia Leibler, Mary Grace-Neville, Karla Phlypo, Charleysee Pratt, Thomas Price, Maryanne Rainey, Tony Silbert, Leslie Sekerka, Suresh Srivastva, Paul Stavros, Amanda Trosten-Bloom, Rita Williams, and Susan O. Wood.

Our clients have contributed to this book in ways visible and subtle. At each of these organizations, hundreds if not thousands of people deserve credit. We are grateful to many people from the following organizations who provided insights, examples, and tools:

- Avon – Mexico
- British Airways
- Canadian Tire
- Cleveland Clinic
- DTE Energy Services
- Fairmount North America
- FCI Automotive
- GTE Telecommunications
- Hunter Douglas Window Fashions Division
- Imagine Chicago
- Imagine Nagaland (India)
- Lawrence Technological University
- Lovelace Health Systems
- McDonald's
- Myrada
- NASA
- North American Steel, Inc.
- Nutrimental
- Princeton Group Health
- Roadway Express
- Save the Children (Zimbabwe, Africa)
- Scandinavian School System
- Syntegra
- Tendercare, Inc.
- United Religions Initiative
- United States Agency for International Development
- United States Navy
- World Vision Relief and Development

And finally, we thank our families and friends for their support and patience during this adventurous journey.

With loving appreciation,
David, Diana, and Jackie

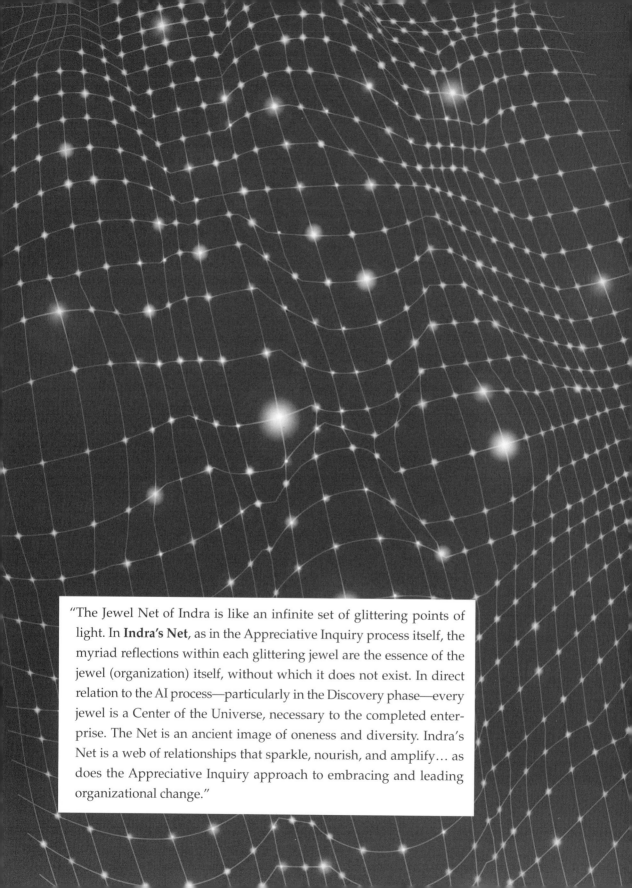

"The Jewel Net of Indra is like an infinite set of glittering points of light. In **Indra's Net**, as in the Appreciative Inquiry process itself, the myriad reflections within each glittering jewel are the essence of the jewel (organization) itself, without which it does not exist. In direct relation to the AI process—particularly in the Discovery phase—every jewel is a Center of the Universe, necessary to the completed enterprise. The Net is an ancient image of oneness and diversity. Indra's Net is a web of relationships that sparkle, nourish, and amplify… as does the Appreciative Inquiry approach to embracing and leading organizational change."

Introduction

Welcome to *Appreciative Inquiry Handbook,* the comprehensive resource manual for learning and creating an AI initiative. This material is usable as is or may be customized to meet specific needs. This section of the book will:

- Provide background information about AI.
- Describe the contents of this book.
- Set the stage for launching an AI initiative.

The Focus of Appreciative Inquiry

AI is an exciting way to embrace organizational change. Its assumption is simple: Every organization has something that works right—things that give it life when it is most alive, effective, successful, and connected in healthy ways to its stakeholders and communities. AI begins by identifying what is positive and connecting to it in ways that heighten energy and vision for change.

AI begins an adventure. Its call to adventure has been experienced by many people and organizations, and it will take many more to fully explore this new paradigm. These people and organizations sense an exciting direction in our language and theories of change; they sense an invitation to "a positive revolution."

The words *positive revolution* were first used by GTE to describe the impact of years of work creating an organization in full voice, a center stage for a positive revolution. Based on significant and measurable changes in stock prices, morale survey measures, quality/customer relations, union-management relations, and so on, GTE's whole system change initiative was given professional recognition by the American Society for Training and Development (ASTD). It won the 1997 ASTD award for best organization change program in the country. AI was cited as the backbone of that change.

Approach of the Handbook

This book provides an approach to launching an AI Initiative. It is written to help people and their organizations take a long-term view of current activities and to achieve positive results by involving stakeholders. AI has proven to be a positive experience of a new way of living and organizing at work. Through the 4-D Cycle, people can transform the present state of their organization into a future state by building on a "positive core" of strengths to create its destiny.

AI is an engaging participative process that, once begun, moves quickly to remarkable results.

This book details the transformational process to design, lead, and implement an AI Initiative anywhere in the organization. It starts with an appreciative interview, by asking four simple but powerful questions:

1. Describe a high-point experience in your organization, a time when you were most alive and engaged.

2. Without being modest, what is it that you most value about yourself, your work, and your organization?

3. What are the core factors that give life to your organization, without which the organization would cease to exist?

4. Assume you go into a deep sleep tonight, one that lasts ten years. But while you are asleep, powerful and positive changes take place, real miracles happen, and your organization becomes what you want it to be. Now you awaken and go into the organization. It is 2013 and you are very proud of what you see. As you take in this vision and look at the whole, what do you see happening that is new, changed, better, or effective and successful?

These questions start a dialogue to discover and dream a new, more compelling image of the organization and its future. From anecdotal images, the future of the human systems within the organization is designed, and the organization moves toward its destiny.

An AI Initiative is more than just a training program. It is an opportunity to create an exciting and dynamic organization. AI recognizes that every organization is an open system that depends on its human capital to bring its vision and purpose to life. AI focuses on what gives life to an organization's system when it is operating at its best. An organization will cease to exist without a human system to lead and support it. AI identifies and leverages the positive core of an organization to ensure its ongoing success.

The outcome of an AI Initiative is a long-term positive change in the organization. AI has helped many organizations increase employee satisfaction, enhance productivity, increase levels of communications among stakeholders, decrease turnover, stimulate creativity and align the whole organization around its vision, mission, objectives, and strategies. AI is applicable to any profit, non-profit, or governmental organization.

Business leaders need to move away from the traditional problem-solving approach to organizational change and toward viewing organizations as a mystery to be embraced. AI provides a fresh approach to organizational change that motivates all stakeholders to contribute to the organization. When an organization uses AI to solve problems, create opportunities, make decisions, and initiate action, the whole system works toward a shared vision.

AI is a powerful tool. The process is simple, yet it can engage everyone in the organization. Through collaborative inquiry and a connection to their positive core, many organizations have co-created whole systems to:

- Create a common-ground vision and strategy for the future.
- Accelerate organizational learning—speeding the spread of innovation and amplifying the power of even the smallest victories.
- Unite labor and management in new, jointly envisioned partnerships.
- Create dialogue to foster shared meanings.
- Improve communications.
- Strengthen implementations of major information technology changes.
- Demonstrate positive intent and trust with stakeholders.
- Build high-performance teams to facilitate change.

AI can revitalize virtually every process or program that may have been deficit-based, such as quality programs, focus groups, surveys, reengineering efforts, and more. AI is important because it works to bring the whole organization together to build upon its positive core. AI encourages people to work together to promote a better understanding of the human system, the heartbeat of the organization.

AI Insight

Appreciative Inquiry can get you much better results than seeking out and solving problems. That's an interesting concept for me—and I imagine for most of you—because telephone companies are among the best problem solvers in the world. We troubleshoot everything. We concentrate enormous resources on correcting problems that have relatively minor impact on our overall service performance.... when used continually and over a long period of time, this approach can lead to a negative culture. If you combine a negative culture with all the challenges we face today, it could be easy to convince ourselves that we have too many problems to overcome—to slip into a paralyzing sense of hopelessness.

And yet if we flip the coin, we have so much to be excited about. We are in the most dynamic and most influential business of our times. We ought to be excited, motivated, and energized. We can be if we just turn ourselves around and start looking at our jobs (and ourselves) differently—if we kill negative self-talk and celebrate our successes. If we dissect what we do right and apply the lessons to what we do wrong, we can solve our problems and re-energize the organization at the same time.... In the long run, what is likely to be more useful: Demoralizing a successful workforce by concentrating on their failures or helping them over their last few hurdles by building a bridge with their successes?

Don't get me wrong. I'm not advocating mindless happy talk. Appreciative Inquiry is a complex science designed to make things better. We can't ignore problems. We just need to approach them from the other side.

Thomas H. White
President, GTE Telephone Operations
Vital Speeches of the Day, 1996

Hundreds of organizations are embracing this positive revolution through AI. Table 1.1 highlights some of these organizations and their initiatives.

Table 1.1 Appreciative Inquiry Initiatives

Organization	AI Initiative/Award
Avon–Mexico	To address the issue of gender equity and a pilot project for Avon globally. Catalyst Award for Best Place to Work in the Country for Women 1997.
British Airways North America	To create and sustain delivery of "Excellence in Customer Service."
Cleveland Clinic	To discover what makes the clinic function successfully (first AI Initiative).
DTE Energy Services	To have the employees create a culture of choice.
FCI Automotive	To improve supply chain management and inventory quality.
Group Health Cooperative	To improve the performance of the health care delivery system in the areas of cost, quality, and service.
GTE Telecommunications	Best Organization Change Project Award from the American Society of Training and Development, 1997.
Hunter Douglas Window Fashions Division	To create a shared vision and reinstill the "positive core" factors (creativity, flexibility, intimacy, and sense of community) that had contributed to the division's original success, while building leadership within the organization that is sustainable.
Imagine Chicago	To discover the hopes and sense of community in a major city. This was the first use of AI intergenerational interviews where young people interviewed the elders. Imagine Chicago has received many awards and today is helping to spawn "Imagine" projects.

Organization	AI Initiative/Award
Imagine Nagaland (India)	To bring various ministries together with young people to discover the future they wanted to create. UNICEF helped guide the project, and a major film producer created a movie documentary showing the movement from hopelessness and conflict to new vision and collaboration.
Lawrence Technological University	To identify the core values of the university to support the strategic plan.
Lovelace Health Systems	To improve nursing retention.
McDonald's	To become the best employer in each community around the world by putting "People First."
Myrada	To build capacity within a network of Southern India NGOs.
NASA	To create a strategic plan for OHR division to align with larger NASA vision and to work to build a more inclusive participative culture.
North American Steel, Inc.	To celebrate its fortieth year anniversary. To tap into the positive core of their history and use the information for strategic planning, 250 factory workers and managers were interviewed.
Nutrimental	To create an innovative whole-system approach to strategic planning and decision making to achieve qualitative and quantitative outcomes; for example, a 600 percent increase in profits as well as a 75 percent reduction in absenteeism rates. The company has used the AI Summit method to do strategic planning for the past six years.
Princeton Group Health	To bring 500 medical people together, including doctors, nurses, administrators, union leaders, patients, and many others for whole system planning by using AI and Future Search.
Roadway Express	To engage its unionized workforce into strategizing about the company's future.

Organization	AI Initiative/Award
Save the Children	To change how the organization could be re-created and led to achieve and sustain its mission.
Scandinavian School System	Award for Educational Achievement, 1998.
Star Island Corporation	To obtain widespread, substantial involvement in the strategic planning system by including the Star Community in the process.
Syntegra – 109	To build a new leadership team and strategy to approach and service its market.
Tendercare, Inc.	To identify the positive care core to increase census while placing the residents in the center of the circle of quality care.
United Religions Initiative	To create a global interfaith organization dedicated to peace and cooperation among people of different religions, faiths, and spiritual traditions.
US Agency for International Development (USAID)	To offer innovative management and leadership training to PVOs and to understand how NGOs could build their capacities.
United States Navy	To create enlightened leadership at every level of the Navy. The Navy brought together admirals and sailors at every level for an AI Summit that included over 250 people. A film was created of the event and now AI Summits have occurred throughout the Navy, including the entire Pacific Fleet.
World Vision Relief and Development	To build collaborative alliances to bring help and developmental assistance to thousands of children in hundreds of orphanages across the country in Romania. Over 300 organizations were connected in a positive change partnership, building on a strength-based analysis of each. Many papers were written about the effort, making possible the new "knowledge alliance" and resulting in millions of dollars in medical support.

Structure of the Book

AI Insight

AI was used in 1980, when David Cooperrider, a young doctoral student at Case Western Reserve University, was helping Al Jensen do his dissertation on physician leadership at one of the top tertiary care medical centers in the world, the Cleveland Clinic. They asked physician leaders to tell stories of their biggest successes as well as their biggest failures. But when David Cooperrider looked at the data, he was drawn only to the success stories. Listening to their narratives of strength and strong leadership, he was amazed by the level of positive cooperation, innovation, and egalitarian governance at the clinic—when it was most effective. With the intellectual collaborations and prodding of his advisor, Suresh Srivastva, and the permission of the clinic's chair, David decided to look at the data only in search of the positives—everything that served to give life to the system and to people when they were most alive, effective, committed, empowered, and so on. Everything else was considered irrelevant. The method of analysis was to systematically and deliberately appreciate everything of value and then use the positive analysis to speculate on the potentials and possibilities for the future. An anticipatory theory of future possibility was created, and momentous stories were used to make vivid the potentials. History was used as a source of positive possibility. In a report to the board of governors, Cooperrider and Srivastva called their method Appreciative Inquiry (AI). This was the first organizational analysis using AI. The results of the study created such a powerful positive stir that the board requested this AI method be used at all levels of the 8000-person organization to facilitate change. Cooperrider wrote his dissertation on the whole process and created a scholarly logic for this, a new form of action research. This experience set the stage for the AI learning community!

To facilitate conceptual understanding and effective practical use of AI, the material in the book is presented in three parts. **Part I: Essential Elements of Appreciative Inquiry** provides a simple but powerful learning approach to: (1) understanding basic AI principles, (2) selecting an affirmative topic to build on from the positive core, and (3) starting an AI initiative. The material presented in this section is a call to working with people, groups and organizations in a more positive, collaborative, and constructive approach than perhaps they have utilized in the past. It provides all of the essential elements to start a "positive revolution."

The 4-D appreciative learning model is the focus of **Part II: Application of the 4-D Cycle of Appreciative Inquiry**. The process is dynamic and interactive. It builds upon imagination and flexibility for its success. It starts with

Discovery. At this stage, the "best of what is" in a system is identified as the positive core. The second stage is Dream. This stages teaches a visioning process to suggest "what might be." The third stage is Design. The Design chapter outlines the steps to create the ideal system for an organization. It builds upon the positive core and the envisioned results of the first two stages. It allows for co-constructing the ideal design, "how it can be." The final stage is Destiny. This chapter covers the implementation and model for sustaining an appreciative learning environment, "what will be." Thus, Part II moves through discovery, dream, design, and destiny. The tools needed for an AI initiative or training program are included in **Part 3: Learning Applications and Resources**. A glossary, index, acronyms, and a list of additional resources are also included.

Audience

This book is for trainers, executives, consultants, and students who want to be catalysts for organizational and social change. AI has been used by senior executives, line and staff managers, specialists in human resources and organizational development, leaders of nongovernmental organizations, and union management teams. The book is designed for those familiar with AI and its potential, as well as for those just beginning to explore the possibilities of AI.

Because the AI focus is innovation and creativity, its effectiveness is not limited to organizations of a particular type, size, demographic, or industry. It has been effective with for-profit and nonprofit organizations alike and works equally well at all levels of the organization. AI is ideal for anyone who wants to be part of a positive revolution in change.

What's in This Book?

This book contains the following:
- 11 chapters of text material and resources
- An exciting selection of AI topic choices, interview guides, reports, and cases
- AI reference and bibliography list
- "Appreciative Insights" by AI users
- A master set of overheads
- Contact information
- Sample participant handouts
- Course outlines
- Detailed description of the 4-D Cycle: Discovery, Dream, Design, and Destiny
- Customizable training workshops

- A series of original classic, published articles on AI
- A Glossary of Terms
- An invitation to be a member of Appreciative Inquiry Consulting, LLC (AIC)

This book contains everything needed to understand the principles of AI and how they apply. It includes a complete set of tools to design and deliver AI initiatives as well as detailed instructions and agendas for setting up multiple types of AI sessions:

- One-Hour AI Introduction
- Two-Hour Executive Overview
- Four-Hour Introductory Meeting
- Two-Day AI Program, plus Detailed Project Plan
- Detailed Project Plan

Each of these sessions can be used by itself or in combination with a planned initiative. Although this book covers a lot of material, it is not exhaustive. The reader is encouraged to develop an appreciative learning library (refer to Bibliography).

How to Use This Book

This book contains everything needed to launch an AI initiative—background information on the topic, sample project plans, designs, agendas and interview guides, overheads, participant worksheets, and resources.

Before starting an AI initiative, it is recommended that the reader review the structure and content of the entire book in order to understand the complete process. **Chapter 3, Introducing, Defining, and Planning an Appreciative Inquiry Initiative**, provides several illustrations and agendas that can help in designing a project plan. **Part 2: Application of the 4-D Cycle of Appreciative Inquiry**, goes into chapter-by-chapter depth to fully explain each phase: Discovery, Dream, Design, and Destiny. More information about AI is available in books, newsletters, articles and web sites cited in the Bibliography.

AI is a robust intervention that can be molded to fit any organization's situation. While the reader or organization is going through the process, comparing **Part 2** and **Part 3** may help show how various organizations have used AI. However, the examples in the book are just that—examples. Creativity and innovation in developing or modifying the existing materials is encouraged.

This book is designed for the novice as well as the experienced AI practitioner. For those just starting out, developing the first AI intervention will likely prove to be a time-consuming task. Sufficient time must be allowed to prepare and modify the plan. New practitioners should be patient and flexible and experience fun in embracing change. Experienced users will find this book a useful reference for further developing their AI initiatives.

How Can AI Make a Difference?

This book is not a recipe; it is an adventure. AI is an effective way to get members of an organization involved to unleash a positive revolution in today's dynamic global environment. The objectives of the book are to teach the founding principles and theories of AI, present a wide range of applications of the theory, and to facilitate the training of trainers to introduce and use AI. Therefore, the final section of this book includes resources to facilitate group teaching.

An organization's guiding force is its people. The book offers those people a framework for an appreciative learning journey that has proven successful for cocreating organizational systems.

Where Can AI Make a Difference?

AI can make a difference with a single person or with any collective human system. To illustrate, AI has been successfully used in the following ways:

- Innovations toward the ideal organization
- Strategic planning
- Leadership and management development
- Work process redesign
- Team development
- Organizational culture change
- Employee development
- HR practices: staffing, orientation, and performance management
- Communications
- Collaborative alliances and joint ventures
- Community relations and customer relations
- Diversity initiatives
- Focus groups
- Generative benchmarking
- Surveys
- Meetings
- Evaluation to valuation of performance systems

AI is a new paradigm for accelerating organizational learning and transformation. It can be used in any situation where the leaders and consultants are committed to building positive, life-centered organizations.

We are ready to begin the journey.

PART 1

Essential Elements of
Appreciative Inquiry

1

The Theoretical Basis of Appreciative Inquiry

Ap-pre'ci-ate, *v.*, *1. to value; recognize the best in people or the world around us; affirm past and present strengths, successes, and potentials; to perceive those things that give life (health, vitality, excellence) to living systems. 2. to increase in value, e.g., the economy has appreciated in value. Synonyms: value, prize, esteem, and honor.*

In-quire' *(kwir), v., 1. to explore and discover. 2. to ask questions; to be open to seeing new potentials and possibilities. Synonyms: discover, search, systematically explore, and study.*

This chapter begins by introducing the theory and creation of Appreciative Inquiry (AI). AI is an organization development (OD) process that grows out of social constructionist thought and its applications to management and organizational transformation. Through its deliberately positive assumptions about people, organizations, and relationships, AI leaves behind deficit-oriented approaches to management and vitally transforms the ways to approach questions of organizational improvement. Such questions include culture change, survey analysis, strategic planning, organizational learning, customer focus groups, leadership development, team building, quality management, measurement systems, joint ventures and alliances, diversity training, performance appraisal, communications programs, internal on-line networks, corporate history writing, and others.

Presented here is a thesis, a proposition regarding the future of OD. It is a significant shift from "traditional" problem-solving methodologies. AI exhibits embedded wisdom that is reminiscent of early pioneers such as Kurt Lewin, Mary Parker Follett, Herb Shepard, and others. The thesis might be summarized this way:

> We may have reached the end of problem solving. AI is a powerful approach to transformation as a mode of inquiry capable of inspiring, mobilizing, and sustaining human system change. The future of OD belongs, instead, to methods that affirm, compel, and accelerate anticipatory learning involving larger and larger levels of collectivity.

The new methods are distinguished by the art and science of asking powerful and unconditional *positive* questions. (Someday there will be an "encyclopedia of questions" that brings together classic formulations like Maslow's interview protocols on peak human experience and Peters and Waterman's studies of organizational excellence or like Vereena Kast's exceptional studies of joy, inspiration, and hope.) The new methods view realities as socially constructed. They will, therefore, become more radically relational, widening the circles of dialogue to groups of hundreds, thousands, and perhaps (with cyberspace) millions. The arduous task of intervention will give way to the speed of imagination and innovation. Instead of negation, criticism, and spiraling diagnoses, there will be discovery, dream, design, and destiny.

AI: A Brief Introduction

AI has been described in many ways. Here is a practitioner-oriented definition:

> *Appreciative Inquiry is the cooperative co-evolutionary search for the best in people, their organizations, and the world around them. It involves the discovery of what gives "life" to a living system when it is most effective, alive, and constructively capable in economic, ecological, and human terms. AI involves the art and practice of asking questions that strengthen a system's capacity to apprehend, anticipate, and heighten positive potential. The inquiry is mobilized through the crafting of the "unconditional positive question," often involving hundreds or thousands of people. AI interventions focus on the speed of imagination and innovation—instead of the negative, critical, and spiraling diagnoses commonly used in organizations. The discovery, dream, design, and destiny model links the energy of the positive core to changes never thought possible.*

AI is based on the simple assumption that every organization has something that works well and these strengths can be the starting point for creating positive change. Inviting people to participate in dialogues and share stories about their past and present achievements, assets, unexplored potentials, innovations, strengths, elevated thoughts, opportunities, benchmarks, high-point moments, lived values, traditions, core and distinctive competencies, expressions of wisdom, insights into the deeper corporate spirit and soul, and visions of valued and possible futures can identify a "positive change core." From this, AI links the energy of the positive core directly to any change agenda. This link creates energy and excitement and a desire to move toward a shared dream.

AI, an approach to organizational analysis and learning, is intended for discovering, understanding, and fostering innovations in social organizational arrangements and processes. In this context, AI refers to two things:

- A search for knowledge
- A theory of collective action designed to evolve the vision and will of a group, an organization, or a society as a whole

AI is deliberate in its life-centric search. Carefully constructed inquiries allow the practitioner to affirm the symbolic capacities of imagination and mind as well as the social capacity for conscious choice and cultural evolution. The art of appreciation is the art of discovering and valuing those factors that give life to a group or an organization. The process involves interviewing and storytelling to draw out the best of the past and set the stage for effective visualization of the future.

The following propositions underlie the practice of AI:

1. **Inquiry into "the art of the possible" in organizational life should begin with appreciation.** Every system works to some degree. Therefore, a primary task of management and organizational analysis is to discover, describe, and explain those "exceptional moments" that give life to the system and activate members' competencies and energies. The appreciative approach takes its inspiration from "what is." This is the first step of the process in the 4-D Cycle: *Discovery*. Valuing, learning, and inspired understanding are the aims of the appreciative spirit.

2. **Inquiry into what is possible should yield information that is applicable.** Organizational study should lead to the generation of knowledge that can be used, applied, and validated in action.

3. **Inquiry into what is possible should be provocative.** An organization is an open-ended, indeterminate system capable of becoming more than it is at any given moment and learning how to take part actively in guiding its own evolution. Appreciative knowledge of "what is" becomes provocative to the extent that the learning stirs members to action. In this way, AI allows use of systematic management analysis to help the organization's members shape an effective future according to their own imaginative and moral purposes.

4. **Inquiry into the human potential of organizational life should be collaborative.** This principle assumes an immutable relationship between the process of inquiry and its content. A unilateral approach to the study of social innovation is a direct negation of the phenomenon itself.

In its most practical construction, AI is a form of organizational study that selectively seeks to locate, highlight, and illuminate what are referred to as the "life-giving" forces of the organization's existence, its *positive core*.

In this sense, two basic questions are behind any AI initiative:

1. What, in this particular setting and context, gives life to this system— when it is most alive, healthy, and symbiotically related to its various communities?

2. What are the possibilities, expressed and latent, that provide opportunities for more effective (value-congruent) forms of organizing?

AI seeks out the exceptional best of "what is" (*Discovery*) to help ignite the collective imagination of "what might be" (*Dream*). The aim is to generate new knowledge of a collectively desired future. It carries forth the vision in ways that successfully translate images into possibilities, intentions into reality, and beliefs into practice.

As a method of organizational analysis, AI differs from conventional managerial problem solving. The basic assumption of problem solving is that "organizing is a problem to be solved." The task of improvement traditionally involves removing deficits by (1) identifying the key problems or deficiencies, (2) analyzing the causes, (3) analyzing solutions, and (4) developing an action plan.

In contrast, the underlying assumption of AI is that an organization is a "solution to be embraced," rather than a "problem to be solved." The phases are shown in **Figure 1.1, Appreciative Inquiry 4-D Cycle.** It starts with selecting a topic: affirmative topic choice. What follows are *Discovery* (appreciating and valuing), *Dream* (envisioning), *Design* (co-constructing the future), and *Destiny* (learning, empowering, and improvising to sustain the future). These are the essence of dialogue woven through each step of the process.

Figure 1.1: Appreciative Inquiry "4-D" Cycle

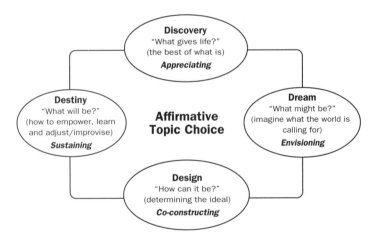

The first step in this process is to discover and value those factors that give life to the organization. For example, the organization might discover and value its commitment and identify when that commitment was at its highest. Regardless of how few or infrequent the moments of highest commitment, the organization's task is to focus on these and discuss the factors and forces that served as fertile ground for that exceptional level of commitment.

The First D is *Discovery*

The list of positive or affirmative topics for *Discovery* is endless: high quality, integrity, empowerment, innovation, customer responsiveness, technological innovation, team spirit, best in class, and so on. In each case, the task is to discover the positive exceptions, successes, and most vital or alive moments. Discovery involves valuing those things that are worth valuing. It can be done within and across organizations (in a benchmarking sense) and across time (organizational history as positive possibility).

As part of the *Discovery* process, individuals engage in dialogue and meaning-making. This is simply the open sharing of discoveries and possibilities. Through dialogue, a consensus begins to emerge whereby individuals in the organization say, "Yes, this is an ideal or vision we value and should aspire to." Through conversation and dialogue, individual appreciation becomes collective appreciation, individual will evolves into group will, and individual vision becomes a cooperative or shared vision for the organization.

AI helps create a deliberately supportive context for dialogue. It is through the sharing of ideals that social bonding occurs. What makes AI different from other organization development methodologies at this phase is that every question is positive.

From *Discovery* to *Dream*

Second, participants *Dream*, or envision what might be. When the best of what is has been identified, the mind naturally begins to search further and to envision new possibilities. Valuing the best of what is leads to envisioning what might be. Envisioning involves passionate thinking, creating a positive image of a desired and preferred future. The *Dream* step uses the interview stories from the *Discovery* step to identify the stories and to elicit the key themes that underlie the times when the organization was most alive and at its best.

Articulated *Dream(s)* to *Design*

Third, participants co-construct the future by the *Design* of an "organizational architecture" in which the exceptional becomes everyday and ordinary. This design is more than a vision. It is a provocative and inspiring statement of intention that is grounded in the realities of what has worked in the past. It enhances the organization by leveraging its own past successes and successes that have been experienced elsewhere with a "strategic intent."

Design to *Destiny*

Fourth, the *Design* delivers the organization to its **Destiny** through innovation and action. AI establishes momentum of its own. Once guided by a shared image of what might be, members of the organization find innovative ways to help move the organization closer to the ideal. Again, because the ideals are grounded in realities, the organization is empowered to make things happen. This is important to underscore because it is precisely through the juxtaposition of visionary content with grounded examples of the extraordinary that AI opens the status quo to transformations in collective action. By seeking an imaginative and fresh perception of organizations, as if seen for the very first time, the appreciative eye takes nothing for granted, seeking to apprehend the basis of organizational life and working to articulate the possibilities for a better existence.

Part 2 of the book covers the 4-D Cycle of AI in detail.

While still fairly new, the principles that underlie AI are deeply grounded in scientific research. While the practitioner need not have a thorough understanding of these principles, it is often helpful when introducing AI to an organization to provide some of the supporting theory and research. The following ideas are organized into eight brief mini-lectures. Each refers to the theoretical constructs upon which AI is based. Practitioners successfully introduce AI by adapting these key concepts to the language and culture of the organization.

Mini-lecture I: Five Principles of AI

The following five principles inspired and moved the foundation of AI from theory to practice:

1. The Constructionist Principle
2. The Principle of Simultaneity
3. The Poetic Principle
4. The Anticipatory Principle
5. The Positive Principle

Launching an AI initiative requires an understanding of these principles to fully grasp AI theory and to internalize the basis of the 4-D Cycle.

For the full conceptual articulation, see D. Cooperrider and S. Srivastva, "Appreciative Inquiry Into Organizational Life," *Research in Organizational Change and Development*, Pasmore and Woodman, (eds.), vol. 1, (Greenwich, Connecticut: JAI Press, 1987).

1. *The Constructionist Principle:* Social knowledge and organizational destiny are interwoven. A constructionist would argue that the seeds of organizational change are implicit in the first questions asked. The questions asked become the material out of which the future is conceived and constructed. Thus, the way of knowing is fateful.[1] To be effective as executives, leaders, change agents, and so on, one must be adept in the art of reading, understanding, and analyzing organizations as living, human constructions. Knowing organizations is at the core of virtually every OD task. Because styles of thinking rarely match the increasingly complex world, there must be a commitment to the ongoing pursuit of multiple and more fruitful ways of knowing.

   The most important resource for generating constructive organizational change is cooperation between the imagination and the reasoning function of the mind (the capacity to unleash the imagination and mind of groups). AI is a way of reclaiming imaginative competence. Unfortunately, the habitual styles of thought include preconscious background assumptions, root metaphors, and rules of analysis that come to define organizations in a particular way. These styles have often constrained the managerial imagination and mind.

2. *The Principle of Simultaneity:* This principle recognizes that inquiry and change are not truly separate moments; they can and should be simultaneous. Inquiry is intervention. The seeds of change are the things people think and talk about, the things people discover and learn, and the things that inform dialogue and inspire images of the future. They are implicit in the very first questions asked. One of the most impactful things a change agent or OD practitioner does is to articulate questions. The questions set the stage for what is "found" and what is "discovered" (the data). This data becomes the stories out of which the future is conceived, discussed, and constructed.

3. *The Poetic Principle:* A useful metaphor in understanding this principle is that human organizations are an open book. An organization's story is constantly being co-authored. Moreover, pasts, presents, and futures are endless sources of learning, inspiration, or interpretation (as in the endless interpretive possibilities in a good work of poetry

---

1 For more information, refer to Kenneth Gergen, *Realities and Relationships* (Cambridge: Harvard University Press, 1994).

or a biblical text). The important implication is that one can study virtually any topic related to human experience in any human system or organization. The choice of inquiry can be in the nature of alienation or joy in any human organization or community. One can study moments of creativity and innovation or moments of debilitating bureaucratic stress. One has a choice.

4. *The Anticipatory Principle:* The most important resource for generating constructive organizational change or improvement is collective imagination and discourse about the future. One of the basic theorems of the anticipatory view of organizational life is that the image of the future guides what might be called the current behavior of any organism or organization. Much like a movie projected on a screen, human systems are forever projecting ahead of themselves a horizon of expectation that brings the future powerfully into the present as a mobilizing agent. Organizations exist, in the final analysis, because people who govern and maintain them share some sort of discourse or projection about what the organization is, how it will function, what it will achieve, and what will likely become.

5. *The Positive Principle:* This last principle is more concrete. It grows out of years of experience with AI. Put most simply, momentum for change requires large amounts of positive affect and social bonding, attitudes such as hope, inspiration, and the sheer joy of creating with one another. Organizations, as human constructions, are largely affirmative systems and thus are responsive to positive thought and positive knowledge.[2] The more positive the questions used to guide a group building an OD initiative, the more long-lasting and effective is the change.[3] In important respects, people and organizations move in the direction of their inquiries. Thousands of interviews into "empowerment" or "being the easiest business in the industry to work with" will have a completely different long-term impact in terms of sustaining positive action than a study into "low morale" or "process breakdowns." These five principles are central to AI's theoretical basis for organizing for a positive revolution in change. These principles clarify that it is the positive image that results in the positive action. The organization must make the affirmative decision to focus on the positive to lead the inquiry.

---

2 See D. Cooperrider, "Positive Image, Positive Action: The Affirmative Basis of Organizing" in Srivastva, S. and Cooperrider, D., *Appreciative Management and Leadership*, Revised (Euclid, OH: Lakeshore Communications, 1999).

3 See G. Bushe and G. Coetzer "Appreciative Inquiry As a Team-Development Intervention: A Controlled Experiment," *Journal Of Applied Behavioral Science*, vol. 31 (March 1995): 13.

Mini-lecture II: Positive Image— Positive Action

The power of positive imagery, as illustrated in the fifth principle, is a key factor in the AI dialogue. There are six main areas of research to support this premise: research into the placebo effect, Pygmalion effect, positive effect, internal dialogue, positive imagery, and metacognitive competence. This section briefly elaborates on each area.

1. *Powerful Placebo:* The placebo effect is a fascinating process in which projected images, as reflected in positive belief, ignite a healing response that can be as powerful as conventional therapy. In the twentieth century, the placebo effect is accepted by most medical professions as genuine. Between one-third and two–thirds of all patients show marked physiological and emotional improvement in symptoms simply by believing they are given an effective treatment, even when that treatment is just a sugar pill or some other inert substance. While the complex mind-body pathways are far from being completely understood, there is one area of clear agreement: positive changes in anticipatory reality through suggestion and belief play a central role in all placebo responses.

2. *Pygmalion Effect:* In the classic Pygmalion study,[4] teachers are led to believe on the basis of "credible" information that some of their students possess exceptionally high potential while others do not. So the teachers are led, on the basis of some expert opinion, to hold a positive image (PI), or expectancy of some students, and a negative image (NI), or expectancy of others. Unknown to the teachers, however, is the fact that the so-called high potential students were selected at random. In objective terms, all student groups were equivalent in potential and were merely dubbed as high, regular, or low potential. As the experiment unfolds, differences quickly emerge— not on the basis of any innate intelligence factor or some other predisposition, but solely on the basis of the manipulated expectancy of the teacher. Over time, subtle changes among students evolve into clear differences, as the high-PI students began to significantly overshadow all others in actual achievement.

   The key lesson is that cognitive capacities are cued and shaped by the images projected through another's expectations. For example, what is seen is believed. As a result, actions take on a whole new tone

---

4 R. Rosenthal, *Pygmalion in the Classroom* (Holt, Rinehart and Winston: New York, 1969).

based on the perceived image. The resulting differential behavioral treatment, in turn, makes the people receiving this treatment begin to respond to the positive images that others have of them. The greatest value of the Pygmalion research is that it provides empirical understanding of the relational pathways of the positive image—positive action dynamic.

3. *Positive Effect and Learned Helpfulness:* While still in the formative stages, early results on this issue suggest that positive imagery evokes positive emotions and positive emotions move people toward a choice for positive actions. Positive emotions are intimately connected with social helpfulness. Somehow, positive emotions draw people out of themselves, pull us away from self-oriented preoccupation, enlarge their focus on the potential good in the world, increase feelings of solidarity with others, and propel them to act in more altruistic and positive ways.[5]

4. *The Inner Dialogue (2:1):* It is argued that all human systems exhibit a continuing "cinematographic show of visual imagery" or ongoing "inner newsreel" that is best understood through the notion of inner dialogue. For example, a study of a stressful medical procedure indicated that people may have thoughts that either impede the aim of the clinical intervention (this procedure may kill me, a negative image) or, alternatively, facilitate the goals of the care (this will save my life, a positive image). Hence, the inner dialogue functions as an inner dialectic between positive and negative adaptive statements, and one's guiding imagery is presumably an outcome of such an inner dialectic. In addition, studies show that there is a definite imbalance in the internal dialogue in the direction of positive imagery for those groups of individuals identified as more psychologically or socially functional. Functional groups are characterized by a 2:1 ratio of positive images to negative images, whereas mildly dysfunctional groups demonstrate equal frequencies, a balanced 1:1 internal dialogue.

     The AI dialogue creates guiding images of the future from the collective whole of the group. It exists in a very observable, energizing and tangible way in the living dialogue that flows through every living system, expressing itself anew at every moment.

5. *Positive Imagery As a Dynamic Force:* Various scholars have noted that the underlying images held by a civilization or culture have an enormous influence on its fate. In his study of Western civilization, the Dutch sociologist Fred Polak argued this point concerning the tendency of the positive image. For him, the positive image of the

---

5 M. Seligman, *Helplessness: On Development, Depression and Death* (W. H. Freeman: New York, 1992).

future is the single most important dynamic and explanatory variable for understanding cultural evolution. Therefore, as long as an organization's or society's image is positive and flourishing, the dynamic culture is growing toward the positive images of the future. When there is a vision or a bright image of the future, the people flourish.

6. *Metacognition and Conscious Evolution of Positive Images:* Metacognition is awareness of one's own cognitive systems and knowledge and insight into its workings. It is the awareness that prompts a person to write reminders to himself or herself to avoid forgetting something.[6] The heliotropic hypothesis states that human systems have an observable tendency to evolve in the direction of those positive images that are the brightest and boldest, most illuminating and promising. To the extent that the heliotropic hypothesis has some validity, questions of volition and free agency come to the fore.

   - Is it possible to develop metacognitive capacity and thereby choose positive ways of construing the world? If so, with what result?
   - Is the quest for affirmative competence, the capacity to project and affirm an ideal image as if it is already so, a realistic aim or merely a romantic distraction?
   - Is it possible to develop the affirmative competence of large collectives, that is, of groups, organizations, or whole societies affirming a positive future together?[7]

With the exception of the last question (where not enough research has been completed), most of the available evidence suggests quite clearly that affirmative competence can be learned, developed, and honed through experience, and disciplined, formal training. One example is that imagery techniques are becoming important to the successful training of athletes. Experimental evidence indicates that the best athletes may be successful because of a highly developed metacognitive capacity of differential self-monitoring. In brief, this capacity involves being able to systematically observe and analyze successful performances (positive self-monitoring) or unsuccessful performances (negative self-monitoring) and to be able to choose between the two cognitive processes when desired. The professional athlete wills himself or herself to succeed by envisioning (imagining) a positive outcome to his or her next action or series of actions.

---

6 Ashcraft, M., *Fundamentals of Cognition* (Addison-Wesley-Longman: Reading, Massachusetts: 1998).
7 Ibid.

These examples demonstrate the power of positive imagery leading to positive actions and demonstrate that such imagery on a collective basis may be the strongest approach to co-creating a positive future. It is time to concentrate as never before on the power of positive images in leading to positive actions. Through these studies, new knowledge and images of possibility have been created. To learn more about these relationships between positive imagery and positive action, refer to the *classic* article in Chapter 11, **Positive Image, Positive Action: The Affirmative Basis of Organizing.**

Mini-lecture III: Social Constructionism

A central premise of AI is that the appreciative process of knowing is socially constructed. In other words, knowing takes place through interaction with and within a social system. This is why AI views organizations as centers of human relatedness. Thus, by getting people to unite on a central theme or idea, AI allows people who share a related objective to project or construct their future—in this case, the future of an organization.

The idea that a social system creates or determines its own reality is known as *social constructionism*. AI takes this theoretical framework and simply places it in a positive context. This positive spin on social constructionism is central to AI. Many of its principles flow from the idea that people control their destiny by envisioning what they want and developing actions to move toward it. There is considerable overlap between the AI model and social constructionism theory. Some areas of overlap include these:

1. The social order at any given point is viewed as the product of broad social agreement.
2. Patterns of social/organizational action are not fixed by nature in any direct biological or physical way; the vast share of social conduct is virtually stimulus free, capable of infinite conceptual variation.
3. From an observational point of view, all social action is open to multiple interpretations, not one of which is superior in any objective sense. The interpretations favored in one historical setting may be replaced in the next.
4. Historical narratives and theories govern what is taken to be true or valid and, to a large extent, determine what scientists and laypersons are able to see. An observation, therefore, is filtered through conventional stories, belief systems, and theoretical lenses.

5. To the extent that action is predicated on the stories, ideas, beliefs, meanings, and theories embedded in language, people are free to seek transformations in conventional conduct by changing patterns of narration.

6. The most powerful vehicle communities have for changing the social order is through the act of dialogue made possible by language. Alterations in linguistic practices, therefore, hold profound implications for changes in social practice.

7. Social theory can be viewed as a highly refined narrative account with a specialized grammar all its own. As a powerful linguistic tool (created by trained linguistic experts), theory may enter the conceptual meaning system of a culture and, in this way, alter patterns of social action.

8. Whether intended or not, all theoretical accounts are normative and have the potential to influence the social order. Therefore, all narrative accounts (including social theory) are morally relevant. They have the potential to affect the way people interact with one another. This point is a critical one because it implies that there is no such thing as a detached, technical, scientific mode for judging the ultimate worth of value claims.

9. Value knowledge or social theory is therefore a narrative creation, not an aspect of the physical world. Social knowledge is not "out there" in nature to be discovered through detached, value-free, observational methods (logical empiricism); nor can it be relegated to the subjective minds of isolated individuals (cognitivism). Viewed from this perspective, social knowledge resides in the stories of the collectivity; it is created, maintained, and put to use by the human group. Dialogue, free from constraint of distortion, is necessary to determine the "nature of things" (social constructionism).

More information on the social constructionst viewpoint can be found in Kenneth Gergen's work listed in the References and Bibliography at the end of the book.

Mini-lecture IV:
Beyond Problem Solving to AI

Since the 1930s, organizations have used a "deficit-based" approach to problem solving. It begins with seeking out the problem, the weak link in the system. Then, typically, there is a diagnosis, and alternative solutions are recommended. AI challenges this traditional paradigm with an "affirmative" approach, embracing an organization's challenges in a positive light. AI offers an alternative—to look for what is good in the organization, its success stories.

In **Figure 1.2**, Paradigm 1's basic assumption is that an organization is a problem that needs to be solved. Paradigm 2's basic assumption is that an organization is a mystery that should be embraced as a human center of infinite imagination, infinite capacity, and potential. The word *mystery* signifies, literally, a future that is unknowable and cannot be predicted. And this is true of organizations, because nobody really knows when or where the next creative insight will emerge that can shift everything or how a fresh combination of strengths will open to horizons never seen before. Paradigm 1 pictures organizations as broken-down machines in need of fixing; they are problems to be solved. Every analysis begins, therefore, with some variation of the same question: What is wrong? What are the problems? What are the causes?

Figure 1.2 Two Paradigms for Organizational Change

Paradigm 1: Problem Solving	Paradigm 2: Appreciative Inquiry
"Felt Need" Identification of Problem	Appreciating "Valuing the Best of What Is"
⇓	⇓
Analysis of Causes	Envisioning "What Might Be"
⇓	⇓
Analysis of Possible Solutions	Dialoguing "What Should Be"
⇓	⇓
Action Planning (Treatment)	Innovating "What Will Be"
Organizing is a problem to be solved.	*Organizing is a mystery (infinite capacity) to be embraced.*

Paradigm 2 says something quite different. Organizations are not problems. Indeed, no organization was created as a problem. Organizations, if anything, are meant as solutions. But even more than that, organizations are not even singular solutions. They are creative centers of human relatedness, alive with emergent and unlimited capacity. Paradigm 2 is "life-centric." It searches for everything that gives life to a living human system when it is most alive. It is creative and in a healthy relationship with its extended communities. AI is an approach to organizational change that is unique and refreshing. Observers of AI say that it is one of the greatest, yet largely unrecognized, models available to the OD field.[8]

Mini-lecture V:
Vocabularies of Human Deficit

AI Insight

While AI was still evolving, Frank Barrett and David Cooperrrider teamed up to work with a hotel that was experiencing low occupancy, with the staff and management locked in a setting of distrust and backbiting. Both sides were extremely negative toward each other, and neither was able to move past this to see a more positive option. In order to turn this hotel around, the AI team knew the first step was to shift the focus from a negative mind-set to one of openness. The AI team took the group to experience a four-star hotel. The staff and management did an inquiry to focus on what made this property an award-winning hotel. They focused on what worked well. From this inquiry, they learned they could work in similar ways to transform their hotel to a four-star hotel. Negative conversations turned into discussions of how they could be more than what they were. The transformation began and the hotel became a top-rated four-star hotel. Frank Barrett and David Cooperrider co-authored a major paper on the breakthrough called "Generative Metaphor Intervention" and it received Best Paper of the Year Award at the Academy of Management's OD Division in 1988.[9]

---

8 See D. Cooperrider and S. Srivastva, "Appreciative Inquiry Into Organizational Life," *Research in Organizational Change and Development*, Pasmore and Woodman, (eds.), vol. 1, (Greenwich, Connecticut: JAI Press, 1987).

9 See F. Barrett and D. Cooperrider, "Generative Metaphor Intervention: A New Approach to Intergroup Conflict," *Journal of Applied Behavioral Science*, vol. 26, 1991.

A fundamental assumption underlying AI is that the language one uses creates one's reality. Therefore, the emotional meaning of words such as *dysfunctional, co-dependent,* and *stressed out* affect one's thinking and acting, as illustrated earlier in the Pygmalion effect. This deficit-based vocabulary can inhibit the vision for a better and brighter future and limit growth.

Examples of deficit-based vocabularies are prolific in everyday conversation. Organizations, too, have adopted this mentality and spend considerable resources to train managers to remain vigilant at uncovering problems and identifying issues. As a result, many believe that a manager's job is to solve problems. This mentality constantly seeks to reinforce the idea that only by focusing on the problems can we create a better organization.

These tremendous expansions in vocabularies of human and organizational deficit can best be illustrated below in **Table 1.1, Vocabularies of Human Deficit,**[10] and **Table 1.2, Vocabularies of Organizational Deficit.**

Table 1.2: Vocabularies of Human Deficit

Depressed	Midlife Crisis	Extremely Controlled
Bulimic	Kleptomaniac	Obsessive-Compulsive
Antisocial Personality	Neurotic	Low Self-Esteem
Paranoid	Anorexic	Identity Crisis
Posttraumatic Stress	Psychopathic Co-dependent	
Sadomasochistic	Dysfunctional Family	
Brief Psychotherapy		

Table 1.3 Vocabularies of Organizational Deficit

Organizational Stress	Theory X	Job Dissatisfaction
Work Alienation	Turfism	Neurotic Organization
Authoritarian Management	Low Morale	Executive Burnout
Role Conflict	Groupthink	Intergroup Conflict
Defensive Routines	Peter Principle	Structural Inflexibility
Bureaucratic Red Tape	Labor-Management Mistrust	Dilbert Bureaucracy
Interpersonal Incompetence	Organizational Diagnosis	Organization Learning Disabilities

To break through this negative vocabulary framework, AI proposes an affirmative vocabulary of organizing for the future. Why? As noted earlier, human systems and organizations move in the direction of what they study.

The sooner the unconditional positive question is asked, the sooner the right answers can be obtained. This principle leads to the Affirmative Theory of Organizing.

Mini-lecture VI: Toward a Theory of Affirmative Organization

The AI adventure truly begins with the appreciative mind-set, eye, thoughts, and vocabulary based upon the following concepts:

1. Organizations are made and imagined.

2. No matter what the durability to date, virtually any pattern of action is open to alteration and reconfiguration.

3. Organizations are "heliotropic" in character in the sense that organizational actions have an observable and largely "automatic" tendency to move in the direction of images of the future.

4. The more an organization experiments with the conscious evolution of positive imagery, the better it will become. There is an observable self-reinforcing, educating effect of affirmation. Affirmative competence is the key to the self-organizing system.

5. Paradoxically, the following is also true: the greatest obstacle in the way of group and organizational well-being is also the positive image, the affirmative projection that guides the group or organization.

6. Organizations do not need to be fixed. They need constant reaffirmation.

7. Leadership = Affirmation.

8. The challenge for organizational learning and development is creating the condition for organization-wide appreciation. This is the single most important act that can be taken to ensure the conscious evolution of a valued and positive future.

Once these simple yet powerful concepts are internalized,[10] the conditions that are essential to becoming an affirmative organization of change fall into place.

---

10 All of these terms have come into common usage only within the past century (several only in the last two decades). See Kenneth Gergen, *The Saturated Self* (New York: Basic Books, 1991).

Mini-lecture VII: Assessing Organizational Inner Dialogue

Too often there is a tendency for OD interventions to become gripe sessions or exercises in problem solving. Transforming the human system and its organization toward an affirmative learning and working environment requires a conscious effort to maintain a positive focus on the dialogue. In so doing, positive affirmations or comments should be encouraged, while negative dialogues should be minimized or avoided altogether. Keeping an ear out for key phrases and/or activities can facilitate this process.

The following positive discourse categories are offered:[11]

I. Positive Categories

1. Positive Valuing: Any mention of positive values, past or present.

2. Hope towards future: Any mention of hope, optimism, or positive anticipation toward the future.

3. Skill or Competency: Any mention of skill, competency, action, or positive quality about self or others.

4. Openness, Receptivity, Learning: Any mention of receptivity in self or others accompanied by a positive outcome; also, any noticing of self or others' learning or interests.

5. Active Connection, Effort to Include, Cooperation, or Combination: Any noticing of efforts to include, cooperate, connect, and relate that may be accompanied by at least an inferred positive outcome.

6. Mention of Surprise, Curiosity, or Excitement: Any mention of curiosity, surprise, openness to fresh insights, or excitement in self or others.

7. Notice of Facilitating Action or Movement toward a Positive Outcome: Any mention of a facilitating action or movement toward a real or imagined positive outcome or any mention of a facilitating object or circumstance. Also, noticing of any event that enhances another event, an effective state, or a person; noticing facilitative or positive cause and effect.

8. Effort to Reframe in Positive Terms: Any mention of a negative emotion or action accompanied by the possibility of a positive desired outcome; also, any mention of a change in mood from negative to pos-

---

11 From F. Barrett, D. Cooperrider, R. Tenkasi, and T. Joseph (unpublished manuscript, Case Western Reserve University).

itive, including any mention of an obstacle that is temporary or getting over a negative static state, or reframing a negative situation into more positive terms.

9. Envisioned Ideal: Any mention of a vision/value end-state articulation of a positive outcome envisioned for a future that is utopian or pragmatic.

Then, for the organization to process, there must be a commitment to let go of the negative discourse categories that drain the organization's resources. These include:

II. Negative Discourse Categories

1. Negative Valuing: Any mention of negative valuing, e.g., fatalism, apathy, or dislike. Any description of person, group, circumstance, or event as a problem or an obstacle.

2. Concern, Worry, Preoccupation, Doubt: Any mention of concern, worry, or preoccupation without mention of a possible model to alleviate concern or to enhance understanding; any mention of doubt, suspicion, or lack of confidence in future outcomes.

3. Unfulfilled Expectation: Any mention of any event, action, state, or person that does not match intention, wish, desire, goal, or other unfulfilled expectation.

4. Lack of Receptivity, Absence of Connection: Any mention of a lack of receptivity in self or others, including a lack of collaboration, a lack of understanding, a failure to listen or failure to agree, or any explicit mention of an absence of connection.

5. Deficiency in Self or Others: Any mention of a sense that something is missing; for example, a deficiency in self or others or a lack of motivation, appropriate effort, skill, or competence or an absence of resources (such as time or money).

6. Negative Effect: Any mention of feelings of dissatisfaction, selfishness, sadness, defensiveness, irritation, or anger without mentioning a possible antidote or relief or effort to understand.

7. Withdrawal or Suppression: Any mention of avoidance, ignoring, withdrawal of energy or surrender, or suppressing self or others.

8. Control or Domination: Any notice of effort or action to disrupt, dominate, wield control, or halt a mood or an action in self or other.

9. Wasted Effort: Any mention of excessive investment of time, resources, or energy without mention of reward or positive outcome.

10. Prediction, Image of a Negative Future: Any mention of prediction, vision, image, or expectation of a negative future.

11. Attribution of Control by Others in Combination with Self-Depracation: Any notice of effort or action in others to disrupt, dominate, or wield control in combination with attribution of helplessness to self or self-pity.

12. Negative Cause-and-Effect Relation: Any explicit notice of a cause-and-effect relationship leading to a negative outcome.

13. Reframing a Situation in Negative Terms: Any mention of a positive emotion with the possibility of a negative outcome; mention of a change in mood from positive to negative or getting into a negative state, focusing on possible obstacles, or reframing a positive situation into more negative terms.

The responsibility of the AI moderator—whether a consultant, a manager, or an appointed team leader—is to facilitate positive discourse and minimize negative discourse in order to foster constructive social change.

Mini-lecture VIII:
History as Positive Possibility

Three factors that give life to healthy organizations are continuity, novelty, and transition. Research[12] has established that visionary organizations and their leadership have the capacity to learn and apply lessons from the best of the past (*continuity*), to surface and develop ideas for creative acts (*novelty*), and to enact actual changes in systems and behaviors to progress toward a desired state (*transition*). The importance and effectiveness of AI stems in part from its natural focus on all three of these generative factors.

AI begins with a focus on organizational continuity, the understanding and appreciation of the system's connective threads of identity, purpose, pride, wisdom, and tradition that perpetuate and connect day-to-day life in the organization. It is paramount to recognize that continuity is a necessary part of change or transformation. As Jim Collins, co-author of *Built to Last* puts it, "…change is good, but first know what should never change."[13] Steven Covey

---

12 See J. Collins and J. Porras, *Built to Last: Successful Habits of Visionary Companies* (New York: Harper Business, 1994) and H. Jonas, R. Fry, and S. Srivastva, "The Office of the CEO: Understanding the Executive Experience," Academy of Management Executive, 3 (4), (1989).

13 Collins, ibid.

also emphasizes the importance of valuing continuity in human development:[14]

> *People cannot live with change if there's not a changeless core inside them. The key to the ability to change is a changeless sense of who you are, what you are about, and what you value.*

In attending to continuity, the dialogue is built around the system's founding stories, turning points, proudest achievements, best practices, empowering traditions, intergenerational wisdom, legacies, and amazing moments. It is a discovery of the organization's history-as-positive-possibility. This inquiry reveals the bases upon which healthy management of continuity can be sustained by:

- Knowing what people do best.
- Ensuring human and technical resources to support basic core tasks.
- Orienting to maintain the most valued aspects of the culture.

The function of continuity is between the individual and the organization.

Table 1.4 Functions of Continuity

For the Individual	For the Organization
Social Connectedness	Strengthened Commitment
Moral Guidance	Better Sense-Making and Decision Making
Confidence to Act	Consistent Values and Mission
Personal Welfare	Decentralized Control
Pride, Hope, and Joy	Basis for Organizational Learning
Freedom	Long-Term Thinking
	Customized Change

In attending to novelty, the AI dialogue and process provides the opportunity for unexpected newness to be offered up. A space for true valuing of novel thinking and acting is created. Hierarchy is suspended; harmony is postponed in favor of curious questioning. Symphonies of logical rationales are replaced with cacophonies of wild, half-baked notions; and typical incentives to conform are supplanted with celebration of those who constructively challenge the status quo. Such flowerings in an organization—what Dee Hock

14 See Stephen Covey, The *7 Habits of Highly Effective People* (New York: Simon & Schuster, 1990): 108.

terms "creative chaos"[15]— enable the healthy management of novelty through:
- Intentional processes for learning from collective experience.
- Practices that actively search for new ideas: internally and externally.
- Investments in individual growth and development as a stimulus for new paradigm thinking.

This is where the affirmative topic choices come into the AI process.

In attending to transition, the dialogue uncovers ways in which new ideals (novelty) are transformed into visible changes that are experienced by everyone as positive movement toward a change target with minimal disruption (threat to continuity). The system is enlivened through a shared sense of enacting a "common script," whereby everyone recognizes the positive reason to change, the desired state to be achieved, and the next few steps to be taken. This allows for healthy management of transition through:
- Common vision, from which priorities are determined.
- Helpful feedback/measurement mechanisms on key success factors.
- Support for real, choiceful experimentation.
- Involvement strategies to promote a common script.

AI: The Foundational Questions

For visionary organizations, continuity, novelty, and transition are necessary capacities that exist in healthy tension. Too much attention on continuity may create myopic, rulebound systems that constrain. Too much attention to novelty can result in ivory-tower leadership that loses credibility with those doing the core work. Too much emphasis on transition can create a sense of directionless change-for-the-sake-of-change. As a process, AI is instrumental in finding and sustaining a healthy balance among these life-giving capacities. The foundational questions below provide an opportunity to address all three elements of **continuity, novelty,** and **transition**. The first three AI generic questions focus on continuity:
- Describe a high-point experience in your organization, a time when you were most alive and engaged.
- Without being modest, what is it that you most value about yourself, your work, and your organization?

---

15 D. Hock, *Birth of the Chaordic Age* (San Francisco: Berrett-Koehler, 1999).

- What are the core factors that give life to your organization, without which the organization would cease to exist?

The next step for the organization is to open itself to **novelty,** the unexpected newness or the new possibilities in its human systems. It is a time to dream. What is it that the organization can become?

- Imagine you have awakened from a long, deep sleep. You get up to realize that everything is as you always dreamed it would be. Your ideal state has become the reality. What do you see? What is going on? How have things changed?

Finally, there is the transition, the intentional change of the human systems in the organization. How will the organization achieve the dream that was discovered? It is in the Design phase that transition begins, continuing through the Destiny phase. The final AI foundational question addresses the future:

- What three wishes do you have…to enhance the health and vitality of your organization?

All organizations have something about their past to value. This element must be appreciated in order that change becomes a positive experience, without encountering unnecessary resistance from the sense of disruption. The AI process helps one to honor the past (continuity) and search for newness (novelty) in order to embrace movement toward the new future (transition), as illustrated in Figure 1.3.

Figure 1.3 Managing Change: Continuity, Novelty, and Transition[16]

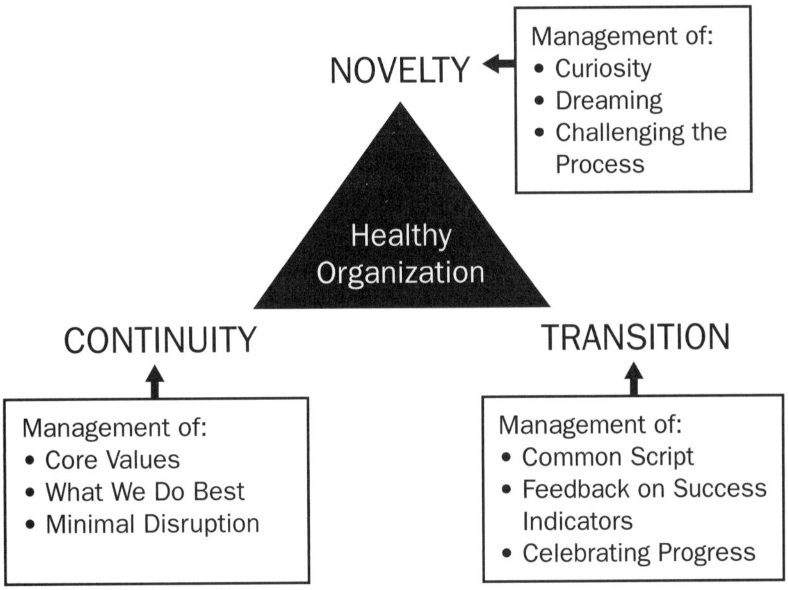

Summary

AI brings all three areas into balance and harmony simultaneously. These eight preceeding mini-lectures provide the theoretical foundations and research citations that move human and organizational systems toward a positive, generative future. In addition, it is manifest that human systems within organizations move in the direction of what they study and that the study begins with an inquiry. The best way to understand AI is to discover how it works. This will be the focus of the next chapter: to show how these theoretical foundations move us into a positive, generative future.

16 From S. Srivastva and R. Fry, *Executive Continuity* (San Francisco: Jossey-Bass, 1992).

2

The Appreciative Inquiry
Process: How It Works

Overview

AI is premised on the idea that organizations move toward what they study. For example, when groups study human problems and conflicts, they often find that the number and severity of complex and problematic issues has grown. In the same manner, when groups study high human ideals and achievements (such as teamwork, quality, or peak experiences), these phenomena tend to flourish. People in organizations construct and enact worlds that, in turn, affect their behavior. In this sense, the AI approach accepts the notion that knowledge and organizational destiny are interwoven: *the way we seek to know people, groups, and organizations is fateful*. Upon this basic premise, AI builds its positive framework. To understand AI at a fundamental level, one needs simply to understand these two points. First, organizations move in the direction of what they study. Second, AI makes a conscious choice to study the best of an organization, its positive core.

To this point in the book, the theoretical foundation for AI has been established, as well as a basic framework of *what* AI is and *why* it works. From this point forward, the focus will be on *how* it works. This chapter begins with an overview of the principle of the positive core. The central theme of the positive core is fundamental to AI. It is the dominant principle and established basis for the 4-D Cycle and how it facilitates the AI intervention. The chapter concludes with an overview of the 4-D process.

The 4-D Cycle is a tool that allows the user to follow a well-coordinated series of steps to help an organization identify its positive core and initiate the concrete operational steps to achieve its goals. *Discovery, Dream, Design* and *Destiny* were discussed briefly in the previous chapter. The concept of the affirmative topic choice, however, is new to this discussion. Yet this is where the AI process begins.

The first step in the AI process involves choosing the positive as the focus of inquiry. This is because what is studied becomes reality. Therefore, the right topics need to be created or chosen. These topics will ultimately guide the formulation of questions. This approach is known as the "affirmative topic choice," and it lies at the center of the 4-D Cycle, illustrated in **Figure 2.1** on the next page.

Figure 2.1 Appreciative Inquiry 4-D Cycle

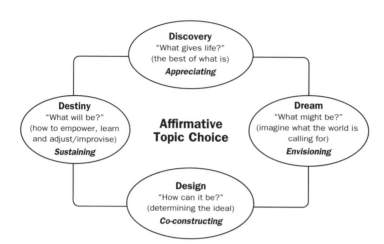

The Positive Core

The *positive core* of organizational life is one of the greatest, yet least recognized, resources in the change management field today. AI has demonstrated that human systems grow in the direction of their persistent inquiries, and this propensity is strongest and most sustainable when the means and ends of inquiry are positively correlated. In the AI process, the future is consciously constructed upon the positive core strengths of the organization. Linking the energy of this core directly to any change agenda suddenly and democratically creates and mobilizes topics never before thought possible.

The concept of the positive core is separate from, yet central to, the 4-D Cycle. It has been stated several times that AI is more than the 4-D Cycle. The cycle is simply a tool that allows the practitioner to access and mobilize the positive core. The positive core lies at the heart of the AI process. In this respect, the organization's positive core is the beginning and the end of the inquiry. This is where the whole organization has an opportunity to value its history and embrace novelty in transitioning into positive possibilities.

This positive core is woven throughout the 4-D Cycle. It is identified in the Discovery phase, mobilizing a whole-system inquiry into the positive core... that which gives meaning to the organization. It is amplified throughout the Dream phase, creating a clear, results-oriented vision in relation to the discovered potential and in relation to questions of higher purpose. It is woven into the "organizational architecture" through the Design phase, creating provocative propositions of the ideal organization, an organizational design that people believe is capable of magnifying the positive core. Finally, it is implemented throughout the Destiny phase, strengthening the affirmative capability of the whole system. Thus, AI begins and ends with valuing that which gives life to an organization. In this sense, the organization's positive core can be expressed in any one of a number of ways, all of which can be identified through the inquiry. The following are some of the ways in which the positive core is expressed:

- Best business practices
- Core and distinctive competencies
- Elevated thoughts
- Embedded knowledge
- Financial assets
- Innovations
- Organizational achievements
- Organizational wisdom
- Positive emotions
- Positive macro trends
- Product strengths
- Relational resources
- Social capital
- Strategic opportunities
- Technical assets
- Values
- Visions of possibility
- Vital traditions
- Strengths of partners
- Capacities worldwide

Affirmative Topic Choice: A Fateful Act

Once the basic concept of the positive core is understood, the 4-D Cycle can be better explained. The first step in an AI intervention is selecting the *affirmative topic choice*. This is, in short, the selection of topic(s) that will become the focus of the intervention.

Selecting the affirmative topic choice begins with the constructive discovery and narration of the organization's "life-giving" story. The topics, in the initial stages, are bold hunches about what gives life to the organization. Most importantly, the topics (usually three to five for an inquiry) represent what people really want to discover or learn more about. The topics will likely evoke conversations about the desired future.

The seeds of change are implicit in the first questions asked. The following two broad questions form a basis by which groups and organizations can create their own customized topics.

- *What factors give life to this organization when it is and has been most alive, successful, and effective?* This question seeks to discover what the organization has done well in the past and is doing well in the present.

- *What possibilities, expressed and latent, provide opportunities for more vital, successful, and effective (vision-and-values congruent) forms of organization?* This question asks the participants to dream about and design a better future.

Since human systems typically grow in the directions about which they inquire, affirmative topic choices encourage people to select topics they want to see grow and flourish in their organizations. The choice sets the stage for AI through the application of the 4-D Cycle.

Careful, thoughtful, and informed choice of topics defines the scope of the inquiry, providing the framework for subsequent interviews and data collection. When AI was first being used, the design was an open topic choice, the "homegrown topic." The power of this type of discovery and dream led to the affirmative topic or topics to be studied by the organization, beginning with the AI foundational questions, as follows:

- Describe a high-point experience in your organization, a time when you were most alive and engaged.

- Without being modest, what is it that you value most about yourself, your work, and your organization?

- What are the core factors that give life to your organization, without which the organization would cease to exist?

- What three wishes do you have now to enhance the health and vitality of your organization?

Pre-selected Topic Choices

Some organizations have succeeded with pre-selected topic choices. For example, a midsized long-term care company located in the Midwest had been struggling with census development (attracting patients) in their nursing homes and assisted living centers. The company's centers provided a high quality of care, as evidenced by both regional and statewide awards received (such as the Governor's Award for quality of care). But many centers were experiencing a declining census base due to increased competition. The company decided to employ an AI Initiative to focus on census development.

The objective of the initiative (called the *Plus 1* campaign) was to jumpstart the census development effort by designing an inquiry that would include the center's stakeholders in working toward this common goal within a six-week budget period.

In an effort to focus the census campaign, the four key topics shown in **Table 2.1** were pre-selected in a subgroup planning discussion based on the four original topics:

Table 2.1 AI Key Topic Choices: "Plus 1 Campaign" Example

Original Topics	Pre-selected AI Topics
Center of Choice	Provider of Choice
Customer Loyalty	Resident Loyalty
Treatment of Staff and Residents	Genuine Appreciation
Teamwork	The Exceptional Team

The company embraced the idea that larger gains would be made and sustained by expanding its initial goal of census development to include these preselected AI topic choices in order to understand best how to collectively achieve its census goal.

Another example is referenced in **Table 2.2**. A large global automotive firm had a rough idea of what it would take to build the positive core of a certain division.[1] However, the company wanted to make its topics more boldly affirmative. Therefore, the AI consultant worked with the group and suggested the following preselected AI topics.

---

1 A helpful resource to assist in determining preselected topic choices is the *Encyclopedia of Positive Questions: Volume One* (Euclid, OH: Lakeshore Communications, 2002).

Table 2.2 AI Key Topic Choices: Automotive Example

Original Topics	Preselected AI Topics
Communications	Compelling Communications
Learning and Development	Continuous Learning
Management Behaviors	Integrity in Action
	Inspirational/Irresistible Leadership
Commitment and Enthusiasm	Culture As a Strategic Advantage
	Fun at Work
	Let's Do It

Who to Involve?

Selecting an affirmative topic choice can be a rich and satisfying experience, especially when it engages large numbers of people. At a minimum, a topic selection team should consist of people who have an important stake in the organization and its future. The team comprises any level of organizational participants from line staff to board of directors, so as to create a "representative" steering committee.

Ideally, the topic selection team involves a microcosm of the organization. More people is better, in terms of the overall organization's commitment to the process. Finally, the team must contain a variety of "voices," for in diversity comes a greater richness of relationship, dialogue, and possibility. **Table 2.3** details a list of potential stakeholders to consider for the topic team.

Table 2.3 Potential Representatives for Topic Team Selection

Potential Team Members

- Senior management
- Board of directors
- Middle management
- Staff or employee groups
- Union
- Customers
- Suppliers (vendors)
- Strategic partners
- Trade and professional associations

An important criterion in selecting participants is their ability to bring viewpoints and experiences from many different levels of and from many different perspectives about the organization. Therefore, the list of potential participants is not necessarily limited to employees. The participant is also the reasoning behind the statement "more is better." The more the intervention allows the participants to capture the true spirit of development, the better. In short, greater input will yield a stronger base of dialogue.

Once participants have been identified, a point about team dynamics becomes important. Every participant in the topic selection team should have an active role and an equal role. The organization's leaders, executives, and/or managers must not control the dialogue. The participants must use a watchful eye to prevent this from happening on either a conscious or subconscious level. All who participate must be encouraged to speak their minds and say what is in their hearts.

The ABCs of Topic Choice: How to Do It

The topic selection team meets for a one- to two-day period. (The material in **Chapter 3** provides examples that can help lead to the affirmative topic choice.) Whether a two-hour executive overview or a one-day introduction, the process begins with a brief introduction to the initiative and then goes directly into "mini-interviews," given the broad categories of topics initially selected. For these interviews, team members should be assigned to partners who are different from themselves with respect to functions, management levels, gender, age, tenure, or ethnicity. The goal is to get diverse opinions and to create dialogue. The mini-interview is an opportunity to create a genuine relationship with the partner, and that opportunity should not be wasted.

The four AI starting questions are generally used for the mini-interviews. These questions have been used in many variations. Thus, tailor the basic questions to suit the needs of the inquiry and the organization. The four questions are given in **Table 2.4**.

Table 2.4 The Four AI Foundational Questions

1. What was a peak experience or "high point"?
2. What are the things valued most about...
   • Yourself?
   • The nature of your work?
   • Your organization?
3. What are the core factors that "give life" to organizing?
4. What are three wishes to heighten vitality and health?

A worksheet for preparing for topic selection using the four foundational AI questions is available in **Chapter 10**.

Following the mini-interviews, topic selection team members should organize into groups of six to eight members, staying with their original partners. In this smaller group, each member should introduce his or her partner, share stories and highlights, and begin to find common threads within the group. The groups must allow adequate time and space for relationship building. They must also do whatever is necessary to prevent people from identifying themes before team members have really talked. The team must take time to dialogue, listen, and reflect. They must take good notes. Within these groups, team members must identify key patterns and/or themes that have emerged.

When the time is right, these groups re-assemble into the full group. The full group shares highlights and feedback from the small groups and discusses emerging themes and patterns. Are any of the themes related? Do any of them speak more loudly than another? Less than another? Will any of them have a greater or lesser impact on the organization? Subgroups continue talking and working, if necessary, moving in and out of the large group.

The facilitator of this session may also be a participant in the process. This is acceptable because the facilitator is a member of the group. The facilitator must not monopolize; however, the facilitator can add value by sharing insights and ideas that have emerged.

On a final note, throughout this process, considerable dialogue and deliberation over particular words or phrases are not "just semantics"; they are essential. In an AI intervention, a fundamental assumption is that "words create worlds"; so the words chosen will have enormous impact on what is shared, what is learned, and where the group is headed with the inquiry. This is especially true at this stage in the inquiry. The selection of the affirmative action topic(s) drives the process from this point forward. A difference of one or several words may create different conclusions later in the process. Therefore, the moderator must allow for ample time and discussion over points that may seem irrelevant to some.

Characteristics of Good Topics

Topics can be anything related to organizational effectiveness. Two such examples are provided in **Table 2.5**. They can include technical processes, human dynamics, customer relations, cultural themes, values, external trends, market forces, and so on. Topics must be positive affirmations of the organization's strengths and the potential it seeks to discover, learn about, and become. In the end, between three and five compelling topics should be identified, all of which meet the following criteria:

- Topics are affirmative or stated in the positive.
- Topics are desirable. They identify the objectives people want.
- The group is genuinely curious about them and wants to learn more.
- The topics move in the direction the group wants to go.

The following principles apply as the group proceeds through the process:

- Organizations move in the direction of their images of the future.
- Their images of the future are informed by the conversations they hold and the stories they tell.
- The stories they tell are informed by the questions asked, so…
- The questions asked are fateful; i.e., they affect the answers given.

Table 2.5 Affirmative Topic Choice Samples

British Airways	Other Company Examples
1. Happiness at Work 2. Harmony and Sharing among All Employees 3. Continuous People Development 4. Exceptional Arrival Experience	1. Revolutionary Partnerships 2. Customer Intimacy 3. Optimal Margins 4. Lightning-Fast Consensus 5. Transformational Cooperation 6. Leadership at Every Level

These topics are used in sample interview guides available in **Chapter 8**. These two examples help illustrate that topics can be anything an organization considers strategically and humanly important, such as technical processes, market opportunity identification, or social responsibility.

Table 2.6 summarizes useful guidelines to help create affirmative topic choices.

In the case of topic choice, the premise is still true: Human systems grow in the direction of their deepest and most frequent inquiries. The AI process truly begins when a conscious choice is made to focus on the affirmative.

Table 2.6 Affirmative-Topic Choice Guidelines

Main Points

Topic choice is a fateful act.
Organizations move in direction of inquiry.
Vocabulary is not "just semantics"; words create worlds.
People commit to topics they have helped develop.
  • Everyone is an active participant.
  • Diversity is essential.

Critical Choice

Build a representative steering committee, or
start with senior executive-level team, or
involve the whole system to whatever extent is possible.

Rules of Thumb

No more than five topics are ultimately selected.
Topics are phrased in affirmative terms.
Topic is driven by curiosity—spirit of discovery.
Topic is genuinely desired. People want to see it "grow."
Topic is consistent with the overall business direction and intentions of the organization.
Topic choice involves those that have an important stake in the future.
Topic choice should take up to two days.

The Discovery Phase

As was indicated in the overview of the positive core, the primary task in the Discovery phase is to identify and appreciate the best of "what is." This task is accomplished by focusing on peak times of organizational excellence, when people have experienced the organization as most alive and effective. Seeking to understand the unique factors (e.g., leadership, relationships, technologies, core processes, structures, values, learning processes, external relationships, planning methods, and so on) that made the high points possible, people deliberately "let go" of analyses of deficits and systematically seek to isolate and learn from even the smallest wins.

In the Discovery phase, people share stories of exceptional accomplishments, discuss the core life-giving factors of their organizations, and deliberate upon the aspects of their organization's history that they most value and want to bring to the future. In the Discovery phase, members come to know their organization's history as *positive possibility* rather than a static, problematized, eulogized, romanticized, or forgotten set of events. Empowering and hopeful conceptions of organization frequently, if not always, emerge from stories that are grounded in organizing at its best. Appreciation is alive and stakeholders throughout an organization or community are connected in a dialogue of discovery. Hope grows and organizational capacity is enriched. This is where the storytelling begins. The distinguishing factor of AI in this phase is that every carefully crafted question of the topic choice is positive.

The Dream Phase

The *Dream* amplifies the positive core and challenges the status quo by envisioning more valued and vital futures. Especially important is the envisioning of potential results and the bottom-line contributions to the world. The Dream phase is practical, in that it is grounded in the organization's history. It is also generative, in that it seeks to expand the organization's potential.

One aspect that differentiates AI from other visioning or planning methodologies is that images of the future emerge out of grounded examples from its positive past. These images are compelling possibilities precisely because they are based on extraordinary moments from an organization's history.[2] Sometimes this data is complemented with benchmarking studies of other organizations. In both cases, the good-news stories are used like an artist uses materials to create a portrait of possibility. Without all of the colors (red, green, blue, and yellow), the painting is less beautiful. So, too, are many visions or re-engineering programs that fail to take notice of organizational history.

The Dream phase is a time for key stakeholders to collectively share their stories of the organization's past and their historical relationship with it. As the various stories of the organization's history are shared and illuminated, a new historical narrative emerges. This narrative engages those involved in much the way a good mystery novel engages a reader. As participants become energetically engaged in re-creating the organization's positive history, they give life to its positive future.

---

2 "Ground theory" is the qualitative research methodology of choice. It is inductively derived from the study of the phenomenon it represents. It is discovered, developed, and provisionally verified through a process pertaining to the phenomena explored. For more information, refer to Anselm Strauss and Juliet Corbin, *Basics of Qualitative Research: Grounded Theory Procedures and Techniques* (Newbury Park, CA: Sage Publications, 1990).

During the Dream phase, organization stakeholders engage in conversations about the organization's position and potential in the world. Dialogue about the organization's calling and the unique contribution it can make to global well-being catalyzes a furtherance of images and stories of the organization's future. For many organization stakeholders, this is the first time to think "great" thoughts and create "great" possibilities for their organization. The process is both personally and organizationally invigorating.

The Design Phase

The Design phase involves the creation of the organization's social architecture. This new social architecture is embedded in the organization by generating *provocative propositions* that embody the organizational dream in the ongoing activities. Everything about organizing is reflected and responsive to the dream, the organization's greatest potential.

By crafting the organization's social architecture, stakeholders define the basic infrastructure. This phase requires in-depth dialogues about the best structure and processes to support the new system. By analogy:

> *To construct a home, one must decide to include or not to include windows, doors, a cooking space, sleeping spaces, spaces to greet visitors, fireplaces and/or walls, and so on.*

> *To construct an organization, one must decide to include or not to include leadership, strategy, structure, human resource management, customer relations and/or culture, and so on.*

As provocative propositions are composed, the desired qualities of organizing and organizational life are articulated. To further illustrate:

> *To construct a home, one must, after deciding to have doors, determine the number and nature of doors to build.*

> *To construct an organization, after deciding to have collaborative leadership, one must describe the quality of organizational life, relationships, and interactions that are desired enactments of collaborative leadership.*

The Design phase involves the collective construction of positive images of the organization's future in terms of *provocative propositions* based on a chosen social architecture.

The Destiny Phase

The Destiny phase delivers on the new images of the future and is sustained by nurturing a collective sense of purpose. It is a time of continuous learning, adjustment, and improvisation (like a jazz group)—all in the service of shared ideals. The momentum and potential for innovation are extremely high by this stage in the process. Because of the shared positive image of the future, everyone is invited to align his or her interactions in co-creating the future.

Stakeholders are invited into an open-space planning and commitment session during this phase. Individuals and groups discuss what they can and will do to contribute to the realization of the organizational dream as articulated in the provocative propositions. Relationally-woven action commitments then serve as the basis for ongoing activities.

The key to sustaining the momentum is to build an "appreciative eye" into all of the organization's systems, procedures, and ways of working. For example, one organization transformed its department of evaluation studies to valuation studies (dropping the e). Others have transformed focus group methods, surveys, performance management systems, merger integration methods, leadership training programs, diversity initiatives, and so on. The areas for application of AI are far-reaching. *Provocative propositions* may require that an organization's processes and system be redesigned.

Frank Barrett's four areas of competency development are central to sustaining appreciative organizing.[3]
1. Affirmative Competence
2. Expansive Competence
3. Generative Competence
4. Collaborative Competence

The Destiny phase is ongoing and brings the organization back, full circle, to the *Discovery* phase. In a systemic fashion, continued appreciative inquiry may result in new affirmative topic choices, continuous dialogues and continued learning.

This chapter presented a basic understanding of how AI works, but it is best learned by doing. A major change program is not necessary to get started. Something as simple as a team building initiative to get two areas within a department communicating is enough. It could be as simple as asking the question at the end of a staff meeting: what is it that we do well as a team? To get started with an AI initiative, a major change program is not required.

---

3 See F. Barrett, "Creating Appreciative Learning Cultures," *Organizational Dynamics* 24, no. 1 (1995): N 36-49.

One of the wonders of AI is that it can be implemented after limited exposure to its theory base (**Chapter 1**) and process overview (**Chapter 2**). Those who wish to have more formal training in AI can find references and a bibliography at the end of this book.

One of the first challenges in planning an AI initiative is how to introduce the concept, theory and process to an organization. The following chapter provides tips, suggestions, selected AI projects and sample agenda to help prepare for an AI initiative.

A good start usually leads to a good finish. An AI initiative is no exception. The way AI is introduced to the organization sets the tone for the process that follows. Getting started involves three key activities: introducing AI; defining the project, purpose and process; and creating a project plan. This next chapter includes an overview and examples of each of these three key activities.

3

Introducing, Defining, and Planning an Appreciative Inquiry Initiative

Introducing AI

Successful AI engagements begin by introducing AI to key stakeholders. Some of the best experiences introducing AI have shared some common characteristics.[1]

Involve the whole system from the beginning

It is important to introduce AI to as many informal opinion leaders as possible, along with formal leaders and keepers of the purse strings. At the very least, this will create a sense of anticipation in the organization. Often it will begin the long-term process of transforming the organization's inner dialogue.

Experience is an inspiring teacher

AI can't be "sold" without giving people an experience of AI.
What kind of experience do people really need in order to become engaged by and attached to this new way of thinking, working, and being? First, they need to experience an appreciative interview that can include some variation of the four generic AI questions presented in **Chapter 2**, as follows:

- Describe a peak experience or high point in your life—personal or professional?
- What do you value most about yourself? your work? your organization?
- What is the core factor that gives life to your organization?
- Describe your vision of the future for the organization and your world.

This interview helps people taste the power, the effect, and what some people have described as the intimacy of the AI process. It begins to build relationships within the team that later becomes the driving force for a whole-system inquiry. Each person finds a partner to interview. Each partner conducts an interview of the other for at least twenty minutes. Then, after the 40-minute interview session, the whole group is reconvened to discuss the experience. Depending on the size of the group, each person may introduce his or her partner to the group.

Second, people must hear the story of AI and its successes should be told. The powerful stories of personal transformation, community development, organizational change, and global organizing that have emerged from the extensive work in the not-for-profit and for-profit sectors are impressive and should be shared. These stories bring a level of inspiration, of "global

---

1 Adapted from D. Whitney and A. Trosten-Bloom, *The Power of Appreciative Inquiry: A Practical Guide to Positive Change*, (San Francisco, CA: Berrett-Koehler, 2003).

relevance," to the process. They touch people's hearts in ways that elevate their decision-making and assessment of AI as a viable tool for their organization. The details of the AI methodology can be explained through stories too, including testimonials to augment the presentation.

AI is a process that speaks for itself, when given the chance. As such, it calls consultants and facilitators of change to new levels of humility. A successful AI engagement depends less on a single person's capacities to communicate and facilitate and more on the wisdom and insight that resides at the heart of people throughout every organization and community.

Use alternative media where possible

Talking and stories are effective, but pictures (and other media) speak a thousand words. Videos, music, and other methods can enhance the story of AI—its assumptions and its successes. The message of AI can be supported by inspirational quotes posted on walls. Excerpts from stories and poems can be read. Movie clips may help describe the phases of the 4-D Cycle. Interviews and outcomes may be quoted. To illustrate, in one introduction to a large workforce, home videos were shown, shot in the company's production plants, of people talking about their peak experiences with the company. People must experience and be stimulated by AI on multiple levels.

Create cultural stretches consistent with the desired outcome

As with any good organizational change effort, each step, including the introduction, should be consistent with the desired outcome. For example, if an outcome is to reduce organizational hierarchies, the process leading to a "flattened" organization may be introduced. If another organizational outcome is to build bridges across functions, cross-functional introductions must be created.

"Surprises" in an AI introduction can be a powerful signal that there will be no more business as usual. For example, several of the most compelling introductory sessions have included field trips to production sites or sister divisions or involvement of external stakeholders in an initial AI mini-interview.

Include impact and first steps conversations

As AI is introduced, participants need space and opportunity to discuss and imagine implementation possibilities and impact while they are still close to the first experience. If first steps or next steps are included in discussions in the introduction, imagining what AI might offer participants' organization can be powerful. After a brief introduction and experience with an AI interview, participants should discuss why AI makes sense for the organization. People should have the opportunity to share how they see AI being used in their organization and to volunteer for upcoming activities. The key is to help people make the transition from the abstract to the practical, while inspiration and insights are high.

Inspire a Team

If a team can be inspired, activities will move faster and have greater organization-wide support. A small group of captivated and engaged people, even in nonleadership positions, can create a momentum for AI-based change. A cohesive group tends to be more creative, more insightful, and more enthusiastic than any one person.

Defining the Project Purpose, Process, and Plan

Purpose

AI can be used for a wide range of organizational initiatives—from transforming a whole-system culture to strategic planning to retention to process redesign. Clarity of purpose is essential to successful large-scale AI work. The purpose of the effort will usually affect the design of the AI process. For example, in the case of a merger or partnership between two organizations, the inquiry process would include cross-organization interviews, dialogues, and presentations. Once the purpose is established, the AI process is then designed. A simple statement should be articulated:

Our organization will use AI because we want to _____ in order to _____.

Process

Each AI process is designed to meet the needs and constraints of the organization(s) involved. Key questions to address in designing the process include:
- Who are the project sponsors and champions?
- What is the time frame for the effort?
- Who are the organization's stakeholders?
- How many people will be involved?
- Who will select topics for the inquiry?
- How many interviews will be conducted? Who will conduct them?
- How will stories collected in the interviews be used, shared, and analyzed?

- Who will be involved in envisioning the organization's future?
- Who will design the ideal organization?
- What communication vehicles will be used to keep people "in the loop"?
- How will logistics be managed?
- How will AI be integrated into the culture and its success sustained?

Some organizations, such as Hunter Douglas and British Airways North America, have used AI processes that span a year and have been fully integrated into the organization. Others, such as Nutrimental Foods and Roadway, have accelerated AI through a whole-system four-day summit.

Plan

The plan must align with the purpose and process. In addition, a most useful plan serves to order activities and point people in a common direction. It specifies who will do what and when, providing guidance for the effort. It must also be flexible because AI is an emergent process, one that unfolds as success builds upon success. As a result, organizations tend to find the most success by combining long-term macro plans, which approximate the activities and time frame of the AI 4-D Cycle, with short-term detailed plans, which clearly specify times and outcomes for specific activities such as meetings, trainings, interviews, and so on.

Samples

The remaining materials in this chapter are sample designs to initiate an AI-based process. The five samples provided can be used independently or in combination with one another.

- **Brief Introduction to AI: One-Hour Agenda**
  This session can be used to acquaint members of the organization with the concept and value of AI. It can build interest in and demand for a more intensive session. It is typically used as a brief, yet formal presentation by the AI practitioner to a decision-making group.
- **Executive Overview to AI: Two-Hour Agenda**
  This session provides a little more time to explore the theory and process of AI, as well as engage in a set of mini-interviews.
- **Workplace Redesign Using AI: Four-Hour Agenda and Slides**
  This session reinforces concepts introduced in the *Executive Introduction to AI* and introduces more of the 4-D model. It also includes more activities that allow participants to begin to practice AI techniques.

- **Values Project Using AI: Detailed Project Plan**
  This sample captures the same conceptual material as the other two options. In addition, it provides a concrete, detailed project plan that demonstrates the key elements of the AI process for the organization and an action plan to get the organization moving towards its destiny.
- **Two-Day AI Workshop, Agenda, Project Roles, and Interview Guide**
  This sample contains materials developed for an AI into the passion for nursing, as an example [Lovelace Health Systems]. It begins with a project overview and includes a steering team meeting agenda, steering team roles, the interview guide, and an interviewer training agenda. It shows responsibilities of the steering team and the organization of the steering team into subteams focused on the interview guide, data collection and synthesis, and communication.

The following materials can be modified or adapted to plan for and conduct an AI initiative for your organization.

Brief Introduction to AI: One-Hour Agenda

This is an outline for a brief informative introduction to AI that was used for a global automotive manufacturer. The goal is to introduce the key concepts and highlight success stories appropriate for the organization. It should include a mini-experience so that people get a sense of AI's potential and its uniquely positive way of looking at the organization's future.

Agenda

1. AI—What's It All About? (10 minutes)
   - Define AI (theoretical and practitioner).
   - Introduce the Five Principles:
     - The Constructionist Principle
     - The Principle of Simultaneity
     - The Poetic Principle
     - The Anticipatory Principle
     - The Positive Principle
   - Highlight AI benchmark success stories.
   - Hand out success stories such as Roadway: AI Summit.[2]
   - Ask why we are here.

2. Opening Interviews—Using two of the four foundational questions (30 minutes)
   - Set up the process by reading the four questions:
     - Describe a peak experience or high point in your life— personal or professional.
     - What do you value most about yourself? your work? your organization?
     - What is the core factor that gives life to your organization?
     - Describe your vision of the future for the organization and your world.
   - State that time is only committed for the following two questions:
     - Think about a time when you were really engaged in and excited about your work. Tell me a story about that time. What was happening? What were you feeling? What made it a great moment? What were others doing that

---

2 See article by Keith Hammonds, "Leaders for the Long Haul," *Fast Company* (July 2001): 56-58.

contributed to this moment? What did you contribute to creating this great moment?
   – If you had three wishes for this organization, what would they be?

- Divide participants into pairs; allow 15 minutes per person.
- Return to the group and discuss **how** it went (e.g., sharing descriptive adjectives).

3. Sample Interview Guide Using Client's Choice Topics (10 minutes)
    - Review traditional problem-solving topics clients provide and rework these topics into affirmative topic choices.
    - Review the newly revised topics in the new AI protocol.
    - Discuss differences from traditional problem-solving questions.

4. Wrap-up—How can it help your organization? (10 minutes)
    - Go around the room and ask: "How does this sound?" "Is it interesting enough to explore further?"
    - Ask: "What applications can you imagine for your organization?"
    - Discuss multiple ways to launch AI initiatives in a large organization.
    - Next steps: Think of one AI project, big or small, with which you might like to experiment.

After a formal introduction, the decision-making team will want to engage in a planning session with the AI practitioner to set up an Executive Overview and/or a half-day to two-day workshop. The AI process is flexible enough to fit the organization's desired design.

Executive Overview to AI: Two-Hour Agenda

This is an outline for a typical two-hour Executive Overview to AI. In a two-hour overview, the stage is briefly set and people should begin interviews as quickly as possible, typically within the first 15 minutes. The keys to the success of a brief introduction of AI are the interview experience, stories of the impact of AI in other organizations, and the opportunity for participants to discuss applications of AI for their organization.

Agenda

1. Context Setting (10 minutes)
   - State that it's time to rethink human organization and change.
   - Describe it as something hopeful…heartfelt (in facilitator's own words).
   - Ask why we are here.
   - Define AI (theoretical and practitioner).

2. Five Principles of AI (5 minutes)
   - Introduce the Five Principles:
     - The Constructionist Principle
     - The Principle of Simultaneity
     - The Poetic Principle
     - The Anticipatory Principle
     - The Positive Principle
   - Acknowledge that these are abstract principles.

3. Opening Interviews—Using the four foundational questions (35 minutes)
   - Set up the process by reading the following questions:
     - Describe a peak experience or high point in your life—personal or professional.
     - What do you value most about yourself? your work? your organization?
     - What is the core factor that gives life to your organization?
     - Describe your vision of the future for the organization and your world.
   - Divide participants into pairs; allow 15 minutes per person.
   - Return to the group and process how it went (e.g., sharing descriptive adjectives).

4. Introduction to AI (30 minutes)
   - Shift from deficit change to positive change.
   - Discuss the 4-D Cycle.
   - Describe a story of the AI process and success in another organization.
   - Discuss the importance of *topics and questions.*

5. A Sample Interview Guide (10 minutes)
   - Hand out a concrete example to participants.
   - Review two or three of the questions.
   - Discuss differences from traditional problem-solving questions.
   - Ask participants to imagine something like this for their organization.

6. The Choice Points: (15 minutes)
   - Decide what the topics are.
   - Decide who to include on the interview team and who to interview.
   - Decide how many interviews to conduct.
   - Discuss many possibilities for Dream and Design.
   - Make the point: "Our job today is not *planning!*"

7. Discussion: (15 minutes)
   - Go around room and ask: "How does this sound?" "Is it interesting enough to explore further?"
   - Ask: "What applications can you imagine for your organization?"
   - Ask what the next steps are.

Workplace Redesign Using AI: Four-Hour Agenda and Slides

Once the purpose of an initiative is determined, it is often necessary to introduce AI to the people who will be leading the overall effort. The following agenda is an example of a four-hour introduction of AI in such a situation.

In this example, the decision had been made to use AI to study and redesign the workplace environments throughout the company, worldwide. In this meeting, thirty people from around the world learned about AI and the project. They were invited to serve on the leadership team to help create the interview guide and to chart the course of the endeavor. This meeting was both an introductory meeting and a working session to get input and to clarify the project plan.

The slides that follow the agenda were used to support the introductory presentation. It provides background information about AI and specific information about the proposed project, including the stakeholders to be interviewed, the broad timeline for the project, and specific outcomes for various meetings. The two slides of assumptions (Slides 11 and 12) are especially noteworthy because they highlight the conditions for success and the constraints that influenced the ultimate design of the AI process. They are a good example of how an AI process can be tailored to the needs and constraints of a specific organization and purpose.

This meeting resulted in widespread support for the use of AI for the proposed project and numerous ideas for other ways the organization could use AI. Consequently, several informal AI initiatives have begun and are spreading best practices in areas related to customer service; employee morale; and, of course, work environment and productivity.

Agenda

1. Introductions and Stage Setting (5 minutes)
    *   State the purpose for this meeting.
    *   Introduce AI consultant.

2. Brief Introduction to AI (15 minutes)
    *   Discuss what it is—philosophy and methodology.
    *   Discuss definitions—Appreciate and Inquiry
    *   State where it's been used and with what results.

3. Mini-interview (45 minutes)
    *   Set up the process by reading the following questions:
        – Describe a peak experience or high point in your life—personal or professional?

- What do you value most about yourself? your work? your organization?
- What is the core factor that gives life to your organization?
- Describe your vision of the future for the organization and your world?
- Allow 20 minutes for each person to interview his or her partner.

4. Debrief Interviews and Dream Question (20 minutes)
   - Debrief interview experience—descriptive adjectives?
   - Debrief dream question—surprises?

5. More about AI (30 minutes)
   - Introduce the Five Principles:
     - The Constructionist Principle
     - The Principle of Simultaneity
     - The Poetic Principle
     - The Anticipatory Principle
     - The Positive Principle
   - Discuss the 4D Cycle; provide examples of how it has been implemented in other organizations.
   - Review the interviews just conducted and discuss their relationship to Discovery.

6. Break (10 minutes)

7. Proposed Process to Use for Workplace Redesign (45 minutes)
   - Discuss assumptions.
   - Discuss preliminary project plan.

8. Discussion and Decisions (45 minutes)
   - Discuss potential revisions to process.
   - Discuss timelines, including endpoint.
   - Discuss selection of core team.
   - Ask whether there are other issues.

9. Wrap-up—Next Steps? (15 minutes)

The following material shows the slides used for the session.

Workplace Redesign Using Appreciative Inquiry—PowerPoint Slides

An AI Approach for Designing a Flexible Workplace

"XYZ" Company

Intro Slide

Agenda

- Introductions
- So, what is AI?
- Mini-interviews
- Interview debrief
- More about AI
- The process we propose to use for this pilot
- Assumptions
- Wrap-up

Slide 1

What is Appreciative Inquiry?

"Ap-pre'-ci-ate, v."	*"In-quire', v."*
". . . to value or admire highly; to judge with heightened understanding; to recognize with gratitude."	". . . to search into, investigate; to seek for information by questioning."

Slide 2

AI . . .

- Focuses organizations on their most positive qualities
- Leverages those qualities to enhance the organization

Appreciative Inquiry is the study of what works well.

3

Slide 3

What's *Different* About AI?

- Purposefully positive
- Builds on past successes
- "Grass roots" and "top down"
- Highly participative
- Nurtures a positive "inner dialogue"
- Stimulate vision and creativity
- Accelerates change

Slide 4   4

The *"4-D"* Cycle

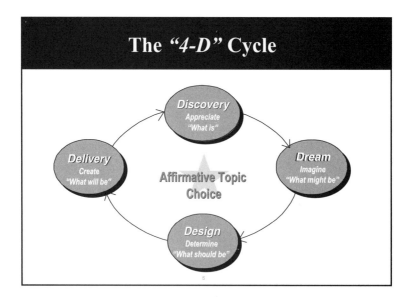

Slide 5   5

AI Success Stories

- **British Airways**
    Customer Service and Culture Change
- **Hunter Douglas Window Fashions Division**
    Culture Change and Strategic Planning
- **GTE Telecommunications**
    Union/Management Relations
- **United Religions Initiative**
    Organization Design
- **Green Mountain Coffee Roasters**
    Business Process Improvement

Slide 6

Questions to Start Us Thinking

- **Think back over your entire career, and all the work you've ever done – for pay, or for volunteer. Now, think about a peak experience or high point – a time when you experienced yourself as most successful and most satisfied.**

    - What was it like?

    - What were the conditions that contributed to that extraordinary level of success and satisfaction? In particular, what was it about the *physical space* that contributed to that experience?

Slide 7

Questions to Start Us Thinking cont.

- **Without being humble, what do you most value about . . .**

  - . . . yourself and your capacities to produce and contribute to your team and your organization?

  - . . . your team and its contribution to *XYZ company* and its clients?

  - What are the core factors that support your highest levels of success and satisfaction?

8

Slide 8

Questions to Start Us Thinking cont.

- **You fell asleep at work and you just woke up! You resume working and you are more successful and satisfied than you have ever been.**

  - Where are you working, and on what?

  - What is it like? (Juicy details, please!)

  - What is it about you, the situation, and the task that makes you so successful and satisfied?

  - What type of support did *XYZ company* provide for you that contributed to this remarkable spike in your performance?

9

Slide 9

Purpose for the Inquiry

To engage XXX location stakeholders in a process of discovering "how we work at our best," in order to:

- Determine the necessary components of a *successful* and *satisfying* "new workplace."

- Generate relevant and meaningful insights related to the physical, technological, sociological, and organizational *design* of the new space(s).

- Create a *positive transition* to the new space(s) by building understanding, support, and buy-in for the change (and all that the change implies).

10

Slide 10

Assumptions

- We want the flexible workplace solution to reduce operational costs.

- We want to increase or maintain employee satisfaction and performance.

- We are limited in our ability to get blocks of committed time from employees serving clients.

- We need to be focused on the future in that the changes we make today are dynamic and flexible enough to meet future needs.

11

Slide 11

Assumptions cont.

- We have a broad population with differing needs and preferences. Not every group or individual employee wants or needs the same setting/services to be optimally productive and engaged.

- This will be a big cultural change and we need to work with other groups to make this successful.

- The flexible workplace solution will reflect the input of our stakeholders.

- The process we use for implementing the change should be inclusive.

12

Slide 12

The "4-D" Cycle

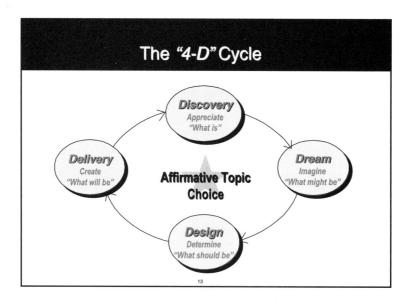

13

Slide 13

"Discovery"

- Getting Started

- Inquiry / Interviews

  - "When we are at our best, what makes work exciting, interesting, invigorating, motivating and productive?"

- Meaning Making / Reflections

- Preparation of report or presentation

14

Slide 14

Getting Started

- Hold an Initial Meeting:

  - 2-1/2-days

  - 17-20 participants (representatives from every related stakeholder group)

  - Early January

15

Slide 15

Meeting Outcomes

- Select Affirmative Topics

- Make Critical Decisions:

  - Who will conduct interviews?

  - Who will we interview?

    - Do we interview clients? Suppliers?

    - Do we benchmark other organizations? If so, which ones?

  - What are our timelines?

16

Slide 16

"Next Steps"

- Set up Sub-Groups

  - Finalize interview guides

  - Prepare interviewers

  - Prepare interview assignments / timelines

  - Make meaning of the "data"

17

Slide 17

Inquiry Process

- Conduct one-to-one interviews with stakeholders:
  - Internal "customers"
  - Clients
  - Vendors/suppliers
  - "Benchmark" organizations
  - Outside "experts" (architectural firms, consultants, other *XYZ company* offices, etc.)
- Answer the question: "When we are at our best, what makes work exciting, interesting, invigorating, motivating and productive?"

Slide 18

Meaning Making / Reflections

- Hold clusters of "synthesis" meetings
  - Keep interviewers *close* to their own data
  - Imagine *implications* and *possibilities*
  - Seek *inspiration,* not "common ground"

- •Meeting outcomes
  - Broad sharing of interview insights
  - Creation of a small team which will meet to create
    the final report / presentation of interview data

Slide 19

The Summit
DREAM, DESIGN and DESTINY

- 1-1/2 days
- As many stakeholders as possible
- Meeting outcomes
  - Determine a variety of *organizing possibilities* that will build upon what we've learned works (from the Inquiry).
  - Agree to a set of *design principles* around which we will organize our "new workplace."
    - These principles will ensure that we will continue to operate at the highest possible levels of customer and client satisfaction and productivity - even as we realize savings in our overall costs.
    - Organize to *implement* the "next steps" that are suggested by our Design.

20

Slide 20

In other organizations, this four-hour topic selection process can be expanded into a longer workshop format that allows organizations to explore other potential topic areas. The next sample is a detailed project plan for a larger AI Initiative.

Values Project Using AI: Detailed Project Plan

The American Red Cross project conducted 5,000 appreciative interviews during a two-month period to discover the values implicit in the services they provide nationwide. Careful and detailed planning were among the many factors that supported the success of this effort. As one might imagine with an organization of this size, commitment was unquestionable and enthusiasm was high. The project plan showed milestones along the way at the president's presentation at the national conference only three months after the Values Project began. This plan showed in great detail all that goes into a mass mobilized inquiry, from creating the interview guide, to identifying interviewers, to conducting interviews to collecting data and stories, to synthesizing the data and preparing a report. In this case, the final report was accompanied by a highly inspirational video showing various Red Cross employees and volunteers demonstrating the values in action as they provided service to people in need. The result of this extraordinary inquiry was the identification of "living values," the values that are embedded in the day-to-day activities of the American Red Cross.

Below is the project plan that illustrates how good project management techniques can be used to help an AI project arrive at various milestones. At the Red Cross, for example, there were important deadlines for the AI interviews. A national convention would be the place the narratives of hope, courage, and excellence would be shared. More than two thousand people from American Red Cross chapters all over the country came together for this convention. In a case like this, the details and time frames can make or break the AI momentum. AI is powerful on its own, but it is even better when the best project management and other consulting techniques are integrated to support the positive AI intentions.

Project Plan—Major Milestones

(**V**–Vince, **H**–Harry, **D**–David, **J**–Jan, **B**–Brian, **R**–Bob, **VT**–Values Technology)

Bold = Major Milestones

Italics = Values Technology

Standard = Appreciative Inquiry, combined activity or other activity

Week	Milestone	Date	Who	Notes	Complete = X
1	Project milestones and plan defined	3/2	V, H, B, R		X
	Interviewer criteria defined identified	3/2	V, H, B, R		X
	Major resource requirements	3/2	V, H, B, R		X
	Contracting with AI and VT vendors begins	3/3	CE&T		X
	Conference rooms reserved for training	3/4	B		X
	President's communication to ARC prepared and approved	3/4	J, B		X
	Chapters, blood regions, NHQ units supplying interviewers selected	3/5	V, H, B, R		X
2	Values project plan presented to OMC	3/8	President, V		X
	President's communication re: Values Project on Cross Link and by mail to board and key leadership	3/8	Comm.		X
	Hotel arrangements completed for AI training	3/9	CE&T	Hotel info and budget numbers needed for interviewer recruitment letters	X
	Interviewer recruitment letters completed and sent to execs.	3/9	J, B	Package contains cover letter specifying exec's recruitment job and due date and letter to interviewers describing process and admin. details	X
	Budget and account number assigned	3/9		B, Finance	X
	Execs. in chapters, blood regions, NHQ who are supplying interviewers are notified	3/10		Comm.	

Week	Milestone	Date	Who	Notes	Complete = X
	Determine requirements (if any) for customizing values inventory	*3/10*	*V, H, VT*		X
2	*Print values inventory forms*	*3/12*	*VT*		X
	Contract process completed with vendors	3/12	Contracts Office		X
3	*Determine values inventory sample range*	*3/16*	*H, VT*		X
	Mailing labels and cover letters sent to VT or mailing service	*3/17*	*H*		X
	Execs. send in names of *committed* interviewers	3/17	Field units	Send as e-mail to CE&T	X
	Interviewers sent notice of acceptance and travel details	3/18–3/19	CE&T	Phone or e-mail to CE&T	X
	Protocol for reporting stories and interview data determined	3/19	R	Demonstrate protocol for sending AI data during training; brief VT on interview reporting process	X
4	*Mail values inventories*	*3/22*	*VT*	Completed 3/19	X
	Determine date for values drafting meeting	3/22	V, H	Meeting date 5/5	X
	Develop participant list for drafting values statement	3/23	V, H		X
	AI training conducted	3/23–3/24	D, CE&T	Washington Marriott	X
4–6	*VT inventories completed and mailed in*	*3/23–4/9*	*HQ and field units*	Completed forms sent directly to VT. Forms processed as received.	
	Appreciative Inquiry interviews scheduled	3/25–3/28	Interviewers		
	Appreciative Inquiry interview protocol developed	3/25–3/28	D	Delivered to CE&T on 3/26, if possible.	
	Interview protocol sheets delivered to interviewers	3/29	CE&T		
4–7	AI Interviews conducted	3/29–4/12	Interviewers		
	Draft letter from president inviting senior leadership to values-drafting meeting	4/5	B, J	Meeting date 5/5	

Week	Milestone	Date	Who	Notes	Complete = X
5–7	Story compilation	3/29–4/13	Interviewers	Interviewers send in story packages as completed; stories sent to VT for analysis	
5	Send invitation to senior leadership meeting to draft values statements	4/7	President, V, H	NHQ, BHQ, field representation	
	Determine convention broadcast options	4/8	V, H, Comm		
	Reserve satellite time for convention broadcast	4/30	Comm	If necessary	
6	All VT forms completed and sent in	4/9	ARC staff		
6–9	Analysis of VT forms	4/9–4/30	VT		
7	All AI stories received by CE&T	4/15	Interviewers, CE&T		
	Electronic versions of stories sent to VT	4/17	R, CE&T		
7–9	Document analysis of stories	4/23–4/30	VT		
7	Purchase (or release) satellite time for convention	5/1	V, H, Comm	Decision and purchase on same day. Might need decision sooner.	
10	Meeting to interpret data	5/3–5/4	V, H, B, R, D, VT		
	Meeting to draft preliminary values statement	6-May	V, H, D, VT	Target date; key leadership from BHQ, NHQ, and field	
10–12	Prepare convention presentation and related activities and materials	5/5–5/20	V, H, B, R, Comm, et al		
	Preliminary values statement presented to president	5/6	V, H		
	Draft values statement revised as necessary	5/7	V, H, B, R		
10	Draft values statement sent to strategic planning comm. of board and appropriate senior leaders for comment	5/11	V, H, B	Involve strategic planning committee of the board	
10–11	Comments on draft values statement received from board members and senior leaders	5/13–5/19	CE&T		

Week	Milestone	Date	Who	Notes	Complete = X
12	Presentation of Red Cross Values at National Convention	5/21–5/23	President, V, H, D		

Two-Day AI Workshop, Agenda, Project Roles, and Interview Guide

This sample contains materials developed for an employee development project focusing on the passion for nursing at Lovelace Health Systems. It begins with a project overview and includes a steering team meeting agenda, steering team roles, the interview guide, and an outline for interviewer training. It shows responsibilities for the steering team and the organization of the steering team into subteams focused on the interview guide, data collection and synthesis, and communication.

LOVELACE HEALTH SYSTEMS
"Discovering the Passion for Nursing"
November 2000 – December 2001

Purpose and Overview

The vision for Lovelace Health Systems is "to be the best place to get care and the best place to give care." Achieving this vision is challenging when nurse turnover at organizational and national levels ranges from 18 to 30 percent per year. In addition to direct expenses incurred from this phenomenon, negative effects such as short staffing, unfilled vacancies, low morale among staff and providers, continuous orientation, and disrupted teamwork are significant.

Although 18 to 30 percent of the nursing staff do leave health care organizations annually, large numbers of nursing staff also continue within organizations. *The aim of this leadership project is to discover why nurses choose to stay at Lovelace and to gather this insight in such a way that the process, in and of itself, contributes positively and minimizes negativity.* The results of the inquiry will be specific actions targeting elements that nurses find engaging and attractive and that contribute to individual tenure. Identifying these attributes will enable nurses to focus on projects, process improvements, and rewards that are aligned to nurses' passion for their profession and Lovelace.

Expected outcomes include an increase in nurse retention from 2000 levels, qualitative findings that articulate positive elements of the nursing organization, and the identification of specific tactics that will enhance future retention. It is anticipated that the AI process will generate positive feedback and goodwill, as measured by the interview guide. Evaluation measurements will include nurse turnover levels, identification of what is working within the nursing organization, and strategies designed to repeat and amplify success.

Primary participants are nursing leaders and hospital nurses at Lovelace. Lynne Frazier, senior vice president of Human Resources; Dr. Martin Hickey, CEO; and Jim Ferando, COO, provide sponsorship to ensure project success.

Progress and Success

As of July 2001, The steering group is alive and active, topics are identified, and the interview guide is pilot-tested and completed. Thirty nurse interviewers have been trained, and interviews are happening in the 300-nurse employee population of the hospital. A goal is to interview at least 120 nurses, with no limit. All who wish to be interviewed will be invited to interview. The inquiry will continue through September, and the Summit will be held in October 2001. Design activities will carry into 2002 and beyond.

Project Leaders

- Kathy Davis, R.N., M.B.A., Vice President Hospital and Nursing Services, Lovelace Health Systems, Albuquerque, NM, *Kathleen.Davis@Lovelace.com*
- Susan O. Wood, M.S., Corporation for Positive Change, *Susanowood@toast.net*

Sponsorship and Funding

Kathy Davis holds a Robert Wood Johnson Executive Nurse Fellowship, a three-year fellowship that includes a leadership project and professional development. She is leading "Discovering the Passion for Nursing" with enthusiastic sponsorship of the Lovelace leadership team.

Steering Group Kickoff Meeting

Purpose: Orient Steering Group to AI; plan and launch inquiry

Goals:
- Understand AI as a foundation of this project
- Select topics for inquiry
- Organize project team and project plan

Deliverables:
- Project timeline and plan
- Steering group roster and role
- Draft interview guide
- Communication plan

Project Stakeholders:
- Medical Council and MSEC
- Recruitment and retention committee
- Marketing
- HR staff
- Senior team

Agenda

Day 1		
Activity	**Leader**	**Time**
Introductions/purpose	Kathy Davis	10 minutes
How we got here—Why AI agenda/roles	Susan Wood	5 minutes
Appreciative Interviews Mural (best stories/themes)	Susan Wood	2 hours
LUNCH		
Introduction to Appreciative Inquiry	Susan Wood	45 minutes
Theory and foundation	Kathy Davis	
Topic selection for inquiry	Susan Wood	45 minutes
A "fateful act"		
What you want more of		
BREAK		
Topic definition/lead-ins	Susan Wood	1 hour
Subgroups		
Definition		
Rotate subgroups/refine		
Review/close	Kathy/Susan	20 minutes
Day 2		
Agenda/goals	Kathy/Susan	5 minutes
Brief interviews 1/1	Susan	10 minutes
2 questions and comments		
Interview guide development	Susan	15 minutes
Qualities of appreciative questions		
Sample guide/structure		
Subgroups develop questions by topic	Susan	1 hour, 15 min
Refine lead-in		
Draft 3-4 questions		
Appreciative feedback and improve questions		
Assemble draft guide		
LUNCH		
Visioning activity for project	Susan	30 minutes
Called to do or be		
Best possible results		
Project Planning	Kathy/Susan	
Timeline		
Stakeholders and interviewers		
Data collection/synthesis		
Steering Group role		
Next steps/commitments	Kathy/Susan	30 minutes
Closing comments	All	15 minutes

STEERING GROUP ROLE

The role of the steering group includes all of the activities listed below. Some have specific time frames for completion; others are ongoing for the life of the project. In addition, three subteams have specific functions related to the interview guide, data collection and synthesis, and communication.

____ Articulate purpose and objectives
____ Identify and enroll stakeholders
____ Select topics for inquiry
____ Refine project plan
____ Form subgroups for tasks and responsibilities
____ Plan Summit
____ Track progress and outcomes during and after inquiry/measurement
____ Feed ideas and information to communication team
____ Integrate subgroup tasks
____ Be an interviewer

STEERING GROUP SUBTEAMS

1. **Interview Guide Team: February through April**
    Cynthia, Penny, Diane, and Barbara
    ____ Draft interview guide and edit
    ____ Pilot test and edit interview guide due by end of April
    ____ Organize interview training May/June
    ____ Enroll first-round interviewers

2. **Data Collection and Synthesis: April through August**
    Marti, Johanna, Mary, Melody, Kathy, and Sandra
    ____ Organize interviews
    - Expand interviewers by enrolling when interviewing
    - Identify and invite interviewees representing all inpatient departments
    - Schedule and track planned and completed interviews
    - Capture stories—database, storyboard, and synthesis meeting
    - Interview all who want an interview
    ____ Prepare data/stories for Summit

3. **Communication Team: Ongoing**
    Kathy, John, Fran, Kerry, Sandra, and Yvette
    ____ Outline communication plan, audiences, and messages
    ____ Design and conduct kickoff for nurses (May)

_____ Help solicit interviewers
_____ Update stakeholders
_____ Produce internal news and updates
_____ Invite stakeholders to Summit
_____ Progress and follow up reporting to all
_____ Link project to strategic objectives and vision

LOVELACE HEALTH SYSTEMS
Discovering the Passion for Nursing
Interview Guide

Thank you for participating in this interview. I am an interviewer for the "Discovering the Passion for Nursing" project. During 2001, we will be inquiring and learning more about why nurses choose to stay at Lovelace and how to amplify the positive aspects of work life there. Nurses will be interviewed directly to collect the "best-case" stories upon which to build the future. The point is to move forward in achieving the vision "to be the best place to get care and the best place to give care" at Lovelace. Your input will be an important contribution to generate meaningful ideas and actions.

Many times in interviews we ask questions about why things don't work well. This time we are going to approach things from a different angle. We are going to learn about your experiences of success here at Lovelace so we can build on those experiences.

This summer we will interview as many nurses who work in the hospital as possible. When the interviews are complete, everyone's input will be synthesized to identify qualities of nursing practice at Lovelace that make it unique. With those qualities as a foundation, we will create specific future steps to build on the strengths.

The conversation will take an hour or so. I'm going to take notes as we talk. During our interview, we will be exploring your experiences in several areas:
1. The Privilege of Nursing
2. Humor: The Other Vital Sign
3. Appreciation
4. The Exceptional Team

Shall we begin?

Topic 1: The Privilege of Nursing

Our profession is based on caring. Nurses blend scientific knowledge with intuition, compassion, and understanding. For the professional nurse, the privilege to participate in the healing relationship is what creates and maintains the passion for nursing. We would like to acknowledge that passion and explore with you how to acknowledge and develop this in everyone who work at LHS.

1. What were your hopes and aspirations when you chose nursing as a profession?
2. What is it about nursing today that keeps you involved?
3. The privilege of caring for others has sparked in many of us the passion for nursing. Describe a situation in which you felt this passion.

Topic 2: Humor: The Other Vital Sign

Humor is an important sign of life, critical to our survival. It enables us to cope with absurdities, sad situations, and the insecurities of our lives. Humor is vital to our ability to handle the stresses of the work environment.

1. Describe a work experience in which humor eased a painful, stressful, or tense situation or enhanced a positive one.

Topic 3: Appreciation

All of us yearn for fulfillment through meaningful work. The most gratifying appreciation is that which is expressed from the heart by active communication, a kind gesture, or written words.

1. Describe a time in which you felt appreciated.
2. What is the most meaningful way your contribution is recognized and appreciated?

Topic 4: The Exceptional Team

An exceptional team is built on individual expertise and excellent collaboration. Cooperative teamwork, clear communication, and wisdom are essential elements in delivering superior patient care.

1. Describe a time in which you participated as a team member where your expertise truly made a difference to the team.
2. Imagine you are working with an exceptional team. Describe the team.
3. What did you value about this team?

Excellence in Nursing Practice Award

Imagine you are representing Lovelace in accepting a national award for "Excellence in Nursing Practice" in 2003.

1. Describe what you admire most about nursing practice at Lovelace.
2. What makes nursing practice at Lovelace unique?

Three Wishes

What three wishes do you have that would make Lovelace the best place to give care and the best place to receive care?

Reflections on This Interview

In closing, I would like to ask you two questions about this interview:
1. What was the highlight of this interview?
2. Would you like to participate in the process of conducting this interview?

Appreciative Interview Summary Sheet

Interviewer: _____

Interviewee: _____ Unit: _____

R.N._____ L.P.N._____ Years of experience_____ Years at LHS _____

1. What were the *best quotes* that came out of this interview?

2. What were the *best stories* that came out of this interview?

3. What were the *best wishes* that you heard in your interview?

4. What were the *best practices* or *specific recommendations* that you heard reflected in your conversation?

Length of Interview: _____

DISCOVERING THE PASSION OF NURSING
Interviewer Training

Purpose:

To prepare interviewers to conduct appreciative interviews

Goals:
- Understand AI as a foundation of this project
- Experience appreciative interview in relation to topics
- Develop comfort and expertise using Lovelace Interview Guide
- Understand expectations and logistics for conducting interviews to include number, timeline, and documentation

Agenda

Activity	Leader	Time
Introductions/purpose	Susan Wood Cynthia or Toni	10 minutes
Agenda/roles	Susan Wood	5 minutes
Appreciative interviews Relate to topics selected	Susan Wood	40 minutes

Introduction to Appreciative Inquiry
    Theory and foundation
    Q&A
	Susan Wood	50 minutes

BREAK		

Interview Guide Review
    Your topics
    Content/structure of a great interview
	Susan Wood	15 minutes

Good Skill question practice—Round 2
    Redirecting negative responses
    Managing time
    Using silence
    Smooth transitions
    Extracting the best stories
    Identifying immediate improvement ideas
	Pairs	30 minutes

Q&A and selected skills practice		30 minutes

Close and next steps (list of interviewees, scheduling, inviting interviewees, data delivery, and so on.)

The agendas, interview protocols, and methods shown in this chapter have been successfully modified and used with hundreds of organizations (large and small, for-profit and nonprofit), governments, and Appreciative Inquiry Consulting (AIC, see p. 423) to accomplish their respective organizational strategies and structures. The purpose of these samples is to provide different ways to launch an AI Initiative for key organizational leaders and their stakeholders.[3]

---

3 For additional information on either a 45-minute AI Introduction or a Four-Hour AI Design, refer to the Jane Watkins and Bernard Mohr book, *Appreciative Inquiry: Change at the Speed of Imagination* (San Francisco: Jossey-Bass/Pfeiffer, 2001).

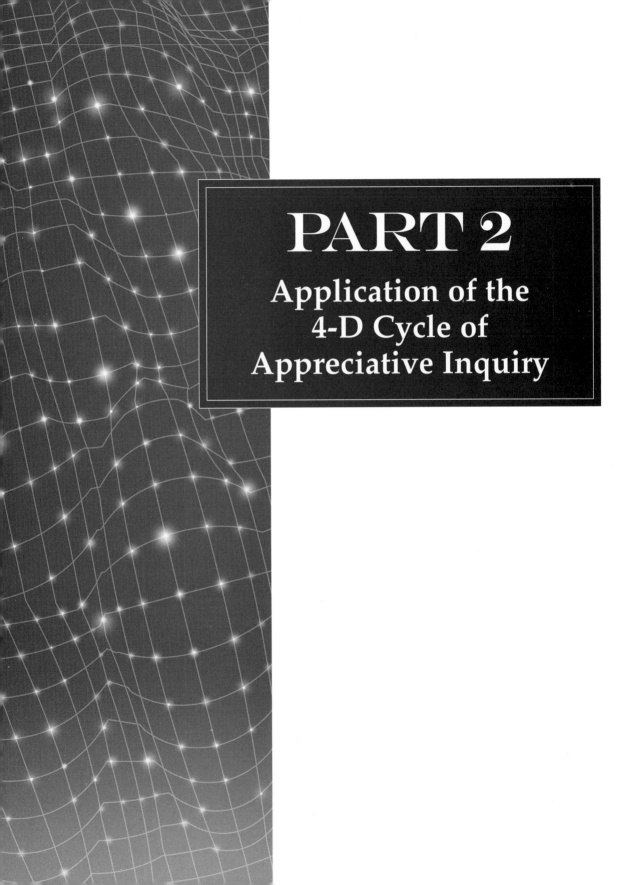

PART 2

Application of the 4-D Cycle of Appreciative Inquiry

The hallmark of AI is an intense exploration of questions, the "unconditional positive questions." The art and practice of asking such questions strengthens an organization's ability to realize its full potential. AI engages the whole organization (often hundreds, sometimes thousands of people) in crafting and posing positive questions.

However, AI is more than crafting questions and conducting interviews. As a process for organizational transformation, AI is best learned and understood through the use of the 4-D Cycle of *Discovery, Dream, Design*, and *Destiny*. This cycle can be as formal as a company-wide process involving every stakeholder. On the other hand, it can also be as rapid and informal as a conversation between two colleagues trying to make a difference in their organization. When individuals or organizations discover and tap rich, inspiring accounts of peak experiences and link the positive core to any change agenda, business transformations never thought possible can emerge. The 4-D Cycle presents AI as a dynamic process of change. This 4-D Cycle, along with supporting information, is detailed in the next four chapters.

- *Discovery:* What gives life? (Chapter 4)
- *Dream:* What might be? (Chapter 5)
- *Design:* How can it be? (Chapter 6)
- *Destiny:* What will be? (Chapter 7)

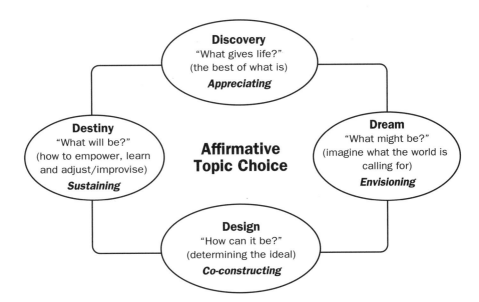

This brief overview of the 4-D Cycle provides the context for the next several chapters. During the first phase, *Discovery*, interviews are conducted to uncover success stories from the company's past and present. These include not only organizational successes, but also the successes of individuals. In order to capture these positive life-giving events, the questions asked during the interview will be intentionally designed to solicit positive affirming answers.

Chapter 4 provides examples of engaging AI interview questions. Once the interviews are completed, the stories are shared and discussed in an attempt to create a shared vision, or *Dream*, of the future for the company. The **Case Clipping** at the end of this chapter is from a Texas insurance company.

Chapter 5 illustrates the movement from Discovery to the Dream stage through an application of AI at the Roadway Express Summit. The chapter ends with an introduction to *Design*, which takes the vision of what the organization can be and creates specific, action-oriented *provocative propositions*, also called *possibility statements* or *design statements*.

Chapter 6 contains the Tendercare, Inc.'s "+1 Census Development Campaign" case study to demonstrate how an organization and its key customers move together from *Discovery* to *Dream* in order to create a set of possibility statements in the Design phase. The chapter introduces the final phase, *Destiny*, in which the core care team publicly declares intended actions and asks for organization-wide support from every level.

Chapter 7 concludes this part with the Destiny phase, using the **Case Clipping** from Hunter Douglas Window Fashions and describing how it has changed and sustained its appreciative corporate culture.

4

Discovery:
What Gives Life?

The most important thing we do as consultants is inquiry. We try to read situations; we do organizational analysis and diagnosis. It all starts with inquiry. The key point is that the way we know is fateful. The questions we ask, the things that we choose to focus on, the topics we choose determine what we find. What we find becomes the data and the story out of which we dialogue about and envision the future. And so the seeds of change are implicit in the very first questions we ask. Inquiry is intervention.

—David Cooperrider

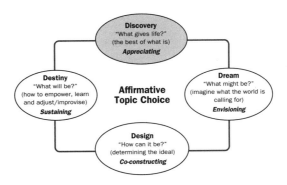

The task in the Discovery phase is to appreciate the best of "what is" by focusing on one's best experiences or moments in time. In this phase, stakeholders share the story of exceptional accomplishments, exploring the "life-giving" factors of the organization. *Discovery* is an inquiry process to begin identifying the themes in the stories told by those interviewed. The data collected during the interviews helps one to locate, illuminate, and understand the distinctive strengths that lend the organization life and vitality when functioning at its best.

Data collection and narrative exploration represent the core of the inquiry process. They serve as the jumping-off point for dialogue and the application of learning to a unique theory of organizational innovation and change. In traditional research processes, data is collected as an objective reality. It is assumed to stand apart from the people involved and the process through which it is generated. In the AI process, collecting objective data is not the goal. It is not the goal because interviewers assume an active role in order to explore and enliven the interview process through their stories of the organization.

When collecting data, an important goal is to stimulate participants' excitement and delight as they share their values, experience, and history with the organization and their wishes for the future. In addition, thinking and dialoguing about positive possibilities are invited into the process. In order to lead the Discovery phase interview, the interviewer must listen and learn. Data collection and it's associated narrative exploration are mutual learning processes. Both the interviewer and the interviewee learn as they explore the participants' values, peak experiences, and aspirations for the organization's future.

This chapter begins by exploring the key steps in Discovery data collection. Considerations for data collection are presented. Instructions are provided to create the interview protocol and guidelines for effective AI questions. Tips for conducting AI interviews are included. This chapter ends with a **Case Clipping** from an insurance company of a completed interview guide. **Chapter 8: Learning Applications and Resources** provides several sample interview guides and a sample AI Report.

Key Steps in Data Collection

Discovery: At this point, inquiry begins. Management genius rests on the ability to craft and ask the unconditional positive question, a powerful, penetrating question that mobilizes an organization-wide inquiry and draws out the best creativity and vision from all. By transcending problem- and deficit-based approaches to change management, AI opens a new path to affirmative growth in human systems. This path begins with discovering who one is when he or she is at his or her very best.

Collecting appropriate, useful, and positive data is the key to the Discovery phase. Data collected at this stage serves as the basis for the next stage of creating the organizational dream. **Table 4.1** summarizes the key steps.

Table 4.1 Key Steps in Data Collection

1. Identify stakeholders.

2. Craft an engaging appreciative question.

3. Develop the appreciative interview guide.

4. Collect and organize the data.
   - How will the findings be recorded?
   - How will the team's data be compiled?
   - Who will do it?

5. Conduct interviews.

6. Make sense of inquiry data.

Step 1. Identify Stakeholders

Successful Discovery data collection requires identifying key stakeholders in the organization and deciding who will interview whom. Stakeholders are typically people who have a vested interest in and/or a strong impact on the organization's growth and future and who can supply valuable insights into selected topic areas. These members become the core AI team or the steering group. **Chapter 2, Table 2.3, Potential Representatives for Topic Team Selection,** provides a list of possible stakeholders.

Once key stakeholders have been identified, this core team (sometimes referred to as the steering committee) creates the interview guide and develops the inquiry architecture. This team can be as small as four people or as large as twenty-five. Ideally, this team involves a microcosm of the whole organization and includes a variety of voices in order to encourage diversity. The goal is to seek out stakeholders who offer unique viewpoints and experiences from many levels and perspectives in the organization. This is why the list of potential participants is not necessarily limited to employees, but also can include customers, suppliers, and community representatives. Inclusiveness is also the reasoning behind the statement that "more is better." Larger representation allows for a stronger base of dialogue.

Step 2: Craft an Engaging Appreciative Question

As stated above, the heart and spirit of the AI process starts in the Discovery phase with the crafting of engaging questions. The questions asked are fateful, in that they ultimately determine the change of direction for the organization. The following guidelines generally produce engaging appreciative questions:

- State questions in the affirmative.
- Begin with a leading question that builds on the affirmative topic choice.
- Give a broad definition to the topic.
- Invite participants to use storytelling and narratives.
- Phrase in *rapport* talk, not *report* talk.
- Allow ambiguity because it gives room to "swim around."
- Value "what is."
- Spark the appreciative imagination by helping the person locate experiences that are worth valuing.
- Convey unconditional positive regard.
- Evoke essential values, aspirations, and inspirations.

AI is based on the premise that the art of inquiry moves in the direction of evoking positive images that lead to positive actions. Therefore, every question must begin with a positive preface. This plants the seed of what is to be studied. It deliberately tells the interviewee what will be learned. Each question has a Part A and a Part B.

Part A: The question must evoke a real personal experience and narrative story that helps participants to see and draw on the best learnings from the past.

Part B: This part of the question allows the interviewer to go beyond the past to envision the best possibility of the future.

This premise explains the need for engaging appreciative questions, as shown below.

Organizations Developing Bold and Enlightened Leadership: Think about the best organization you have seen, heard, or read about or directly experienced outside of your organization. We are looking for exemplary, even radical, models or places that attract great people because of the positive culture or enlightened leadership at every level. Please share what you have heard or know of this organization and its approaches to leadership or leadership development. What is its story? What characteristics do you most admire about this organization and its leaders? Why? What is it doing? How is it doing it? What are the benefits? Where can we take this model?

Step 3: Develop the Appreciative Interview Guide

Once the stakeholders are identified, the core team must arrange, develop, and distribute an interview guide. Creating the interview guide is an exciting task. A complete interview guide incorporates a formal introduction to explain the project and the purpose of the interview, the desired questions to be asked, and a summary report sheet. This process includes three types of questions:

1. Opening questions:
   - Describe a "peak experience" or "high point."
   - What are the things valued most about:
     – Yourself?
     – The nature of your work?
     – Your organization?
2. Questions centering on three to five affirmative topic choices selected by the core team.
3. Concluding questions:
   - What are core factors that "give life" to organizing?
   - What are three wishes to heighten the vitality and health of your organization?

Opening Questions
The first and second of the opening questions capture the tone and direction that set the stage for the entire inquiry. For example:

- Let's start with something about you and your work—and a larger sense of purpose. What is it you do now… and what most attracted you to your present work that you find most meaningful, valuable, challenging, or exciting?
- One could say a key task in life is for everyone to discover and define his or her life purpose. As you look back over important times in your life, can you share a story about a moment or a milestone, where clarity about your life purpose emerged for you? For example, perhaps you experienced an important event or the gift of a special mentor or teacher or perhaps you were given unexpected opportunities or faced difficult challenges.

Topic Questions

The second set of questions relate to the affirmative topic choices. They should be in the form of questions with lead-ins that assume the subject matter in the question already exists. For example, one possible topic choice is "positive change initiatives":

- We have all been part of initiatives, large or small, where we have joined with others to create positive change, that is, change that brings ideas and dreams of a better world into being. As you scan the years of your work, certainly there have been ups and downs, high points and low points. For the moment, we would like you to reflect on a "high-point" experience, a time that is memorable and stands out, when you felt most engaged, alive, challenged, or effective as part of a positive change initiative.

  - Please share the story of the experience. Where was it? What happened? What were your feelings and insights about change?

  - Now beyond this story, let's imagine I had a conversation with people who know you quite well I asked them to share the three best qualities they see in you and the qualities or capabilities… you bring to the leadership of change. What would they say?

  - As you continuously seek to develop into the best leader you can be, would you be willing to share with me how you generate your own inspiration to lead positive change initiatives? What are the personal, spiritual, and developmental practices you have found most useful?

This second set of topic questions is the heart of the inquiry and allows the participants to collect the data that is necessary to advance the human system or the organization being studied to achieve the desired objectives.[1]

Concluding Questions

The concluding question is most effective when it incorporates and follows upon the third and fourth foundational questions. For example:

- It is now 2010. We are able to preserve our core strengths, and we have innovatively transformed our ways of doing business to best serve our customers. It is an organization you want to be part of and others want to join. How would you now describe this division's relationships with its business partners? How does this business work to achieve strategic business objectives? What are people doing? How are you working differently in 2010? What was the key to your success and the organization's success? How did you get there?
- What was the smallest change the division made that had the most significant impact?

Two options for a generic concluding question that have often been used to good effect are:

- Looking toward the future, what are we being called to become?
- What three wishes do you have for changing the organization?

Each **Case Clipping** in the following chapters offers complete interview guides. Additional sample interview guides are provided in **Chapter 8.**[2]

An interview guide should contain instructions for preparing, conducting, and reporting the interview. **Table 4.2,** on the next page, provides tips for creating an AI interview guide.

---

1 These questions were selected from the *Business as an Agent of World Benefit (BAWB) Interview Guide.* This is a project co-sponsored by The Weatherhead School of Management at Case Western Reserve University, Spirit in Business, The Society for Organizational Learning and Appreciative Inquiry Consulting, LLC.

2 Much of the material from Part III—slides, worksheets, examples, and Classic articles—is available in CD-ROM form, from Lakeshore Communications (see last page).

Table 4.2 Tips for Creating AI Interview Guides

AI Interview Guides should include:

– Project background and description.
– Interview instructions.
– List of questions to ask.
– Instructions to collect and record data.
– Information summary sheet.
– Demographic summary sheet (if applicable).
– Interviewee/respondent consent form.
– Description of follow-up activities.
– Thank you to the interviewee/respondent.

Step 4: Collect and Organize the Data

Designing appreciative questions requires some thought regarding how the data will be collected and organized. Careful consideration is needed because the design entails the discovery of the life-giving forces. **Table 4.3, Data Collection and Organizing Considerations,** highlights information that must be taken into consideration in order to discover, re-create, and understand the positive core of the organization.

Table 4.3 Data Collection and Organizing Considerations

Methods of data collection	Interviews
	Participant observations
	Focus groups
Agents of data collection	Outside party
	Core team or steering committee
	Everyone—the interview chain
Information that is meaningful to collect	Best quotes and wishes
	Best stories and practices
	Exemplars
	Illustrations of the positive core
The AI Report	Rich narratives
	Exemplary stories
	Description of the positive core
	Multi-media presentations

Finally, there are some side benefits to the process of inquiry, beyond the content. A typical question asked is "how many interviews should we conduct?" The answer: "Do as many interviews as possible." Why? For one thing, it is clear that inquiry and change are a simultaneous event and the changes begin at the moment of inquiry. It makes sense to involve all relevant and affected parties in any change. This has been demonstrated from years of change research. Secondly, the methods make it easy and possible to engage everyone. The cascade interview approach works well. For example, thirty or so people are trained in AI and they each interview three others in their system. After their interviews, they ask the person interviewed how the interview went and whether he or she would be willing and interested in conducting three interviews? Many people instantly say yes, and the process is off and running. The first thirty people interview an additional ninety people. Those 90 then interview 270. The whole process builds momentum quickly. At the Red Cross Values Project, 5,000 people shared their hopes and dreams for the future within two months.[3]

Another major benefit is what happens to the interviewers themselves. As they sit down with people from different departments and with different functions and meet with stakeholders at every level, they often report how their own visions of possibility expand. It is often exciting for people to experience this view, and the resulting networks become major resources. These people begin to see the organization much as any CEO would, taking in the big picture. In the early stages of AI work, the careers of people doing the interviews are often accelerated.

At Touche Ross in Canada, for example, John Carter conceived the Discovery phase as a leadership development process. Thirty or so of the high-potential junior partners conducted the interviews, first with each other as training and then with 400 senior partners of the firm. These junior partners then analyzed the themes and stories and kicked off the partnership's strategic planning process. They played a prime–time role. They learned the industry's trends and opportunities. They developed a consciousness of the whole, and they built relationships. At the same time, "the elders" were valued. The younger people showed the deepest kind of respect: listening to the best of history and recording insights, acquiring hard-won wisdom, and helping to transmit values. The elders not only felt valued, but also felt like teachers. This created a positive atmosphere of trust and regard. Whereas many change initiatives are a threat, this kind of AI generates positive feelings. Consider Margaret Mead's observation about the intergenerational nature of societal learning. The best learning, she argued, was always intergenerational, with the young people alongside the elders and together with the middle generation

---

3 Refer back to **Chapter 3, Introducing, Defining, and Planning an AI Initiative,** for the ARC Values Project.

adults.[4] Bringing people together in these kinds of natural ways, across the whole system, quite simply brings out the best in human behavior.

These examples illustrate a key point: There are tremendous developmental benefits for organizations in the Discovery phase alone. All of this is missed if one simply thinks of the data collection in scientific "sampling" terms. Again, inquiry and change are a simultaneous event, and the system can benefit as much from the process as if can from the succeeding content.

Step 5: Conduct the AI Interviews

The final section provides helpful tips for conducting the AI interviews. The following tips should be reviewed before the first interview begins.[5]

1. **Explaining Appreciative Inquiry:** Like anything new, appreciative interviewing may seem awkward at the beginning. It may be equally awkward for the interviewee. He or she may be caught up in looking at the organization as a problem-to-be-solved and may not immediately understand this positive approach. Saying something like the following may help:

   Before we start, I would like to explain a little bit about what we are going to do because it may be a little different from what you are used to. This is going to be an appreciative interview. I am going to ask you questions about times when you saw things working at their best in your workplace. Many times we try to ask questions about things that aren't working well, the problems, so we can fix them. In this case, we try to learn about the things at their best, the successes, so we can find out what works and find ways to infuse more of the positive core into the organization's performances. It is much like what we do with children or athletes when we affirm their smallest successes and triumphs so they will hold a positive image of themselves and envision even greater possibility. The end result of the interview will help me understand the "life-giving" forces that provide vitality and distinctive competence to your organization. Do you have any questions?

2. **Respecting Anonymity:** Tell the interviewees the information will be kept anonymous. The data from this interview and others will be compiled into themes. No names will be associated with the overall

---

4 To learn more about Margaret Mead and her work on intergenerational learning, visit the Mead Centennial 2001, The Institute for Intercultural Studies at *www.mead2001.org*.

5 P. Johnson. "Organizing for Global Social Change: Toward a Global Integrity Ethic" (unpublished manuscript, Case Western Reserve University).

summary or report. Stories and quotes from interviews will not have names associated with them.

3. **Managing The Negatives:** Sometimes people work with individuals and places they don't like. An explanation like the one above can generally get a person to identify things at their best. However, people should feel free to talk about things they believe require fixing. Depending on the interviewer's empathic understanding of the interviewee, this can be managed in several different ways:

   - *Postponing:* Tell them you would like to make a note of what they have said and come back to it later. The question "What would you change if you could change anything about the organization?" is a place to collect this "negative" data. Make sure to come back to it at the appropriate time.

   - *Listening:* If someone feels real intensity about what he or she wants to say about issues, let the person say it. If it is "up close and personal," you are not going to get any appreciative data until the person speaks his or her mind. This may mean muddling through quite a bit of organizational "manure," and the biggest threat is that you will absorb it and lose your capacity to be appreciative. You must be empathic, but remember that you cannot take on that person's pain. You cannot be a healer if you take on the patient's illness. Maintain a caring and affirmative spirit.

   - *Redirecting:* If you have listened sufficiently to the seemingly negative issues, find a way to redirect the interviewee back to the task at hand. "I think I understand some of the problems...." Paraphrase a few you've heard. "Right now, however, I would like to focus on times when things were working at their best. Can you think of a time, even the smallest moment, when you saw innovation (for example) at its best?" If the interviewer says it never happened where he or she works, before giving up find out whether the person ever had the experience in any organization or work context anywhere.

4. **Using Negative Data:** Everything people find wrong with an organization represents an absence of something they hold in their minds as an ideal image. What organizational processes, if present (rather than absent), might create the ideal organization, which the negatives

imply? Data is data. Use it. But use it affirmatively. One could argue that there is no such thing as negative data, for every utterance is conditioned by affirmative images.

5. **Starting With Specific Stories—The Interview Rhythm:** There is a rhythm to these interviews. When you begin to address your topic, start with specifics relevant to the person interviewed. Try to get him or her to tell a story. A useful beginning might be "Tell me a story about a time when you experienced cooperation (the topic) at its best." Probe deeply and intently—not like a dentist or like a piranha going after the bait, but like an interested friend hanging on to every detail. Listen and learn from this experience. Try to find out "who did what when?" and "what were you thinking?" and "what you did then?" Be an active listener. Your goal is to learn not only what the person did (behavior), but also what the person thought or felt (values) while he or she was doing it.

6. **Generalizing About "Life-giving" Forces:** After you have thoroughly heard the interviewee's story, go for the generalizations. "What is it about this organization—its structure, systems, processes, policies, staff, leaders, and strategy—that creates conditions where cooperation (for example) can flourish?" If your topic (e.g., cooperation) was a plant, you would be trying to find out what kind of soil, water, and sunlight conditions nourish it. Sometimes people will not understand what you mean by organizational conditions, factors, or forces. Give examples: "Are jobs designed a certain way, for example, to foster cooperation?" "How does the culture or climate of the organization foster cooperation?" Try to get them to think a bit abstractly about what is present in the organization when peak experiences have occurred with the topic (i.e. cooperation).

7. **Listening For Themes—"Life-giving" Factors:** In order to get a sense of some of these factors, listen for information about what the structure was like, as well as the systems, rewards, and so on. It may not be necessary to ask systematically about each of these; the stories may contain information about them. If they do not, gently probe. Listen for a theme, an idea, or a concept presented or defined in the stories being told during the interview. Present these themes in the dialogue session during the Dream phase to see if the group thinks these are important.

8. **Keeping Track Of The Time:** An interview typically has a fixed schedule, so keep track of the time. If more time is needed, ask the person if he or she has more time. It is best to pace questions appropriately to the time scheduled.

9. **Having Fun And Being Yourself: It's A Conversation:** Try not to approach the interview as a piece of drudgery, or the interview will be lost before it has begun. Welcome each interviewee as if he or she is a special person. Take time to listen and value the best of whom he or she is. Be humble; the interviewee is the teacher. Be yourself. Do not put on an expert role or pretend that every word in the interview protocol must be exactly right. Be a learner. Realize that everyone likes to share his or her knowledge and wisdom with people who genuinely want to listen and learn. If you have an affirmative spirit going into the interview, mistakes in wording will not impede the collection of data. Finally, have fun. This is an opportunity to get to know someone new and hear some fascinating and important stories.

Following these guidelines will help ensure that the Appreciative Interview has the key characteristics shown in **Table 4.4, Key Characteristics of the Appreciative Interview.**

Table 4.4 Key Characteristics of the Appreciative Interview

- Assumption of Health and Vitality
- Connection through Empathy
- Personal Excitement, Commitment, and Caring
- Intense Focus through "Third Ear" and "Third Eye"
- Generative Questioning, Cueing, and Guiding
- From Monologue to Dialogue

Creating the interview guide, collecting the data, and locating the themes that appear in the interview stories represent the key activities of the Discovery phase. It is where the dialogue begins in the AI process.

Sense-Making from Inquiry Data

After the interviews are completed, it is time to make sense of the data. What is the best way to capture and transform the stories from the interviews in order to be able to understand the positive core of the organization? What does one want to learn more about?

A diversity of approaches have been used-from formal narrative analysis to narrative forms of best stories and moral tales.[6] Data can be reduced and displayed in diagrams, charts, tables, pictures, storybooks, newsletters, and other visual aids. The search for one perfect method to make sense of data is not the point. There is no single right way to analyze the data. What is important is to find creative ways to organize, listen, and understand what is being said from multiple perspectives, both during and after the interviews. Look for common threads and anomalies in the data. Specifically, what are the best stories, practices, and wishes that came out of the interviews? The goal is to identify themes in order to know how to do more of what worked well in a situation.

Focus on the meaning of the data. The meaning of this data forms the foundation of dialogues that inspires the dreams based on the best stories told (continuity) and the best of what will come (novelty). The Design and Destiny phases transform (transition) the data into the desired future.

AI is a method, a type of action research, that attempts to discover "the best of what is" in any organizational/human system. In completing the interviews, the objective should be to understand when organizations are operating at their best and what are the core capabilities, the positive core, that contributed to such operation.

In managing the information and structuring it to a meaningful analysis, the data collection step outlined earlier coincides with data interpretation and narrative reporting and writing. Code the data under key themes. It may require recoding under new, emerging themes.

A primary goal is to reduce and interpret the meanings and, through dialogue, make sure these are the interviewees' meanings. That is why Interview Summary Sheets are helpful. An example of a generic **AI Interview Summary Sheet** is shown below.

---

6 See A. Coffery and P. Atkinson, *Making Sense of Qualitative Data* (Newbury Park, CA: Sage Publications, 1996).

Summary Sheet

Please use as much or little space as you need in order to answer each question.

1. What was the most appreciative quotable quote that came out of this interview?

2. What was the most compelling story that came out of this interview? What details and examples did the interviewee share? How were the interviewee and/or others changed by the story?

3. What was the most "life-giving" moment of the interview for you as a listener?

4. Did a particularly intriguing "golden innovation" emerge during the interview? If so, describe what you learned about it, including who is doing it and where.

5. What three themes stood out most for you during the interview?

6. What small steps toward positive change emerged as possible?

7. What broader steps of positive change emerged?

AI is exploratory and descriptive. It allows for an open-ended discovery of an organizational system. The objective is to generate themes, descriptors, and key ingredients for dialogue and design of possibility propositions. This topic will be covered in more detail in **Chapter 6**.

Case Clippings: Texas Insurance

The Texas Insurance Company employed an AI approach to facilitate the transformation of its IT organization, approximately 2,000 employees, from a traditional internal IT function to a business/client-facing operating model. The goal of the transformation was threefold: 1) to create a culture of service, 2) to demonstrate the strategic value of IT, and 3) to ensure high levels of productivity and effectiveness during the transformation to the new operating model. Central to this transformation was the strategic inquiry (Discovery) into the "life-giving" factors of the organization and three positive transformation themes. Of primary importance were the affirmative topic choices to guide the successful design of the new operating model: Revolutionary Partnerships, Continuous Transformation, and Innovative and Adaptive Environment.

The following interview packet illustrates affirmative topic choices and meets the criteria for an engaging AI question. It includes the following:
- Purpose of the interviews
- Overview of the interview process
- Tips for conducting interviews
- Interview Guide
- Interview Summary Sheet

The Discovery phase was carried out over a three-week period and included approximately 130 interviews of a broad cross section of the IT organization and key clients. The Discovery outputs were used extensively as input into the design of the three-day Dream and Design Summit that followed. In alignment with the intent of the Discovery process, the goal of the Interview Guide was to obtain information on the three factors that give life to organizations—continuity, novelty, and transition. (Refer to Mini-lecture VIII in **Chapter 1**). The following outcomes resulted from the Discovery phase:
- Quotable Quotes wall
- Texas Insurance's Positive Core (continuity)
- Individual visions of a best-performing IT organization (novelty)
- Positive Deviant Profile (novelty/transition)
- Positive Transformation Themes (transition)

Purpose of the Interviews

Thank you very much for participating in this information-gathering process. The Application Services group is actively involved in a business transformation that will focus on the design and development of a business/client-facing operating model that will accelerate time and results. In this way, Application Services will better serve our internal business partners and strengthen the overall Texas Insurance competitive position. To this end, we will be gathering specialized input from colleagues across the organization. These interviews are part of an intense effort to discover our internal best practices and high points, use this rich experience as leverage for the Application Services Transformation, and apply this learning to the development and implementation of our future-state operating model. Additionally, the results of the individual and group IT fact-finding discussions, along with information and research on external best practices, will be integrated into our design process.

As part of this process we will look at:
- What the core factors are that enable success in our organization.
- What we can learn from our experiences, especially when we examine closely those moments when we have been at our best.
- What our most effective practices, strengths, and best qualities are—what we need to preserve as we transform.
- What important lessons can we draw from our experiences.
- What kind of organization we want to create in the future—the organization that we and others want to be part of.
- How our positive past, the best of our experiences, can help us become more daring and innovative as we think about our true potential as an organization.
- In the context of Texas Insurance, what our specific hopes and images are for the future for Applications Services.

Application of Interview Feedback
- All interviews will be reviewed and summarized for thematic content.
- Themes will be shared and discussed based on relevance to the Application Services Transformation.
- (At a three-day off-site design session Accelerated Solutions Environment (DesignShop),) attended by multiple Texas Insurance participants in August, these themes will be used as key input in designing the Application Services future-state operating model.

- An additional output from the DesignShop is an implementation road map, which will outline key activities and workstreams to support our new operating model. Interview themes will be applied directly to some of the resulting workstreams and indirectly to many of the other workstreams.
- All comments from the interviews will be anonymous. Names will not be attached to any of the stories, suggestions, or examples.

Overview of the Interview Process

Part I—Completing Four to Six Interviews
- You will be provided a list of four to six names of colleagues to interview. You will typically be assigned individuals with whom you may not interact on a regular basis. This is a good opportunity to get a fresh perspective.
- The Transition Team will notify your interviewees that they have been selected as participants. Contact your interviewee to schedule the interview. Explain that each interview should take approximately one hour to complete.
- Complete your interviews and post your summary forms to the **Phase I-Interviews** folder in the Transition Team Folder as soon as they're completed, but no later than July 18.
- Assure your interviewees that all comments are anonymous, but not confidential. In other words, stories and quotes will be shared, but no names will be attached to them.
- If you're having difficulty scheduling an interview, please call and we will help you by supporting scheduling of the interview or by providing an alternative interview participant.

Part II—Returning the Interview Summaries
- Please use the space after each question for taking notes during the interviews. (Notetaking is usually very individualized, but we want you to be able to recall your interview to best assure your summarization.)
- It is recommended that you summarize the interview immediately after the interview session. Use the attached two-page summary template at the end of this guidebook.
- Be sure to note your name, the date of the interview, and the interviewee's organizational group and service date on the summary page.

- Post the electronic summary forms to the **Phase I-Interviews** folder in the Transition Team Folder *no later than July 18.*

Try to not wait until July 18th to send all of the interview summary forms. Please post them as you complete them.

Part III—Leveraging the Interviewing Feedback: Next Steps
- All interview summaries will be reviewed and integrated. In this way, we will document major themes to better understand our internal best practices, high-point moments, and images of the future.
- These internal best practices and positive transformation themes will be shared and leveraged during the August off-site DesignShop to support the development and implementation of our Application Services operating model. Additionally, the results of the individual and group IT fact-finding discussions, along with information and research on external best practices, will be integrated into our design process.
- Following the DesignShop, the new operating model, the benefits of the new model, the positive transformation themes, and the general timeline for implementation will be shared.
- We will make a special effort to share positive transformation themes with all interview participants in late July.

Tips for Conducting Interviews

Use the interview question section for script guidelines and notetaking.
- Use these questions to probe further:
  - Can you tell me more?
  - Why was that important to you?
  - How did that affect you?
  - What was your contribution?
  - How did the organization/business area/team support you? *For example, information systems, leadership, resources, and structures.*
  - How has it changed you?
- Let the interviewee tell his or her story.
- Take notes and listen for great quotes and stories.
- Be genuinely curious about their experiences, thoughts, and feelings.
- Some people will take longer to think about their answers. Allow time for silence.

- If somebody doesn't want to or can't answer any of the interview questions, that's OK. Let it go.
- Use the questions as guidelines. You may choose not to use of all the questions or to adapt the questions to what works best for your interviews.
- Allow the interviewee to interpret whether the questions apply to work or to personal situations.

Interview Guide

Suggested Opening

I'm (name). Thank you for meeting with me and participating in this process of gathering information from colleagues across the organization. These interviews are part of an intense effort to discover our internal best practices in key strategic business areas. These best practices will be leveraged by our Application Services Transformation project to develop our future-state operating model. In addition to these interview findings, we will be leveraging information related to external best practices and the individual and group IT fact-finding discussions.

This interview is divided into three sections:
- Celebrating Texas Insurance's Rich Heritage and Past Successes
- Carrying Forward What We Value Most
- Wake Up. It's 2010: Your Vision of a Best-Performing Application Services

Before we start, I would like to explain a little bit about what we are going to do because it may be a little different from what you are used to. I am going to ask questions about times when you were at your best in your work. You may be more familiar with interviews that ask questions about things that aren't working well—the problems—so we can fix them. In this case, we are going to find out about your work and the organization at its best—the successes—so we can find out what works and find ways to integrate what we learn into the Application Services Transformation moving forward. This *positive-change approach* has been widely researched and proven effective in a variety of situations (i.e., transformation efforts, education, building learning organizations, parenting, athletics, increasing team and organizational effectiveness, health care, and so on). The end result of the interview will help us understand those positive factors, which will increase our vitality, effectiveness, and success going into the future together. Specifically, we are gathering

information on what we are calling *Positive Transformation Themes*. In order to surface these themes, the interview questions focus on areas that we believe are critically important to the successful design of our new Application Services operating model:
- Continuous Transformation
- Revolutionary Partnerships
- Innovative and Adaptive Environment

What questions do you have?

OK. Let's begin.

I. **Celebrating Texas Insurance's Rich Heritage and Past Successes**
    To start, I'd like to learn about your beginnings at Texas Insurance. When did you come to the organization, and what attracted you to Texas Insurance? What keeps you at Texas Insurance? What sets us apart and makes the difference for you?

    In your work at Texas Insurance, you have probably experienced ups and downs, twists and turns. For a moment, I would like you to think about a time that stands out to you as a high point at Texas Insurance– a time when you felt energized, passionate about your work, and most effective— a time when you were able to accomplish more than you imagined.

    Please describe in detail the situation and the people involved and what made it a high-point experience for you. What actions did you and others take? How did these actions translate into business results?

    Let's talk about some things you value most—specifically, about yourself and Texas Insurance as an organization.
    - Without being humble, what do you value most about yourself as a human being? What are the most important qualities or strengths you bring to Texas Insurance?
    - What is it about the nature of *the work you* do here that you value the most? What is most interesting or meaningful?

    Continuous Transformation:
    Organizations today must continually change and evolve to remain ahead of the competition and to thrive in this rapidly changing economy and business environment. Organizations that have passion

and energy for continual transformation display business excellence and are distinguished from their peers—leading the way and creating their future, instead of reacting to it.

Tell me about a time when you were involved with a significant transformation or change effort, a time where you positively influenced the results. What was exciting about the transformation? What did you and others do to make it effective?

Revolutionary Partnerships:
The mark of a revolutionary partnership is doing things together radically different—not only different, but quicker, with a common focus, leveraging each other's diverse strengths. It is also establishing new ways of doing business that are based on trust, mutual respect, and a shared vision.

Think of a time when you were part of a revolutionary partnership, a time in your life (at work or in your personal or community life) when you not only met the other person(s) halfway, but also met and exceeded needs on both sides. Describe the situation in detail. What made it feel radically different? Who was involved? How did you interact differently? What were the outcomes and benefits you experienced?

Innovative and Adaptive Environment:
"Nature has been learning to adapt for four billion years; maybe we need to pay attention." Stuart Kauffman—molecular biologist
    As this is true in nature, it is also true in the business world. An effective environment enables risk taking, empowers leadership throughout the organization, is agile, and thrives on change. These powerful environments are able to balance speed and discipline, are liberating yet standards-based, and support growth and innovation.

Think of a time when you were in an innovative and adaptive environment. Please describe how the environment supported your success (i.e., leadership, creativity, tools, recognition, resources, and so on). How did it feel? What were the keys to success? What were some of the significant breakthroughs you achieved? Again, this could be personal, community-oriented or work-life based.

II. **Carrying Forward What We Value Most**

Good organizations know how to "preserve the core" of what they do best and are able to let go of things that are no longer needed. In transforming Application Services, what are three things—core strengths, values, qualities, ways of working—you want to see preserved and leveraged moving into the future?

III. **Wake Up. It's 2010: Your Vision of a Best-Performing Application Services**

Fast forward. It is now 2010 and we were able to preserve our core strengths and transform Application Services. Revolutionary partnerships, continual transformation, innovation, and adaptability are the way we do business. It is an organization you want to be part of and others want to join.

- How would you describe Application Services' relationships with their business customers? How do they work together differently in 2010 to achieve Texas Insurance's business objectives?
- What are people doing? How are you working together differently in 2010? What was the key to your success and the organization's success? How did you get there?
- What was the smallest change Applications Services made that had the most significant impact?

This is the end of the interview. Thank you very much for your time. Your input will be summarized and used for design of the Application Services Operating Model.

Interview Summary Sheet

Complete and post by Wednesday, July 18 to the Application Services Transition Team shared drive in the **Phase I-Interviews** folder. Save the document with the filename Interviewerlastname-interview#.doc (e.g., Smith-interview3.doc).

Name of Interviewer (your name): _____

Date of Interview: _____

Interviewee's Organizational Division: _____

Interviewee's Service Date (year is optional): _____

What was the most quotable quote that came out of this interview?

What was the most compelling story that came out of this interview? (Use as much space as you need.)

Overall, what was your sense of what was most important to this individual?

What three positive themes stood out most for you during the interview related to each of the following?

Revolutionary Partnerships	Continuous Transformation	Innovative and Adaptive Environment
1. _____	1. _____	1. _____
2. _____	2. _____	2. _____
3. _____	3. _____	3. _____

Carrying Forward What We Value Most

• _____

• _____

• _____

Vision of the Future

1. _____

2. _____

3. _____

5

Dream:
What Might Be?

"One of the basic theorems of the theory of image is that it is the image which in fact determines what might be called the current behavior of any organization. The image acts as a field. The behavior consists of gravitating toward the most highly valued part of the field."

—Kenneth Boulding

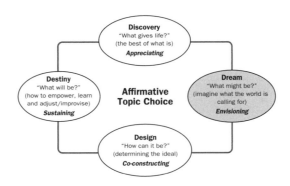

Once an organization discovers its positive core, the next step is to imagine and envision its future. The Dream phase of the AI 4-D Cycle accomplishes this step.

The Dream phase is an invitation for an organization to amplify its positive core by imagining the possibilities for the future that have been generated through the Discovery phase. During the Dream phase, the participants are encouraged to talk about (and dream about) not what is, but what might be a better organization and a better world. The Dream phase is both practical, in that it is grounded in the organization's history, and generative, in that it seeks to expand the organization's true potential. It is the time to challenge the status quo of the organization. It is intended to create synergy and excitement. Once the group gets into the spirit and acknowledges the possibility of greatness, the positive core can be channeled, focused, and used to design how it will be and create the destiny of the envisioned dream.

The primary goal of the Dream phase is twofold. First, it is to facilitate a dialogue among stakeholders in which they begin to share positive stories in a way that creates energy and enthusiasm. This is accomplished by asking those who participated in the Discovery phase to share their stories with the entire group. These stories are the vehicles for bringing out the *positive core* of the organization. Therefore, those who are telling the stories must be encouraged to share the essence of the stories, not a bullet point description of events. Giving the storyteller the latitude to share the story in full and rich detail generates more data for theme building. It is, therefore, the job of the facilitator to gently probe for details in order to continue identifying themes. One tool used to encourage these conversations is called dream dialogues. The *dream dialogue* is often integrated into the appreciative interviews with questions about wishes, hopes, and dreams for a better organization and world. Some interview guides probe for best practices and peak experiences from outside the organization in question. Thus, interviewers might learn through discovery of positive possibilities that have existed elsewhere and that might be transported into their system.

The second goal of the Dream phase is to allow the participants to start to see common themes. At this point, it is important to encourage the group to observe and value the stories rather than critique, judge, or analyze them. Unlike other organizational change methodologies, AI does not focus on solving a problem. Dreaming is a journey of mutual discovery, not an analytical journey. Therefore, it does not emphasize identifying one best idea. Instead, participants look for broad themes or "life-giving" forces that contribute to the organization's success. These positive themes are the building blocks for the rest of the AI process. They are the short answers to the question "What do people describe in the interviews as the "life-giving" forces of this organization?"[1]

---

1 See J. Watkins and B. Mohr, *Appreciative Inquiry: Change at the Speed of Imagination* (San Francisco: Jossey-Bass/Pfeiffer, 2001): 115.

Accomplishing these two goals helps the participants to imagine the organization as they would like it to be. By building energy, excitement, and synergy and by extracting the common themes or "life-giving" forces, the participants can begin to envision an organization of the future, an organization that embodies the images, hopes, dreams, and visions of its people.

The remainder of this chapter deals with creating the Dream activity, introduces the concept of dialogue that creates vision consensus, and provides an example of Roadway's Express AI Summit. A complete project plan for the Roadway Express AI Application is available at the end of this chapter.

Creating the Dream Activity

Organizations tend to move in the direction of what they study. The crafting of questions and activities during the Discovery and Dream phases has strategic significance to eliciting the information needed to identify the themes that will become the starting point for the next phase of the 4-D Cycle.

Many of the best Dream activities share common components:[2]
- They take place on the heels of some sort of brief Discovery process, one that brings the spirit of the original inquiry into the room in personal and creative ways.
- They often involve large groups of people, anywhere from a couple dozen to hundreds at a time.
- They begin with some kind of energizing activity (i.e., guided visualization, a walk, a high-energy activity, yoga, and so on).
- They use a focal question that "primes the pump" for rich, creative dream dialogues. (Facilitators select the question, along with an appropriate time frame for individual and group discussions.)
- As participants complete their individual dreaming reflections, they move into groups (ideally, no more than twelve people per group) to talk about what they've seen, heard, and experienced in this world of the future during the Discovery interviews. This "dream dialogue" takes up to an hour. This dialogue is finished when people have had a chance to share fully what they have seen and imagined and to create a collective verbal picture of the desired future.
- The group creatively depicts what they have seen. The more playful the depictions, the better. The facilitator (whose role was introduced

---

2   See D. Whitney and A. Trosten-Bloom, *The Power of Appreciative Inquiry: A Practical Guide to Positive Change* (San Francisco: Berrett-Koehler, 2003).

in the organizational overview) can offer a variety of ways in which the dream may be depicted. Some examples might include a picture, a story, a skit, a commercial, a newspaper, a song, or a poem. The facilitator should be ready with a variety of supplies and props to aid in this process.

- Each dream team prepares a brief Appreciative Report from its dreams (often a good bit less than five minutes each). Although each team has a spokesperson, everyone on the team is included in the presentation. All presentations are made to the entire group.
- Small-group discussions of common themes and common threads often follow these presentations.

The Dream phase is the time to push the creative edges of positive possibilities and to wonder about the organization's greatest potential.[3] To illustrate, in January 2001, an AI initiative was launched with Roadway Express at the Akron, Ohio, terminal. Roadway is one of the largest trucking companies in America, with about 30,000 employees. The company is unionized and the relationship between Roadway and the Teamsters is strong. Roadway's goal is to create an organization with leaders developing leaders at every level, a "high-engagement organization."

The inquiry started with the opening question:

When did you fell most alive, most engaged, in your job at Roadway?

On Day 2, the Dream phase began when participants were divided into small groups to envision the organization's potential for positive impact. The next foundational question was asked:

Imagine you've awakened after being asleep for five years. What would you want Roadway to look like? What will the company look like in five years and ten years? What will be happening in the world outside? What is the best outcome we can imagine?

The *Discovery* was about the positive core and valuing the best in Roadway's history. The Dream phase included two activities. The first activity was a collective conversation on "images of the future"; the second activity was the creation of an "opportunity map." In moving from Discovery to Dream, the Akron terminal employees focused on the following purpose:

---

3 For more information on a visual approach to dreaming, see LifeScapes at *www.avikus.com*.

To begin to build a future you want, an Akron Roadway team that is truly dedicated to "maximizing throughput with unsurpassed speed, driven by employee pride and involvement."

The dream dialogue focused on the following three statements:
- Share your wishes and dreams from the interviews you did yesterday morning (Question 3). Add any ideas or thoughts about changes or improvements you think will have a major impact on improving our throughput.
- Brainstorm a list of opportunities to improve throughput at the Akron complex.
- As a group, choose the three to five opportunities your team believes will have the greatest impact on throughput.

From this map, each team created aspirations and visions of the future. For example:

Aspiration Statement

Measurement, Technology, Procedures, and Equipment Team

Roadway is No. 1 because employees take pride and are engaged in ensuring that customers are receiving unsurpassed service and error-free delivery that is unequaled by any other carrier.

Employees know and understand cost impacts of all decisions and information is shared through technology so all employees are empowered to make customer-focused and profitable decisions.

The Dream activity gave them the opportunity to summarize key success factors collectively and preserve the past. Together they mapped the highest impact opportunities. More details on the Dream activity are available at the end of this chapter.

Dreaming is a strategically significant activity that leads to higher levels of creativity, commitment, and enthusiasm for the organization and its future. It is this new level of enthusiasm and images embedded in the dreams that facilitate the creation of specific actions and propositions for the future (Design phase).

Evolution of Dialogue to Create Vision Consensus

A *vision* is a direction for an organization. It is what the organization wants to be. It expresses a desire by the organization to be more than what it is. It is strategic in providing a focal point for direction and movement. It is fateful in defining what an organization holds dear and creating excitement for ways to achieve it.

Sometimes a vision is a statement created by senior management and passed down to employees. If so, it is at best a sneak preview of what the leaders of the company believe is important, providing some indication as to why decisions are made. At its worst, it is ink on paper without significance or meaning for stakeholders. The power of AI lies in its ability to breathe life into a vision; to make it speak to all stakeholders; and to provide some value, consequence, and direction in stakeholders' daily lives.

Through the Discovery and Dream processes, participants have been asked to share times and events during which they operated at their peak, felt most alive, and were inspired to push beyond the mundane. Now while riding on the enthusiasm and energy created by sharing these high points, the group should be asked to imagine an organization in which these sporadic glimpses at brilliance are the norm. What would this organization look like?

Once the group begins to create a shared vision of the new and improved organization, the power of AI becomes apparent. Unlike other visioning exercises, AI creates a vision for the future that is grounded in examples from the organization's past. It is the greatness demonstrated in the past that will allow stakeholders to achieve their vision for the future. In short, there is no question as to whether the new vision is achievable; the participants have already demonstrated their desire, willingness, and ability to make it possible. This energy and synergy is what will carry the group to the Design phase. The Design phase is where the key stakeholders regroup and work to transfer the dreams into a concrete plan of action.

Sample Dream Questions

The following Dream questions may prove helpful in shaping the dialogue to achieve the vision for the future of the organization.

- It is the year 2010, and you have just awakened from a long sleep. As you look around, you see the world just as you always wished and dreamed it would be.

What is happening? How is the world different? How is your organization contributing to this new world? What are you doing that makes a difference?

- As you reflect on the industry and business environment in which your organization works, what do you see as the two or three most significant macro trends emerging? How might they change the way your industry and business operate? In your opinion, what are the most exciting strategic opportunities on the horizon for your organization?

- Imagine it is 2010 and your organization has just won an award as the outstanding socially responsible business of the year. What is said about your organization as the award is dedicated? What are customers saying? What are employees saying? What did it take to win the award?

AI Summit: Using Large Groups to Mobilize Positive Change

"AI Summit" is a large-scale meeting process that focuses on discovering and developing the organization's positive change core and designing it into an organization's strategic business processes, systems, and culture.[4]

Participation is diverse by design and includes all the organization's stakeholders. The duration is generally four days and involves 50 to 2,000 participants or more. AI serves as the framework for an AI Summit. The AI Summit can be used to conduct the *Dream* and *Design* phase if data is available from the *Discovery* phase. Many variations are possible; therefore, planning, creativity and flexibility are required.[5]

The AI Summit is designed to flow through the AI 4-D Cycle of *Discovery, Dream, Design,* and *Destiny* in real time. Figure 5.1 illustrates the **Akron Roadway Summit: AI 4-D Cycle**.

4　We want to acknowledge the important role Marvin Weisbord and Sandra Janoff played. Their pioneering work with Future Search impressed us most with the principle of the whole system in the room as well as the clarity of worksheets and some of the exercises in a typical Future Search. For more on Future Search, refer to *Future Search: An Action Guide to Finding Common Ground in Organizations and Communities*, 2d ed. (San Francisco: Berrett-Koehler, 2000).

5　Material contributed and adapted from *The Appreciative Inquiry Summit: A Practitioner's Guide for Leading Positive Large-Group Change*. The book details the strategies for whole system participation and activities before, during, and after an effective summit. (Available from Berrett-Koehler, Spring 2003, by Ludema, Mohr, Whitney, and Griffin.)

Figure 5.1 Akron Roadway Summit's 4-D Cycle

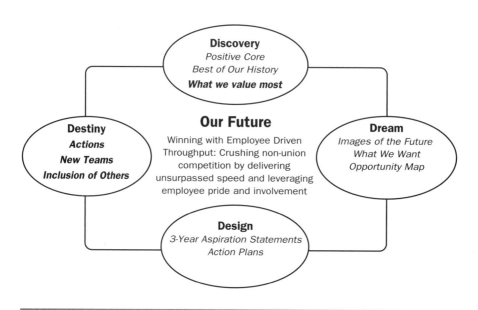

Day 1—*Discovery*: Participants discuss the organization's positive core, which was discovered in earlier interviews. They look at characteristics of which they are most proud and discuss those characteristics that create success and build a competitive future for Roadway. They are asked, who are we? Whom do we represent? As a group, they dialogue about why they are here and what they hope for.

Key activities include defining the context and purpose of the summit, conducting more AI interviews, highlighting stories from prior AI interviews, mapping out the positive core, and launching a continuity search. A *continuity search* is seeking out and then preserving what the organization does best. For example, Roadway wanted to build optimal margins; therefore, it first wanted to learn what things Roadway did best organizationally.

Day 2—*Dream*: Participants break into small groups and envision their organization's potential for positive influence and impact. What will the company look like in 2010? What is happening? What is better? What positive things are the stakeholders saying? After the small breakout discussions, the groups report back to the entire Summit to share their stories.

Key activities include sharing of dreams, enlivening the dreams, and enacting or imaging the dreams.

Day 3—*Design*: Participants focus on co-creating an organization (that includes the positive core and dreams in every element possible). The design results for Roadway were "Aspiration Statements," describing the organization participants hoped Roadway would become, and "Action Plans," describing how the organization will function.

Key activities include creating the organization's architecture, selecting high impact organization design elements and crafting possibility propositions (possibility or aspiration statements).

Day 4—*Destiny*: Participants define the newly created organizational design into a list of inspired action-oriented tasks. Task groups emerge around each aspiration statement. Then each group establishes principles for working together after the AI Summit and agrees on immediate steps they will take next.

Key activities include generating possible action steps, selecting possible action tasks, forming task teams, and closing the large-group summit.

Little if any AI training occurs during a Summit. After a Summit, organizations may decide to develop their capacity in AI by conducting a training program for key employees in leading organizational change. In this situation, AI is taught as a process for management, leadership, and organizational development and change.

The AI Summit process from start to finish invites the whole organization to participate. A successful summit takes time and attention. The task must be clear. It is usually a three- or four- day event that can include from 100 to 2,000 participants. The typical results from a summit are:

- More informed and ultimately more effective change efforts.
- A critical mass of people making changes in which they all believe.
- A total organization mind-set.
- simultaneous change.
- a perception of change as "real work."
- a fast-change organizational network.

The following Roadway example illustrates an AI Summit.

Case Clippings: Roadway Express

The work at Roadway has been very powerful. Again, Roadway's goal was to create an organization with leaders developing leaders at every level, a high-engagement organization. An important part of this goal was building a strong financial literacy at every level, where everyone was thinking and acting as owners of a business. As a result, the main topic in one of the early AI's at Roadway had to do with "optimizing margins." Topics in AI work can be on human, technical, environmental, or financial issues. The same principle still holds true: Human systems move in the direction of what they most persistently, actively, and deeply ask questions about. When reviewing the questions below on optimizing margins, think about potential changes that might take place in the future.

In this case, something remarkable did happen at the Akron terminal of Roadway. In 2002, a few years after the start of the AI work at Roadway, one of the AI teams came up with a ten-million-dollar-per-year-cost savings idea. When this happened, the excitement was understandably quite high. This illustrates the principle that the seeds of change are implicit in the first questions asked. Keep this in mind while reading the interview questions that follow.

The Case Clipping includes:

- *Interview Guide*
- *Summit Preworksheets*
- *Summit Working Agenda*
- *Summit Agenda Overview*
- *AI Organizational Summit*
- *Discovery Worksheet #1*
- *Discovery Worksheet #2*
- *Discovery Worksheet #3*
- *Dream Worksheet #1*
- *Dream Worksheet #2*
- *Dream Worksheet #3*
- *Design Worksheet*

The following resulted from the Dream phase:
- *An Opportunity Map of needs and priorities*
- *Identification of which needs and priorities were most pressing*
- *Action teams to address organizational trust, drivers as strategic sales representatives, employee communications, performance measurements, and monitoring and education*

The most surprising learning was that it did not matter what your job was; everyone wanted the same thing—to win.[6] Shared goals included sustained growth, happy customers, and job security.

Interview Guide

A Roadway Inquiry into Optimal Margin
Opening Dialogue

(In diverse pairs complete an interview. [across functions and levels])

- **Results you want:** With revenues, tonnage, and sales at record levels, one of the most important opportunities we face is to engage everyone in increasing positive margins now. To do so will call on discovery of new strengths, build on old strengths, and carry us to higher levels financially.
  A. As you look at Roadway from the perspective of our capabilities and as you think about the business context and opportunities, how do you define "optimal margin" for us? What is the positive margin you want **and** believe we have the capability to create right now? What is a moderate time frame looking long term?
  B. What results do you want from this meeting? What would make this day a good one for you?

- **Insights from your work:** We all pride ourselves on the things we do that add the most value in terms of creating margin. Some of our work activities add a lot of value, while others do not. Likewise, there are some things we do as leaders—our style, our approaches to managing people—that engage everyone else in increasing margins. Let's reflect using the essential things you do that you believe add the most value.
  A. When you think of your precious time and how you spend it, what are the things you do that, in your view, add the most value in terms of creating margin? Any examples?
  B. In the ideal, if you were able to recraft what you do, what parts of your work (from the perspective of creating margin) would you want to keep doing, let go of, or do new and differently?

---

6 For more information on this story, see the *Fast Company*, July 2001 article, "Leaders for the Long Haul" by Keith Hammond, pp. 56-58.

- Keep doing?
- Let go of (things that are not really needed)?
- Do new or differently?

C. As you reflect on your leadership role here at Roadway—times when you have mobilized or helped develop others—there have been high points and low points, successful moments, and so on. Please describe one situation or change initiative you are proud of, an achievement in which you believe you had an impact in realizing better margins. What happened? What were the challenges? What was it about you or your leadership style? What lessons were learned?

D. Let's think about other leaders or successful stories of change—situations you have heard about or seen here at Roadway as they relate to engaging people to achieve good margins. Is there a story or an example that stands out for you—something that exemplifies the kind of leadership approaches we should aim for more often? Can you describe the leadership and insights?

- **Continuity search:** good organizations know how to preserve the core of what they do best and are able work out or let go of things that have built up or are no longer needed. Preserving the right things is key. Letting go of other things is the next step.

  A. In relationship to building optimal margins, what are the things we do best organizationally—for example, measurement systems, leadership systems, ways of developing others, accountability systems, ways of delegating and building trust, and technologies—things that should be preserved even as we change in the future?

  B. Assuming that things do build up, there is a need to "work out" and streamline. There is a need to let go of things that, given precious time constraints, are not needed. Assuming that very few things are sacred, what things (small or large) do you think we should consider letting go of?

- **Novelty:** Novelty is imagining new possibilities for optimal margins. If anything imaginable were possible, if there were no constraints whatsoever, what would the ideal Roadway organization look like if we were delivering optimal margins? Describe, as if you had a magic wand, what we would be doing new, better, or different? Envision it happening. What do you see happening that is new, different, or better?

- **Transition:** Transition is moving from A to B, asking how we get from there to here.
   A. What is the smallest step (an action, a decision, an initiative) we could take that would have the largest impact?
   B. What is one thing we have not even thought of yet — something that could have a payoff?

Summit Preworksheets

During the Summit meeting, we will be creating a shared history of Roadway's strengths and best past experiences to help in deciding the future we all want to be a part of. It is important that all the of the different participants are heard and appreciated so we truly work from a shared sense of what we already do well and why.

Please take 5–10 minutes and fill out the two attached sheets. Bring them with you to the Summit. We will use them on the first day.

Preworksheet #1

How Are Our Industry And Company Changing?
What Is Our Story? Our Competitive Strengths?
Key Moments In Our History?

Purpose: To develop a collective picture of our changing world, the industry, and the core of our history (strengths, achievements, challenges, changes, and so on).

- Make notes below on memorable industry events and changes in society that have had an impact on Roadway: things you believe are notable milestones, trends, and/or turning points. (At the Summit meeting, you will use a magic marker to add your notes or pictures to timelines on the wall.)

INDUSTRY/SOCIETAL Events, Changes, and Trends
What happened in the trucking and transportation business? (Why was it important?)

1930s–1950s _____

1960s _____

1970s _____

1980s _____

1990s–2000 _____

The future you think is coming:

Preworksheet #2

How Are Our Industry And Company Changing? What Is Our Story? Our Competitive Strengths? Key Moments In Our History?

- Make notes below on notable achievements, changes, events, trends, or turning points here at the Akron complex. (At the Summit meeting, you will use a magic marker to add your notes or pictures to timelines on the wall.)

COMPANY Changes, Events, Trends, and Accomplishments
What happened at Akron Roadway?

1930s–1950s _____

1960s _____

1970s _____

1980s _____

1990s–2000 _____

Where is our company going (the future changes you see coming)?

Summit Working Agenda

Day 1	DISCOVERY	PRESENTERS
8:00–8:15	Welcomes and comments on topic	Mark O. & Jim B.
8:15–8:45	Why doing this / using AI	Terry G.
8:45–9:00	Intro facilitators and topic more	Pete & Ed
9:00–9:20	Community-building activity	Ed
9:20–10:00	AI introduction (Time to rethink. What is a Summit Prep for 1:1 interviews.)	Dave & Ron
10:00–11:00	AI interviews (including Break)	
11:00–11:45	Max-mix subgroups: themes and expectations	Pete
11:45–12:30	Group reports (only some tables)	Pete
12:30–1:30	Lunch (Customer Panel)	
1:30–2:00	Map Timelines on Walls and convene in Stakeholder groups	Cindy & Ed
2:00–2:45	Stakeholders: Proudest Moments and Key Success Factors	Cindy & Ed
2:45–3:00	Break	
3:00–3:45	Group reports: Story and Factors to Keep	Cindy & Ed
3:45–4:45	Positive Image –> Positive Action	Dave & Ron
4:45–5:00	Summary of day & Close	Dave & Ron

Summit Working Agenda

Day 2	DREAM	PRESENTERS
8:00–8:30	Community activity: Labeling Positive Core Freight to be shipped to the future….(stakeholder groups)	Pete
8:30–9:30	Mix/max groups: Generating Opportunities for Improving Throughput	Dave
9:30–10:15	Opportunity Mapping (& dot voting)	Ed & Pete
10:15–10:30	Break (Facilitators cluster and label action groups)	
10:30–10:45	Self selection into Opportunity Groups	Ron
10:45–12:00	Dream: 3-yr. Aspiration draft & skits	Ed
12:00–12:45	Working Lunch	
12:45–2:15	Presentations of Aspirations & Visions	Ed
2:15–2:30	Gallery Aspiration Statements for feedback	Ed
2:30–2:45	Break	
2:45–3:00	Task for new groups: 3 yr. and 1 yr. statements	Pete
3:00–4:30	Group work: new Opportunity Groups	Pete
4:30–5:00	Community: Loading our Aspirations for shipping	Pete

Summit Working Agenda

Day 3	DESIGN AND DESTINY	PRESENTERS
8:00–8:30	Community: Naming the Destination for our Positive Core and Aspirations	Pete
8:30–10:30	Design and Action planning (ready for reports)	Pete
10:30–10:45	Break (and turn in pot. Disks)	
10:45–12:00	Presentations (3 x 15 minutes: 10 min to present + 5 min discussion)	Ron & Dave
12:00–1:00	Lunch (Prep/coach for closing comments in community session)	
1:00–2:30	Continue Presentations	Ron & Dave
2:30–3:00	Teams reconvene for last minute detail and next steps	Ron & Dave
3:00–3:15	Break	
3:15–3:45	Community: 1:1 interviews re. Personal commitments – One message I'd take back… – One thing I can do on my own… – My commitment to my team, going ahead…	Ron
3:45–end	Community: Open Microphone forum	Dave + all

Summit Agenda Overview

Akron Roadway

Winning with Employee-Driven Throughput: crushing nonunion competition by delivering unsurpassed speed and leveraging employee pride and involvement.

Day 1
- Welcomes and overview
- Introduction to topic
- Community-building exercise

Discovery: 1:1 appreciative interviews
Mixed groups of pairs search for themes and factors
that "give life" to our topic

Lunch-(customer panel)

Creating our shared-history stakeholder groups:
Identifying proudest moments and what we want to keep

Input: Where does positive change come from?
- Summary and closing

Day 2
- Summarizing key success factors and practices to preserve

Dreaming: Mixed groups: Improvement possibilities for our topic
Mapping highest impact opportunities
Images of our future around opportunities of most interest
(New self-selected groups)

Lunch

Presentations of images
Declaring aspirations for the future: five-year, goal and one-year steps

- Summary reflections and closing

Day 3
  • Summarizing our five-year aspirations

Design: Work on one-year, targets and action steps
                Prepare presentation of "yes-able proposals for action"
                Community forum:
                Presentations from 3-4 action groups
                Lunch
                Presentations from 3-4 action groups
Delivery: Team formation: Action groups convene to agree on
                (immediate next steps the will take next.)
  • Personal commitments to act on after this Summit
  • "Open microphone" to entire community for comments/reflections
  • Closing

NOTE: All sessions will begin and end on time. There will be breaks each morning and afternoon, with refreshments. All sessions will be video-taped so a summary of deliberations and action plans can be communicated (if we want) to the whole organization.

AI Organizational Summit

ROADWAY
What is an "AI" Organizational Summit?
This is not your typical planning meeting!

- The **WHOLE SYSTEM** participates—a cross section of as many interested parties as is practical. That means more diversity and less hierarchy than is usual in a working meeting and a chance for each person to be heard and to learn new ways of looking at the task at hand.

- Future scenarios—for an organization, a community, or an issue—are put into **HISTORICAL** and **GLOBAL** perspective. That means thinking globally together before acting locally. This feature enhances shared understanding and greater commitment to act. It also increases range of potential actions.

- People **SELF-MANAGE** their work and use **DIALOGUE**—not problem solving—as the main tool. That means helping each other do the tasks and taking responsibility for our perceptions and actions.

- **COMMON GROUND** rather than conflict management is the frame of reference. That means honoring our differences rather than having to reconcile them.

- **APPRECIATIVE INQUIRY (AI)** is a combination of the following: To appreciate means to value—to understand those things worth valuing. To inquire means to study, to ask questions, to search. AI is, therefore, a collaborative search to identify and understand the organization's strengths, its potentials, the greatest opportunities, and people's hopes for the future.

- **COMMITMENT TO ACTION** involves the whole system, allowing for more rapid decision making, and committing to action in a public way—in an open way that everyone can support and help implement.

SELF-MANAGEMENT and GROUP LEADERSHIP ROLES

Each small group manages its own discussion, data, time, and reports. Here are useful roles for self-managing this work. **Leadership roles can be rotated.** Divide up the work as you wish.

- **DISCUSSION LEADER**—Assures that each person who wants to speak is heard within time available. Keeps group on track to finish on time.

- **TIMEKEEPER**—Keeps group aware of time remaining. Monitors report-outs and signals time remaining to person talking.

- **RECORDER**—Writes group's output on flip charts, using speaker's words. Asks person to restate long ideas briefly.

- **REPORTER**—Delivers report to large group in time allotted.

Discovery Worksheet #1

Interview Conversations
(Turn to person next to you…. Complete by _____ o'clock)

Our current reality. Today's transportation environment is characterized by fierce competition in the one- and two- day regional markets. Every day we lose market share as current and former Roadway customers give more and more freight to nontraditional, nonunion carriers who beat us at the game we "invented"—service! Why? How? Because they get the freight to its destination faster than we do. We are better at rating bills and building "high-n-tight" claim-free loads. We have better computer systems and more dock doors. We have the best-trained and most-skilled employees. On price, our base rates are better than the regionals. Yet they still beat us out of market share because they get the goods delivered quicker. But by leveraging the pride and involvement of our people, we can respond and recapture lost business as well as establish new business. Our key to success in this arena is:

Throughput

Throughput is the measure we use to monitor how quickly we can process the freight through our facility. We win the battle for the one- and two- day market when we accelerate the processing of freight from pick-up, through the 211 gate, across the dock, and down the road. System speed… that's our need. If we achieve maximum throughput, we can crush the nonunion regionals and dominate the market.

Question 1:

Think back to a time at work that you recall as a high point, an experience or a moment you remember as having left you with an intense sense of pride, excitement, or involvement in having been a part of something that was meaningful, a time when you truly believed you had contributed to the betterment of a fellow employee(s), the customer, or the organization.

Describe that experience. What was going one, who was involved, and what made it so memorable?

Question 2:

Tell me about a time when you thought throughput (speed) was at its best at 211 or when you were involved in moving a shipment quickly through facility to final destination in order to meet a customer requirement.

- Tell the story of what was going on, who was involved, and what happened.
- What did you do? What did you value most about your involvement in that story?
- What do you value most about the contribution of others in that story?

Question 3:

Tomorrow's reality. Imagine that you have awakened from a deep sleep and three years have passed. It is 2004 and the landscape of regional LTL is different. Roadway dominates the nonunion regional carriers in the marketplace! Wall Street is buzzing over the dramatic success Roadway has had in the regional markets! Articles in Transport Topics describe how Roadway—by tapping into the pride and involvement of its employees—has leveraged a dramatic improvement in speed at the 211 complex! This muscular, yet agile, system has catapulted Roadway Akron to the forefront in reducing costs while establishing unparalleled levels of customer service and employee satisfaction. For customers, it's now imperative that they do their one- or two-day regional business with 211/Akron! For employees, 211 is they prefer to work over!

- What happened to allow for this kind of success?
- What part did you play in this success?
- What three wishes do you have to help Akron Roadway reach and sustain this success?

Discovery Worksheet #2

Discovery at Roadway:
Discovering the Resources and Strengths in this Community
Group reports will begin at _____ *o'clock.*

Purpose: To appreciate and welcome each other and to learn about the special experiences, commitments, capabilities, and resources people bring to this conference.

Self-Manage: Select a recorder, reporter, timekeeper and discussion leader.
- **Introduce the person you interviewed.** Go around the table. Introduce your interview partner to the group and share one highlight from your interview (high-point story and vision of Roadway).

- As a group, talk about (each person shares):
  - What interests or excites you about being here? What results are you hoping for?
  - From the stories you have heard, what stands out as key factors or themes that cause effective throughput with unsurpassed speed that is driven by employee involvement here at the Akron complex?

- Recorder/reporter listens for and prepares a two-minute summary on:
  - Hopes we have for this meeting and results we want.
    - 3-5 key factors that give life to throughput with unsurpassed speed that is driven by employee pride and involvement.

Discovery Worksheet #3

Discovery at Roadway:
Root Causes of Success: When Are We Most Effective
and Why?
Reports are due at _____ o'clock.

Purpose: To look at the things we are doing of which we are most proud and to understand the things that create success and build competitive advantage.

Self-manage: Select a reporter, recorder, timekeeper and discussion leader.

- On a flip chart, list what you and this stakeholder group are doing (or have done) that you are most PROUD of in relationship to our task— Achieving Maximum Throughput with Unsurpassed Speed, Driven by Employee Involvement and Pride: **"We are most proud of... "**

  (Use the historical timelines to remind the group of significant moments, turning points, achievements, and so on.)

- Select your "proudest prouds" and come up with two actual examples/stories of successful "high-throughput moments"

  NOTE: These might be stories you told or heard in your opening interviews in pairs this morning.

- Now do an analysis of the two stories. Have someone tell the story and listen for patterns. **What were the root causes of success? What happened new or different? What was it about the people and customers? What was it about the work group? What was it about the organization (e.g., procedures, resources, equipment, leadership, communications, training, and so on)?**

- RECORDER: List 5-10 root causes of success, things we want to keep doing or do even better no matter what else changes.

- REPORTER: Prepare a three-minute summary. Choose one story to retell with the whole group and review the list of the root causes of success.

Dream Worksheet #1

Roadway Moving from Discovery to Dream
Mapping the Opportunities for Improvement
Summaries are due at _____ o'clock.

Self-Manage: Select a discussion leader, recorder, and timekeeper.

Purpose: To begin to build a future you want—an Akron Roadway team that is truly dedicated to "Maximizing Throughput with Unsurpassed Speed, Driven by Employee Pride and Involvement."

1. Share your wishes and dreams from the interviews you did yesterday morning (Question 3). Add any ideas or thoughts about changes or improvements you think will have a major impact on improving our throughput.

2. Brainstorm a **list of opportunities for improving Throughput** at the Akron complex.

3. As a group, choose 3-5 opportunities you all believe will have the greatest impact on throughput.

Dream Worksheet #2

Dreaming the Future Roadway Wants
Ideal Future Scenarios
Presentations are due at _____ o'clock.

Self-Manage: Select a discussion leader, recorder and timekeeper.

Purpose: To imagine and define the future you want to work toward—
an Akron Roadway team that is truly dedicated to "Crushing the
Nonunion Competition by Maximizing Throughput with Unsurpassed
Speed, Driven by Employee Pride and Involvement."

- Put yourselves three years into the future. It is 2004. **Visualize the
  Akron complex you really want from the perspective of the oppor-
  tunity area you have chosen.**
  What is happening?
    - How did this come about? What helped it happen?
    - What are the things that support this vision— leadership,
      structures, training, procedures, and so on?
    - What makes this vision exciting to you?
    - How does this vision maximize throughput with unsur-
      passed speed?

- Capture this dream in a three-year aspiration statement draft on one
  flip-chart page: "By 2004, what we most aspire to in terms of (your
  chosen opportunity area), is…"
  (See two examples on next page.)
    - Use vivid language.
    - Be positive.
    - Be bold and provocative. Make it a stretch that will attract
      others.

- Choose a creative way to present your vision to the rest of us in a
  five-minute "portrayal," as if it existed now. Use as many members
  of your group as possible in the presentation.

       Examples: * A TV News Report * A Song or Poem * A Day
       in the Life ** A Skit * A Hiring Interview *

Dream Worksheet #3

Dreaming the Future Roadway Wants
Ideal Future Scenarios

Example Aspiration Statements:

Opportunity Area: Delegation and Trust

> "Roadway 2003: Roadway is an organization that is world-class in terms of its leaders developing leaders at all levels. We are known throughout the industry for our core competency of delegation. People want to work at Roadway because all employees are trusted and empowered to create value."

Opportunity Area: Career Opportunity/Training/Mentoring

> "Roadway is a proactive organization that enables employees to achieve their personal career goals by taking advantage of career opportunities, centrally administered and personally initiated training/education, and mentoring.
>
> Career opportunities are provided by vehicles such as internal job fairs, intranet job postings, use of a skills database, career assessment inventories, and a formalized mentoring process—with a key emphasis on promoting from within. All employees are provided time for various training where tuition reimbursement for continuing education is "boundary-less" (i.e., all departments, job levels, and interest levels), fully supported, budgeted, and funded.
>
> Training includes soft skills for all employees, leadership training, advanced and technical training, while using experienced personnel as a training asset."

Design Worksheet

Designing for Optimal Throughput at Roadway

Self-Manage: Select a discussion leader, recorder, and timekeeper.

Purpose: To begin translating your three-year aspiration statement into one-year goals and steps to be taken in the next 6-12 months.

- Using the feedback and comments from other groups, take 10-15 minutes to revise, edit, or improve on your aspiration statement.

- Begin formulating one-year targets or goals that can be achieved and demonstrated showing we are on our way to your three-year aspiration:
  - Brainstorm ideas about specific things that can occur or be changed, in the upcoming year, that will put us on a course to realize your vision for 2004.

  - Agree on key targets and scenarios for how to get there. Who would need to do what and by when?

Guidelines for Action Steps:
  - Is it a "yes-able" idea (likely to get support)?
  - Does it address/reflect the underlying principles in our aspiration statement?
  - What are we already doing (key success factors from yesterday) that can be continued or enhanced?
  - What new actions would create an impact?

6

Design:
How Can it Be?

"*Organizational transformation is much more than the critical mass of personal trans-formation. It requires macro level changes in the very fabric of organizing, the social architecture.*"

—Diana Whitney

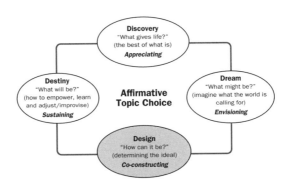

The *Dream* phase articulated the strategic focus, such as a vision of a better world, a powerful purpose, and a compelling statement of a strategic intent. In the *Design* phase, attention turns to creating the ideal organization in order to achieve its dream. Future images emerge through grounded examples from an organization's positive past. Good-news stories are used to craft provocative propositions[1] that bridge the best of "what gives life" with a collective aspiration of "what might be." This is where the organization's social architecture is designed.

The *Design* phase of the 4-D process is key to sustaining positive change and responding to the organization's most positive past and highest potential. Grounded in the best of what has been, good appreciative designs address all three of the elements necessary for effective organizational change discussed in **Mini-lecture VII**. The positive core identified and expounded in the first two phases begins to take form.

The design starts by crafting provocative propositions. Sometimes referred to as *possibility propositions*, they bridge "the best of what is" (identified in *Discovery*) with "what might be" (imagined in *Dream*). They are written in the present tense. They re-create the organization's image of itself by presenting clear, compelling pictures of how things will be when the positive core is fully effective in all of its strategies, processes, systems, decisions, and collaborations. In this way, provocative propositions redirect daily actions and create future possibilities and a shared vision for the organization and its members. It is important that the design fully integrate the "best of past and possibility" and that it be consistent with the intended outcome of the inquiry.

The following pages present the concept of social architecture and its relationship to AI-based design. The elements of a good provocative proposition are defined. This chapter includes additional provocative propositions to stimulate imagination and creativity. The **Case Clippings** in this chapter are from a long-term health care organization, Tendercare, Inc. They illustrate how this organization incorporated AI into its "+1 Census Development Campaign" at an assisted-living center. The clippings demonstrate how Tendercare's Core Care Team moved from Discovery to Dream and through the Design phase.

---

1 Provocative propositions have also been referred to as *possibility propositions*, *possibility statements*, and *design statements*. The different wording depends on the language desired by the organization.

Social Architecture for Organizing

When creating a building, an architect considers many elements in the design, as previously stated. A building requires certain key elements: foundation, roof, walls, windows, doors, and floors. But within the constraints of those necessary elements, the architect and client have a number of choices, ways in which to accommodate their unique preferences. For example, they may choose a brick or adobe exterior, a flat roof or one with a pitch, a glass or solid wall, and a traditional or cathedral ceiling.

In many ways, a set of provocative propositions is a kind of *social architecture* for the ideal organization. It addresses the "design elements" critical to an organization (e.g., systems, structures, strategies, and so on) to support the positive core. The design steps are outlined in **Table 6.1**.

Table 6.1 Four Design Steps

- Select design elements.
- Identify internal and external relationships.
- Identify themes and engage in dialogue.
- Write provocative propositions.

Step 1: Select Design Elements

The first step in AI *Design* is to select design elements. Organization members may choose to articulate their own social architecture, or they may choose to write provocative propositions based on other common models, such as Marvin Weisbord's Six Box Model, Watkins and Mohr's process, or McKinsey's 7-S model.[2] In Tendercare's situation, the Core Care Team selected those elements that best fit the organization's architecture for each affirmative topic choice, as illustrated in **Table 6.2**.

The Design phase defines the basic structure that will allow the dream (or vision) to become a reality. Like the other phases, the Design phase requires widespread dialogue about the nature of the structure and processes. This is what is meant by co-constructing the organization's future.

---

2 For more alternative approaches on whole system design, see McKinsey's 7-S Framework in Cornelis DeKluyver's *Strategic Thinking: An Executive Perspective* (Upper Saddle River, NJ: Prentice Hall, 2000), pp. 51-52; Marvin Weisbord and Sandra Janoff, *Collaborating for Change: Future Search* (San Francisco: Berrett-Koehler, 2000); Marvin Weisbord, *Discovering Common Ground* (San Francisco: Berrett-Koehler, 1994); and Bernard Mohr and Jane Watkins, *Appreciative Inquiry: Change at the Speed of Imagination* (San Francisco: Jossey-Bass/Pfeiffer, 2001).

Table 6.2 Design Elements

Design elements to Consider When Designing a Social Architecture

– Business Processes	– Management Practices	– Stakeholder Relations
– Communication	– Policies	– Strategy
– Competencies	– Relationships	– Structure
– Culture	– Results	– Systems
– Customer Relations	– Shared Values	– Technology
– Education (Training)	– Social Responsibility	– Beliefs about Power
– Vision and Purpose	– Practices and Principles	and Authority
– Governance Structure	– Societal Purposes	– Alliances and Partnerships
– Leadership	– Staff/People	– Knowledge of Manage-
- Distribution of Wealth	– Ecological/Environmental	ment System

For example, if "leadership" is an element selected, questions might be "what kind of leadership structure is needed," or "what is the preferred behavior of the leaders?"

In the Tendercare example, "+1 Census Development Campaign" project, the Core Care Team created a unique business and social architecture based on an image of three rings. Tendercare's architecture placed the residents in the center ring, the stakeholders in the second ring, and the design elements in the outermost third ring.

Step 2: Identify Internal and External Relationships

In the second step, staff and residents worked from the inside out to identify those relationships that helped build the positive core. They listed those key relationships that affected "resident loyalty," as shown in the two boxes labeled "Internal" and "External" in **Figure 6.1**. Therefore, when designing the provocative proposition, these key relationships had to be considered.

Figure 6.1 Tendercare's Business and Social Architecture

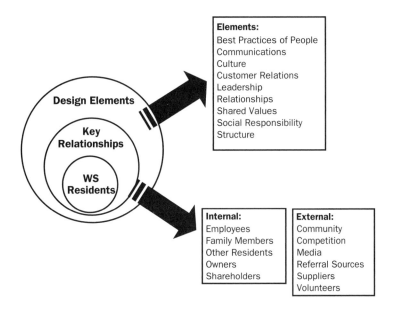

Step 3: Identify Themes and Engage in Dialogue

The third step was to go back to the AI analysis report and the Interview Summary Sheets (ISS) to identify those key themes that supported resident loyalty. The Core Care Team called these themes "the key ingredients needed to build and sustain resident loyalty." These key ingredients were listed on a large sheet of newsprint. During this step, a lot of open dialogue took place and stories were told about what contributed to resident loyalty.

Looking through the data and listening to the conversations, the team attempted to pick out statements and/or stories that seemed to exemplify the essence of resident loyalty. Examples included:

- Building relationships between staff and residents, staff and family, staff and community, and residents and community.
- Caring and consistent follow-through on residents' requests.
- Showing genuine interest and compassion in the residents (staff acted like an extended family).
- Knowing each resident by name and something special about him or her.
- Taking time to do something helpful for a resident, such as tying a shoe or putting on her makeup.

- Developing trust through the managing of a resident's finances, such as monthly budgeting for amenities, or balancing a checkbook.
- Keeping the physical grounds nice.
- Helping residents to keep their dignity and independence.

From these statements, the team selected the best words and even created new concepts they believed captured their meaning of resident loyalty. Words such as *positive relationships, nurturing, listening, understanding, trust, compassion, quality care, service,* and *independence* were listed. Then the group took time to reflect on the list and make changes, additions, and alterations. At this point, a deeper conversation took place, ensuring that just the right words were listed. For instance, the word *communication*, which was initially listed, was changed to *understanding* because the group believed this word better captured what the staff and residents wanted in their relationship in order to enhance resident loyalty.

Step 4: Write Provocative Propositions

Next, each member of the Core Care Team worked independently to write a preferred possibility statement[3] about resident loyalty. At this point, the group was quiet and reflective, as each member attempted to use the words the group identified as significant. The themes and key ingredients were posted to capture resident loyalty in their version of a possibility statement. The participants were instructed to incorporate these ingredients into the possibility statements, as well as to include the key relationships that were identified earlier. After adequate time was allotted, each team member read his or her statement aloud. As each statement was read, it was transcribed and posted for everyone to see. This resulted in ten affirmative possibility statements for further dialogue. Many statements were very similar, yet each one had a unique offering. For example, several statements helped to develop the framework of the possibility statement. Other statements provided key ingredients to make the dreams a reality. Another possibility statement provided the concluding sentence that captured the essence of resident loyalty.

This participative process allowed each member to capture or highlight his or her aspect of what he or she believed was important for resident loyalty. The team ended the Design phase with one collective possibility statement. The group worked together to integrate the ten possibility statements into one shared possibility statement.

---

3 For this **Case Clipping**, Tendercare used the term *possibility statements* instead of *possibility propositions*.

Resident Loyalty Possibility Statement:

"At Wayne Seniors, residents are our lifeline. We maintain this lifeline by building relationships with our residents and their families to ensure a caring, consistent, and positive living experience.

We always strive to nurture relationships by creating an environment of listening, understanding, and trust.

Residents trust us with their lives — a responsibility we hold sacred. We earn trust through unwavering commitment to superior care tempered with compassion and respect.

To provide superior care, we provide knowledge to residents, staff, and families to ensure consistent and compassionate service delivery.

With dedication to these ideals, our center for seniors nurtures resident loyalty, thereby effectively serving the community."

Typically, the core team or steering group coordinates this effort, but it is important to incorporate the feedback of all stakeholders who will be affected. Once the design elements and stakeholders have been selected and most stakeholders identify with the dream, the provocative propositions can be written. The next section covers suggested criteria for writing a provocative proposition. These propositions articulate the desired organizational qualities, processes, and systems (created in the Dream phase) to help guide the organization to its higher purpose.

In order to get buy-in from the entire organization, a process must allow all those affected to offer their contributions. In the Tendercare example, a dietary aide later suggested creating a dining committee made up of both residents and staff to explore how to improve the residents' dining experience. This suggestion resulted in a flexible meal program with more menu choices and different meal times, while also providing the residents with a greater sense of independence and control over their surroundings. This fostered greater resident loyalty. Such contributions move the provocative propositions forward to implementation of the dream in the Destiny phase.

Criteria for Good Provocative Propositions

A provocative proposition is a statement that bridges the best of "what is" and "what might be." It is provocative to the extent that it stretches the realm of the status quo, challenges common assumptions or routines, and helps suggest desired possibilities for the organization and its people. At the same time, it is grounded in what has worked in the past. It conveys the positive images (from the Dream phase) of the ideal organization.

The following questions serve as a guideline or checklist for crafting engaging provocative propositions:

- Is it *provocative*? Does it stretch, challenge, or interrupt the status quo?
- Is it *grounded*? Are examples available that illustrate the ideal as a real possibility? Is it grounded in the organization's collective history?
- Is it *desired*? Do *you* want it as a preferred future?
- Is it stated in *affirmative* and bold terms?
- Does it follow a *social architecture* approach?
- Does it expand the *"zone of proximal development"*?[4]
    —Used with a third party (outside appreciative eye)
    —Complemented with benchmarking data
- Is it a *participative* process?
- Is it used to stimulate *intergenerational learning*?
- Is there balanced management of *continuity, novelty, and transition*?

Provocative propositions provide a clear, shared vision for the organization's destiny. The following are samples of provocative propositions. These focus on a specific design element and theme or topic of the organization's social architecture.

---

4 The Zone of Proximal Development was developed by Lev Semenvoich Vygotsky (1896-1934). He suggested that the mind is not fixed in its capacity, but rather provides a range of potential possibilities. For more information on ZPD and how it relates to AI, refer to Stavros's (1998) dissertation entitled "Capacity Building Using an Appreciative Approach."

Sample Provocative Propositions

DESIGN ELEMENT: Culture

THEME/TOPIC: Recognition and Celebration

The AI Advocates Standing Committee understands and honors the pivotal role of recognition and celebration within the formation of a true "appreciative organization." Therefore, frequent and visible recognition and celebration of the value of life, people, and ideas are an integral part of the AI Advocates' philosophy and practice.

We value diversity of people and ideas. We nurture and support people to express who and what they are. We begin all meetings and gatherings with positive storytelling and recognition. Whenever we are engaged in a discussion or decision-making process, we consciously use "appreciative feedback" with one another and with coworkers outside the team. We collect and publicly disseminate stories that communicate the richness of individual and collective contributions within the community. We purposefully recognize and celebrate those individuals in the community who regularly recognize and celebrate other people, ideas, and accomplishments.

DESIGN ELEMENT: Human Resources Management System

THEME/TOPIC: Performance Appraisal

Our organization acts on its value of high-level trust in the belief that people are committed to personal accountability by using appreciative performance appraisals. It focuses on employee competence and exemplary service to our stakeholders. Our employees are valued.

DESIGN ELEMENT: Shared Values

THEME/TOPIC: Authenticity

Authenticity in human relationships is a key foundation for true organizational transformation and excellence. When we are authentic, we recognize and share our thoughts, feelings, and experiences with others in the spirit of deepening relationships and in service of collaborative achievement. This dialogue allows us to:

- Unleash the best of who we are.
- Become energized and unite around our heartfelt focus.
- Meet the goals of the business.
- Contribute to the greater good.

Being authentic is a shared individual, interpersonal, and organizational responsibility. In practical terms, we:

- Each commit to reflecting and contributing openly.
- seek out other's viewpoints so we can get the best of everyone's thinking.
- build in pauses to allow people to know their own thoughts.
- embrace the philosophy of slowing down so we can finish sooner.

DESIGN ELEMENT: Organizational Purpose

THEME/TOPIC: Shared Vision

Partners in all regions share a basic common vision of the firm's core mission, intent, and direction. It is an exciting, challenging, and meaningful direction, which helps give all partners a feeling of significance, purpose, pride, and unity. The firm uses whatever time and resources are needed to bring everyone on board and thus continuously cultivates the thrill of having "a one firm feeling," of being a valued member of one outstanding national partnership.

DESIGN ELEMENT: Structure

THEME/TOPIC: Ownership

We have created an organization where everyone experiences himself or herself as an owner of the business. People at all levels believe the organization is theirs to improve, change, and help in order to reach its potential. We recognize that there is a big difference between owners and hired hands. Ownership happens in three ways: (1) on an economic level, where everyone is a shareholder and shares in the profit; (2) on a psychological level, wherein people are authentically involved; and (3) on a business level, when the "big-picture" purpose is shared by all and all take part at the strategic level of business planning.

Case Clippings: Tendercare

This AI project was designed and adapted to discover the positive core of one of Tendercare, Inc.'s assisted-living centers to enable the staff to focus on projects, process improvements, and rewards that are aligned to increase the number of residents, occupancy (census).[5] At the same time, it was designed to build a team spirit, thereby creating a better environment for the residents and staff.

Since 1990, Tendercare, Inc., has become Michigan's largest provider of long-term care services. It has 35 health centers located throughout the state and over 3,400 employees. In an effort to build census, the marketing department created the "+1 Census Development Campaign" and invited the center's staff and residents to participate in this project. This campaign had three primary goals:

- *To educate the entire staff as to the importance of increasing occupancy and how having more residents positively impacts them on a daily basis*
- *To educate the staff as to how they can help with the census development efforts*
- *To establish a census goal and create an environment of energy and excitement toward the center's census goal*

An AI intervention was designed and combined with the "+1 Census Development Campaign" to enhance the education and participation while identifying and sustaining the positive core of the center.

Four topics were selected as the focus of this project: Provider of Choice, Resident Loyalty, The Excellent Team, and Appreciation. (The other three possibility statements created by the core care team with the input of the entire staff and residents are as follows):

Provider of Choice

We are the provider of choice because we have a high-quality, trained, experienced, and caring staff to meet the needs of our residents. We create a positive culture that radiates energy and life through a superior dining experience and activities that encourage participation and increase the quality of our residents' lives. We offer a fun, clean, and friendly community that caters to the individual's needs.

---

5 Assisted-living organizations generate their revenue by increasing resident occupancy levels. As another company works to increase sales, long-term care providers work to increase census.

The Exceptional Team

We are proud to be an exceptional team. Our team is driven by our commitment and ability to communicate with those we are privileged to work with and care for.

Our respect for each other is a value that is carried to every aspect of service delivery. Through appreciation, we build strong connections that result in a fun, high-energy work environment that supports friendship and loyalty to our Wayne Seniors Community.

Appreciation

At Wayne Seniors, EVERYONE is appreciated. We take the time to make our residents, families, staff, and community feel welcome. We listen, care for, and support each other by:
- Greeting each other.
- Remembering special moments.
- Celebrating holidays.
- Getting to know residents.
- Sending gifts and cards.
- Sharing time.
- Valuing daily contributions.
- Recognizing accomplishments.
- Seeking out the best in one another.
- Asking if anyone needs help.
- Giving heartfelt thank-you's.
- Taking care of our environment.

Appreciation is a gift we give each other every day.

The center is now using these possibility statements as guiding philosophies to make the center the provider of choice by building an excellent team through appreciation and development of resident loyalty, thereby creating a better environment for the residents and staff.

*The **Case Clippings** include:*
- *Project Proposal*
- *Interview Guide and Summary Sheet*
- *Project Summary*
- *Sample Master Wish List*
- *Agenda: AI Discovery and Dream*
- *AI: Discovery and Dream Minutes*
- *Agenda: AI Design and Destiny*
- *AI: Dream and Design Minutes*

The AI approach was favorably received by the staff and residents and yield- ed highly insightful information about how the staff relates to each other and to the residents and how the residents relate to each other. Four managers at Tendercare remarked how drastically the culture had changed. They observed that the culture had gone from a negative to a very hopeful and positive one in a matter of weeks. Three individuals, who were reported to be skeptical and the most negative of the employees, at one point cried during their AI interviews and offered excellent ideas for improvement.

The Master Wish List has become an action plan used by management and employees to implement the ideas to improve the overall quality of work life and living conditions. The positive core of the staff lies within the genuine compassion and sincere caring for the residents and for each other.

The census at the beginning of this project was 92. Within six weeks of the campaign launch, it had increased to 99. Monthly in-service meetings for the staff were reinstated. The employees of this center, who were unionized, initiated a union decertification campaign. Additionally, a cross-disciplinary team of employees within the center completed a marketing action plan based on the information collected from the interviews and within the framework of the four possibility statements.

The following outcomes resulted from the Design phase:
- Creation of the social-technical architecture
- Crafting of the possibility propositions
- Dream becoming a reality in these statements

Project Proposal

Tendercare Assisted Living
"Discovering the Positive Core to Best Achieve Census Growth"
April 2002–July 2002

Purpose and Overview
Our vision is "to be the **provider of choice** for both our residents and our staff." Our team is committed to our residents and to each other.
"Caring people, caring for people"
The "+1 Census Development Campaign" is a six-week census development program designed to accomplish three goals. The first goal is to educate the entire staff as to the importance of census and how it impacts them on a daily basis. The second goal of the campaign is to educate the staff on how they can help with the census development efforts. The third goal is to create an environment of energy and excitement toward the center's census goal. It is expected that by creating this air of enthusiasm, teamwork, and synergy and by educating the staff as to the importance of census and how they can help increase the center's census, that census (and revenue) goals will be greatly enhanced.

This campaign will be combined and enhanced by integrating it into an Appreciative Inquiry (AI) intervention. The project will consist of completing an AI interview at the assisted-living center to identify and sustain the positive core of the center. This positive core will best help to achieve census growth while placing the resident in the center of the circle of quality care. This change process will incorporate the entire staff. The results of the AI intervention will be specific actions targeting elements that will help increase census.

Identifying these attributes will enable the staff to focus on projects, process improvements, and rewards that are aligned to increase census while building a team spirit.

Expected outcomes include:
- An increase in average daily census of 8 (from 92 to 100).
- Qualitative findings that articulate elements of the positive core.
- Identification of specific tactics that will enhance teamwork and cooperation.

It is anticipated that the AI process will generate positive feedback and goodwill as measured by the Interview Guide. Other evaluation measurements will include turnover levels, customer satisfaction scores, and identification of what is working well within the center, as well as strategies designed to repeat and amplify success.

Primary Participants
    Champions—Census Care Team (CCT):
- Vice President of Marketing
- Marketing Development Consultant
- Administrator
- Director of Care
- Community Relations Representative
- Dietary Manager
- Activities Coordinator
- AI Coordinator and AI Facilitator
- Direct Care Staff (5)
- MBA Student Interns (2)

Project Scope
The scope of this project is to learn and use an AI process to discover and sustain the qualitative elements of the positive core, identify specific tactics that will enhance teamwork, and report findings to all participants for the purpose of increasing the daily average census. A series of meetings to train a core team of participants on the AI techniques will be conducted, as well as interviews and additional meetings to collect, theme, analyze, and interpret the data sets (or outcomes) of the interviews. The final deliverable will be a report of the key findings and outcome of this project.

    The AI process will be integrated with the "+1 Census Development Campaign." It will begin with the Discovery phase to learn about the positive core of the group, and the following key topic issues/themes will be addressed:
- Provider of Choice à Best in Care
- Resident Loyalty
- The Exceptional Team: Working and Winning Together
- Appreciation

    An AI Interview Guide will be designed around these core topics, and each team member will be interviewed to help identify the positive care core and what is most valued. The Dream phase begins with a visioning dialogue among the team members to identify the key themes. As a team, we will create images of the future of what everyone wants and requires.

These themes will be designed into possibility statements based on the center's (organizational architecture – care statement.) The final phase will be creating the Destiny, census action plans to implement these design elements to ensure continued success of the campaign. In addition, the Census Care Team (CCT) will learn about a change process called AI to use throughout their work at the center.

Interview Guide and Summary Sheet

Tendercare Assisted Living
Discovering the Positive Core to Best Build Census
Interview Guide

Thank you for participating in this interview. I am an interviewer for "Discovering the Positive Core" in our "+1 Census Development Campaign." We will be asking questions to learn more about why we choose to work here and why residents choose to live here. We want to learn about the positive core of our people and how to increase the positive aspects of the work life.

Staff and residents will be interviewed to collect the "best-case" stories on which to build the future. The goal is to move forward in achieving the vision "to be the provider of choice for both staff and residents." Your input will be an important contribution to generate meaningful ideas and actions.

Many times in interviews we ask questions about why things don't work well. This time we are going to approach things from a different angle. We are going to find out about your experiences of success at TENDERCARE so we can build on those experiences.

We will interview everyone who works and lives here. When the interviews are complete, everyone's input will be reviewed to identify the positive core that makes us unique. With those qualities as a foundation, we will create specific steps to build on our strengths and to build census.

The conversation will take an hour or so. I'm going to take notes as we talk. During our interview, we will be exploring your experiences in several areas:
- Provider of Choice à Best in Care
- Resident Loyalty
- The Exceptional Team à Working and Winning Together
- Appreciation
Shall we begin?

Introduction: The Privilege of Caring

Our profession is based on caring with compassion and understanding. The privilege to participate in the aging and healing relationship is what creates and maintains the passion for health care providers. We would like to acknowledge that passion and explore with you how to acknowledge and develop this in all of those who work here.

First, I would like to know what attracted you to our center? What were your initial excitements and impressions when you joined this center?

Can you recall a high point when you felt most alive, most involved about your work at the center? What made it exciting? Who was involved? Please tell me the story.

- What were your hopes and dreams when you chose to work here?
- What is it about caring for others today that keeps you involved?

Before we get into our interview topics today, can you tell me what is it that you value about yourself, the nature of your work, and the center?

Topic 1: Provider of Choice

Provider of choice means we are the place where residents want to live and employees want to work. We can be the provider of choice by identifying and nurturing the "best-in-class" qualities within our departments and job responsibilities.

The provider of choice means that we demonstrate levels of caring and excellence that are beyond the reach of other "good" assisted-living centers. The way we need to do things allow us to accomplish exceptional results, along with high levels of care and employee satisfaction.

Please tell me what is it about you and the way you do your job that's "best-in-class"? What effect do these skills or behaviors have on you and your sense of belonging to the team? What effect do they have on your coworkers and the residents?

Topic 2: Resident Loyalty

Today's best companies create and maintain exceptional levels of customer loyalty. Loyal customers are great customers. They provide information and, in time, this helps us give them what they need. They share great ideas. They invite new customers.

Resident loyalty is something we must earn. We can earn it by listening to what our residents and their families or referral sources tell us they want. If possible, we can exceed our residents' expectations by treating them with genuine respect and caring and by creatively anticipating ways we can provide the services they want more of in order to be happy, safe, and cared for.

By earning resident loyalty, we build ourselves a caring competitive edge that puts each of us in a position of being the provider of choice for our residents.

1. Think of a time when you were a very loyal customer (to a large organization or, for example, simply a neighborhood babysitter).
   - What were the most significant things this company or person did to earn your loyalty in the first place?
   - How did this company or person learn about what was important to you? How did this company or person stay current with what you needed?
   - Describe a time when this loyalty was tested. What did your "provider" do to keep you as a loyal customer and, if necessary, rebuild the relationship?

2. Put yourself in the place of one our most loyal residents or referral sources.
   - How would this person describe us to a new resident?
   - Why would this person say he or she is so committed to our center?

3. Suppose we could choose just three things to do more of or do differently in order to dramatically enhance our resident loyalty. What would they be?

Topic 3: The Exceptional Team à Working and Winning Together
An exceptional team is built on individual expertise and excellent cooperation. Cooperative teamwork, clear communication, and wisdom are essential elements in delivering superior patient care.

1. Describe a time when you participated as a team member where your expertise truly made a difference to the team.
2. Imagine you are working with an exceptional team. Describe it.
3. What do you value about this team?

Topic 4: Appreciation
All of us want fulfillment through meaningful work. The most gratifying appreciation is that which is expressed from the heart by active communication, a kind gesture, or written words.

1. Describe a time when you felt extremely appreciated.

2. What is the most meaningful way your contribution is recognized and appreciated?

Excellence in Long-Term Care Award
Imagine you are representing our center in accepting a national award for "Excellence in Care" in 2003.
1. Describe what you admire about working here.
2. What makes caring for our residents unique?

Three Wishes
What three wishes do you have to make our center the best place to give care and the best place to receive care?

Reflections on This Interview
In closing, I would like to ask you two questions about this interview:
1. What did you like most about this interview?
2. Would you be interested in conducting this interview with one of your residents?

Appreciative Interview Summary Sheet

Interviewer: _____

Interviewee: _____

Years of Experience in Caring _____

Years Employed _____

What are the best quotes that came out of this interview?

What were the best stories that came out of this interview?

What were the best wishes that you heard in your interview?

What were the best practices or specific recommendations that you heard reflected in your conversation?

What contributes to the positive core?

What do residents and staff want more of?

Length of Interview _____

Project Summary

A "+1 Census Development Campaign" kick-off meeting was held on April 25 at the assisted-living center with the following three goals as its focus:

1. To educate the entire staff as to the importance of census and how it impacts them on a daily basis
2. To educate the staff as to how they can help with the census development efforts
3. To establish a census goal and create an environment of energy and excitement toward the center's census goal

This AI project coincided with the "+1 Census Development Campaign" in an effort to build on the momentum and to discover and sustain the positive core of the group to enable the staff to focus on projects, process improvements, and rewards that are aligned to increase census while building a team spirit, thereby creating a better world for our residents and staff.

Four topics were chosen as our project focus: Provider of Choice, Resident Loyalty, The Excellent Team, and Appreciation. Our main goal in using the AI tool was to obtain constructive information as to what is working well today and to learn what we can do to improve with regard to the four focus topics.

The following key objectives were met:

- Learned and used an AI tool to discover the qualitative elements of the positive core at the center
- Identified specific tactics that will enhance teamwork
- Conducted a series of meetings to train a core team of participants on the AI techniques
- Conducted interviews with the staff and residents
- Collected, themed, analyzed, and interpreted the data sets (or outcomes) of the interviews
- Reported findings to all participants for the purpose of increasing the daily average census

The initial training of AI with the core team (identified as the Census Care Team [CCT] in the proposal process) was conducted on April 29. The significant outcome of this meeting was eleven appreciative inquiry staff interviews and an introduction of the Discovery, Dream, Design, and Destiny concepts of AI to the CCT team.

The next meeting, on May 6, discussed the common themes of the eleven interviews and an in-depth overview of the Dream and Design phases. The significant outcome was the development of possibility statements for the **Resident Loyalty** and **Provider of Choice** topics. At this point, each member of the CCT was given a list of staff and resident names to interview. The next two weeks were spent conducting interviews.

Method

A combination of both qualitative and quantitative methods was used in the process of data collection and data interpretation. A comprehensive survey was designed to identify attributes of as many staff and resident respondents as possible, relating to the four focus topics. The survey information was collected over a two-week period via a face-to-face interview format with the individuals. This method was used to build an environment of trust and openness and received very favorable feedback, as it gave each individual an opportunity to talk about what was important to him or her.

The total number of AI interviews conducted was 74 (24 staff and 50 residents). All staff and resident interviews were collected, themed, and summarized. From this information, a Master Wish List was created.

Sample Master Wish List

Master Wish List:

	Wish	Ideas/Solutions	Time frame	Resource	Cost
1	More Activities: Give everyone a chance to do more around here. They just want to have more options and do and go places. Get out more—more activities instead of just smoking. Group activities outside. You're only as old as you feel; activities schedule keep their minds going. More outings. Have more family-oriented activities. Get staff more involved in resident activities. More field trips for the residents. Have more games. More outings. More family-oriented activities which involve the families. Should have the most awesome activities in the world. More entertainment. More outings for residents. To have more family-oriented events. More functions with residents and staff.	A Exercise Program 1. Square dancing or some kind of dancing 2. Resident picnic 3. Go to a ball game 4. "Ask" program —volunteers: Recruit agencies, churches, and schools 5. Tabletop bowling 6. Vegas Night, Black Jack Night, Roulette 7. Shopping: Dollar Store or mall walking 8. Call day camps to have children come in, do activities at WS 9. Create Resident Recreation Committee: need buttons			
2	Facility: When someone walks in the front door, it should smell clean, look and feel cozy and inviting. Just make it a nice place for the residents and us. Pride in physical plan—building itself. More private areas.	1. Fresh flowers from weddings, churches 2. Put air-conditioning in the halls; some are very hot 3. Why isn't our bathroom as nice as their bathroom up front? Air freshener in employee's bathroom 4. What about new lockers? 5. Photographs of staff and residents in halls 6. A more comfortable place to sit outside (lawn chair) 7. Call landscape companies, funerals, flower shops to send overflow to center 8. Create a gardening club 9. Create Historical Room or Century Wall			
3	Appreciation, more appreciation from each other and corporate office.	1. Send letters or certificates based on corporate calendar. Give facilities funds to recognize their employees; i.e., employee of the month, and so on			
4	More Training/Communication	1. New employee orientation 2. Customer service 3. White board to communicate supplies needed			
5	Food: Do something with menu, give a choice or two. Get a list of things they like to eat.	1. Survey residents on food preferences 2. Coffee all day 3. Create Food Committee: Have residents volunteer to cook their specialties with the staff 4. Presentation and serving of food			

AI Discovery and Dream Meeting
April 29, 2002
9:30 a.m. – 1:30 p.m.

Facilitators: Jackie Stavros and Anne Meda
Purpose: Orient CCT to AI, plan and launch inquiry

Goals:
- Understand AI as an integral foundation of this project
- Complete AI interviews
- Explain Project Plan and Timelines

Deliverables:
- Complete the Discovery and Dream phases
- CCT group roster and role

Project Stakeholders:
- Tendercare
- Residents
- Marketing Team

Activity	Leader	Time
Introductions/purpose How we got here? Why AI?	VP Marketing	10 minutes
Agenda/roles	Jackie	15 minutes
Appreciative Interviews Mural (best stories/themes)	Jackie	1.5 hours
Discovery and Dreaming (Working lunch)	Jackie/Anne	1 hour
Report-Outs	Jackie/Anne	30 minutes
Interview Plan – Define – Rotate subgroups/refine – Need a list of employee shifts for the interviews and how to best set up interviews with the residents	Jackie/Anne	15 minutes
Review/close AI: Discovery and Dream Minutes	VP Marketing/Jackie	15 minutes

---

AI: Discovery and Dream Minutes

Monday, April 29, 2002

10 a.m.— Introductions: "If I owned the company, I would...."
Ideas:
- Hold classes for new employees (new employee orientation)
- Invite family of residents and family of workers to functions
- Hold monthly in-services with each department; mandatory staff
meetings
- Hold an Appreciation Day
- Pay overtime
- Keep employees
- Ensure accountability among staff
- Change budget, build census, make sure residents are well cared for
- Add staff—lighten workload and have better care
- Move into the twenty-first century and have more technology (would like to see residents using e-mail to keep in contact with family members living far away)
- Have more social activities for employees and residents
- Build teamwork

96% full to break even

10:15 a.m. — Handout: Develop an Appreciative, Caring Environment
"What do we do really well?"

Core Team—Whole-System Representation

Focus on common ground.

Interview Guide—Intro, (question walk participants through the Interview Guide)

10:15 a.m. – 12:15 p.m.— Interviews

　　　Debrief:

　　　Fun, informative, more commonality—we're after the same
　　　thing; we need to know the person better; it's nice to be lis-
　　　tened to.

12:15 p.m. – 12:30 p.m.— The Unconditional Positive Question
　　　1. Discovery ⇒ 2. Dream ⇒ 3. Design ⇒ 4. Destiny

Today we covered the Discovery phase wherein we interviewed each other. The next step is to Dream. Based on the stories you heard in your initial interviews, select 3 – 5 positive topics. We will cover this in our next meeting. We will also cover the Design and Destiny phases in our next meeting.

12:30 p.m.— "How are the rest of the folks going to be interviewed?"
- Try talking about things from the other side, such as: What works well here?
- Create a shared dialogue, stop and listen to people, create positive intent to trust each other.
- Make a difference in the attitude of people you work with; build self-esteem.
- Create a course of action—capture the rich, thick dialogue of what people say.
- During interviews, listen and TAKE GOOD NOTES!
- CCT is responsible for its interviews.

12:55 p.m.— Read first question and state the answer that was given.
Common themes:
- Tendercare cares about employees
- Culture
- Family feeling
- Elderly care and support
- Acceptance
- Rapport with residents
- Staff (care group)
- Activities
- Appreciation
- Tenure of staff
- Likes to solve problems and impart knowledge
- Likes to help seniors, especially those who don't have family
- Extended family—residents ask employees about their weekends
- Likes to listen to residents
- Likes to be treated as his or her family is treated

Focus on what is good and not what is wrong. What will give life to your center, what should it be, what energizes you about your well-being?

Next meeting is Monday, May 6, 9:30 a.m. – 2:30 p.m.

Agenda: AI Design and Destiny

AI Design and Destiny Meeting
May 6, 2002
9:30 a.m. – 2:00 p.m.

Facilitators: Jackie Stavros and Anne Meda
Purpose: Create Possibility Statements

Goals:
- To make "dream" themes a reality
- To learn how to create an appreciative learning culture

Deliverable:
- Defined Possibility Statements

Project Stakeholders:
- Staff
- Residents
- Marketing Team

Activity	Leader	Time
Welcome Back	VP Marketing	5 minutes
Explain Design Phase	Jackie	30 minutes
Theme Selection	Anne	15 minutes
Design Team Activity	Jackie/Anne	2 hours
Destiny Discussion (Working lunch)	Jackie	1 hour
Report-outs	Jackie/Anne	30 minutes
Review/Close	VP Marketing/Jackie	10 minutes

AI: Dream and Design Minutes

May 6, 2002

9:40 a.m.— Debrief from last week's meeting

+1 Blitz went very well, heard nothing negative, made a good connection; eight people got pins that day. Picnic appears popular. Hard to choose a good time that people will attend. Just purchased a grill, can make a lunch for employees. Did you notice / get feedback from last week?
Nothing in particular, other meetings were scheduled all week, ratifying contract today. Marketing Consultant is getting together with group on Thursday to brainstorm, has received great ideas. The attention from corporate has been great. Have always felt neglected; impressed to meet upper management.

9:48 a.m.— Question posed to the group by VP Marketing: If you had one super power, what would it be?

BC: Photographic memory
BS: The ability to mind read and know what other people are thinking
DC: Five minutes to ponder the impact of the decision you just made (see into the future)
LJ: The ability to see into the future
TF: Time travel—observe and get actual/real perspective
TS: Wants a magic wand
JP: Wants super energy
JS: The power to be in two places at the same time
AM: Wisdom
PS: The ability to control other people's minds
MH: To also be in two places at the same time
FG: To have perfect employees
JH: To control time: stop and have enough time to do everything, and then start time back up again

9:54 a.m.— Agenda overview

Handed out schedule of all interviewers/interviewees. Everyone is to call Terry or Mabel to obtain information about assigned interviewee's schedule and availability.

Shift hours run: 7 a.m. – 3 p.m., Days
3 p.m. – 11 p.m., Afternoons
11 p.m. – 7 a.m., Midnights

Copies of the Staff and Resident Interview Guide will be provided, and a master copy of both was given to Tony.

10 a.m.— Handed out meeting notes from 4/29 meeting
Reviewed notes

A table of 'wish list' items will be created and quantified so we can see each wished-for item and how many times it was mentioned in the interviews.

DESIGN PHASE
A handout was given to the group. We are trying to do a positive revolution of change. There are things we can do now that do not cost money. When we hit census, there is a $200 census incentive that will be added into the monthly budget. When we exceed census, we will be able to do more things. Looking at the data, (JS) came up with eight things—four can be implemented next week, and four will need help.

DISCOVERY
Appreciating—critical to people. We have chosen four topics that we discovered and turned into possibility statements. Take idea and turn it into a possibility statement. The four topics are as follows:
1. Resident Loyalty
2. Provider of Choice
3. The Exception Team—Teamwork
4. Appreciation

Making everyone understood—take time to be an active listener.

Design ⇒ What should be the ideal? Construct possibilities.

Destiny ⇒ After we leave, how do you continue to keep this going? Cycle—every 6 months conduct another discovery/inquiry, find consensus.

Getting to transformational topics:

Ideas: Extra care, shoe untied, customer service: What specifically is this? Define, demonstrate. How do you change mind-set? Develop happier employees (via appreciation programs) to change culture. By doing things for the employees, leading by example. Change starts one step at a time. Have policy for employees to use.

10:30 a.m.— Two ways to deal with things (after we finish):

1. Focus on problem
2. Ask: What possibilities exist that we haven't thought about yet? The smallest change makes the biggest impact.

Four Fundamental Questions (from handout):

Discover optimal margins—census.

DESIGN PHASE
The social-technological architecture:

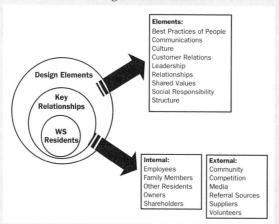

Ingredients: The themes from the interviews.

Key Relationships—Who's affected? How does it affect the center?

You design what you want and then make it happen in Destiny phase, creating a grand possibility statement.

Department heads are part of the core team, must extend to a larger group and get rid of the "us versus them."
**Idea: Stress Call: pick up page – "meet me in the Dining room," play the Hustle.

11:15 a.m. – Noon— Theme Exercise

Topic: Provider of Choice

As a group we:
1. Identified the inner circle: Family, Residents, Responsible Party (guardian, lawyer, and so on), and Staff. This is who we are providing care for.

2. Identified the next outer circle: Key Relationships: Community, Corporate Office, Referral Sources, FIA and Hospitals, Transportation (taxis, bus pickups), and Volunteers.

3. Identified outer circle components: Elements that affect the center and being a provider of choice: Training (i.e., CPR, new-employee orientation, consistent care), Culture, Leadership, Strategy (continuous), Energy/Life, Activities, Stability, and so on.

What makes our center the provider of choice? What is it that people would say make us the best provider of care? What does our "ideal" center consist of?

We brainstormed the following list to answer the last question. Each team member got to vote for the four top elements on the list that he or she thought most significantly impacted the center's ability to become the provider of choice. The chart illustrates the number of votes each item received. (Items in bold were the top picks.)

Ideal Environment	Team Members				
Physical Plant					
Clean	•	•	•		
Fun	•	•	•	•	
Friendly	•				
Services (i.e., medical, nonmedical)	•				
Security/Comfort	•				
Delicious food	•	•	•		
Highly Trained Staff	•	•	•	•	•
Empathetic Staff					
Mentor System					
Concierge/Amenities (i.e., massage therapy, cable TV, and so on)	•				
Energy/Life	•				
Activities	•	•			

We also brainstormed what makes the "ideal" food environment so great. We came up with the following:
- Taste
- Quality and quantity
- Variety and choice
- Presentation
- Ambience/atmosphere
- Special meals/themes
- Salad bar

We then constructed the possibility statement using the elements that were the most frequently selected.

Provider of Choice Possibility Statement:

...We are the provider of choice because we have a high-quality, trained, experienced, and caring staff to meet the needs of our residents. We create a positive culture that radiates energy and life through a superior dining experience and activities that encourage participation and increase the quality of our residents' lives. We offer a fun, clean, and friendly community that caters to the individual's needs...

Topic: Resident Loyalty
- Identified the inner circle: Wayne Seniors Residents
- Identified the components of the next outer circle: Key Relationships: Referral Sources, Guardians, Families, Staff (food), Volunteers, and R.A.
- Identified the outer circle components: Social Responsibility, Follow-up, Follow-through, Culture, Systems, Customer Relations, Education, and Community.

The following was the result of a brainstorm session on the definition of resident loyalty: **What makes a resident loyal?**

Resident Loyalty:
- Relation building, show loyalty to family members, referrals
- Consistency—same-grade service (temp/resident), what? Follow-up and through
- Genuine vested interest, how? Know thy resident, know what is important (by listening)
- Compassion—staff residents (extended family)
- Knowledge—(staff), why? In what they do,: i.e., tie shoe, mash potatoes; level of service
- Finance—(trust), at ease; What are we doing with their money? Budgeting, amenities, balance checkbooks, manage money, keep independence; demonstrate by staff being members
- Physical plant

Common Parts among the Group
- – Trust
- – Compassion
- – Interest
- – Knowledge
- – Dedication
- – Listening
- – Relationships (effective)
- – Respect

Each member of the group wrote an individual possibility statement based on the definition brainstorm elements of resident loyalty. The combined possibility statement is as follows:

Resident Loyalty Possibility Statement:

"At Wayne Seniors, residents are our lifeline. We maintain this lifeline by building relationships with our residents and their families to ensure a caring, consistent, and positive living experience.

We always strive to nurture relationships by creating an environment of listening, understanding, and trust.

Residents trust us with their lives — a responsibility we hold sacred. We earn trust through unwavering commitment to superior care, tempered with compassion and respect.

To provide superior care, we provide knowledge to residents, staff, and families to ensure consistent and compassionate service delivery.

With dedication to these ideals, Wayne Center for Seniors nurtures resident loyalty, thereby effectively serving the community."

7

Destiny:
What Will Be?

*"Allow yourself to **dream** and you will **discover** that **destiny** is yours to **design**."*

—Jackie Stavros

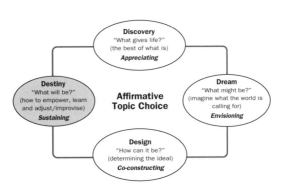

The final phase of the 4-D Cycle is known as Destiny (sometimes called Delivery). The goal of the Destiny phase is to ensure that the dream can be realized. The AI perspective looks at the role of improvisation in building appreciative management into the fabric of organizational culture. The design team publicly declares intended actions and asks for organization-wide support from every level. Self-selected groups plan the next steps for institutionalization and continued vitality. This is where the dream becomes reality.

Like the other phases, Destiny is full of continuing dialogue. Provocative propositions should be revised and updated. Additional AI interviewing may take place with new members in the organization and/or new questions for existing members.

The Destiny phase represents both the conclusion of the Discovery, Dream and Design phases and the beginning of an ongoing creation of an "appreciative learning culture." This chapter explores both aspects of the Destiny phase:

- Aligning the actual organization with the provocative propositions created in the Design phase
- Building AI learning competencies into the culture

The techniques associated with the final phase of the 4-D Cycle are self-organized and often resemble Open Space processes. Individuals and small groups self-organize to implement the Design statements (provocative propositions). This approach involves neither prioritization of needs nor an imposed sequence of management. Instead, people who are passionate about implementing a particular aspect of the design step forward and join with like-spirited collaborators. It is a time of continuous organizational learning, adjustment, and improvisation.

Collective focus on actions to be taken is high as a result of the extensive involvement of large numbers of people in the Discovery, Dream and Design phases. The massive number of people engaged in interviews, large group meetings, and critical decision-making help participants get a strong sense of what the organization is really about and how they can contribute to the future through their personal actions. It is a time of continuous innovation and inquiry, which continues to implement and sustain the newly created social architecture.

This chapter begins with an overview of why the name of this phase was changed from *Delivery* to *Destiny*. Then a summarization of Frank Barrett's material on *Appreciative Learning Cultures* helps organizations learn how to build AI-based learning competencies. The chapter also highlights GTE in its Destiny phase and concludes with a Destiny case clipping of the Hunter Douglas story. Excerpts from this study illustrate some of the outcomes that were experienced upon completion of the Destiny phase. The connections among the four phases, along with the outcomes that such an approach can deliver, are quite apparent.

Rethinking Destiny

In the early years of AI work, the fourth D was called Delivery. This phase emphasizes planning for continuous learning, adjustment, and improvisation in the service of shared ideals. It was a time for action planning, developing implementation strategies and dealing with conventional challenges of sustainability. But the word *delivery* did not go far enough. It did not convey the sense of liberation AI practitioners were experiencing. A perfect example is the well-documented hotel case, where an organization transformed itself from a one-star to a four-star hotel by using AI and literally putting a moratorium on all the traditional problem-solving efforts it had been using.

AI practitioners soon discovered that momentum for change and long-term sustainability increased as "delivery" ideas of action planning, monitoring progress, and building implementation strategies were abandoned. What was done instead, in several of the most exciting cases, was to focus on giving AI away to everyone and then stepping back.

The GTE story told in the **Introduction** of this handbook is still unfolding. It shows that organizational change needs to look a lot more like an inspired movement than a neatly packaged or engineered product. Dan Young, the head of Organizational Development at GTE, and his colleagues, Maureen Garrison and Jean Moore, call it "organizing for change from the grassroots to the frontline." It can be considered the path of positive protest, or a strategy for positive subversion. Whatever it is called, it is virtually unstoppable once it is up and running.

GTE calls it the Positive Change Network (PCN). GTE trained 2,000 people in AI so anyone could use it anywhere in the organization to launch a positive change initiative. One especially dramatic moment gives the sense.[1]

> The headline article in GTE Together described what was spreading as a grassroots movement to build the new GTE. Initiated as a pilot training to see what would happen if the tools and theories of Appreciative Inquiry were made available to frontline employees, things started taking off. All of a sudden, without any permission, frontline employees are launching interview studies into positive topics like innovation, inspired leadership, revolutionary customer responsiveness, labor-management partnerships and "fun." Fresh out of a training session on AI, one employee, for example, does 200 interviews into the positive core

---

1 See David Cooperrider and Diana Whitney, *Collaborating for Change: Appreciative Inquiry* (San Francisco, CA Berrett-Koehler, 2000).

of a major call center. Who is going say "no" to a complimenta-
ry request like, "would you help me out? I'm really trying to find
out more about the best innovations developing in your area and
I see you as someone who could really give me new insight into
creating settings where innovation can happen. It is part of my
leadership development. Do you have time for an interview? I
would be glad to share my learnings with you later!"

Soon the topics are finding their way into meetings, corridor
conversations, and senior planning sessions. In other words
the questions, enthusiastically received, are changing corporate attention, language, agendas and learnings. Many start
brainstorming applications for AI. Lists are endless. Ever done
focus groups with the 100% satisfied customer? How about
changing call center measures? What would happen if we
replaced the entire deficit measures with equally powerful
measures of the positive? How can we revitalize the TQM
groups, demoralized by one fishbone analysis after another?
What would happen if we augmented variance analysis with
depth studies that help people to dream and define the very
visions of quality standards? How about a star stories program
to generate a narrative-rich environment where customers are
asked to share stories of encounters with exceptional employees? How about a gathering with senior executives so we can
celebrate our learnings with them, share with them how seeing the positive has changed our work and family lives, and
even recruit them to join the PCN?

The pilot had acquired a momentum all its own. The immediate response,
an avalanche of requests for participation, confirmed that large numbers of
people at GTE were ready to be called to the task of positive change. To grow
the network by the hundreds, even thousands, GTE decided to do a ten-region
training session, all linked and downloaded by satellite conferencing. A successful pilot of three sites confirmed that the same kind of energy and response
could happen through distance technologies. Quite suddenly, the power of a
thousand-person network caught people's attention. Very rapidly, by connecting and consistently noticing breakthroughs, new patterns of organizing
could become commonplace knowledge. Changes could happen not by organized confrontation, diagnosis, burning platforms, or piecemeal reform, but
through irresistibly vibrant and real visions. PCN was becoming a lightning
rod for energy and enthusiasm that was previously underestimated.

Then the unions raised questions. There were serious concerns, including the fact that they were not consulted in the early stages. The employees were told the initiative was over. There was to be a meeting of the unions and GTE at the Federal Mediation Offices in Washington, D.C., to put the whole thing to rest.

But at the meeting, leaders from both groups recognized something fresh and unique about AI. They agreed to bring two hundred union leaders together for a two-day introduction. Their purpose was to evaluate AI to see if it should have any place in the future at GTE. A month later as the session began, the room was full of tension and overt hostility. Over the two-day session, the group of 250 went from polarized hostility to appreciative dialogue. Then there was the moment of decision. Thirty tables of eight were instructed to evaluate the ideas and cast a vote as a group: "Yes, we endorse moving forward with AI" or "No, we withhold endorsement." For thirty minutes the groups deliberated. Tensions were high. The vote was called:

> Table 1, how do you vote? The response was ready: We vote 100% for moving forward with AI and believe this is a historic opportunity for the whole organization.

> Then the next table: We vote 100% with a caveat that every person at GTE have the opportunity to get the AI training and that all projects going forward be done in partnership with the unions and the company.

On and on the vote went. Thirty tables spoke. Then thirty tables voted. Every one voted to move forward. The outcome was stunning. Eight months later AI was combined with the "conflictive partnership" model of the Federal Mediation Services at the kickoff session announcing a new era of partnership. The historic Statement of Partnership stated:

> The company and the unions realize that traditional adversarial labor-management relations must change in order to adapt to the new global telecommunications marketplace. It is difficult to move to cooperation in one quantum leap. However, the company and the unions have agreed to move in a new direction. This new direction emphasizes partnership.

This story boldly illustrates how AI can accelerate the nonlinear interaction of organizational breakthroughs. Putting historic, positive traditions together with strengths creates a "convergence zone," facilitating the collective repatterning of human systems. At some point, apparently minor positive discoveries connect in an accelerating manner. Suddenly, quantum change, a jump from one state to the next that cannot be achieved through incremental change alone, becomes possible.

The Destiny phase of AI suggests what is needed: the networklike structures that liberate not only the daily search into qualities and elements of an organization's positive core but the establishment of a convergence zone for people to empower one another to connect, cooperate, and co-create. Changes never thought possible are suddenly and democratically mobilized when people constructively appropriate the power of the positive core and simply "let go" of accounts of the negative.

Creating Appreciative Learning Cultures

An important task for an organizational leader is to create cultures in which members can explore, experiment, extend capabilities, improvise, and anticipate customers' unspoken needs. Frank Barrett has called such cultures appreciative *learning cultures*. Organizations need to innovate and strive to create new ideas and new products. The push for innovation requires a different kind of learning, one that goes beyond adapting to challenges and solving problems. Such learning focuses instead on imagining possibilities and on generating new ways of looking at the world. Innovation requires willingness to think "outside the box." It involves an appreciative approach, an ability to see radical possibilities, and a willingness to go beyond the boundaries of problems.

The challenge in the Destiny phase is to do just that. Whether trying to create a radically new, innovative organization or tweaking an already well-run organization, appreciative learning cultures nurture innovative thinking by creating a positive focus, a sense of meaning, and systems that encourage collaboration.

To review: AI begins with the assumption that something in the organization is working well. When engaged in appreciative learning, managers attempt to discover, describe, and explain those exceptional moments in which the system functioned well, those moments when members were highly motivated and their competencies and skills activated. The art of appreciation is the art of discovering and valuing those things that give life to the organization, of identifying what works well in the current organization. This positive approach creates what Senge calls "generative conversations" as the dialogue expands from valuing the best of "what is" to envisioning "what might be." While problem solving emphasizes a dispassionate separation between observer and observed, appreciation is a passionate, absorbing endeavor. Appreciation involves the investment of emotional and cognitive energy to create a positive image of a desired future.

Likewise, appreciative learning cultures accentuate the successes of the past, evoke images of possible futures, and create a spirit of ongoing inquiry that empowers members to new levels of activity.

Destiny: An Improvisational Capacity

AI has achieved remarkable results in the areas of productivity improvement, efficiency, and performance. However, the "goal" of the process is to create highly *improvisational organizations*. These are organizations that, according to Frank Barrett, demonstrate consistent strength in four key kinds of competence: affirmative, expansive, generative, and collaborative. In the end, these four key areas of competence are expanded through ongoing application of the skills applied during Discovery, Dream, Design and Destiny.

- *Affirmative Competence.* The organization draws on the human capacity to appreciate positive possibilities by selectively focusing on current and past strengths, successes, and potentials. In nurturing affirmative competence, leaders of a high-performing organization celebrate members' achievements, directing attention to members' strengths as the source of the organization's vitality.
- *Expansive Competence.* The organization challenges habits and conventional practices, provoking members to experiment in the margins. It makes expansive promises that challenge them to stretch in new directions, and it evokes a set of higher values and ideals that inspire them to passionate engagement. High-performing organizations create a vision that challenges members by encouraging them to go beyond familiar ways of thinking; they provoke members to stretch beyond what have seemed to be reasonable limits.
- *Generative Competence.* The organization constructs integrative systems that allow members to see the results of their actions, to recognize that they are making a meaningful contribution, and to experience a sense of progress. High-performing organizations inspire members' best efforts. Their systems include elaborate and timely feedback so members sense that they are contributing to a meaningful purpose. In particular, it is important for people to experience progress, to see that their day-to-day tasks make a difference. When members perceive that their efforts are contributing toward a desired goal, they are more likely to feel a sense of hope and empowerment.

- *Collaborative Competence.* The organization creates forums in which members engage in ongoing dialogue and exchange diverse perspectives to transform systems. Collaborative systems that allow for dialogue promote the articulation of multiple perspectives and encourage continuous, active debate. The high-performing organization creates the environment that fosters participation and highly committed work arrangements.

Sustaining appreciation and inquiry into the way work is completed requires some of the same "design elements" that were central to the original crafting of provocative propositions. High-impact systems into which AI can be integrated can make this way of working "everyday and ordinary" rather than being viewed as a distinct cultural or change program that fades away. **Table 7.1** identifies areas in which AI and the 4-D Cycle can be integrated into business operations.

Table 7.1 Areas for Integrating AI into Business Operations

Organization Design	Employee Satisfaction	Process Improvement	Learning & Development	Measure-ment	Customer Satisfaction	Planning
Communication Architecture	Employee Orientation	Work Process Redesign	Supervisory Development	Performance Management	Focus Groups & Surveys	Strategic
Joint Ventures	Staffing & Development	Continuous Quality Improvement	Leadership & Management Development	Metric Standards	Customer Feedback	Business
Strategic Alliances	Coaching	Benchmarking	Team Development	Reward & Recognition	Supplier Feedback Systems	Operations
	Diversity Initiatives	Innovations	Training	Surveys	Public Relations	Marketing

There is no one best way to carry out the Destiny phase. Each organization has chosen a different approach to sustain the design from the dream that it discovered. One example is still unfolding in the Destiny phase of the Hunter Douglas story. Within three weeks of the AI Summit launched in the Dream phase, the groups were formalized in the Design phase into "innovation teams" to co-construct their future. What follows is the narrative of the Destiny phase of the AI process as experienced by Hunter Douglas.

Case Clippings:
Hunter Douglas Window Fashions Division[2]

In 1993, Hunter Douglas Window Fashions Division embarked on a whole-system AI process. Branded **Focus 2000**, *the purpose of the process was to enhance employee engagement in creating the future of the organization. In addition, it aimed to build leadership bench strength needed for the fast-growing, highly successful organization. The entire workforce of 950 people was involved in discovering best practices and creating the future. They interviewed employees, customers, vendors, and members of their local community. They hosted a 100-person AI Summit, and they launched 14 action teams. The results were transformative for the organization and its employees.[3]*

From Discovery to Destiny: Appreciative Inquiry Full Cycle

Topic Selection—Education: Given that Hunter Douglas was seeking to build the informal leadership capacities of its workforce, education was of prime interest to the 90-person topic selection team. It was selected as one of five affirmative topics.

Appreciative Interview Question: Two weeks after the selection of the topics, a ten-person subgroup finalized the interview guide and published the following question related to the topic of Education.

Education: Knowledge empowers people and people power Hunter Douglas. We each contribute to Hunter Douglas' position of market leadership through personal knowledge of our jobs and equipment, other functions in the company, our customers, our competition, and the industry.

To maintain our position as market leaders, we must continue to invest in each employee's training and education through individual coaching, challenging work assignments, cross training, tuition assistance, on- and off-site classes, and family scholarships for our children.

1. If knowledge empowers people and people power Hunter Douglas, what kind of learning opportunities would turbo-charge Hunter Douglas?

2. If you could learn more about our customers, our competitors, the industry, and all functions of our company, how could that

---

2 Refer to Frank Berrett, "Creativity and Improvisation in Jazz and Organizations: Implications for Organizational Learning," *Organization Science*, (1998), 9(5), pp. 605-622.

3 For a fuller discussion, see Whitney and Trosten-Bloom, *The Power of Appreciative Inquiry: A Practical Guide to Positive Change.* (San Francisco: Berrett-Koehler, 2003). Adapted by permission.

information help you to take ownership in your role for continued success at Hunter Douglas?

3. What is the best training you have ever experienced? Why? How did this influence your development as a professional? How did it influence the training you passed on to others?

4. Reflecting on your past and where you are today, what types of training have proven the most beneficial to you?

5. Robert Fulghum wrote a book entitled **All I Really Needed to Know I Learned in Kindergarten.** If this were kindergarten, what would you like to learn for the future?

Sense-Making: Three months and 500 interviews later, hundreds of people had responded to this and four other questions. A group of 30 people gathered for two days of sense-making. Sticky notes were everywhere and conversations were energetic.

The Report: Two weeks later a written report went to press, the **Inquirer 2000 Special Edition.** It was a newspaper-like report distributed to the entire workforce, including 100 people who would attend the upcoming three-day summit.

Dream: The following excerpts from the Inquirer 2000 reflect the dreams shared in the interview process.

HD WFD Supports People Through Training And Education

In a series of discussions, Synthesis team members exploring the topic of education made two important discoveries.

First, Hunter Douglas employees, customers, suppliers, and community members are committed to enhancing their work performance, career potential, and relationship with Hunter Douglas through job-related training.

Second, and perhaps more striking, employees look to the company to support their development as human beings. Some of the richest comments, stories, and dreams referred to people's desire for education, for skills that will help them not only live their lives better, but also become stronger on the job. Many interviewees shared a dream that HD would help educate them for higher levels of personal as well as professional success.

Those who gave details suggested classes and programs that would help them in their personal lives as well as at work. These would include a wellness program that teaches how health is essential to a good attitude and good performance. Others asked for classes in stress and moneymanagement. Still others shared dreams for access to experts in career and life counseling, including an on-campus career guidance center or counselor. They believed this resource would help people understand the steps needed to better themselves at work and at home.

Possibility Design Statement: Turn the clock forward again by a month. It's the second day of the Summit. Participants are self-organizing into "design teams." Not surprisingly, one of the seven design statements is on the topic of education. Here is the Education Design Statement:

> Education and training are cornerstones of Hunter Douglas. Individuals partner with the company to achieve a sense of inner purpose, direction, and continuous growth. This, in turn, nurtures the strength and confidence people need to achieve their full personal and professional potential.

> Hunter Douglas sponsors a learning center, Hunter Douglas University (HDU), which provides such things as mentoring, customer training, career counseling, and skills development.

The Design phase interprets the organization's dreams about the future. It is the collective commitments, principles, processes, actions, programs, structure, and tasks necessary to make the dream come alive.

Destiny: It is now the third day of the Summit. All 100 participants have self-organized into groups that have been inspired by the seven Design Statements. Several of the 14 groups deal with issues of education, training, and development.

Fast forward now in the still-unfolding Destiny phase. Beginning six months later, the following are implemented within the Hunter Douglas Window Fashions Division:

- **A formal mentorship program.** With an advisory team consisting of both leaders and floor staff, this program solicits mentors and matches them with people requesting mentoring. It offers formal "accreditation" for people's personnel files. More than thirty people completed the program within the first year.
- **Appointment of a half-time career planning professional.** This person—a latecomer to the effort AI—bids for and is awarded a job transfer. She goes through formal training in career planning and moves to spending half her time at this activity, with the other half dedicated to internal communication (in response to one of the other Design Statements).
- **Establishment of an "English as a Second Language" program.** One of the original third-shift employees conducted interviews during the original inquiry with some of the Laotian refugees who were also employed on her shift people whom she'd seen but never spoken to. Shocked and saddened by some of what she learned in her conversations, she informally committed herself to teaching English on her lunch hour in order to "make right" on the wrong that fate had done to her colleagues.

  She approached the Vice President of Human Resources about her intention. He talked her into serving as on-site coordinator for the local community college's professionally developed ESL classes. Human Resources had been trying to get these classes under way for over two years. They had previously been unable to get a critical mass of non-English speaking employees to sign up for the classes.
- **Initiation of a state-of-the-art "new-hire orientation" program.** This is yet another program that the Human Resources Department tried unsuccessfully to design for over three years. Following the Summit, it becomes a regular monthly event. A year or so after its initial implementation, long-time employees also begin rotating through the program. The innovation team that designs this program commits that every employee will develop a sense of his or her relationship to the entire business.

- **Establishment of a Hunter Douglas University.** Initially launched as a virtual university, it becomes the clearinghouse for all on- and off-campus classes available to HD employees. A year later the company breaks ground on an on-site learning center, dubbed Hunter Douglas University (HDU). A year after that, HDU contains two classrooms (each seating up to 50 people, fully equipped with sound and visual equipment and a break-down wall between rooms), two conference rooms, a computer laboratory, and a library. It has a kitchen and a serving area for on-site training program.

  In its first two years of existence, HDU hosted hundreds of training and planning meetings, several of which have included 100 or more people. Its regular schedule now includes training classes in "Focus on Excellence" (continuous improvement), English as a Second Language, Interaction Management for supervisors; Dale Carnegie, personal financial planning, and Toastmasters training for presenters.

*The following material in this **Case Clipping** traces the Hunter Douglas process from start to finish. It shows how affirmative topic choices led to discovery, organizational learning, dream, design, and innovative actions.*

   *The **Case Clippings** include:*
   - *Leadership Introduction Agenda*
   - *Town Meeting Agenda*
   - *Employee Interview Guide*
   - *Interview Summary Sheet*
   - *Design Statements*

Results: A year later Hunter Douglas Window Fashions Division conducted a mini AI interview. The first question in the inquiry solicited people's input on what is best within the Division... most worthy of holding on to... with the greatest capacity to influence the organization positively as it grew. Almost to a person, the response was "this company's commitment to employee and customer training and education is second to none."

   This story is a clear reminder that **organizations move in the direction of the things they study.** Therefore, it is necessary to continually seek ways to gain a deeper understanding of those things that give life to an organization and its people. Finding ways to tell the stories, to build the conversations, and to enhance the relationships and dialogue will bring the best to life.

Leadership Introduction Agenda

One-Day Leadership Introduction
(Hunter Douglas Window Fashions Division)

Agenda
Leadership Team Meeting
March 3, 7:30 a.m. – 5 p.m.
Location: Doubletree Inn

Participants: Entire Leadership Team

Key Roles: Facilitators: Amanda and Linda
Timekeeper, Scribes, Gatekeeper: Volunteers

Focus of Meeting: Introduction to and Applications of Appreciative Inquiry to Identified Organizational Issues

Time	Presenter	Item
7:30–7:40	Rick	Welcome and Meeting Opening
	Linda	Agenda, ground rules
7:40–7:55	Amanda	Background of Appreciative Inquiry • ABC Model (reviewed) • Foundational principles • Introduction to 4-D Cycle (ABC superimposed)
7:55–8:35	All	Mini Appreciative interviews (pairs) (Core questions)
<8:35–8:45>	<BREAK>	
8:45–9:40	All	Debrief appreciative interviews. Answer questions: "What was it like to be interviewed?" "What was it like to interview?" • Witness interviews. • Extract and record highlights/themes. • Prepare to share highlights with large group (entire subgroup involved).

9:40–10:35	All	Extract highlights key themes Present to larger group / choose a theme. • Highlights of the interview/ witnessing experience • Key themes • Multivote to choose a topic
<10:35–10:50>	<BREAK>	
10:50–11:05	Amanda	Introduction to Interview Protocols • Overview—purpose of the interview • Sample of protocols • Give assignments
11:05–11:25	All	Construction of a protocol for selected theme Subgroups (4 of 6, 2 of 5) construct preambles and questions for chosen topic.
11:25–11:45	All	Piloting of Interview Protocol/ Debriefing in Paired Teams • Fishbowl format • Debriefing questions: Note similarities and differences between two groups' approaches.
11:45–12:00	Amanda/Linda	Summary / Lessons Learned • Main point: There isn't a "right/ wrong" question It's only a question of whether it takes you where you want to go. • Tie back to Foundational Principles and Charter issues.
<12:00–12:45>	<LUNCH>	
12:45–1:05	All	Review of morning's learnings/ Setup pending activity • Describe on-site interviews. • Select interviewees.

1:05–3:00	All	Applications activity (on-site interviews)
<3:00–3:15>	<BREAK>	
3:15–3:45	All	Shared learnings
3:45–4:10	Amanda	Final stages of Appreciative Intervention (4-D cycle) Questions about AI
<4:10–4:15>	<BREAK>	
4:15–4:45	All	Design Steering Team for overall intervention
4:45–5:00	Linda	Next Steps / Meeting Review • Select meeting date. • Questions to Ponder: • How do we interview everyone and still run the business? • Parameters within which intervention must be designed? • Meeting review (Most meaningful for you today? Insights?) • What do you hope for in our next intervention? • Thumbs up/down?

Town Meeting Agenda

1½ Hour "Town Meeting" (introduction to general workforce)
(Hunter Douglas Window Fashions Division)
Hunter Douglas WFD "Town Meeting"

Meeting Objective: Preview of plans to engage everyone in Hunter Douglas in making this organization the best workplace possible.

What	**Who**	**Time**
Opening, welcome, and introduction	Rick	9 minutes

- Welcome to everyone. Thank you for being here.
- Turn to someone who's near to you in the room and introduce yourself. Tell them who you are, where you work in the company, and how long you've been with HD.
- Today is about introducing a way of working that draws upon the wisdom of the entire organization. The need to listen to and involve everyone in creating our future is the most important insight that the leadership team has gotten from the surveys of the past few years. By working this way, we will all create an even more fun, exciting, rewarding, and alive place to work.
- What we'll be talking about over the next hour is tied to a need to pay attention to our people and service our customers, which was a key theme in the employee opinion surveys we conducted last summer.
- We're going to be asking for your help today. We're looking for people who want to get involved and affect the organization's future. Part of the help you can give us included speaking up and participating in this meeting.
- The process we're going to use to make this happen is different than anything we've done before.
- The way this meeting is structured is different. Look around. There are people from all different shifts, functions, and business units around you.
- We have a few guests from outside HD who'll be speaking to you today. Some may be familiar to you.
  - GTE folks (detail later)   Rick (continued)
  - Linda and Amanda (detail later)
  - Turn over to Amanda

What	Who	Time
The change that's already started	Amanda	17 minutes

- Let me tell you two stories that explain better than anything what we're beginning to do (Medic Inn and Imagine Chicago).
- What did people in these stories do to get results and change their thinking?
  - Asked questions
  - Focused on the positive
  - Made changes based on things that were already shown to work
  - Asked and involved everyone
  - Mixed up people of different backgrounds, levels, and so on.
  - It was good experience for the people being interviewed and the people asking questions

What	Who	Time
Introduce and show video	Todd	7 minutes

- The video you're about to see will show you three things:
  - Slices of the types of interviews that will be conducted within HD over the coming months
  - The many different types of answers—and the moving answers—you can get when you ask the right questions
  - The enthusiasm and energy that this type of questioning generates
- KICK BACK and enjoy it!

Discuss the video	Amanda	3 minutes

- What inspired you, about what people shared about Hunter Douglas?
- What did you learn about the best of who we are?

Making it come alive: guest stories	Guests	20 minutes
- What we did (overview)
- Why we did it
- Who was involved
- What's now different as a result
- (Consider having personal testimonials as well as guests)

Lessons learned
(Tie the lessons learned and main points heard in the guest stories back
to what they saw in the video.)

The plan to make this happen   Amanda   5 minutes
Introduction
I'm going to discuss the three general phases we'll go through using
this new way of working. In general, we will be creating interview
questions, conducting interviews, and pulling together the highlights
of all interviews in order to make permanent changes within HD. The
interviews we conduct will focus especially on peak experiences and
successes from the past. (Once we understand what really works, we
are more likely to do it again.)

1. Create interview questions—This work starts when we identify the
   qualities that "give life" to HD. We do this by bringing together
   about seventy people from all around the organization who have
   different kinds of experience and who do different kinds of jobs.
   These people will work together for three days to create interview
   questions that everyone in the organization (and even some people
   outside of HD) will answer. **This will be their only work for these
   three days.**

2. Conduct interviews—Every employee in the company, as well as
   some people from outside of HD (such as customers, suppliers,
   other divisions of HD, and other manufacturing companies) will be
   interviewed using the questions that were developed by the group
   of seventy. The interviews will focus especially on peak experiences
   and successes.

   This will not be a survey. Though we'll be asking questions, they
   are not the same types of questions we've all answered on surveys
   over the past years. The interviews are more like guided conversations, which will help us understand the best of what we've been
   doing so we can do more of it.

   These "conversations" will create **immediate changes** in how we
   do things. For example... (use the bowling example here to show
   how positive images can create immediate positive changes.)

3. Preview of coming attractions—After we've completed the interviews, there will be lots of information that needs to be pulled together. We'll go back to the original group of 50+ to do this. This group will find the highlights from the interviews and make recommendations for permanent changes in the organization that will build on what we've learned, allowing HD to be the very best workplace it can be.

What	Who	Time
How this is all going to happen	Amanda	3 minutes

- Amanda is now on staff for several days a week as resident expert on this process.
- Linda Sorrento will be an outside consultant who can help us get this done.
- Five-day intensive training, five HD people (introduce and give names) in how to work in this way
- A team of people created by the Interview Design Team will develop the plan for how we'll do this work at HD (i.e., who gets interviewed and how, how feedback gets synthesized, who and how many get trained as interviewers—in other words, plan the logistics of the implementation).

Timing	Rick	5 minutes

- Started the process in January when members of the Leadership Team were trained in this way of working, and practiced some new skills through unscheduled one-on-one interviews in the plants. (Raise your hand if you were interviewed that day.)
- Since then we've done additional planning and training of the business leadership team and of some individual departments.
- We waited to have this meeting until after the ISO audit, to be sure we'd be ready to go forward with the training and interviews of the whole workforce.
- We plan to interview everyone (inside and outside the company) between the middle of June and the end of July. We will begin acting on the changes that are recommended by the middle of September.

- You'll all be getting regular updates on how things are going between now and mid September, and you'll have a chance to see and comment on the results at other Town Meetings and gatherings such as the Leadership Round Table.

Questions and Answers	All	10 minutes
Action items	Rick	1 minute

- As we said a few minutes ago, we need a team to meet for two or three days to help create the questions we'll use for our interviews
- Show and explain matrix
- 56 people representing 27 offices and 29 floors
- extra 10 to assure diversity
- total of 66

Amanda's will explain to you how we're going to figure out who's on the team.

What	**Who**	**Time**
	Amanda	4 minutes

- Each of you has two pieces of paper on your seat. First, pick up the yellow paper. Use this paper to write the name of at least one person **other than yourself** who you believe should be part of the interview design team. Consider nominating two or three people from inside or outside your immediate work area whose work and feelings about HD you know well. We want a variety of people, who have very different opinions. This means we want people who love working here, and we also want people who feel improvements can be made. All the opinions are important.
- Now pick up the blue piece of paper on your seat. If you would like to be part of this team, write your name on this page. (We're separating the nominations for other people and self so everybody's nomination will count the same.)
- Show example
- On your way out the door at the end of this meeting, turn this paper in to one of the people wearing a red hat.

What's next?	Amanda	3 minutes

- We'll put all the names of the people who were nominated onto a matrix.
- The people who were nominated most frequently will be asked to work on a team to finalize the list of nominees for their business area.
- As you can already see, this work will not be done in a top-down kind of way. Everyone on this team of 50+ will have an equal vote and an equal say in the questions we ask and an equal chance to make HD the best workplace possible for all of us.

Meeting debrief   TBD   5 minutes

- What was most meaningful about this meeting for you?
- What do you want to see happen next as part of this activity?

Adjourn   Rick   2 minutes

- Closing comments
- People turn in their nominations on the way out the door.

Employee Interview Guide

Hunter Douglas Window Fashions Division
Interview Guide

Name: _____ Phone Ext. (if available):_____

Position: _____

Business Unit/Function: _____

Years of Service: _____ Date: _____

Interviewed by: _____

OPENING

Thank you for participating. I'm looking forward to what I'll be learning from this conversation, and I hope it will be a rewarding experience for you as well. As Rick Pellett explained in his letter to you, these interviews are critical to the future of our company.

Many times in interviews we try to ask questions about things that aren't working well so we can fix them. This time we are going to approach things from a different angle. We are going to find out about your experiences of success here at Hunter Douglas or in other parts of your life so we can find ways to create more of these types of experiences in our organization.

Later in the summer everyone in the Window Fashions Division will have been interviewed. At that time, everybody's input will be compiled to identify the qualities that make Hunter Douglas a rewarding place to work. With those qualities as a foundation, we will dream about our vision for the year 2000 and beyond.

There are just a few more things you'll want to know about this process. Our conversation will last between 1-1/2 and 2 hours. I'm going to take notes as we talk. Sometimes if you tell a really great story or say something in a way that's especially striking, I might write down what you say word for word. But the information I collect will still be confidential and anonymous, unless you ask to have your name attached to it. I am the only person who will see the detailed notes from this interview. A **summary** of our conversation will be turned into an independent consultant, who will work with a group of people later in the summer to pull together all of our results.

Now before we begin, do you have any questions? Okay, then. Let's get started.

1. What were your initial excitements and impressions when you first joined the company?

2. What has been your most positive or pleasurable experience since you've been here?

3. Without being humble, explain what you value most about:
   - Yourself.
   - The people you work with.
   - Your business unit or functional area here at Hunter Douglas.

PEOPLE

The foundation of any great organization lies in the strengths of its people. The experiences and diverse backgrounds are assets that any organization must utilize to be successful. When we look at Hunter Douglas, it is obvious why it has been so successful. Looking back, we have grown from a small company to a worldwide market leader. How have the people contributed to this success? Hunter Douglas has fostered personal growth through teamwork, two-way respect, communication, and creativity.

When employees have the freedom to express themselves openly and to be involved in the decisions that affect their future, they gain confidence and authority to perform at their best.

1. Describe the most memorable event that illustrates your contribution to the success of a team or organization. What strengths did you bring to that success?

2. Reflect back on someone in your life you have admired and describe his or her qualities. How do you feel those qualities have influenced your growth?

3. If you could look into a crystal ball and see the haute of Hunter Douglas and its employees, what would you like to see? How do you think we can get there?

EDUCATION

Knowledge empowers people and people power Hunter Douglas. We each contribute to Hunter Douglas' position of market leadership through personal knowledge of our jobs and equipment, other functions in the company, our customers, our competition, and the industry. To maintain our position as market leaders, we must continue to invest in each employee's training and education through:

- Individual coaching.
- Challenging work assignments.
- Job cross-training.
- Tuition assistance.
- On- and off-site classes.
- Family scholarships for our children.

1. If knowledge empowers people and people power Hunter Douglas, what kind of learning opportunities would turbo-charge Hunter Douglas?

2. If you could learn more about our customers, our competitors, the industry, and all functions of our company, how could that information help you take ownership in your role for continued success at Hunter Douglas?

3. What is the best training you have ever experienced? Why?

   • How did this influence your development as a professional?

   • How did it influence the training you passed on to others?

4. Reflecting on your past and where you are today, what types of training have proven the most beneficial to you?

5. Robert Fulghum wrote a book entitled All I Really Need to Know I Learned in Kindergarten. If this were kindergarten, what would you like to learn for the future?

QUALITY OF LIFE

Quality of life is achieved in part through a balance of work and family. By ensuring personal and professional well-being, employees can reach their highest level of performance and self-satisfaction.

Throughout the past, Hunter Douglas has been sensitive to its employees' changing personal and professional needs through flexibility and awareness. We can ensure success for today and in the future by continuing to acknowledge this need for balance.

1. Describe your definition of what a perfectly balanced personal and professional life is.

2. Envision a time when you were able to balance the personal and professional aspects of your life.
   • Describe how this balance was achieved.
   • What was it about the experience that made you feel this balance?

3. If you could travel over the rainbow, what do you think the quality of life would be like there?

COMMUNICATION

An ongoing and productive exchange of information and creative ideas is vital to the success of Hunter Douglas. Information about how our business is doing, our customers and competition, our plans for the future, and business processes in other parts of the company allows each of us to make the most effective decisions possible. As we grow, this kind of complete communication ensures our continued success in delivering innovative and quality products to our customers.

By exercising active listening and two-way communication, we secure our future as a fair and open organization where every voice is heard.

1. Describe the best example you have experienced of open two-way communication?
   • What did you learn from that experience?
   • How have you applied this to your daily interactions (for example, with your supervisor, coworkers, other business units, customers, and suppliers)?

2. What do you believe would be the ideal situation in which your questions, concerns, or ideas could be heard and responded to?

3. What do you foresee would be the most effective process of receiving Hunter Douglas information concerning products, employees, competitors, and the Window Fashions industry?

MORALE

We, as a company, appreciate the importance of each individual's contributions to our success. Recognition, commitment to excellence, and a sense of being stretched or challenged provided the motivation to do our best and go beyond our realm of responsibility. This, in turn, creates:

- Job satisfaction.
- Self-worth.
- A sense of value.
- Ownership.

Continuous focus on positive morale ensures a fun and appreciative work environment.

1. When you reflect on your own experiences, tell me about a high point in your life that gave you a sense of ownership and value.

2. Think of someone who brings a sense of value and pride to his or her job and how he or she projects this level of ownership towards his or her peers. Tell me about it.

3. How do you think receiving recognition from your leadership and others and having the resources and equipment needed to get the job done would contribute to morale?

4. How can we continue to improve morale, build camaraderie, and have fun in the workplace?

CLOSING

In conclusion, I'd like to ask you just a few final questions.

1. What direction would you like to see yourself going with Hunter Douglas in the future?

2. Five years from now your best friend wants to work for Hunter Douglas. What would you like to be able to tell him or her?

3. If you had three blank memos signed by Rick Pellett, the general manager of Window Fashions, that would become company policy, how would you use them?

4. In your opinion, what was the highlight of this interview? What do you hope comes out of this process?

5. Would you like to become a future Focus 2000 interviewer? If so, it will involve your meeting with between two and five people over the next month or so, using the same process you and I just used. (Interviewer note: Please fill out the Future Interviewer Notice at the end of this packet for those who say yes to this question.)

Interview Summary Sheet

Information requested from each interviewer

- Complete in full after each interview.
- Be sure to gather information from EACH SECTION of the Interview Guide.
- Review your notes with your interviewee before submitting, if at all possible.

What were the best quotes that came out of this interview?

What were the best stories that came out of this interview?

What were the best practices or specific recommendations that you heard reflected in your conversation?

Interviewer Name　_____

Interviewee Name (optional)　_____

Date of Interview　_____

Please complete this summary sheet within 30 minutes of your interview and send it promptly to the Focus 2000 mailbox in Building One.

Design Statements

Hunter Douglas Design Statements
Possibility Propositions

CREATIVITY

Hunter Douglas thrives on creativity. It is the source for new ideas, the lifeblood of the company, and the catalyst for positive change. It is the basis for leadership in products and processes that are both proprietary and innovative.

Hunter Douglas leads the industry in creative ideas that involve all of the company's stakeholders, including employees, customers, and suppliers. We vigorously promote a creative culture to help reinvent and improve products, services, and organizational and business processes. We actively solicit, implement, and reward ideas generated by all people.

We foster an environment that inspires unique ideas, and we provide resources and opportunities for people to develop their creativity and bring their ideas to fruition. Decision makers actively listen to all ideas to enhance creativity and enable people to realize their dreams.

LEADERSHIP

Visionary leadership permeates Hunter Douglas and is the catalyst for our success. Leadership exists in three areas: individual, managerial, and industry. We seek out and develop leadership qualities among our employees. Leadership strongly supports hands-on involvement and mentoring; defines leadership opportunities; and actively listens to all voices, all opinions, and all ideas with fairness and impartiality.

PEOPLE

Hunter Douglas Window Fashions Division's success as a company is built on the ideas, dreams, and diversity of our people and business partners.

We encourage, challenge, and support people in the pursuit of their ideas, dreams, and aspirations through 1) utilizing and participating in the Appreciative Inquiry process, 2) enhancing the quality of life through the balance of work and personal life, 3) providing opportunities and resources for continuous personal and professional growth and, 4) providing a safe and open work environment while honoring and rewarding individual and team, accomplishments.

The future of the company is dependent upon employees' participation, ownership, integrity, and respect for others. Commitment to people and their ideas ensures continued success, enhanced profitability, and product quality for Hunter Douglas and its partners, while resulting in happier, more productive people.

EDUCATION

Education and training are cornerstones of Hunter Douglas. Individuals partner with the company to achieve a sense of inner purpose, direction, and continuous growth. This, in turn, **nurtures the strength and confidence people need to achieve their full personal and professional potential.**

Hunter Douglas sponsors a learning center, "Hunter Douglas University" ("HDU"), which provides such things as:
- Mentoring.
- Customer training.
- Career counseling.
- Skills development.

COMMUNICATION

Hunter Douglas demands open, honest, high-quality, and ongoing communication among its employees, business partners, and communities. We provide all stakeholders the **opportunity to express and be actively listened to on all ideas and opinions.**

The organization:
- Promotes continuous two-way exchange of information and ideas across all cultures and languages.
- Actively shares the big picture through open access to all appropriate information about the company, its history, and its business environment.
- Maximizes use of the most effective communication tools.
- Expects individual ownership of and responsibility for effective communication.

CUSTOMERS

Customers are Hunter Douglas' lifeblood and future. We delight customers (fabricators, dealers, consumers, suppliers, employees, and the community) by understanding and exceeding their expectations in the areas of:
- Product quality and innovation.
- Customer service and technical support.

- Customer relations.
- Training and education.
- *Community involvement.*
- *Promises kept.*

We provide professional and seamless service, create strong partnerships, and significantly contribute to customer success. The Hunter Douglas family embraces customers through commitment to excellence, innovation, imagination, dreams, and "small company values." Our culture demands an atmosphere of respect, trust, integrity, honesty, reliability, and responsibility. We expand our customer base by nurturing current and new relationships. Customers eagerly do business with us because "we are easy to do business with." We set the benchmark for others to follow!

PRODUCTS

HDWFD's market leadership is built on the strong foundation of its products. Critical driving forces behind our market leadership are product innovation, improvements, quality, and marketing. We create high-fashion, high-function, reliable, branded products. In addition, we are committed to:

- Continually reinvent our business through the creation of profitable, new, proprietary products.
- Extend, defend, and continuously improve our existing products.

Our challenge is to develop and deliver "whole" products that provide total satisfaction for our fabricators, dealers and consumers through:

- Creation of new products that are imaginative, fashionable, and robust.
- Thoughtfully designed and engineered products, with processes that have high yields, zero defects, and minimal return rates—and that are easy to install and fabricate.
- Products that are positioned and marketed effectively so their place in the market is easily understood by dealers and consumers.
- Supportive sampling and sales efforts that communicate product features and benefits effectively.
- Low-maintenance products that require minimal care and cleaning.

This results in products that consumers display with pride and enthusiasm.

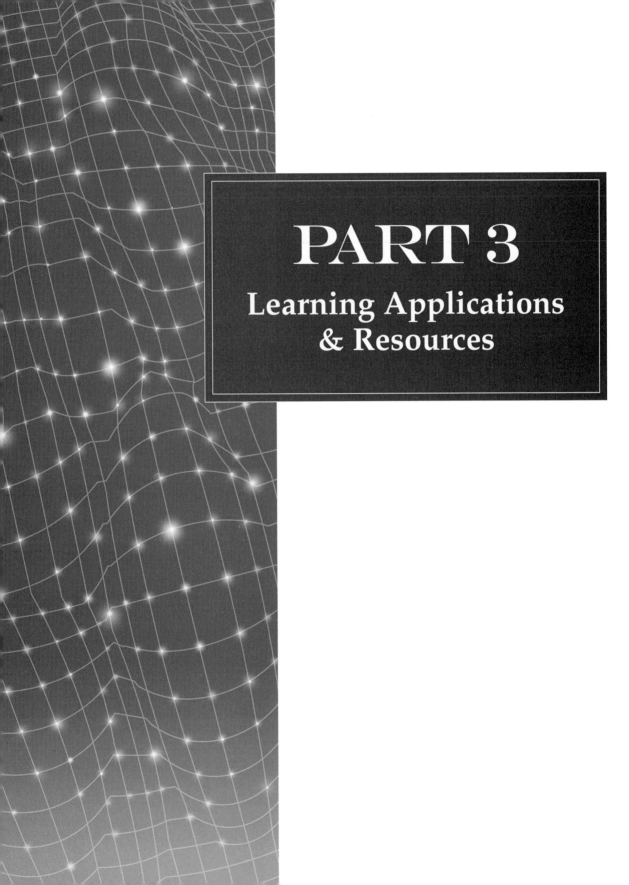

PART 3
Learning Applications & Resources

This final section provides a collection of sample materials and resources. These resources are offered not as a formula for success, but rather as guides for your own AI Initiative. Many of these resources were contributed by consultants who worked collaboratively with their clients to tailor AI to their needs and context.

These range from interview guides to a sample AI Summary Report and a detailed project plan in **Chapter 8**. Examples range from services, manufacturers, and not-for-profit to retail organizations. There are a range of formats, affirmative topics, and interview summary sheets. **Chapter 9** includes a master set of slides that can be used for a workshop. (These slides are available on CD-ROM, available separately from Lakeshore Communications [see last page].) **Chapter 10** contains a set of worksheets for use in training sessions or workshops. **Chapter 11** concludes this handbook and contains four key AI classic articles.

Chapter 8: Sample Interview Guides, Summary Report
and a Detailed Project Plan

Sample Interview Guides
- First American National Bank - service
- North American Steel, Inc. – manufacturer
- World Vision Relief and Development– not-for-profit
- Canadian Tire – retail

AI Summary Report
- Fairmont North America

Detailed Project Plan
- British Airways, NA – Customer Service

Chapter 9: Master Set of AI Overheads for Use in Training

Chapter 10: AI Worksheets

Chapter 11: *The AI Classics:* Selected Articles (reprinted by permission of the respective publishers; copyright protected).

8

Sample Interview Guides, Summary Report and a Detailed Project Plan

SAMPLE INTERVIEW GUIDE—Service

First American National Bank
Appreciative Inquiry Questionnaire

Name _____

Title _____ Date_____

Group/Department _____

Years of Service_____ Phone _____

Interviewed by _____

OPENING:

As part of a special study, we are conducting interviews with employees about their work experience. In particular, our goal is to locate, illuminate, and understand the distinctive values, management practices, and skills that lend the organization its organizational vitality. In other words, we are interested in understanding more about what is happening when we are at our best.

The information you provide in this interview will be used to help prepare a corporate vision statement as seen and valued by members at all levels in the corporation. Our interest is in learning from your experience. The collected comments, experience, and suggestions from all of the employees interviewed will be summarized and reviewed with senior management.

The interview takes about one hour. The interview will tend to focus on the organization when it is operating at its best in the following (preliminary) topic areas:

1. Being the Best   4. Integrity
2. Shared Ownership Commitment   5. Empowering People
3. Cooperation

QUESTIONS:

EXPERIENCE OF ORGANIZATION
  1. First, I'd like to learn about your beginnings with the organization.
     • What attracted you to the organization?
     • What were your initial feelings and impressions when you joined the company?

2. Looking at your entire experience, can you recall a time when you felt most alive, most involved, or most excited about your involvement in the organization?
    - What made it an exciting experience?
    - Who were the most significant others?
    - Why were they significant?
    - What was it about you that made it a peak experience?
    - What were the most important factors in the company that helped to make it a peak experience? (Probe. Leadership qualities, structure, rewards, systems, skills, strategy, and/or relationships?)

3. Let's talk for a moment about some things you value deeply— specifically, the things you value about 1) yourself, 2) the nature of your work, and 3) the organization.
    - Without being humble, what do you value the most about yourself as a human being, a friend, a parent, a citizen, or a son or daughter?
    - When you are feeling best about your work, what do you value about the task itself?
    - What is it about the organization…you value?
    - What is the single most important thing the company has contributed to your life?

BEING THE BEST

4. The organization builds on "proven strengths" and has a history of being a pioneer in a large number of areas. In your opinion, what is the most important achievement you can recall that illustrates this spirit of being the best?

5. What is the most outstanding or successful achievement you have been involved in pulling off—a piece of work or project of which you are particularly proud?
    - What was it about you (unique qualities you have) that made it possible to achieve this result?
    - What organizational factors (e.g., leadership, teamwork, and/or culture) fostered this determination to excel or achieve?

SHARED OWNERSHIP AND COMMITMENT

Organizations work best when people at all levels share a basic common vision in relation to the company's core mission, intent, and direction. When people know the big picture, they often experience a feeling of purpose, pride, significance, and unity.

6. In your mind, what is the common mission or purpose that unites everyone in this organization? How is this communicated and nurtured?

7. Think of a time you felt most committed to the organization and its mission. Why did you feel such commitment?
   - Give one example of how the organization has shown its commitment to you.

COOPERATION / TEAM SPIRIT

A cooperative team spirit is important to our company. Important initiatives usually depend on the support and goodwill of others within work groups and/or between groups that cross department, specialization, and hierarchical levels. Cooperation requires trust, open channels of communication, responsiveness to others' needs, and interpersonal competence.

8. Can you think of a time when there was an extraordinary display of cooperation among diverse individuals or groups in the company?
   - What made such cooperation possible? (Explore planning methods used, communication systems or process, leadership qualities, incentives for cooperation, skills, team development techniques, and others).

9. Give an example of the most effective team or committee you have been part of. What are the factors/skills that made it effective?

EMPOWERING PEOPLE

Our organization's strength rests with its people. It has a tradition of providing structures or opportunity for members of the corporation to excel. This requires consideration of individual goals, ideas, and aspirations as well as providing developmental opportunities to learn, to grow, and to take risks.

10. What individual qualities are most valued in this organization?

11. What qualities are necessary for people to excel?
    - In empowered organizations people feel significant. People believe they have a chance "to make a difference." They believe that what they do has significance, and they are recognized. What does the organization do best (at least three examples) when it comes to empowering people?

12. How do people develop these qualities?

IN CONCLUSION

13. What is the core factor that gives vitality and life to the organization (without which the organization would cease to exist)?
    - If you could develop or transform the organization in any way, what three things would you do to heighten its vitality and overall health?

SAMPLE INTERVIEW GUIDE—Manufacturer

North American Steel, Inc.
Learning from 40 Years of Experience

INTRODUCTION

Thank you very much for agreeing to be interviewed for the organization study we are conducting in preparation for North American Steel's 40th-year celebration. As you may know, the majority of organizations in our society die before they reach the age of forty (40). But there are exceptions. North American Steel is one of them. Even more important, North American Steel is stronger than ever. Over the years, North American has proven itself resilient. In good times and bad, it has provided a stable base of employment for many people. It has adapted, changed, and grown with the times. And its future looks positive and promising. The question is "why?"

What are the core factors that give life to this organization? What can we learn from our history, especially when we examine closely those moments when we have been our best? What are North American Steel's most effective practices, strengths, or best qualities — things we should try to preserve about our organization even as we change? What important lessons can we draw from our history? Building on all of this, what kind of organization do we want to be in the future? What is our potential? Can our positive past, the best in our past, help us become more daring as we think about our true potential as an organization? What is your dream for North American Steel? What ideas do you have for helping us move to a whole new level as a business?

The information you provide will be used to help accelerate our continuous improvement as an organization and to help us prepare for our 40th-year anniversary celebration in September 1994. The important thing is learning from everybody's experience. The collected comments will provide the basis for a report to be reviewed by all. Your comments will be put together with others anonymously. Your name will not be attached to any of the stories, suggestions, examples, or comments you make. The interview will take about 30 to 45 minutes.

    A. Experience with North American Steel, Inc.
       1. To start, I'd like to learn about *your* beginnings at NAS.
          a. When did you start at NAS, and what were your first impressions?
          b. Why have you stayed with NAS?

       2. What is one of the most rewarding experiences you have had at NAS, something that was a *real high point*? Can you

tell me about a time when *you felt best*, most alive, most effective, proud, and so on.

3. Let's talk a moment about some things you value most specifically about (1) yourself and (2) the organization.
   a. What do you believe is the strongest, most important asset you offer to NAS? What are your best qualities?
   b. What is it about NAS as an organization that you value the *most?*

4. Brief History of NAS: From what you have experienced or heard of NAS's history since 1954, name two or three key events, decisions, innovations, achievements, or challenges that were important turning points in the life of the organization.

B. Exploring Best Qualities and Hopes for the Future
   1. **Team Mind-set:** Organizations work best when team spirit and enthusiasm are high and everyone is a valued member of a group where his or her ideas are heard. To be effective over time, organizations need cooperation within groups as well as between groups that cross department lines, jobs, and levels in the hierarchy. Teamwork requires trust, open channels of communication, appropriate business information, responsiveness to others' needs, good training, and interpersonal skills.

   Think of an example of the most effective team or group effort *you* have been part of at NAS. Tell the story of what happened. Who was involved? What made the teamwork effective? What were the important lessons?

   2. **Customer Satisfaction and Market Responsiveness:** Central to the vision statement of NAS is an organization that is market driven and totally responsive to customer satisfaction, which time and time again is the lifeblood of the business.
   a. Think of a time when NAS was most effective in terms of customer responsiveness or market innovation? Tell me a story of what happened. What was most noteworthy?
   b. Possibilities for the Future: What things could NAS do to improve or even revolutionize its responsiveness to and connection with its customers?

3. **Continuous Learning:** In a changing world, the competitive edge goes to the company that is able to change, grow, or learn faster than any of its competitors. When at its best, NAS is a "learning organization" in which people are continuously challenging themselves to move out of their comfort zones, think in new ways, acquire new knowledge and skills, and experiment with new management and production methods.

   a. Describe a time at NAS when you believed you were learning something new, meaningful, and helpful to the business. More importantly, what lessons can be drawn from your example? What does NAS do *best* as it relates to building good learning opportunities or strengthening the learning spirit of the whole company?

   b. As you look to the future, describe one thing you think NAS could or should do more of to strengthen the learning capacity of the company.

4. **Shared Vision and Ownership:** Organizations work best when everyone thinks and acts they are an owner of the business. That sense of ownership is highest when as if a shared vision exists for where the business is headed in the future, when people are involved in major decisions that are relevant to them and their work, when appropriate information about the business is shared openly, when people know the whole picture in terms of others' tasks or jobs, and when people believe they are at the center of things rather than on the outside.

   a. Describe a time when you felt most involved in the big picture of the organization, a time when you felt most like a partner or even an owner of the business. What can we all learn from this experience?

   b. Thinking about the future, what could NAS do *more of* to create a shared vision of the future and a heightened sense of ownership at all levels?

5. **Resiliency and Managing Change:** Over the years, NAS has proven its resiliency and its ability to manage change when small and large challenges have confronted the organization. Many of the changes introduced (for example, in the early 1990s) were positive, healthy, and successful.

a. Thinking of all the changes you have seen, what changes have most positively affected you, your work, or the company?

b. What could NAS do more of, less of, or the same in the future to become more resilient, more flexible, and more able to manage change?

SAMPLE INTERVIEW GUIDE—Not-for-Profit
World Vision Relief and Development
Interview Questionnaire for Appreciative Inquiry

GENERAL INFORMATION

Name: _____

Title: _____

Group/Department: _____

Years of Service: _____

Extension: _____

Interviewed by: _____

Date: _____

INTERVIEW PROTOCOL

As part of a special study, we are conducting interviews with employees and other individuals about work experience and perceptions of our organization.

The information you provide will be used to prepare a corporate vision statement as seen and valued by members at all levels in the organization. Our intent is to learn from your experience. The collected comments, experiences, and suggestions from all of the employees and others interviewed will be summarized and reviewed with senior management. We assure you that your name will not be attached to any of the final data.

The interview will take about one (1) hour. The interview will tend to focus on the organization when it is operating at its best in the following topic areas:

1. Integrative Process
   a. Partnership
   b. Programs
   c. Holistic Communication
2. Innovation
3. Empowerment
4. Quality
5. Diversity
   a. Transnational
   b. Faith
   c. Specialization
6. Organizational Ethos (Sharing and Learning)

A. **Experience with WVRD**
(The following three questions are stage setting.)

1. To start, I'd like to learn about your beginnings and/or awareness of WV/your organization.
    a. What attracted you to WV/your organization?
    b. What was your initial excitement/impression when you joined/participated with WV/your organization?

2. Looking at your entire experience, can you recall a time when you felt most alive, most involved, or most excited about WV/your involvement?
    a. What made it an exciting experience?
    b. Who were the most significant people involved?
    c. Why were they significant?
    d. What was it about you that made it a peak experience?
    e. What were the most important factors in the organization that helped make it a peak experience? (Probe. Leadership, qualities, structures, rewards, systems, skills, strategies, and/or relationships?)

3. Let's talk a moment about some things you value deeply; specifically, the things you value about (1) yourself, (2) the nature of your work, and (3) WV/your organization.
    a. Without being humble, what do you value most about yourself as a human being, a friend, a parent, a citizen, and so on?
    b. When you are feeling your best about your work, what do you value about the task itself?
    c. What is it about WV/your organization that you value?
    d. What is the single most important thing WV/your organization has contributed to your life?

B. **Communication**
   Global organizations often create a special feeling of alignment among their members, wherein individual, believes that they "live" the values and goals of the organization in their work and personal lives.
    a. What does your organization do to heighten a sense of understanding, alignment, or attunement among its members?

b. When new members enter the organization, what does WV/your organization do particularly well to educate them about the mission and values of the organization?

c. Does your organization provide its members with meaningful opportunities so they can consider how their personal values fit with organizational values?

C. Empowerment

Global organizations need members who can act and make decisions that are aligned with organizational values and goals. People who are empowered are given latitude to make decisions related to their position and work. They are also given information and support to carry out these decisions and actions.

a. When have you felt most empowered by WV/your organization?

b. What does your organization do to encourage members to take action in whatever ways they can?

c. How does your organization succeed in empowering its members?

d. What factors in WV/your organization serve to empower people outside of the organization to help themselves?

D. Quality

Global organizations often face the strategic issue of an effective transition from a "Growth" model to a "quality" model of organizational development for all aspects of programmatic, fund-raising, and organizational activities.

1. How does your organization face the challenges of donor relations and demands in light of shifting from a northern-dominated international partnership to one of engagement with southern participants as full partners?

2. How does your organization shift from resource quantity to resource quality?

E. Diversity (Transnational, Faith And Specialization)

Global organizations encounter incredible diversity among their members—diversity in cultures, goals, backgrounds, experience, age, sex, religion, and values.

1. What does your organization do to embrace the diversity among its members?

2. What does your organization do to create common goals and beliefs that allow diverse people to work together effectively?

3. What does your organization do to prevent diversity among its members from becoming divisive or interfering with the success of its overall efforts?

4. How does your organization respond to the need for local groups to determine their own approaches to accomplishing tasks?

F. **Sharing And Learning Organization**
    An effective global organization must always be in a state of evolution in order to remain effective in the current world's rapidly changing political, technical, and economic paradigms.
    1. What does your organization do to maintain a "current" perspective?
    2. What does your organization do to help its members think about the global perspective of their work and to encourage reflective thinking?

G. **Conclusion**
    1. What is the core factor that gives vitality and life to this organization (without which the organization would cease to exist)?
    2. If you could now envision, develop, or transform this organization in any way, what would you do to heighten its overall vitality and health? (List three things in order of priority.)

SAMPLE INTERVIEW GUIDE—Retail

Canadian Tire
An Inquiry into What Our Customers Value Most

PURPOSE OF INTERVIEWS

Thank you very much for participating in this process of gathering information from colleagues across Canadian Tire. These interviews are part of an intensive effort to connect all parts of Canadian Tire to truly become **the best at what our customers value most.**

(To rally around clear,) a robust customer value is not only strategic, it is also fundamental to our success and central to Canadian Tire's statement of purpose. It is a journey we are in for the long term.

What do our customers want? At the top of the list, studies show our customers want:

- Enthusiastic, knowledgeable help from our people.
- Us to deliver on our promises.
- To be respected (for their time, caring, and rapid service).
- To trust in our quality and price.
- To work with people who are empowered (people who are resourceful and able to think, act, and serve with enthusiasm).
- To have an exciting shopping experience (a memorable experience that leaves a lasting impression).

This Appreciative Interview Guide forms the start of our conversation. On the following pages, you will find a set of questions that invite you and your interview partner to reflect on and look with an appreciative eye to the topics we will address during this meeting.

The questions are offered to engage you in the best thinking you can do about customer values. Give your partner your full attention and draw out the richness of the stories and images that he or she shares with you. After the first interview, simply thank your partner and shift roles.

To begin: First, some things about you and your background at Canadian Tire…

1. Think back to the moment in your career at Canadian Tire when you were offered a position at Canadian Tire and you said yes.
    - What were some of the attributes that attracted and excited you?
    - What set us apart and made the *difference* for you?

2. In your work at Canadian Tire, you have probably experienced ups and downs, twists and turns, high points and low points. For a

moment, I would like you to think about a time to you as a high point. This is a time that stands out when you felt most engaged, alive, effective, or really proud of your involvement in the organization. It might have been a special change or innovation, a great team, or even a special year.

- Please tell me the story about a "high-point" experience for you?
- What made it a high-point experience?
- What was it about **you** that made it successful—more specifically, *what are your best skills or qualities*—as a leader, manager, or change agent?

Now let's shift specifically to an exploration of Canadian Tire's customer values.

3. **Enthusiastic, Knowledgeable Help For Every Customer:** Central to Canadian Tire's statement of purpose is to be the best at delivering what our customers value and want. One of those values is **"to have enthusiastic, knowledgeable help"** from every person at Canadian Tire.

   a. To begin, I would like you to think about *your own work*—times when you have best served or responded to your valued customers. Can you share with me one story, something you were involved with, of a time that best illustrates what it means **"to deliver enthusiastic, knowledgeable help"**? Please share with me the whole story. What did you or your group do, and what was the impact?

   b. Now let's build on that story and think about the future and what you would most like to see at the Canadian Tire stores. Let's fast-forward into the future; it is 2005. What is your vision of "enthusiastic, knowledgeable help"? Please describe it. What does it look like?

4. Now let's take a look at another value our customers say they are looking for, **"an exciting shopping experience"**—an experience that is enjoyable, exciting, different, or fun. We all know stories that make us proud and show us what we can be when we are at our best. Learning from these stories is important. A famous proverb says "stories have wings and they fly from mountain-top to mountain-top."

   a. From something you observed or heard about (from any store or dealership at Canadian Tire), can you share a story of a place or person delivering "an exciting shopping experience"? Where does the story take place? When? Why does it stand out for you?

b. In a changing world, the competitive edge goes to the company that is able to change, grow, or learn faster than any of its competitors. We need to become great at sharing and amplifying stories like the ones we have been talking about—helping them fly "from mountain-top to mountaintop" all across Canadian Tire. *As you look to the future, describe one thing you think we as a whole could do more of to strengthen our learning capacity and our ability to replicate new "customer value" successes all across the company?*

5. **Continuity Search:** Good organizations know how to "preserve the core" of what they do best and are able to work out or let go of things that have built up or are no longer needed. Preserving the right things is key. Letting go of other things is the next step.
   a. With regard to being the best in our industry at providing customers with what they value and want, what **are** three things we do best *at the stores* today that we should keep, things that should be preserved or amplified even as we change in the future?
   b. What are three things we do best *at the corporate level* that we should keep, things that should be amplified or preserved even as we change in the future?

Wrap-up and looking to the future...

6. **Images of the Canadian Tire of the Future:** Let's assume that tonight, after this session, you go to sleep and don't wake up until ten years from now. The year is 2010. While you were asleep, significant and exciting changes happened. Canadian Tire became exactly as you wanted to see it. It is No.1—*the best at delivering what our customers value most.*
   a. Imagine you wake up and it's 2010. You go into the Canadian Tire stores and the corporation. What do you see and feel happening that's new and different and better? How do you know? Describe the Canadian Tire of the future.
   b. What is the smallest step (an action, a decision, an initiative) we could take today that would have the largest impact on creating the future you want?
   c. What is one thing have we not thought of yet—something new we could do that would improve, or even revolutionize, our ability to become **the best at what our customers value most?**

SAMPLE AI SUMMARY REPORT
Fairmount North America
Our Future Begins with Our Strengths

Teaching note: This Appreciative Inquiry Report goes on to describe eight "Ideal-Type" Themes with illustrative quotes and stories. It ends with a compilation of all the visions for the future. We are including only one "Ideal-Type" Theme here for review.

This kind of report is useful as background material for building provocative propositions. Reports like this have been distributed prior to people coming to a Future Search conference. Before an artist paints a picture, he or she assembles his or her: red, green, blue, yellow, and so on. The Appreciative Inquiry Report serves exactly the same purpose, it is the material that will help the collective imagination come alive.

Overview
On behalf of all the people at Fairmount North America, the Committee on Appreciative Inquiry (AI) is pleased to present its first report: **"Vision 2000: It Begins with Our Strengths."**

Our hope is that this report serves as both a catalyst and an invitation. The invitation: To participate in an organization-wide process where everybody at each location has the opportunity to think strategically and imaginatively about "our common vision for the organization of the future." As a catalyst: The report provides inspiring snapshots of many of the strengths of the organization "when it is working at its very best." There is, it must be acknowledged, an undeniable positive quality about this report. Some of it stems from the nature of the questions that were asked of you in the interviews. But equally important, much of it comes from the real sense of optimism people feel about the company and its prospects for the future. We, too, as a committee, found ourselves energized and excited about the organization's future when we began letting our imaginations go.

> What will Fairmount North America look like in 2000? What will it look like if all of its best qualities are magnified, extended, or multiplied, let's say, by a factor of ten? Are we really ready, as many have said in interviews and private conversations, to jump to a whole new level as an organization? What is our dream? What do we really want this organization to be in the future?

How This Document Was Put Together

We constructed this analysis from interviews with 329 of you, comprising all locations and all levels of personnel. The questions used in the interviews (which lasted from one to two hours each) were generated in several three-day workshops on Appreciative Inquiry held in August and September. During those workshops, several topics were identified: **care and respect for people, teamwork, leadership, empowerment, common goals and direction, commitment, and recognition**. The interviews were designed to explore these topics in several ways. When, for example, have people felt really empowered in this organization? What supports or strengthens empowerment? What are the organization's "best practices" when it comes to good people management, or empowerment? What would we like to do more of to build a more empowered organization?

On the basis of the interviews, the data was put together first by location and then as a whole corporation. This particular report is a summary overview for the whole of Fairmount. It draws on information from each site report, attempting to discover those ideals that are common throughout the company.

In terms of analysis, we first typed up all the interview responses and grouped them together by question. The next step was to code each comment to discover, for example, what the most important factors are that create, maintain, or strengthen **empowerment**? We then grouped examples (and quotes) of empowerment together and attempted to put words to the **topic ideals**. What do people really mean when speaking about empowerment? What are people really saying is **ideal**? We figure if we did our homework well, the topic ideals, as written, will resonate strongly with what people **want** the organization to be. Two things are important to keep in mind when reading through the report. First, these topic ideals are fashioned from people's actual experiences. There are examples, many examples, of each of the ideals (see actual quotes). Thus, the topic ideals express the corporate culture of Fairmount as we understand it from appreciation of our proven strengths. But the statements go a step further. They also, hopefully, represent a bold extension of those strengths—focused vision to which people are saying they aspire to as an organization. The topic ideals are stated, therefore, in the present tense, not because they have been totally attained, but because people are saying this is their present "ideal" based on experiences when they/we have been at our best. We invite you to think of this document as a resource, as a catalyst, to help you think seriously about what you want this organization to be like in the future.

How to Use This Document

The most thorough approach we have in mind is as follows:

1. Read the **summary** at the beginning of each section to get a feeling for the topic ideal. Ask yourself: If we could be this way all the time, would I want it?

2. Read each of the **sample quotes** to get an idea of what people actually talked about. Ask yourself: Do these quotes illustrate the topic ideal? Do you have other examples from your own experience that help illustrate the way things could be like in the ideal? What are those illustrations?

3. Read through the **analysis**. Ask yourself: Does the analysis sound plausible? What else would you add to the analysis?

4. Remember: A future does not arrive uninvited. It is built. Organizations begin in the imagination. And when an organization as a whole takes time to give voice to its preferred future, it is all that more likely to bring about that future. Put simply, it is easier to do things together when there is common focus.

Next Steps

Over the next several weeks, meetings will be held to discuss the report. We hope these meetings will serve three purposes:

1. As a vehicle for discussing the discoveries — to confirm, restate, debate, and elaborate.

2. As an opportunity to appreciate the organization for what it is today and to expand our thinking about what it can be in the future.

3. As an invitation for people at each location to become part of a Vision 2000 team.

We believe the Appreciative Inquiry approach is a powerful way of building a common focus. One management thinker, Peter Senge, calls it building "a learning organization." He writes:

> If anything, the need for understanding how organizations learn, and accelerating that learning, is greater today than ever

before. The old days when a Henry Ford, Alfred Sloan, or Tom Watson learned for the organization are gone. In an increasingly dynamic, interdependent, and unpredictable world, it is simply no longer possible for anyone to "figure it all out at the top." The old model "the top think and the locals act" must now give way to integrated thinking and acting at all levels. While the challenge is great, so is the potential payoff. "The person who figures out how to harness the collective genius of the people in his or her organization" according to former Citibank CEO Walter Wriston, "is going to blow the competition away."

It has been an exciting task thus far. We look forward to the feedback sessions.

Ideal-Type Theme #1: A Team-Based Organization

Fairmount North America has become a multifaceted business where the mind-set of teamwork has become a critical success factor in continuous innovation and responsiveness to customers (internal and improvement). Said one person, "There are hundreds of examples of positive impact and innovation because of teamwork. Our history keeps teaching us that none of us is so smart as all of us."

More than a set of empty slogans or words, the call for teamwork has been a call for fundamental change. Fairmount is an organization that has, in fact, dared to experiment with advanced organizational changes and management approaches. It is an organization that has shown its change efforts even when there are inevitable setbacks and learning pains. The movement to a team-based organization at Fairmount is not cosmetic. "It is inevitable," said one person.

But it is not just the spirit or mind-set of teamwork. When working at its best, the organizational structure eliminates unnecessary hierarchy and division and engages people as partners. At Fairmount, the so-called organizational chart, with its hierarchy of reporting relationships and separation of jobs, reflects only one reality. The "other structure," not generally shown on the chart, is an overlay of person-to-person networks, cross-functional project groups, teams, information-seeking meetings, new-business planning groups, and the like. While this kind of "ad-hoc teamwork" often seems a bit confusing (from a standard organizational-chart perspective), it can be argued that it is precisely this, the ability to create fast, focused, free-formed, flexible (even fun) teamwork that has brought Fairmount so much success in recent years. Through the use of this "parallel" organizational form (i.e., the nonhierarchical team-based organization), Fairmount fosters the cross-fertilization of ideas, minimizes the building of empires, harnesses the synergy of group cooperation, and cultivates the pride of being a valued member of "one outstanding corporation."

Sample Quotes:

1.   *Early last year we had a serious situation in California. It was a dangerous situation where the product could jeopardize someone's safety. We never had an experience like that. We never had a recall before. Lives could be at stake. Liability laws in California were strict. It put us in an unbelievable pressure-filled situation. Some of our customers were afraid for their business. The negative situation grew darker. Our customers became adversarial. But we dug down deep. I remember sitting in the room when we made the decision to respond. People were shouting, arguing, searching for what to do. Gerry stepped forward and the made the decision. We acted immediately, came up with a war plan and launched a campaign. A team went to Escardo, California, hunting down all the big tanks. Bob at our Ontario warehouse was a hero, helping to make everything happen in California. Millions of dollars were at stake. At home, FRP was heroic. They made 700 replacement tanks in a matter of months. It probably cost us a half million dollars to do what we did. But we were taking the long-term view.*

2.   *Teams: This is what the place is really all about. It's about people working with one another. Why have an organization if people don't need other people? We are what we are because of our teamwork, and not just individual parts. It's how the parts fit together. You see, you could try to make a car from all the best parts: engine of a Mercedes, body of a Corvette, brakes from a Cadillac, and so on. But you know what? The car won't work. It is how the parts mesh, how the parts act as a team. The same is true here. Teamwork is not an option. It's got to be a way of life.*

3.   *The most effective team effort was on an integrated product development team. It was about large tanks. We were working out the concept of flanges and various ports. Fifteen people were involved. The group was too large but worked OK. To make these teams work really well we need to (1) involve only six to eight people, (2) recognize people's contributions, (3) recognize people in written minutes and (4) utilize democratic leaders who are dynamic and positive and give people the recognition they deserve.*

4.   *I felt most involved when we redid the whole back on the FRP line. We cut the water bath down, re-arranged equipment, figured out how to run it with six people instead of sixteen — and we did it together. It was fantastic. We met once a week. Tim was a great listener. All of our ideas were used. There wasn't anybody in the area not involved unless a person chose not to be. This is a model of how we can be all the time. We need more of this.*

5. *Great teamwork happened when the marketing group decided to introduce a new product. We were all kind of intoxicated !! It was a universal tank concept. We had all the pieces and parts, ad it cost no money. A team took the ideas from concept to production in less than six months. We had twelve people from every part of the company. We can draw three lessons: (1) The goal was sold to the team—veryone agreed 100%. (2) Everyone wanted to make it a success. (3) We had lots of communication—lots of meetings. At times, we met once a week for a couple of hours. We also had good leadership.*

6. *I've been here almost twenty years, and I'm really sure that my high point was the beginning of the teams and the team training. But it was also a low for me. The high point was being in the training session with the managers. Just being in the same room together broke down lots of negative stereotypes we had for each other. I wish this would continue. The company needs it. A low point was not being accepted by coworkers anymore. Lots of people were negative about the team idea, saying it wouldn't work. As it turns out, maybe their predictions were right. But we shouldn't let the thing die. Sure, there were mistakes with two steps forward and three back for a while. But the team idea is critical for our future. Nobody wants to go back to the authoritarian style where workers are to "leave their brains at the time clock."*

Commentary:

Fairmount North America is an organization that has dared to experiment with advanced organizational changes and management approaches. The most controversial, and arguably the most productive, has been the idea of teams. My reading is that the organization has been overly hard on itself as it relates to inevitable "learning pains." The idea of a more group-based, less hierarchical or paternalistic form of management is a major change, and Fairmount is not alone in its love-hate affair with complex transformation like this. In my reading of the sentiment of the organization, there is no going back to more authoritarian management relations ("where people check their brains at the time-clock").

The question is not whether to have team-based processes, but how to persist and work through inevitable learning pains even when there are voices of cynicism. In this case, **even** the cynicism should be valued. The cynical voice puts into words the doubts we all have. We have no doubts only about things we do not care about. That's the point. People care. They see a promise in the team idea that they really want. The idealism in this area is extremely high at Fairmount. In my more adventurous moments, I find myself wanting to suggest a giant step forward with the team idea, much like the examples given in an important new book, *Real Time Strategic Change*. With recommitment, the team idea can and will thrive at Fairmount, and making it work will be a big key to the company's success in the future.

SAMPLE DETAIL PROJECT PLAN: Airline
British Airways, NA—Customer Service

Background
The British Airways Appreciative Inquiry Core Team, made up of forty people from all different departments and levels in the company, determined that the following topics are key to success in British Airways Customer Service:
1. Happiness at work
2. Harmony and sharing among all employee groups
3. Continuous people development
4. Exceptional arrival experience

Appreciative Interviews were conducted among employees to learn more about what makes us successful in these four important areas. Each interview was 45 minutes to one hour. The information collected during this time of Discovery was shared throughout the customer service organization so employees could learn from one another and bring the best of who they are and how they work to their customers.

The set of case materials includes the following:
- Interview Guide
- Interview Summary Sheet
- Immediate Attention Flag Sheet
- Station Discovery Meeting
- Station Discovery Meeting Agenda
- Presentation Slides

Interview Guide
Appreciative Interview Tips for Success

When you call or contact someone to schedule an interview:

1. Introduce yourself and explain the purpose of the interview—to learn about what makes British Airways one of the world's greatest airlines. Explain that all British Airways North America employees will be interviewed.

2. Explain the interview process in your own words. Share what it was like, for you, when you were interviewed. Was it informative, fun, positive?

3. If the person asks about confidentiality, tell him or her that the purpose of the interview is to discover and share best practices and good ideas throughout the organization. Explain that the interview is focused on positive ideas and information—things that people are generally proud to share.

4. Schedule one hour for the interview and agree to a location that is quiet, comfortable and private.

When you conduct an interview:

Remember—The interview is a time for you to put the spotlight on your interviewee. It is a time for you to listen and to learn from your interviewee. Your turn to talk will be later when you share all the interesting stories that you hear as an interviewer.

1. Read a question, or say it in your own words and then allow time for your interviewee to reflect and answer. Silence is okay, don't talk to fill the empty space, repeat the question if necessary.

2. Encourage your interviewee to talk. To use an expression; it is "their nickel." Listen with curiosity and wonder—like a curious child wondering what makes British Airways such an amazing place.

3. Demonstrate your listening by nodding your head, taking notes, and asking probing follow-on questions.

4. Enjoy the experience of learning about someone else and how that person does what he or she does. Smile and remember, the more at ease you are, the more at ease your interviewee will be.

5. Make notes as you go and then record key points on the Summary Sheet that follows the interview questions.

6. When the interview is complete, tell your interviewee what you learned that most interested you and thank the person for his or her time.

Opening

1. Tell me about your *beginnings with British Airways*. What was it that first attracted you to British Airways and excited you about working here?

2. We have all had our ups and downs while working here at British Airways. For now, I'd like you to tell me about one of your ups—a *high-point experience* you have had while working with British Airways, a time when you were most involved, engaged, and alive at work. Describe the situation.
   • What made it a high point for you?
   • Who else was involved?
   • What did they do?
   • What did you do that contributed to its being such a high point?

Happiness at Work

Happiness at work means different things to different people. It may mean social connections, job satisfaction, and/or self-worth. We believe that we, the people, are the most important assets of British Airways. Our happiness at work is crucial to the success of the company. Keeping this in mind, we would like to explore what makes you happy and how we can build on it.

1. Tell me about a time when you felt most happy at work—a time when you were having fun and doing a great job of customer service. Describe the situation.
   • What was it that created a sense of happiness and fun at work?
   • Who was involved? What did they do?
   • What did you do that contributed to your own sense of happiness and fun?
   • What effect did your happiness have on customers?

2. Tell me about a time when you were pleased with a decision you made. Describe the situation. What made you especially happy about your decision?

3. What ideas do you have for how we can foster positive morale, build camaraderie, and have fun in the workplace while being the best at customer service?

Harmony and Sharing Among All Employee Groups

A cooperative, harmonious, and supportive relationship among all employee groups is vital to the success of our company. Harmony among all employee groups is built upon open and honest sharing of information and creative ideas. We thrive on dialogue and communication among employees, which includes listening as well as speaking, in an atmosphere of respect, understanding, and cooperation. It is our capacity to work in harmony with one another that makes us a great customer service team.

1. Tell me a story about the best example of open two-way communication and honest dialogue you have experienced within the workplace. It might be between you and a coworker, between you and your manager, between an employee and a customer, or between different departments.
    • Who was involved and what made it great communication?

2. Tell me a story of successful conflict resolution—a time when a conflict or difference between people was resolved successfully.
    • Who was involved?
    • What was it that enabled the conflict to be resolved?
    • What can we learn from this situation to help us all be successful with daily customer service challenges?

3. What, in your opinion, are the best ways to share information among all employees that are fun, informative, and meaningful?
    • Flight information
    • Customer information
    • Employee information
    • Business information

Continuous People Development

British Airways is committed to continuing its investment in people development, enabling us to exceed our expectations. Exceeding our expectations and our customers' expectations makes British Airways great!

People development happens every day at British Airways. We maintain our position as market leader by investing in each employee's learning and development through individual coaching, tuition assistance, opportunities to utilize current expertise in new areas, learning centers, and passionate learning leadership.

1. Learning is a continuous process. It happens every day. Taking that into consideration, think about last week and what you learned at work. Specifically, what have you learned in the last week that helped you better understand British Airways—how it operates, our customers, or how to do your job?
   - How did the learning occur?
   - Who did you learn this from?
   - What impact has that had on you?

2. Tell me about a time when you encouraged or influenced another person's personal development at British Airways.
   - What was the situation?
   - What did you do?
   - How did you positively encourage the other person's learning?
   - How did you know you were making a difference?
   - What can others who wish to mentor learn from this experience?

3. Fast forward into the future. You're now doing the job you always wanted to do. Describe it!
   - Why did you choose this job?
   - How did you choose it?
   - What two or three things can you do right now to get yourself on the path to that job?

Exceptional Arrival Experience

British Airways' goal is to provide an exceptional travel experience both in the air and on the ground. The handling of a flight's arrival and baggage reconciliation is of equal importance to any other component of the passenger's journey. The arrival experience is the time to leave a positive lasting impression. It also provides the opportunity to recover from any service shortfall the customer may have encountered. Focusing on Exceptional Arrival Experience demonstrates commitment to our customers and to one another.

1. Describe your most memorable arrival experience, as a customer or as airline personnel.
   - What was the situation?
   - Who was involved?

- What made it memorable for you?
- How did you feel?
- What effect did it have on the customer?

2. Tell me a story about your most powerful service recovery. Describe the situation.
    - What was it about you that made it happen?
    - Who else was involved and why were they significant?
    - What tools did you use, or what did you do that others in British Airways might be able to do in a similar situation?

3. If you had a magic wand, how would you use it to enhance our overall arrival experience for our customers?
    - What ideas do you have to ensure exceptional arrival experiences for all of our customers?
    - What ideas do you have to make the process easier for us, as well!

Final Thoughts

1. In your opinion, what is the *core factor that gives life* to British Airways North America? What is it that makes us uniquely and exceptionally British Airways North America?

2. If you had three blank memos signed by David Erich that would become company policy once you filled in your ideas, how would you use them? What are your three best ideas to improve the well-being of British Airways North America?

Interview Summary Sheet

Please complete this summary sheet within 30 minutes of your interview. Reflect on what you heard and make note of the best ideas, stories, and quotes. Make notes that will remind you of the stories and information you heard.

1.   What was the most interesting story you heard during this interview?

2.   What were the best practices you heard in this interview? Especially make note of good ideas we should share around the company—practices worthy of being replicated in other stations.
     • Happiness at work
     • Harmony and sharing among all employee groups
     • Continuous people development
     • Exceptional arrival experience
     • Other

3.   What was the most compelling hope or dream for the future of British Airways that you heard?

4.. What was the best idea, thought, or phrase that came out of this interview—something you would want to quote to other people?

PLEASE PRINT THIS INFORMATION

Interviewer: _____

Contact Information: _____

Interviewee: _____

Date of Interview: _____

Immediate Attention Flag Sheet

If during your interview, you learned about an issue or a situation that requires immediate attention, write a brief summary here. For example, you may have discovered:

- Someone who should be acknowledged and rewarded for a job well done.
- An issue that needs the attention of management at your station.
- An opportunity for your station that may not last long.
- Something worthy of being reported in the British Airways newsletter.
- Other

PLEASE PRINT THIS INFORMATION

Interviewer: _____

Contact Information: _____

Interviewee: _____

Date of Interview: _____

Remove the pink "Immediate Attention Flag Sheet" if it has been filled in and send it to your station manager, making note of the date and request. The rest of the Interview Guide should remain intact. Do not remove any other pages.

Station Discovery Meeting

Purpose of Meeting:
To review station appreciative interview information and stories in order to share discoveries, learnings, and best practices throughout Customer Service.

Objectives/Outcomes:
1. Station Discoveries Report (Document #2, enclosed)
2. Station story for Customer Service Power of Two Video at April workshop
3. Station Best-Practices Canvas Banner (Due 4/3/00 in Dallas)
4. Station plan for recognizing and celebrating best practices (Due 4/3/00)
5. Station photograph using a digital camera (if you have one)

Time: 3 hours

Participants:
A group of at least six people, including all AI interviewers, the AI coordinator, at least one manager, and several interviewees. With the exception of JFK, we recommend no more than eighteen people.

Specific Roles: Please determine who will serve these roles before the meeting begins.

> **Facilitator:** Direct the meeting in an appreciative manner, including as many people as possible. Keep everyone on task. Follow meeting agenda and support completion of each activity.

> **Timekeeper:** Support facilitator by monitoring time spent on each task and keeping the meeting moving.

> **Photographer:** Take station photograph and send it to AdEssence.

> **Bannerkeeper:** Direct the creation of the station banner and take responsibility for delivery of the banner to the April workshop in Dallas.

> **Recorder:** Capture meeting information for station report of Appreciative Inquiry Discoveries.

Distribute this page to all attendees before conducting the station meeting.

Station Discovery Meeting Agenda

(5 minutes)
- Welcome everyone and review the purpose of the meeting.
- Review the agenda and timeline for the meeting.
- Ask participants to get into small groups of six to eight people.

(30 minutes)
Go around the small group and have each person answer the following three questions. As each person shares, record his or her ideas on a flip chart in three columns or on three separate pages. (This information will go into your station report.)
1. What was the high point for you in the interview process? Describe it.
2. What did you learn in the interview process that has positively impacted the way you work with others at British Airways (colleagues and customers)?
3. What are some of the things you know people are already doing differently as a result of the interview process?

(15 minutes)
Explain that there will be a video made of British Airways Customer Service: The Power of Two. People from each station will be interviewed on the video about a story that represents the station at its best. The task now is to select the story we would like to tell about our station.

Go around the small group and ask everyone to share the **best** story he or she heard during the interviews—the story that best illustrates one of the four topics (happiness at work, harmony and sharing among all employee groups, continuous people development, and exceptional arrival experience) in action. It should be a story that makes you and others really proud to be part of British Airways.

(15 minutes)
After all the stories have been shared, as a whole group, collectively decide the one you would like told on the video. **Create a name for the story** and record the names of everyone involved in the story and the name of the interviewer who discovered the story.

Tell why it was selected. Do this in a way that honors the people involved.

(30 minutes)
Complete worksheet now.
Explain that this next section is to identify best practices in the four topic areas (happiness at work, harmony and sharing among all employee groups, continuous people development, and exceptional arrival experience)—practices and processes that were described in the interviews as being done exceptionally well in your station and as contributing to your station's success.

> *A best practice does not mean that everyone is doing it perfectly all the time. It does mean that it is very important to your station's success and some of the time it is done exceptionally well.*

Go topic by topic and list the best practices described in the interviews. Upon completion of this exercise, you will have four lists on your **Worksheet A**. Worksheet A will go into your station report.

Ask everyone to close his or her eyes and to relax. Now guide the group by reading the following: *Imagine it's three years from now. We are the British Airways we want to be. We are truly everyone's favourite airline.*

(15 minutes)
Note: These are thought-provoking questions. We are not expecting answers.

What do you see happening?
<pause>
Who are we serving?
<pause>
What are they saying?
<pause>
What is the gift you have contributed to make this happen?
<pause>
What have you done to help BA be the best?
<pause>
What is your station's greatest gift to this success?
<pause>
What one thing is being done in North America that makes the difference?
<pause>

(25 minutes)
Complete worksheet now.
Tell everyone to open his or her eyes and to prepare to share his or her dreams.

In each of the four topic areas (happiness at work, harmony and sharing among all employee groups, continuous people development, and exceptional arrival experience), identify the one item your station will commit to doing in order to:

- Positively impact employees
- Positively impact customers
- Positively impact the business

After identifying the most important best practice in each area, go around the whole group and share, add to, and compile the ideas.

Worksheet B will go into your station report.

(30 minutes)

In the kit of materials you received about this meeting is a large piece of canvas. Each station received a piece of equal size. During "the Power of Two: A Time For Action" workshop in April, you will bring this completed banner and use it to communicate visually the best practices of your station to all.

Using any medium you choose, construct a creative illustration of your station's best practices. Don't be shy. Include as much information as you like on your banner that illustrates your station at its best. We have supplied an art box to get you started, but please don't limit yourselves. **Be as creative as you like and have fun!**

- Display the station banner and let people contribute to it.
- Do this now or set another time to complete the banner.

(15 minutes)

Complete worksheet now.

This is your opportunity to share one best practice from all of the learning today.

What is the one best practice your station is recommending to be put into practice all across North America?

(10 minutes)

Now decide as a group what you will do at the station to recognize and celebrate the affirmative discoveries made during the interview process.

Determine who will take all of the information from today's meeting and create your station's report.

The report is to be sent to Edward by Friday, March 24.

(5 minutes)

All station reports will be shared at the April workshop.

(15 minutes)
Take a few minutes to go around the group and ask people to share their most significant learning for the day. Ask them to describe it and the impact it will have on the way they do business at British Airways.

Station Discovery Meeting Checklist
After your station meeting, you should have completed the following:
Selection/naming of a **Station Story** for the Customer Service Power of Two Video at April Workshop

Station Best-Practices Canvas Banner created or a new time set to complete the banner (Remember that you will be transporting the finished banner to the April workshop in Dallas)

Station plan for recognizing and celebrating best practices

Station photograph using a digital camera (Send this photo via e-mail to your facilitator for use in reports (and AI collection of information) and stories for your **Station Discoveries Report**)

The completed **Station Discoveries Report** (including Document #2 Station Discoveries Report and Worksheets A, B, and C) sent to Edward by **Friday, March 24**

Meeting Agenda

The Power of Two: A Time for Action
Agenda for April 4–5

Purpose: To realize the value of "The Power of Two" for customer satisfaction and retention. To share, dialogue about and celebrate BA customer service at its best—to dream about the most promising future for BA, its customers, and employees; to design practices that realize the dream; and to chart a path of action that will align all of BA Customer Service NA in delivering on "The Power of Two."

Participants: 100 people (12 tables of 8 to 10) from all positions, all stations, and all functions of BA Customer Service NA as well as stakeholders from departments interdependent with Customer Service.

Setup:
- Preassigned table groups to maximize the mix of people at each table
- Easel, flip chart, and markers for each table
- LCD player for DW PowerPoint slides and/or overhead projector

Outcomes:
1. Video: "The Power of Two"; the completed video will be distributed to all stations as follow-up to the workshop
2. A cross-station innovation team focused on *happiness at work* in the year 2000 that will plan, sponsor, and communicate activities and celebrations for Customer Service NA
3. A cross-station innovation team focused on *continuous people development* that will create a set of principles of people development to be put into practice at all stations
4. A cross-station innovation team focused on *exceptional arrival experience* as a year 2000 initiative
5. A cross-station innovation team focused on *harmony and sharing among employee groups* as a year 2000 initiative

   Note: Champions of these teams may be determined in advance or may be selected during the workshop. Each team champion, if not already a member of the Power of Two steering committee, will join the steering committee.

Tuesday, April 4

7:00–8:00   Registration for the Workshop and Continental Breakfast

8:00–8:30   Opening Session
- Welcome—Dave Erich (15 minutes)
- Purpose and agenda for this workshop—Diana Whitney (Worksheet 1)
- Overview of 4-D Model—Discovery, Dream, Design, and Destiny
- (Worksheet 2)

8:30–9:15   Appreciative Interviews (2 interviews 20 minutes each)
- High-point experience – The Power of Two
- Your positive contribution to BA, your legacy: What would you like to be known for at BA after you leave
- Hopes and dreams for the future of BA
- A time for action: What Actions are needed now to realize your dream for BA?
- (Worksheet 3 – Interview Guide)

9:15–9:30   Break

9:30–10:15   Table group dialogues
- Introduce partners with high-point and legacy stories
- (Worksheet 4—Table Tasks)

10:15–10:45   Formative Events in the Life of British Airways
Individuals make notes on worksheets and then record on time-lines:
- Airline Industry
- British Airways
- Personal
- (Worksheet 5—Key Events in the Life of British Airways)

Break while recording and reviewing timelines

10:45–11:15   Table groups study timelines and interpret implications for BA (Worksheet 6—Table Tasks)

11:15–11:30   Presentations from table groups (2 minute each with whistle)

11:30–12:30   Stations present Their banners (six stations: 10 minutes each)—
                Connie Cali facilitates
                (Worksheet 7—for taking notes about best practices at the sta-
                tions)

12:30–1:30   Lunch

1:30–3:30   Stations present their banners (10 stations, 10 minutes each)—
                Connie Cali facilitates

                Stretch break mid way

3:30– 4:15   BA Customer Service Positive Core
                Table groups discuss BA best practices/ banner presentations:
                • List best practices.
                • Determine three to five BA customer service core competen-
                  cies—things we do *uniquely* that give us a competitive
                  advantage in the eyes of our customers, that give life to us
                  as an organization.
                • Post lists of best practices and of core competencies for
                  walk-around.
                • (Worksheet 8)

4:15–4:45   Walk Around to Review Lists

                Break

4:45–5:00   Tables Review Lists and Discuss
                • Each table picks one item it believes is the core factor that
                  gives life to BA Customer Service NA—one core competen-
                  cy they would build upon for the future.
                • (Worksheet 9)

5:00–5:30   Dreams for BA Customer Service
                • Table groups share stories of dreams described by their
                  interview partners.
                • Table groups imagine in practical terms what it would be
                  like if their dreams were alive—a vision for BA Customer
                  Service 2005.
                • Each person prepares to report one dream image.
                • (Worksheet 10)

5:30–6:00	Dream Map As dream images are called out, they are recorded on a Mind Map. As folks leave for the day, they are invited to add to the Dream Map.
6:00	Closing • Highlights of the Day • Preview of Next Day • Homework—Review Station Reports
7:00	Dinner

Wednesday, April 5

7:00–8:00	Continental Breakfast
8:00–8:15	Welcome Back – Overview of the Day
8:15–9:00	Table Groups Discuss Station Reports (especially the recommendations) • Each group determines one recommendation that would be the best next step to realize the dream. • (Worksheet 11)
9:00–9:15	Design Overview: Designing Competencies for the Organization—Living the Dream
9:15–9:45	Writing Design Principles • Each table group reviews the item it listed as the core factor that gives life to BA and the recommendation it believes would be the best next step to realize the group's dream. • Each group writes one design principle—its recommendation stated in the present tense. These statements will be stretch statements, something highly desired and stated as if it already exists. • (Worksheet 12)
9:45–10:00	Break

10:00–10:30   Reading of Design Principles
(We the people of BA Customer Service NA are committed to each group reads their design principle)

10:30–10:45   Destiny
• Overview Organization Improvisation – Innovation and Performance
• Positive Regard Enhances Capacity for Improvisation...

10:45–11:15   Table Groups Give Each Other Positive Regard in Order to Close and Dissolve the Group
• (Worksheet 13)

11:15–11:45   Set Up The Power of Two Innovation Teams
• Kate Spector provides an overview of Appreciative Inquiry at BA (10 minutes).
• Review list of teams and tasks (some for today only, others, long-term).
• David Erich issues the charge to the groups.
• David Erich gives book as gift.
• Everyone self-selects into one working group. (Need some criteria for how to chose a group.)

11:45–12:00   Innovation Teams Meet
Introduce one another

12:00–1:30   Lunch Working in Innovation Teams

1:30–2:30   The Power of Two Innovation Teams—Reports
• Happiness at work
• Harmony and sharing among groups
• Continuous people development
• Exceptional arrival experience
• Appreciative Inquiry applications
• Sharing stories and best practices across stations
• Closing ceremony for this workshop
• Follow-up communications to the stations

2:30–2:45   Break

2:45–4:00   Closing
                 • Personal commitment dialogues with initial interview
                   partners
                 • (Worksheet 14)

                 Closing Ceremony (30 minutes)

4:00   Out the Door

Presentation Slides

Slide 1 – Title
> British Airways North America
> Appreciative Inquiry Workshop
> April 4-5

Slide 2 – Purpose of the Workshop
> To realize the value of "The Power of Two" for Customer Satisfaction and Retention.
>
> To share, dialogue about, and celebrate BA Customer Service at its best; to dream about the most promising future for BA, its customers, and its employees; to design practices that realize the dream; and to chart a path of action that will align all of BA Customer Service NA in delivering on The Power of Two.

Slide 3 – AI 4-D Model and Workshop Agenda
> - Discover: Station Best Practices
> - Dream: BA 2005
> - Design: Design Principles
> - Destiny: Innovation Teams

Slide 4 – Workshop Interview Guide
> **Task:** To conduct an Appreciative Interview with one other member of your table group.
>
> **Time:** 45 minutes (20 minutes for each interview)
>
> **Process:**
> - Select a partner at your table, someone you don't know or don't know well.
> - Using the questions below, interview your partner for 20 minutes.
> - Take notes. You will use the information you hear later in the workshop.
> - At the end of your interview, briefly tell your partner what was most outstanding for you during the interview.

Slide 5 – Interview Questions #1:
> As we all know, excellent customer service depends on excellent relationships—The Power of Two. Our ability to create and maintain great relationships, with one another and with customers, contributes to our capacity to provide excellent customer service. Tell me about a time when you experienced the "Power of Two"—a time when your ability to create and maintain positive relationships contributed to British Airways' success. What was the situation?

Who else was involved? What did you do? What relationships were important in this situation? How did positive relationships contribute to the success of this situation?

Slide 6 – Interview Questions #2:

It is often said that people like to work for a cause greater than themselves. When you think about your future with British Airways, what is your cause? To put it another way, when you leave British Airways, what positive legacy do you personally want to be remembered for having contributed? In what ways would you like to leave British Airways a better place than you found it?

Slide 7 – Interview Questions #3:

Imagine that the year is 2005 and we have all just awaken from a very long sleep—5 years! As you look around, you see that British Airways is very successful and just as you always wished it could be. What do you see going on? What are people doing? Saying? What is different from today? How has technology advanced customer service?

As you reflect on your dream, your mind comes back to today, April 4. You recognize that to make your dream come true, we have to start now. What are the 2 – 3 actions that you believe we should begin now to realize your dream of British Airways 2010?

Slide 8 — Introductions of Interview Partners

Task: Introduce your interview partner to your Table Group.

Time: 30 minutes (3 minutes each for 8 people)

Process:
- Go around the table and each person introduces his/her partner.
- Introduce your partner by sharing what it was in his/her interview that touched you, inspired you, and/or excited you.
- Focus on the highpoints of your partner's "Power of Two" story and your partner's legacy.

Slide 9 – Key Events in the Life of British Airways

Task: To make note of key events in the life of British Airways and then to record these ideas on the timelines posted on the walls around the room.

Time: 30 minutes (10 minutes to record on this worksheet, 10 minutes to record on the timelines, and 10 minutes to walk around and review all the information posted on the timelines).

Slide 10 – Key Events in the Life of British Airways

Process:

- In the spaces below, make notes for yourself of key events that occurred in each of the three areas over the past _____ years.
  1. The Transportation and Airline Industries
  2. British Airways
  3. Your life
- After you finish making notes on this page, go to the timelines on the walls and record your ideas and information.
- As you record, make note of what others are writing, ask them about the events they are documenting, and get familiar with the information on the timelines.

Slide 11 – Interpretations and Implications of Time Lines

Task: To review the timelines and consider the implications for British Airways' future.

Time: 30 minutes (group dialogue and preparation for presentation)

Process:

- Tables 1 – 2 – 3 Review the timeline titled "Transportation and Airline Industries"
- Tables 4 – 5 – 6 Review the timeline titled "British Airways"
- Tables 7 – 8 – 9 Review the timeline titled "Personal"
- Tables 10 – 11 – 12 Review all 3 of the timelines
- Prepare a presentation to the whole group:
  - What is the story that this timeline(s) is telling?
  - What are the implications of this story for the future of British Airways?
  - What is this timeline(s) saying that gives you the greatest hope for the future?
- Put your ideas on a flip chart and select a spokesperson to report for your group.

Slide 12 – Discovery Notes on Station Best Practices

Task: Listen to the Station Banner Presentations with an ear for what you can take back to your station. Use this page to make notes of the most significant ideas you hear. Make notes in the spaces below:

- List practices that you believe positively impact customer satisfaction.
- List practices that you believe positively impact employee satisfaction.
- List practices that you want to learn more about.
- List practices that you will take back to your station and share.

Slide 13 – The Positive Core of British Airways Customer Service

Task: To dialogue with your Table Group about the Station Banner Presentations and to identify core competencies of British Airways Customer Service. Core competencies are things:

- that are unique in the industry,
- done better than the competition,
- that give BA a competitive advantage in the eyes of customers.

Businesses that are built to last develop and provide products and services based on core competencies. They organize their business around the strengths they have in the eyes of their customers.

Time: 45 minutes for dialogue and posting.

Process:

- Discuss what you heard during the Station Banner Presentations. First, go around the table and share what you learned that you will take back to your station.
- As a group, list all the best practices you heard. Record your list on a flip chart.
- Discuss the practices listed and determine the 3 – 5 that your group believes are BA Customer Service core competencies—they are at the heart of customer satisfaction and retention. Record your 3 – 5 core competencies on a flip chart.

Slide 14 – One Core Competency for the Future of Customer Service

Task: To review the work of all the groups and to determine the one core competency that your group would build upon for the future of British Airways Customer Service.

Time: 30 minutes (10 minutes to walk about and review the work of all the groups and 20 minutes to meet with your Table Group to determine the one core competency your group would build upon for the future of BA Customer Service).

Process:

- Walk about the room and review the lists posted by all the Table Groups.
- Make notes on this page.
  - What are the most frequently identified core competencies?
  - What, for you, are the most unique core competencies listed?
  - What, for you, are the core competencies that BA does better than the competition?
  - What, for you, is the one core competency most strategic to the future of BA Customer Service?

- Reconvene with your Table Group and discuss what you have learned during the walk-about. As a group, select the one core competency that you would build the future of BA Customer Service upon. Circle it on your flip chart or record it alone on a separate flip chart.

Slide 15 – British Airways' Dream

"A Vivid Image Compels the Whole Body to Follow"
—Aristotle

Task: To create a vivid image of a highly successful future for BA Customer Service.

Time: 45 minutes (30 minutes to share interview stories and to create the dream story and 15 minutes to prepare to present the dream story in a creative and inspiring manner).

Process:
- Go around your table and share your interview partner's answer to interview question # 3—BA 2005. Make notes on common images of the future.
- Brainstorm as a group—wild ideas for how air travel can make the world a better place.
- Now, considering the core competency your group chose as the one to build the future upon, the images of the future shared in your interviews, and your brainstorm about air travel and a better world, describe BA 2005: the world's most revered airline.
- Prepare to present your image of BA 2005 to the whole group. Do it in a creative and inspiring manner. You may chose to do a skit, present a TV or radio commercial, present an award, read a London Times article July 2005, etc.

Slide 16 – Notes on Station Reports
Task: Look over all of the Station Reports and determine the one recommendation you would make for all of BA Customer Service NA in order to realize your greatest hope and dream for BA.

Make notes below and be prepared to discuss the reports with your group.
1. What, for you, is the main message being conveyed in the reports, taken as a whole?
2. What in the reports makes you proud to be a part of BA and gives you hope for the future?
3. What is the path forward being suggested in the reports? In other words, what actions stand out as being significant and strategic for future success?

4. If you could do one thing to enhance the health and vitality of BA Customer Service, as indicated by these reports, what would it be?

Slide 17 – Review of Station Reports

Task: To discuss the content of the Station Report and to select one recommendation that you believe has the greatest potential for helping BA to realize **your dream.**

Time: 30 minutes

Process:
*   As a Table Group, discuss the four questions you answered on Worksheet 11, as you reviewed the Station Reports.
*   Select one action that you would recommend (because it will help you realize your greatest dream for BA) as part of the path forward for BA Customer Service.
*   Record your recommendation on a flip chart.

Slide 18 – Design Principles

Task: To write one Design Principle.

A Design Principle is a statement of what you want the organization to be. It is a stretch statement. It affirms that the organization is a bit more like your ideal than it may actually be. It is a positive statement—in the present tense—of what you want the organization to become. It is a statement of what you believe BA must be in order to realize your dream and to be the airline of choice for employees and customers.

Sample Design Principles:
1. We learn and work best in collaboration with one another. To foster the continuous learning essential to our success, all employees of BA Customer Service have a peer mentor.
2. Our customers depend on our ability to make decisions on their behalf in a timely and informed manner. To support our capacity for on-the-spot decision making, BA Customer Service has a world-recognized, Customer-Oriented, Online Knowledge Management System.

Time: 30 minutes

Process:
*   Review the core competency your group selected.
*   Review the key aspects of your group's image for BA 2005.
*   Review the one recommendation your group selected as strategic for the future of BA Customer Service.
*   Write one Design Principle that pulls it all together.

- Record your Design Principle on a flip chart and select a spokesperson to read it to the entire workshop group.

Slide 19 – The Power of Two: Giving Positive Regard

Task: To take time and give each member of your Table Group positive regard as a way of ending the group and getting ready to reorganize for other work.

Time: 30 minutes

Process:
- Take turns having each member of the group be in the spotlight. While they are in the spotlight, all other members of the group tell them what they admire about them, what they appreciate about working with them (for these two days and otherwise at BA), and/or what they have learned from them.
- The person in the spotlight is to listen and not talk back. At the end of their turn in the spotlight, they can say "thank you" to everyone in the group.
- When you are giving positive regard, make it short and to the point; there is no need to tell long stories. Focus on giving the person in the spotlight an experience of sincere appreciation for who they are and what they do.

Slide 20 – Follow-up Dialogues

Task: To reflect on the workshop and to say what it is that you will personally do as follow-up to support the ongoing success of BA Customer Service.

Time: 30 minutes (10 minutes of personal reflection and 20 minutes sharing with your interview partner from Tuesday).

Process:
- Take a few minutes alone and answer the questions on this page.
- Meet with your interview partner from Tuesday and share your thoughts, especially share the one project you are going to do.
- After you have shared with each other, agree to a time when you will check in by phone to see how you are doing with your projects.
- Say good-bye for now.

As you think about the two days and all we have discovered, dreamed, and designed for the future, answer the following questions:
1. What do you already do that brings Appreciative Inquiry—"The Power of Two" alive?
2. What one project, large or small, will you take on at your station to spread the stories of success and/or to further the success of BA Customer Service?

3. What support and resources do you have for this endeavor? What other support and resources might you need? Who will you get to help you?

4. What beliefs do you hold about yourself that will ensure your success?

Slide 21 – The Power of Two Innovation Teams—Topics

- Happiness at work
- Harmony and sharing among employee groups
- Continuous people development
- Exceptional arrival experience
- Knowledge exchange: Sharing stories and best practices across stations
- Appreciative inquiry culture: training and applications
- Follow-up communication to the stations (from this workshop)
- Closing ceremony (for this workshop)

Slide 22 – Innovation Teams—Purpose

To plan, introduce, and carry out, within all of BA Customer Service NA, one innovative process, practice, or event that will positively impact customer satisfaction and retention.

Slide 23 – Innovation Teams—Workshop Task

Task: To determine and plan one initiative that your team will undertake—in its specific innovation topic—to enhance customer satisfaction and retention.

Time: 1 hour 30 minutes including lunch

Process:
1. Introduce yourselves—where you work and what you do.
2. Make a list of Innovative Ideas for Action—be sure they are related to your specific innovation topic.
3. Select the one Idea for Action that your group will plan, introduce, and carry out in the next 6 months.
4. Create a plan of action. Who will do what? By when?
5. Determine how your group will stay connected to complete its Innovation.

9

Master Set of AI Slides

Appreciative Inquiry:

A Positive Revolution in Change

Slide 1

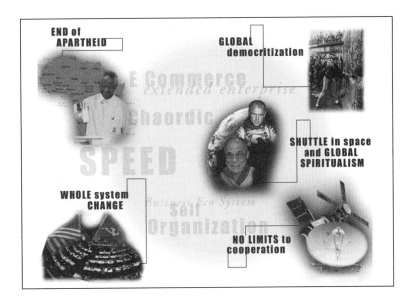

Slide 2

A Time For Re-thinking...
Human Organization And Change

- Global context of democratization

- End of Apartheid

- No limits to cooperation, e-company connect now

- Shuttle into space & reality isn't what it used to be

- "Whole system" change
  - Large groups...
  - "Positive revolution": aiming higher

Slide 3

Appreciative Inquiry is a Shift

- *"No problem can be solved from the same level of consciousness that created it. We must learn to see the world anew."*

- *"There are only two ways to live your life. One is as though nothing is a miracle. The other is as though everything is a miracle."*
  - *- Albert Einstein*

Slide 4

An Open Moment
We Are "In It" Now.

"We are at the very point in time when a 400-year old age is dying and another is struggling to be born, a shifting of culture, science, society, and institutions enormously greater than the world has ever experienced. Ahead, the possibility of the regeneration of relationships, liberty, community, and ethics such as the world has never known, and a harmony with nature, with one another, and with the divine intelligence such as the world has never dreamed."

—*Dee Hock, Founder & CEO—Visa*

Slide 5

Exciting Stories and Results

- Hunter Douglas
  - ✧ Culture Change
  - ✧ Strategic Planning
  - ✧ Total Quality

- Results
  - ✧ Employee Engagement
  - ✧ Leadership "Bench Strength"
  - ✧ Strategic Vision & Alignment

Slide 6

Exciting Stories and Results

- Tendercare Assisted Living Center
  - ✧ Business Results: Increasing Revenue Base from Census Development
  - ✧ Provider of Choice

- Results
  - ✧ 10% Increase in Census within six weeks
  - ✧ Union decertification vote initiated
  - ✧ Improved employee morale

Slide 7

Exciting Stories and Results

- United Religions Initiative
  - ✧ Annual Global Summits
  - ✧ Organization Design

- Results
  - ✧ June 2000 Charter Signing
  - ✧ The Birth of a Global "Chaordic" Organization
  - ✧ Centers on Every Continent
  - ✧ Over a Million Pledges of Support

Slide 8

Exciting Stories and Results

- GTE
  - ✧ Positive Change Network
  - ✧ Culture Change
  - ✧ Union Management Partnership
  - ✧ Call Center Excellence

- Results
  - ✧ 1997 ASTD Award
  - ✧ Employee Surveys
  - ✧ Contract Negotiations

Slide 9

Six Principles of Appreciative Inquiry

1. Constructionist Principle: The way we know is fateful.
2. Principle of Simultaneity: Change begins at the moment you ask the question.
3. Poetic Principle: Organizations are an open book.
4. Anticipatory Principle: Deep change = change in active images of the future.
5. Positive Principle: The more positive the question, the greater and longer-lasting the change.
6. Principle of Wholeness: The whole system can have a voice in the future.

Slide 10

Positive Image → Positive Action

- Powerful Placebo
- Pygmalion
- Positive Affect
- Imbalanced "Inner Dialogue"
- Rise and Fall of Cultures
- Affirmative Capability

Slide 11

A Theory of Affirmative Organizing

- Organizations are made and imagined
- No iron laws
- Metaphor: heliotropic hypothesis
- Healthy organizations = 2:1
  positively imbalanced "inner dialogue"
- Educative effect of positive imagery
- Positive image (discourse) as an obstacle
- Organizations do not need to be fixed
- Leadership = affirmation

Slide 12

Where Do Positive Images and Stories Come From?

Slide 13

#1 Moments of Magnified Meaning Making

Peak experience or a high point in your life.

Slide 14

Exploring Moments of Leadership in Your Life?

- A story or "high point" experience ... leading positive change.
- What things do you value most about ...
  - ✧ Yourself?
  - ✧ The nature of your work?
  - ✧ Your organization?

Slide 15

Your Vision of a Better World

Business as an agent of world benefit?

How is it organized?

What are its practices?

How to bring out the best in human beings?

Slide 16

An AI Interview
Activity #1: *Discovery*

DISCOVERY

- A dialogue in pairs.
- A interviews B, and B interviews A (45 minutes each).
- Engage in a spirit of **Discovery.**
- Listen and take good notes.
- At the end… summarize and thank you.

Slide 17

Problem Solving   *vs.*   Appreciative Inquiry

- Identify Problem.
- Conduct Root Cause Analysis.
- Brainstorm Solutions & Analyze.
- Develop Action Plans.

- *Metaphor: Organizations are problems to be solved.*

- Appreciate "What is" (What gives life?).
- Imagine "What Might Be."
- Determine "What Should Be."
- Create "What Will Be".

- *Metaphor: Organizations are a solution/mystery to be embraced.*

Slide 18

Deficit Theory of Change, and Cultural Consequences of Deficit Discourse

"The key accomplishment of the industrial age was the notion of continuous improvement. It remains the secular religion of most managers ... has reached the point of diminishing returns in incremental improvement programs."

Gary Hamel
Leading The Revolution

Slide 19

Cultural Consequences of Deficit Discourse

- Fragmentation
- Few New Images of Possibility ... Self-Fulfilling Frames/Questions
- Exhaustion & Visionless Voice
- The Experts Must Know
- Dependence on Hierarchy
- Spirals in Deficit Vocabularies
- Breakdown in Relations/Closed Door Meetings/Decrease in Public Space

Slide 20

Deficit Based Change:
Unintended Consequences

◆ Much lamented fragmented responses

◆ Slow: Puts attention on yesterday's causes

◆ No *new* positive images of future

◆ Visionless voice... fatigue

◆ Weakened fabric of relationships &
   defensiveness...negative culture

◆ Out of sync with the embedded economy of speed,
   partnerships, alliances, & e-commerce

Slide 21

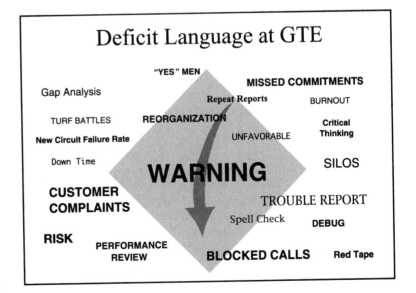

Slide 22

Organizations Grow In The Direction Of What They Study

REGION	JUNE RESULTS			Business			Commitments Met			Residence		
	'95 YTD	'95 YE	6/96	'96 YTD	'96 OBJ	FAV/UNF	'95 YTD	'95 YE	6/96	'96 YTD	'96 OBJ	FAV/(UNF)
California	96.3	96.5	95.7	96.6	96.5	0.1	96.9	97.6	97.8	98.1	96.1	2.0
Florida	93.4	94.6	96.5	96.0	96.5	(0.5)	96.2	96.7	96.3	97.2	96.1	1.1
Hawaii	89.9	90.7	94.2	94.4	96.5	(2.1)	95.9	95.5	97.7	97.1	96.1	1.0
Midwest	90.9	92.2	89.8	92.4	96.5	(4.1)	95.0	95.8	95.1	96.0	96.1	(0.1)
North	90.8	91.0	91.9	92.1	96.5	(4.4)	96.3	96.5	94.0	95.2	96.1	(0.9)
Northeast	91.7	93.0	94.4	95.2	96.5	(1.3)	94.9	96.1	95.7	96.8	96.1	0.7
Northwest	94.9	94.4	94.2	93.4	96.5	(3.1)	96.1	95.4	95.4	95.1	96.1	(1.0)
South	87.1	89.2	87.6	91.8	96.5	(4.7)	93.6	94.5	90.3	94.5	96.1	(1.6)
TX/NM	94.2	93.7	95.6	95.5	96.5	(1.0)	94.6	94.7	96.7	97.2	96.1	1.1
Virginia	92.9	93.5	92.2	94.4	96.5	(2.1)	96.6	97.1	94.6	96.5	96.1	0.4
Total Telops	92.7	93.3	93.6	94.5	96.5	(2.0)	95.7	96.2	95.3	96.5	96.1	0.4

Objective Not Met

Slide 23

Words Are Tools

To a hammer everything is a nail!

Slide 24

Ap-pre'ci-ate, v.,

1. valuing; the act of recognizing the best in people or the world around us; affirming past and present strengths, successes, and potentials; to perceive those things that give life (health, vitality, excellence) to living systems
2. to increase in value, e.g. the economy has appreciated in value.

•   Synonyms: VALUING, PRIZING, ESTEEMING, and HONORING.

Slide 25

In-quire' (kwir), v.,

1. the act of exploration and discovery.
2. to ask questions; to be open to seeing new potentials and possibilities.

•   Synonyms: DISCOVERY, SEARCH, and SYSTEMATIC EXPLORATION, STUDY.

Slide 26

What is Appreciative Inquiry?

It is the discovery for the best in people, their organizations, and the relevant world around them. It is an art and practice of asking the unconditional positive questions that strengthen a system's capacity to apprehend, anticipate and heighten positive potential. Instead of negation, criticism and spiraling diagnosis, there is discovery, dream, design and destiny. It works from accounts of the "positive change core". AI links the energy of the positive core directly to any change agenda and changes never thought possible are suddenly and democratically mobilized.

Slide 27

What would *you* call it?
(all these things taken together)

- Achievements
- Strategic opportunities
- Product strengths
- Technical assets
- Innovations
- Elevated thoughts
- Best business practices
- Positive emotions
- Financial assets
- Cooperative moments

- Organization wisdom
- Core competencies
- Visions of possibility
- Vital traditions, values
- Positive macrotrends
- Social capital
- Embedded knowledge
- Business ecosystem +s eg. suppliers, partners, competitors, customer

Slide 28

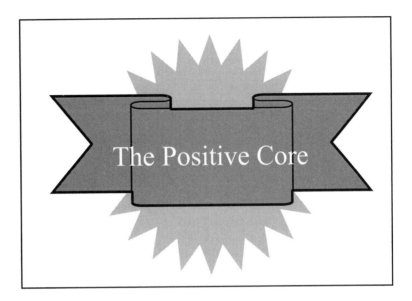

Slide 29

Whole Organizational Connection to the Positive Core

- ELEVATES: positive emotions of hope, inspiration, confidence, joy; raises intelligence; expands the language of life (internal dialogue); increases in appreciative interchange and mutually elevating relationships; high creativity, better decision making, increased collective capacity.

- "Undo" NEGATIVE IMPACTS: letting go, makes irrelevant, finishes the residual of negative past.

- PROTECTION IN FUTURE: Increases health-ability; resilience; accumulation of power; like an increase in immune system functioning.

Slide 30

- WHAT IS (NON-DEFICIT) POSITIVE CHANGE …
  "Any form of organization change, re-design, or
  planning that begins with comprehensive analysis of
  an organization's "positive core" and then links this
  knowledge to the heart of any strategic change agenda.

- Because human systems move toward what they
  persistently ask questions about, positive change
  involves the deliberate discovery of everything that
  gives a system "life" when it is most effective in
  economic and human terms.

- Link the positive core directly to any strategic agenda,
  and changes never thought possible are more rapidly
  mobilized while simultaneously building enthusiasm,
  corporate confidence, and human energy".

Slide 31

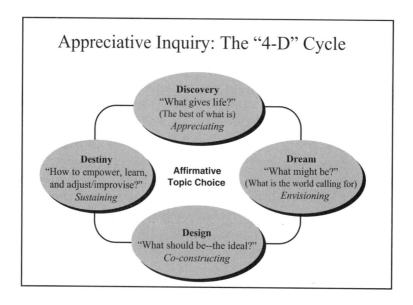

Slide 32

Best Way to Build High Enthusiasm?

- Do an organization survey of **low morale**?

- Magnify and learn from moment of **highest** enthusiasm?

Slide 33

Topic Choice

A Fateful Act:

Organizations Move in the Direction of What We Most Frequently and Systematically Ask Questions About!

Slide 34

Deficit Problems & Affirmative Topics

Deficit Issues

Sexual Harassment

Mid-mgmt. Turnover
Fear of Job Loss
Low Morale
Turfism/Silos
Delayed Orders
Customer Complaints
Lack of Training
Missed Commitments

Affirmative Topics

Positive Cross-Gender Working Relationships

Slide 35

Recent Topics

- Lightning-Fast Consensus
- Optimal Margins
- Magnetic Connections With Customer
- Outstanding Arrival Experience
- Environmentally Sustainable Enterprise
- Digital Spirit

- Crushing the Non-Union Competition
- Transformational Dialogue (Improbable Pairs)
- Revolutionary Customer Response
- Courageous Acts of Goodness
- Empowering and Enlightened Leadership
- Business as An Agent of World Benefit

Slide 36

Groups
Create "Topics" for Our Future

- Build on AI from this morning…patterns
- Now go beyond the data: 3-5 topics
- Good topics are -
  - ✧ Bold…a stretch….beyond status quo
  - ✧ Desired…you want it
  - ✧ Potential to energize, mobilize, strategic
  - ✧ Can "link" seeming opposites (both/and)
- List topics on flip chart….(make the case!)

Slide 37

Websites for other AI slides and
for sharing AI Tools

http://appreciativeinquiry.cwru.edu
This is the Appreciative Inquiry Commons at the
Weatherhead School of Management, Case
Western Reserve University.

Please submit/share your new tools, stories and
studies.

Slide 38

British Airways

- Approximately 1000 employees
- 22 Stations throughout North America
- "Pecos River" Workshops
    - ✧ Personal Awareness for all Employees
    - ✧ Target of Change - the People
- Appreciative Inquiry
    - ✧ "How to engage everyone in creating a culture of outstanding service?"
    - ✧ Target of Change: *the Organization*

Slide 39

Getting to Transformational Topics

From	To
Baggage Problems ⟶	*Service Recovery*
Service Recovery ⟶	*Exceptional Arrival Experience*

- Final Topics:
    - ✧ People are Owners
    - ✧ Continuous People Development
    - ✧ Big Picture Harmony Among Work Groups
    - ✧ Exceptional Arrival Experience

Slide 40

Selecting Significant Topics
Activity #2: *Dream*

DREAM

- Based on the stories you heard in your initial interviews.
- Select 3 - 5 affirmative topics.
- Record your topics on a flipchart.
- Prepare to present your topics to the whole group and explain why they are relevant to the future success of the organization.
- Time: 1.5 hours.

Slide 41

Genius is Creating the Question

"What would the universe look like if I were riding on the end of a light beam at the speed of light?"

—*Albert Einstein*

Slide 42

The Art of the Question

- What's the biggest problem here?
- Why did I have to be born in such a troubled family?
- Why do you blow it so often?
- Why do we still have those problems?

- What possibilities exist that we have not thought about yet?
- What's the smallest change that could make the biggest impact?
- What solutions would have us both win?
- What makes my questions inspiring, energizing, and mobilizing?

Slide 43

Basic Elements to the Typical AI Question

- A Positive Preface (introduce your TOPIC)

- Then a 2-part question
  - ✧ High point discovery
  - ✧ Image of desired future

- Refer to *The Encyclopedia of Positive Questions*

Slide 44

4 Foundational Questions

Q1: Peak experience or high point?

Q2: Things valued most about …
- ✧   yourself?
- ✧   the nature of your work?
- ✧   your organization?

Q3: What are the core factors that give "life" to organizing?

Q4: What are three wishes to heighten vitality and health?

Slide 45

Creating the New Question

From a study of customer
dissatisfaction and complaints to …

Slide 46

"Magnetic Connections"
(Example of a Positive Preface)

"In the physical world, all matter is held together by the
pull between opposite electric charges. Successful e-
companies are equally magnetic. People connect in new
and innovative ways. Suppliers and customers are
pulled together and become seamless edge-to-edge
organizations. Communities of interest form and are pulled
together by shared values and interests. Knowledge
networks form as catalysts for innovation and creativity."

Slide 47

Part A *(past)* & B *(future)*

A. Think of a time when you felt "magnetically"
connected to your client, your colleagues, and
your community. . . Connected in a way that
the force was so strong that it could not be
broken. What was that experience like?

B. As you look into the future, describe how we
are connected to our customers and our
colleagues in a way that is so strong that we
are seen as inseparable business partners.

Slide 48

Example #1

From an analysis of Grievance
Reduction to ...

Slide 49

Engagement & Positive Energy

- Organizations work best when they are vibrant, alive and fun. You know, when the "joint is jumping!" You can sense that the spirit of the organization is vital and healthy and that people feel pride in their work. Everyone builds on each other's successes, a positive can do attitude is infectious and the glow of success is shared. What's more, this positive energy is appreciated and celebrated so it deepens and lasts.

  A. Tell me about a time when you experienced positive energy that was infectious. What was the situation? What created the positive energy? How did it feel to be a part of it? What did you learn?

  B. If positive energy where the flame of the organization, how would you spark it? How would you fuel it to keep it burning bright?

Slide 50

Example #2

From Analysis of Baggage Delays to …

Exceptional Arrival Experience

- Our goal is to provide an exceptional travel experience both in the air and on the ground. The handling of a flight's arrival and baggage reconciliation is of equal importance to any other aspect of a passenger's journey. The arrival experience is the time to leave a wonderful lasting impression. It also provides the opportunity to recover from any service shortfall the customer may have encountered. Focusing on Exceptional Arrival Experience demonstrates commitment to both our customers and to one another.

  A. Describe your most memorable arrival experience, as a customer or, as airline personnel. What made it memorable to you? How did you feel?

  B. Tell me a story about your most powerful service recover. Describe the situation.

  C. Looking to the future how would you enhance the arrival experience?

Example #3

From Poor Performance and Margins to …

Slide 53

Discovering Optimal Margins

- With revenues, tonnage and sales at record levels one of the most important opportunities we face is to engage everyone in increasing positive margins now and to do so will call on discovery of new strengths, build on old strengths and carry us to higher levels financially.
    - ✧ As you look at Roadway from the perspective of our capabilities, and you think about the business context and opportunities, how do you define "optimal margin" for us? Define it: what is the positive margin you want and believe we have the capability to create? Right now? In the moderate time frame? Longer terms?

Slide 54

Discovering Optimal Margins

- As you reflect on your leadership at Roadway, times where you have mobilized or helped develop others, there have been high points and low points, successful moments, etc. Please describe one situation, or change initiative that you are proud about ... an achievement in which you feel you had impact in realizing better margins. What happened? What were the challenges? What was it about you or your leadership style? Lessons learned?

- If anything imaginable was possible, if there were no constraints whatever, what would the nature of an ideal Roadway organization look like if we were to rapidly move into stage of delivering optimal margins? Describe it. What is better, new or different? Envision it!

Slide 55

Groups
Crafting the Question

- Select one topic that has energy for your group (you can work more if there is time)
- Crafting the AI question(s): 3 PARTS
  1. Positive Preface
  2. A question to evoke a story from persons history
  3. A question to evoke images of future

Slide 56

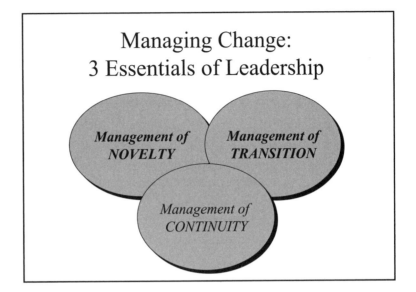

Managing Change:
3 Essentials of Leadership

Management of
NOVELTY

Management of
TRANSITION

Management of
CONTINUITY

Slide 57

Functions of Continuity

- For individuals: pride, confidence to act, ethical guidance connection to others, freedom.

- For the organization: strengthened commitment, better decision making; decentralized control; mission stability; organizational learning; long term thinking; customized change.

Slide 58

What Makes AI Questions Important?

- Language: questions & statements...
- Focus attention
- Heighten energy...drive to complete, to answer
- Every creative act
- Rapport and relationship (people are honored)
- Fulcrum change: connect to strength, imagination
- Break automatic thinking, essence of learning
- Alter internal dialogue & storytelling
- *Specific* positive future (the fairway)

Slide 59

The AI
Organization Summit Method

Increasing positive capacity through
large group methods

Slide 60

Dream & Design
The AI "Organization Summit"

- "Whole System" in the Room
- Task is Clear...
- Future Focus--In Historical and Global Perspective
- Self-Management and Dialogue
- Common Ground
    (not conflict management as the frame of reference)
- 3-Day event/100 to 1000 Participants
- Uncommon Action/Follow Through

Slide 61

Typical Results from Whole System AI Summit

- More Informed and Ultimately More Effective Change Efforts
- A Critical Mass of People Making Changes that they All Believe Are Needed
- A Total Organization Mindset
- Simultaneous Change
- Change is Perceived as "Real Work"
- Fast…Entire Organization…Strong Implementation…Action…Unifying…Spirit

Slide 62

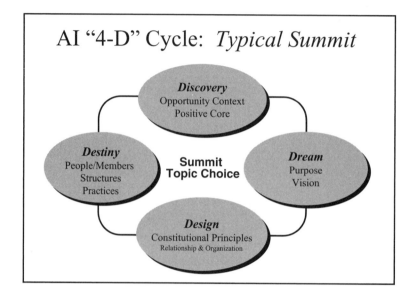

AI "4-D" Cycle: *Typical Summit*

Discovery
Opportunity Context
Positive Core

Destiny
People/Members
Structures
Practices

**Summit
Topic Choice**

Dream
Purpose
Vision

Design
Constitutional Principles
Relationship & Organization

Slide 63

Nutrimental Foods

- Why is this so easy?
- The experience of wholeness…an amazing power….why? how?

Slide 64

A Story on Organizational Design:
The Birthing of a "Spiritual United Nations"

- A call from the UN: the UN 50th
- A Bishop's vision
- Hans Kung… "there will be no peace among nations until there is peace among religions, no peace among religions until…"
- Huntington's thesis…clash of civilizations
- Can we make a contribution?

Slide 65

Three Types of Relations Between: The Past 100 Years

1. Canceling Conversation
2. Tolerating Conversation
3. Honoring or *Strength-Building* Conversation

Slide 66

How People Feel About the Initiative

- The World Context
- The "surprise of friendship"
- Unifying power of going to sacred places
- Continuity,"long term"
- From friendship & dialogue to action
- Enormous potential
- Many requests…

Slide 67

Insights on Success

- Holographic Beginning
- Polyphonic--Multiple Voices
- Dislodgement of Certainty…Appreciative
- From Negotiation to Narrative (Stories)
- From Common Ground to Higher Ground
- Retrospective Consensus…
- Inspired Action on Behalf of the Whole
- "Chaordic" Organizing

Slide 68

Design Phase

- Create the social-technical architecture
- Craft a provocative proposition
- Dream becomes a reality

Slide 69

Good Provocative Proposition

- Bridge the best of "what is" and "what might be"
- Challenge the "status quo"
- It should be desirable
- State it in affirmative and bold terms
- Fit within the architecture
- Zone of Proximal Development (ZPD)
- Participative process
- Balance the management of continuity, novelty and transition

Slide 70

Activity #3: *Design*
(for business and society)

DESIGN

- Your Dream (theme)
- Key Relationships → Stakeholders
- Corporate & Society Elements
  - ✧ Vision & Purpose
  - ✧ Practices & Principles
  - ✧ Communication Infrastructure
  - ✧ Culture
  - ✧ Structure
  - ✧ Distribution of Wealth
  - ✧ Other ....

What Matters Most?

- Being a **student** of "organization alive"
- Power of the **unconditional positive question**
- Relational basis of knowing: **communicamus ergo sum**
- Our **positive images of the future** lead our positive actions...words create worlds, "nothing so practical..."
- Yoga with the **positive change core**
- Ai accelerates the **non-linear interaction of the positive--** a "convergence zone" for sudden dialogic repatterning
- The best in people...**wholeness heals**
- **Letting go** of deficit based change vocabularies
- AI is not a "thing"; in its **infancy (5 %)**; many questions...

Activity #4: *Destiny*

DESTINY

- Delivery the design.
- Back to *discovery, dream* and *design.*
- Build AI learning competencies into the culture.
- No one best way to do it.

Destiny: Creating a Positive Change Network (PCN)

- GTE :How to invite 67,000 people to create a new culture?
- Storytelling and hope
- AI at the front line
- The "zealots are coming"
- Labor & management: an impasse
- The positive change network…ongoing!!

The PCN: What is it?

- Special invitation & *call* to people to be change leaders…
- AI program on positive change
- Many applications
- Self-organizing...
- Connected in knowledge sharing

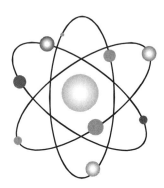

Success Factors

- Great AI training
- e-Knowledge management
- Strategic business opportunities
- Annual Summit (face-to-face)

Impact Areas

- Reduce cycle time of change--change ready
- Cost efficient leadership education
- A positive culture
- Rapid *whole-system mobilization* capability for strategic planning
- The power of digital storytelling
- Measurable change in unit performance and company morale

Slide 77

Applications Appreciative Inquiry

- Strategic change... "Org Summit"
- Core business redesign
- Quality…surveys…culture change
- Customer partnerships
- Labor-management relations
- Transformation of measurements
- Knowledge exchange: the "PCN"
- Business ecosystem analysis...

Slide 78

Destiny – What Will Be?

Allow yourself to *dream* and you will
discover that *destiny* is yours to *design.*

- *Dr. J. Stavros*

Slide 79

Activity #4: It's all About You
(take a time out for yourself)

- What do you do best already--from an appreciative perspective? The way you work with people?
- What would you like to do more of….(work or home)?
- <u>One</u> AI project (small or big) you would like to experiment with and do?
- Beliefs you have about yourself will help you succeed?

Slide 80

10

AI Worksheets

Worksheet 1:

Topic Choice Four Key Questions in Discovery

Take a few minutes to jot down some notes to yourself in response to the following questions. Your partner will interview you and help you to explore these questions in-depth.

Describe a peak experience or high point in your organization. This would be a time when you were most alive and engaged.

Without being modest, what is it that you most value about yourself, the nature of your work, and your organization?

What are the core factors that give life to your organization, without which the organization would cease to exist?

What are three wishes you have to enhance the health and vitality of your organization?

Worksheet 2:

Topic Team Selection

Use this worksheet to create the best topic team or core steering team for the Appreciative Inquiry initiative.

Suggested Team Member, Title, Organizational Area and Best Reason for Invitation to Team

Suggested Team Members

Name	Title	Organizational Area	Best Reason for Invitation to Team

Worksheet 3:

Getting Started Discussion Checklist

This worksheet can help with the initial discussions to help a team get started with an AI project.

Our organization will use AI because we want to _____
in order to _____.

Who will sponsor and lead this AI initiative?

What is the timeframe for the effort?

Who are the organization's stakeholders?

How many people will be involved?

How will we select topics for the inquiry?

How many interviews will be conducted? Who will conduct them?

How will stories be collected, shared and analyzed from the interviews?

What communication vehicles will be used to keep people "in the loop"?

Who (or what groups) will be involved in each stage of the project?

How will logistics be managed?

How will costs be shared?

How will AI be integrated and sustained in the organization's culture?

Worksheet 4:

Engaging AI Question Checklist[1]

This worksheet can be used to ensure that the questions in the interview guide are framed in a positive tone and engaging. In reviewing the question, ask yourself does the question…

state an affirmative tone?

build on a "half full assumption"?

give a broad definition to the topic?

present an invitation that is:
    expansive?
    positive feeling words?
    locating energizing stories?

enhance the possibilities of story telling and narratives?

phrase itself in rapport talk not report talk?

value "what is?" This will help to spark the appreciative imagination by helping the person locate the experiences that are worth valuing.

move beyond common ground and elevate conversation to higher ground?

convey an unconditional positive regard?

evoke essential values, aspirations and inspirations?

---

1 This material is adapted from Dr. Marge Schiller's work in Appreciative Inquiry.

Worksheet 5:

Interview Packet Checklist

Creating the interview guide is an exciting task because what we "ask" determines what we "find." What we find determines how we talk. How we talk determines how we imagine together. How we imagine together determines what we achieve. The interview guide should incorporate the following components:

Introduction to explain the project and purpose.

Instruction for preparing, conducting and reporting the interviews.

Stage setting questions:

Describe a peak experience or high point in your organization. This would be a time when you were most alive and engaged.

What do you value most about yourself, your work and your organization?

Affirmative topic questions: formulate engaging questions with lead-ins (positive free-fall) that assume the subject matter in question already exists.

Conclusion questions to wrap up the interview:
- What are the core life-giving factors that life to this organization?
- Looking toward the future, what are we being called to become?
- What three wishes do you have for changing the organization (or the "miracle questions")?

Interview Summary Sheet to collect the best interview stories, quotes and ideas.
What was the best story that came out of the interview?
What was the best quote that came out of the interview?

Demographic Summary Sheet (if appropriate)

Interview Consent Form

A sincere thank you!

Worksheet 6:

Dreaming the Organization's Future

The goal is to create ideal future scenarios. The following activity can help to create and visualize the discovery of the dream:

Self-manage the process to include:

- Discussion leader

- Recorder

- Timekeeper

Visualize the dream that you really want from the themes or conversations identified in the discovery phase. Ask yourself:

- What is happening?

- How does this happen?

- What are the things that made this happen? (i.e. leadership, structures, systems, etc.)

- What makes this dream (the vision) exciting?

Capture the dream in a narrative statement.

- Use vivid language.

- Be positive and uplifting.

Choose a creative way to present your dream (vision) to all the participants. It can be the format of a new report, song, poem, skit, interview or a picture.

Worksheet 7:
Criteria for Creating Provocative Propositions

In creating provocative propositions that begin to build positive images of the ideal organization, ask yourself if the provocative proposition meets the following criteria::

Is it provocative... does it stretch, challenge or interrupt?

Is it grounded... are there examples that illustrated the ideal as real possibilities?

Is it desired... if it could be fully actualized would the organization want it? Do you want it as a preferred future?

Is it stated in affirmative and bold terms?

Does it follow a social architecture approach?

Does it expand the zone of proximal development?

Use of third party (outside appreciative eye)

Complimented with benchmarking data

Is it a high involvement process?

Is it used to stimulate intergenerational organizational learning?

Is there balanced management of: continuity, novelty and transition?

Worksheet 8:

Design to Destiny Worksheet

To begin to translate your provocative proposition into goals, strategies and/or action items, complete the following:

Self-manage the process to include:

- Discussion leader

- Recorder

- Timekeeper

Select the provocative proposition to work with. Based on the feedback from others, take 15-20 minutes to revise, edit or improve it.

Write down targets, goals, strategies and/or action items that can achieve the desired provocative proposition.

Brainstorm ideas about specific things that can occur now or in the near future to realize the dream.

Discuss and agree on key targets and goals, plus the strategies and action items on how to get there and to be completed by whom and when.

Worksheet 9:

How to Build or Map the Positive Core

There is a field of work called graphical recording that can help to guide the mapping of the positive core" of the organization. Below is a suggested process:

Form into teams and ask participants to:

- Share their stories collected in the interview process.

- Write down those key factors that create the organization's successes.

Use a visual creation to map the positive core such as:
- graphical metaphor
- mosaic or collage

Display and communicate the visual of the positive core to the stakeholders.

Worksheet 10:

AI: Valuation and Learning Worksheet

At the end of an Appreciative Inquiry initiative, workshop or Destiny session, you may want to ask the participants the following questions:

What about the Appreciative Inquiry approach most enlivened you?

What excites you most about introducing or using Appreciative Inquiry in your work or personal life?

What Appreciative Inquiry competencies have you discovered that you already have?

What's your elevator story about Appreciative Inquiry that you would like to share?

What can you envision to take Appreciative Inquiry to a higher level for yourself, someone else or your organization?

What is one simple appreciative idea or action that you can do tomorrow?

11

AI Classics: Selected Articles*

A Positive Revolution in Change:

Appreciative Inquiry[1]

David L. Cooperrider and Diana Whitney
(Draft)

Introduction

Appreciative Inquiry (AI) begins an adventure. The urge and call to adventure has been sounded by many people and many organizations, and it will take many more to fully explore the vast vistas that are now appearing on the horizon. But even in the first steps, what is being sensed is an exciting direction in our language and theories of change—an invitation, as some have declared, to "a positive revolution".

The words just quoted *are* strong and, unfortunately, they are not ours. But the more we replay, for example, the high-wire moments of our several years of work at GTE the more we find ourselves asking the very same kinds of questions the people of GTE asked their senior executives: "Are you really ready for the momentum that is being generated? This is igniting a grassroots movement…it *is* creating an organization in full voice, a center stage for the positive revolutionaries!"

Tom White, President of what was then called GTE Telops (making up 80% of GTE's 67,000 employees) replies back, with no hesitation: "Yes, and what I see in this meeting are zealots, people with a mission and passion for creating the new GTE. Count me in, I'm your number one recruit, number one zealot". People cheer.

Enthusiasms continue, and they echo over subsequent months as lots of hard work pays off. Fourteen months later —based on significant and measurable changes in stock prices, morale survey measures, quality/customer relations, union-management relations, etc.— GTE's whole system change initiative is given professional recognition by the American Society for Training and Development. It wins the 1997 ASTD award for best organization change program in the country. Appreciative inquiry is cited as the "backbone".

How Did They Do It?

This paper provides broad update and overview of AI. The GTE story mentioned at the outset is, in many ways, just beginning but it is scarcely alone. In the ten years since the theory and vision for "Appreciative Inquiry Into Organizational Life" was published (Cooperrider and Srivastva, 1987; Cooperrider 1986) there have been literally hundreds of people involved in co-creating new practices for doing AI, and for bringing the spirit and methodology of AI into organizations all over the world.[1] The velocity and largely informal spread of the ideas suggests, we believe, a growing sense of disenchantment with exhausted theories of change, especially those wedded to vocabularies of human deficit, and a corresponding urge to work with people, groups, and

---

1 Cooperrider, D., Whitney, D. (1999). *A Positive Revolution in Change: Appreciative Inquiry.* Taos, NM: Corporation for Positive Change.

The interested reader will find, at the book's end, references and resources to many pieces of published accounts of AI work drawn from large and small corporations, with communities and cities, and with international organizations working across cultural boundaries.

organizations in more constructive, positive, life-affirming, even spiritual ways.

In this paper we hope to serve as conduit to this impulse as we touch on exciting examples and concepts, and provide references for future study. And while the outcomes and illustrations we have selected are often dramatic, we do want to emphasize, throughout, that AI is clearly only in its infancy. Questions are many, and we believe they will be a source of learning for many years.

Could it be, for example, that we as a field have reached "the end of problem solving" as a mode of inquiry capable of inspiring, mobilizing and sustaining significant human system change? What would happen to our change practices if we began all of our work with the positive presumption—that organizations, as centers of human relatedness, are "alive" with infinite constructive capacity? If so how would we know? What do we mean by infinite capacity? What would happen to us, lets say as leaders or catalysts of change, if we approached the question of change only long *after* we have connected with people and organizations through systematic study of their already "perfect" form? How would we talk about "it"—this account of the ideal-in-the-real? Would we, in our work, have to go any further once we and others were connected to this positive core? *How can we better inquire into organization existence in ways that are economically, humanly, and ecologically significant, that is, in ways that increasingly help people discover, dream, design and transform toward the greatest good?*

What is Appreciative Inquiry?

Ap-pre'ci-ate, v., 1. *valuing; the act of recognizing the best in people or the world around us; affirming past and present strengths, successes, and potentials; to perceive those things that give life (health, vitality, excellence) to living systems* 2. *to increase in value, e.g. the economy has appreciated in value. Synonyms: VALUING, PRIZING, ESTEEMING, and HONORING.*

In-quire' (kwir), v., 1. *the act of exploration and discovery.* 2. *To ask questions; to be open to seeing new potentials and possibilities. Synonyms: DISCOVERY, SEARCH, and SYSTEMATIC EXPLORATION, STUDY.*

AI has been described by observers in a myriad of ways: as a *paradigm of conscious evolution* geared for the realities of the new century (Hubbard, 1998); as a methodology that takes the idea of the *social construction* of reality to its positive extreme— especially with its emphasis on metaphor and narrative, relational ways of knowing, on language, and on its potential as a source of generative theory (Gergen, 1996); as the most important advance in *action research* in the past decade (Bushe, 1991); as offspring and "heir" to Maslow's vision of a *positive social science* (Chin, 1998; Curran, 1991); as a powerful second generation *OD practice* (French and Bell, 1995; Porrras, 1995; Mirvis, 1993); as model of a much needed *participatory science*, a "new yoga of inquiry" (Harman, 1991); as a radically affirmative approach to change which completely lets go of problem-based management and in so doing vitally transforms strategic planning, survey methods, culture change, merger integration methods, approaches to TQM, measurement systems, sociotechnical systems, etc. (White, 1997); and lastly, as OD's *philosopher's stone* (Sorenson, et. al 1996). Indeed it is difficult it is to sum up the whole of AI—as a philosophy of knowing, a normative stance, a methodology for managing change, and as an approach to leadership and human development. However for purposes here, it might be most useful to begin with a pracitice-oriented definition of AI, one that is more descriptive than theoretical and one that provides a compass for the examples to follow:

Appreciative Inquiry is about the coevolutionary search for the best in people, their organizations, and the relevant world around them. In its broadest focus, it involves systematic discovery of what gives "life" to a living system when it is most alive, most effective, and most constructively capable in economic, ecological, and human terms. AI involves, in a central way, the art and practice of asking questions that strengthen a system's capacity to apprehend, anticipate, and heighten positive potential. It centrally involves the mobilization of inquiry through the crafting of the "unconditional positive question" often-involving hundreds or sometimes thousands of people. In AI the arduous task of intervention gives way to the speed of imagination and innovation; instead of negation, criticism, and spiraling diagnosis, there is discovery, dream, and design. AI seeks, fundamentally, to build a constructive union between a whole people and the massive entirety of what people talk about as past and present capacities: *achievements, assets, unexplored potentials, innovations, strengths, elevated thoughts, opportunities, benchmarks, high point moments, lived values, traditions, strategic competencies, stories, expressions of wisdom, insights into the deeper corporate spirit or soul— and visions of valued and possible futures.* Taking all of these together as a gestalt, AI deliberately, in everything it does, seeks to work from accounts of this "positive change core"—and it assumes that every living system has many untapped and rich and inspiring accounts of the positive. Link the energy of this core directly to any change agenda and changes never thought possible are suddenly and democratically mobilized.

The positive core of organization *alive,* we submit, is one of the greatest and largely unrecognized resources in field of change management today. As said earlier, we are clearly in our infancy when it comes to tools for working with it, talking about it, and designing our systems in synergistic alignment with it. But one thing is evident and clear as we reflect on the most important things we have learned with AI: *human systems grow in the direction of what they persistently ask questions about and this propensity is strongest and most sustainable when the means and ends of inquiry are positively correlated. The single most prolific thing a group can do if its aims are to to liberate the human spirit and consciously construct a better future is to make the positive change core the common and explicit property of all.*

Lets Illustrate: The Appreciative Inquiry "4-D" Cycle
You have just received the following unsettling phone call:

My name is Rita Simmel; I am President of a New York consulting partnership. Our firm specializes in dealing with difficult conflict in organizations: labor-management issues, gender conflict, issues of diversity. We have been retained by a fortune 500 corporation for the past several years. The contract is around sexual harassment, an issue that is deeper and more severe than virtually any corporation realizes. The issues are about power, the glass ceiling, and many things. As you know millions of dollars are being expended on the issues. Our firm has specialized in this area for some years and now I'm beginning to ask myself the Hippocratic oath. Are we really helping? Here is the bottom line with our client. We have been working on the issues for two years, and by every measure— numbers of complaints, lawsuits, evaluations from sexual harassment training programs, word of mouth—the problem continues in its growth. Furthermore people are now voting with their feet. They are not coming to the workshops. Those that do seem to leave with doubts: our post-workshop interviews show people feel less able to communicate with those of the opposite gender, they report feeling more distance and less trust, and the glass ceiling remains. So here is my question. How would you take an appreciative inquiry approach to sexual harassment?

This was a tough one. We requested time to think about it, asking if we could talk again in a day or two. We can do the same for you right now (give you a bit of time) as we invite you to think about things you might seriously propose in the callback.

So before going further with the story lets pause and look at a typical flow for AI, a cycle that can be as rapid and informal as in a conversation with a friend or colleague, or as formal as an organization-wide analysis involving every stakeholder, including customers, suppliers, partners and the like.

Figure 1: Appreciative Inquiry "4-D" Cycle

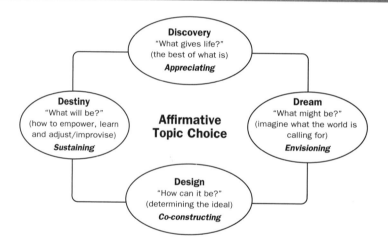

Figure one shows, on the outside, four key stages in AI: **Discovery**—mobilizing a whole system inquiry into the positive change core; **Dream**—creating a clear results-oriented vision in relation to discovered potential and in relation to questions of higher purpose, i.e., "What is the world calling us to become?" **Design**—creating possibility propositions of the ideal organization, an organization design which people feel is capable of magnifying or eclipsing the positive core and realizing the articulated new dream; and **Destiny**—strengthening the affirmative capability of the whole system enabling it to build hope and momentum around a deep purpose and creating processes for learning, adjustment, and improvisation like a jazz group over time (see the excellent article by Barrett, 1993).

At the core of the cycle, is **Affirmative Topic Choice**. It is the most important part of any AI. If in fact if knowledge and organizational destiny are as intricately interwoven as we think it, then isn't it possible that the seeds of change are implicit in the very first questions we ask? AI theory says yes and takes the idea quite seriously: *it says that the way we know people groups, and organizations is fateful. It further asserts the time is* *overdue to recognize that symbols and conversations, emerging from all our analytic modes, are among the world's paramount resources.*

Topic Choice

So back to our phone call. If inquiry and change are a simultaneous moment; if the questions we ask set the stage for what we "find"; and if what we "discover" (the data) creates the material out of which the future is conceived, conversed about, and constructed—then how shall we proceed with an appreciative approach to sexual harassment? Here is an excerpt from the response:

> D.C.: Hello Rita. Before we get into our proposal we have an important question. What is it that *you* want to learn about and achieve with this whole intervention, and by when?

> Rita: We want to dramatically cut the incidence of sexual harassment. We want to solve this huge problem, or at least make a significant dent in it.

> D.C.: O.K. Rita… But is that all?

> Rita: You mean what do I *really* want to see? (Long pauses…then she blurts out). *What we really want to see is the development of the new century organization—a model of high* **quality cross-gender relationships in the workplace!**

> DC: Great topic. What would happen if we put an invitation out in the company newsletter, asking people in pairs to step forward to nominate themselves as candidates to study and share their stories of what it means to create and sustain high quality cross-gender relationships in the workplace? It might be interesting to do a large conference, and really put a magnifying lens to the stages of development, contextual factors, tough questions of adult attraction, breakthroughs in terms of power relations, and so on. What do you think?

To move fastforward, a relatively small pilot project was created which surpassed everyone's expectations. Hundreds, not dozens, of pairs nominated themselves. That was surprise number one. Then other organizations got word of the pilot and a truly major effort, moving through the 4-D framework, was conceptualized by another consulting firm, Marge Schiller and Associates. The pioneering organization she worked with, which now can happily be named, was the Avon Corporation in Mexico. The issues here were not about harrasment but there were other hopes about women and men in shared leadership contexts—including dealing with the glass ceiling at senior management levels—but again there was interest in framing the whole thing in terms of an inquiry.

To begin, a hundred people were trained in the basics of AI interviewing. They in turn went out into every part of the organization and over the next several weeks completed many more interviews, about 300 in all. At the end of each interview the interviewers asked the person interviewed if they too could help do some interviewing. A waterfall was experienced. Stories poured in—stories of achievement, trust building, authentic joint leadership, practices of effective conflict management, ways of dealing with sex stereotypes, stages of development and methods of career advancement.

The second two "Ds"— articulating the new century dream and creating designs for an organization that maximally supported the development of high quality cross-gender relationships— came next. These were combined in a large group format much like a future search. Using stories from the interviews as a basis for imagining the future, expansive and practical propositions were created like, for example, "Every task force or committee at Avon, whenever possible, is co-chaired by a cross-gender pairing". The significance of even this simple proposal proved to be big. Likewise propositions in other areas of organization design were also carefully crafted. Soon literally *everything* in the organization was opened to discussion: corporate structures, systems, work processes, communications, career opportunities, governance, compensation practices, leadership patterns, learning opportunities, customer connections, and more.

In the end some 30 visionary propositions were created. Marge Schiller has written about the whole thing eloquently. Subsequent changes in system structures and behaviors were reported to be dramatic (Schiller, 1998). As it turns out the story, like GTE's, gets even better. Avon Mexico was just recently singled out, several years later, by the Catalyst organization. *They were given the 1997Catalyst Award for best place in the country for women to work.*

It is a classic example of the power of topic choice. Affirmative topics, always homegrown, can be on anything the people of an organization feel gives life to the system. As a rule of thumb most projects have between 3-5 topics. Words like empowerment, innovation, sense of ownership, commitment, integrity, ecological consciousness, and pride are often articulated as worthy of study. Topics can be on anything an organization feels to be strategically and humanly important. AI topics can be on technical processes, financial efficiencies, human issues, market opportunities, social responsibilities or anything else. In each case of topic choice, the same premise is firmly posited: human systems grow in the direction of their deepest and most frequent inquiries.

The Phase of Discovery

The inquiry we are talking about is anything but wishful. If we were to underline one of the two words— appreciative or inquiry—our pen would immediately move to the later. In *Vital Speeches of the Day* (1996) Tom White, President of what was then called GTE Telephone Operations puts his interpretation of AI in executive language, months before GTE's change effort was recognized by ASTD:

> *Appreciative Inquiry can get you much better results than seeking out and solving problems. That's an interesting concept for me—and I imagine most of you—because telephone companies are among the best problem solvers in the world. We trouble shoot everything. We concentrate enormous resources on correcting problems that have relatively minor impact on our overall service and performance (and which)...when used continually and over a long period of time, this approach can lead to a negative culture. If you combine a negative culture with all the challenges we face today, it could be easy to convince ourselves that we have too many problem to overcome—to slip into a paralyzing sense of hopelessness....Don't get me wrong. I'm not advocating mindless happy talk. Appreciative Inquiry is a complex science designed to make thing better. We can't ignore problems—we just need to approach them from the other side".*

What Tom White calls "the other side" we are describing as the positive change core. AI, most simply, is a tool for connecting to the transformational power of this core. Willis Harman (1991) talks about AI as a participatory science, a yoga of inquiry, where the term yoga comes from the Sanskrit root yug which means link or bond. In that sense if we remember something or someone, it can be said that there is a form of yoga happening. Ai helps make the memory link by concentrating systematic inquiry onto all aspects of the appreciable world, into an organization's infinite and surplus capacity—past, present and future. By concentrating on the atom, human beings have unleashed its power. AI says we can do the same in every living system once we open this ever emergent positive core—every strength, innovation, achievement, resource, living value, imaginative story, benchmark, hope, positive tradition, passion, high point experience, internal genius, dream— to systematic inquiry.

The core task of the discovery phase is to discover and disclose positive capacity, at least until an organization's understanding of this "surplus" is exhausted (which has never happened once in our experience). AI provides a practical way to ignite this "spirit of inquiry" on organization- wide basis. Consider this example:

> *At Leadshare in Canada AI was used to help this big eight accounting firm make the tough transition in the executive succession of a "legendary" managing partner. The managing partner seized the moment as an incredible leadership development opportunity for all 400 partners. Everyone was interviewed with AI. An extensive interview protocol was designed (it ended up taking about 2 hours per interview) focusing on affirmative topics like innovation, equality, partnership, speed to market, and valuing diversity (in Canada between francophone and anglophone). And not one outside consultant did the interviews. All were done internally, by 30 junior partners as part of a leadership development program. A powerful and instant intergenerational connection was made, and organizational history came alive in face-to-face story. Instead of amnesia, or a problem-to-be-solved, people began to relate to their history in a whole new way. Like a good piece of poetry filled with endless interpretive meaning, people at Leadshare ascended into their history as a reservoir of positive possibility. At the next annual partners meeting with over 400 people in the conference hall, the material was showcased and coupled to the future, as the strategic planning became one of the "best" the partners could ever remember (Rainey, 1996)*

Perhaps it is obvious but the process of doing the interviews is as important as the data collected. When managers ask us how many people should be interviewed or, who should do the interviews, we increasingly find ourselves saying "everyone". It is not uncommon in AI work to talk about doing thousands of interviews. A hospital in Seattle recently did 3 thousand interviews in preparation for an organization-wide Appreciative Inquiry Summit (Whitney and Cooperrider, 1998). People themselves, not consultants, generate the system-wide organization analysis using questions like this: " Obviously you have had ups and downs in your career here at GTE. But for the moment I would like you to focus on a high point, a time in your work experience here where you felt most alive, most engaged, or most successful. Can you tell me the story? How did it unfold? What was it organizationally that made it stand out? What was it about *you* that made it a high point? Key insights for all of us at GTE?"

In Chicago, in one of the most exciting AI's we have seen, there is talk of over a million interviews. And guess whose interviews have produced the best data—the most inspiring, vision-generating stories? It is the children. It is happening through intergenerational inquiry where the elders are valued and share hopes in settings with the young. On of our favorite papers is about the Imagine Chicago story and the leadership of Bliss Browne. It is titled *"The Child as the Agent of Inquiry"* (Cooperrider, 1996).

It argues that the spirit of inquiry is something all of us in change work need to reclaim and aspire to: openness, availability, epistemological humility, the ability to admire, to be surprised, to be inspired, to inquire into our valued and possible worlds.

What distinguishes AI, especially in this phase of work, is that every carefully crafted question is positive. Knowing and changing are a simultaneous moment. The thrill of discovery becomes the thrill of creating. *As people throughout a system connect in serious study into qualities, examples, and analysis of the positive core —each appreciating and everyone being appreciated— hope grows and community expands.*

From Discovery to Dream

When an artist sits in front of a landscape the imagination is kindled not by searching for "what is wrong with this landscape" but by a special ability to be inspired by those things of value worth valuing. Appreciation, it appears, draws our eye toward life, but stirs our feelings, sets in motion our curiosity, and provides inspiration to the envisioning mind. In his analysis of esthetics and the origins of creative images Nietzsche once asked of the power of appreciation: " Does is not praise? Does it not glorify? Does it not select? Does it not bring {that which is appreciated} to prominence?" (In Rader, 1973, p. 12). Then in the same passage he takes a next step, linking valuing (discovery) and imagination (dream). He elaborates: "valuing is creating: hear it, ye creating ones! Valuation is itself the treasure and jewel of valued things".

During the dream phase the interview stories and insights get put to constructive use. As people are brought together to listen carefully to the innovations and moments of organization "alive", sometimes in storytelling modes, sometimes in interpretive and analytic modes, a convergence zone is created where the future begins to be discerned in the form of visible patterns interwoven into the texture of the actual. The amplified interaction among innovators and innovations makes something important happen: very rapidly we start seeing outlines of the New World. Some organizations turn the data into a special commemorative report celebrating the successes and exceptional moment in the life of the organization (Liebler, 1997). Others have created a thematic analysis—careful to document rich stories and not succumb to "narrative thin" one line quotes (Ludema, 1996). In all cases the data onto the positive change core serves as an essential resource for the visioning stages of the appreciative inquiry 4-D model.

Before their strategic planning session session in 1997, Nutrimental Foods of Brazil closed down the plant for a full day to bring all 700 employees together for a day of Discovery into the factors and forces that have given life the system when it had been most effective, most alive, and most successful as a producer of high quality health foods.With cheers and good wishes a "smaller" group of 150 stakeholders—employees from all levels, suppliers, distributors, community leaders, financiers, and customers—then went into a four day strategy session to articulate a new and bold corporate dream. The stories from the day before were used just as an artist uses a palette of colors—before painting a picture the artist assembles the red paints, blue, green, yellow and so on. With these "materials" in hand people were asked to dream: "What is the world calling us to become? What are those things about us that no matter how much we change, we want to continue into our new and different future? Lets assume that tonight while we were all asleep a miracle occurred where Nutrimental became exactly as we would like it to be—all of its best qualities are magnified, extended, multiplied the way we would like to see…in fact we wake up and it is now 2005…as you come into Nutrimental today what do you see that is different, and how do you know?"After four days of appreciative analysis, planning, and articulation of three new strategic business directions the organization launches into the future with focus, solidarity, and confidence. Six months later record bottom line figures of millions of dollars are recorded—profits are up 300%. The co-CEOs Rodrigo Loures and Arthur Lemme Nettto attribute the dramatic results to two things: bringing the whole system into the planning process, and realizing that organizations are in fact "centers of human relatedness"(Loures and Lemme Netto, 1998) which thrive when there is an appreciative eye—when people see the best in one another, when they can dialogue their dreams and ultimate concerns if affirming ways, and when they are connected in full voice to create not just new worlds but better worlds.

Design

Once the strategic focus or dream is articulated (usually consisting of three things in our model— a vision of a better *world*, a powerful purpose, and a compelling statement of strategic intent) attention turns to the creation of the ideal organization, the social architecture or actual design of the system in relation to the world it is part. What we have found is that the sequencing is crucial, moving first through in-depth work on Dream before Design, followed with back and forth iterations. In Zimbabwe we recently worked with a partner organization of Save the Children. It was fascinating to observe how easy it was to re-design the organization in terms of structures and systems once broad agreement was reached on a powerful Dream. The articulation of the image of the future was simple: "Every person in Zimbabwe shall have access to clean water within five years". The critical design shift, demanded by the large dream, was to a new form of organization based on a network of alliances or partnerships, not bureaucracy's self-sufficient hierarchy.

One aspect that differentiates Appreciative Inquiry from other visioning or planning methodologies is that images of the future emerge out of *grounded* examples from an organization's positive past. Sometimes this "data" is complimented with benchmark studies of other organizations creating a "generative metaphor" for circumventing common resistances to change (Barrett and Cooperrider, 1988). In both cases, the good news stories are used to craft possibility propositions that bridge the best of "what is" with collective speculation or aspiration of "what might be". In the working of the material people are invited to challenge the status quo as well as common assumptions underlying the design of the organization. People are encouraged to "wander beyond" the data with the essential question being this: "What would our organization look like if it were designed in every way possible to maximize the qualities of the positive core and enable the accelerated realization of our dreams?"

When inspired by a great dream *we have yet to find an organization that did not feel compelled to design something very new and very necessary.* Here is an example of a possibility proposition, one of about twenty organization design visions that were created at DIA Corporation, a rapidly growing distributor of consumer products. Today this proposition is modus operandi at the corporation:

DIA has become a learning organization that fosters the cross fertilization of ideas, minimizes the building of empires, harnesses the synergy of group cooperation, and cultivates the pride of being a valued member of one outstanding corporation. DIA accelerates its learning through an annual strategic planning conference that involves all five hundred people in the firm as well as key partners and stakeholders. As a setting for "strategic learning" teams present their benchmarking studies of the best five other organizations, deemed leaders in their class. Other teams present an annual appreciative analysis of DIA, and together these data-bases of success stories (internal and external) help set the stage for DIA's strategic, future search planning.

Recently we have had the opportunity to team up with Dee Hock, one of the truly visionary CEOs we have ever worked with. Dee was the founder of VISA, a breakthrough organization that has over 20,000 offices, and since 1970 has grown something like 10,000%; this year annual sales expected to pass $1 trillion. The whole Visa system, from Calcutta to Chicago in over 200 countries is completely unmanageable from the perspective of using centralized, command-and-control design principles.

If General Motors once defined the shape of the old model, perhaps Dee's "chaordic organization" –combining chaos and order in ways which interweave (like nature's designs) infinite variety and self-organizing order—is a foreshadowing of an emerging prototype. What we have learned by working with Dee is how to move pragmatically and substantively from appreciative Discovery and Dream to truly post-bureaucratic Design that distributes power and liberates human energy in a way we have never seen. Most recently we have collaborated on a re-constitution of the United Way of America as well as an initiative to design something akin to a United Nations among the world's great religions and spiritual traditions (it is called United Religions). In each case helping people agree on a set of design principles is crucial. That is "principles" as in "We hold these truths to be self evident: that all people are created equal…" Again, this is not a set of platitudes but a manifesto, what people believe in and care about in their gut.

Destiny
Of all the creatures of earth, said William James in 1902, only human beings can change their pattern. "Man alone is the architect of his destiny".

In our early years of AI work we called the 4th "D" Delivery. We emphasized planning for continuos learning, adjustment, and improvisation in the service of shared ideals. It was a time for action planning, developing implementation strategies, and dealing with conventional challenges of sustainability. But the word delivery simply did not go far enough. It did not convey the sense of liberation we were seeing, like the well documented hotel case, where the system tranformed itself from a one-star to four-star hotel by using AI and literally putting a moratorium on all the traditional problem solving efforts that it had going (Barret and Cooperrider, 1989).

Executives like Jane Watkins (former Chair of the Board at NTL) and Jane Pratt (executive at the World Bank and now CEO of the Mountain Institute) argued that AI engenders a repatterning of our relationships not only with each other but also our relationship to reality itself. Reminiscent of Paulo Friere's concept of pedagogy of the oppressed—where people move in their relationship to reality from "submergence" to "reflexive awareness" to "co-participation"—these leaders insisted that Ai's gift is at the paradigmatic level. AI is not so much about new knowledge but new knowing. Indeed people frequently talk, as they move through the pedagogy of life-giving Discovery, Dream, and Design, that something suddenly hits home: *that interpretation matters*—that the manner in which they/we read the world filters to the level of our imaginations, our relationships, and ultimately to the direction and meaning of our action. We create the organizational worlds we live in.

What we discovered quite honestly was that momentum for change and long-term sustainability *increased the more we abandoned "delivery" ideas of action planning, monitoring progress, and building implementation strategies.* What was done instead, in several of the most exciting cases, was to focus only on giving Ai away, to everyone, and then stepping back. The GTE story, still unfolding but already attracting national recognition, is suggestive. It is a story that says organization change needs to look a lot more like an inspired movement than a neatly packaged or engineered product. Dan Young, the head of OD at GTE, and his colleagues Maureen Garrison and Jean Moore call it "organizing for change from the grassroots to the frontline". Call it the path of positive protest, or a strategy for positive subversion—whatever it is called it is virtually unstoppable once "it" is up and running. Its structure is called the Positive Change Network (PCN). One especially dramatic moment gives the sense:

> The headline article in **GTE Together** described what was spreading as a grassroots movement to build the new GTE. Initiated as a pilot training to see what would happen if the tools and theories of appreciative inquiry were made available to frontline employees, things started taking off. All of a sudden, without any permission, frontline employees are launching interview studies into positive topics like innovation, inspired leadership, revolutionary customer responsiveness, labor-management partnerships, and "fun". Fresh out of a training session on AI one employee, for example, do 200 interviews into the positive core of a major call center. Who is going say "no" to a complementary request like—"would you help me out…I'm really trying to find out more about the best innovations developing in your area and I see you as someone who could really give me new insight into creating settings where innovation can happen… It is part of my leadership development. Do you have time for an interview…I would be glad to share my learning's with you later!" Soon the topics are finding their way into meetings, corridor conversations, and senior planning sessions—in other words the questions, enthusiastically received, and are changing corporate attention, language, agendas, and learnings. Many start brainstorming applications for AI. Lists are endless. Ever done focus groups with the 100% satisfied customer? How about changing call center measures? What would happen if we replaced the entire deficit measures with equally powerful measures of the positive? How can we revitalize the TQM groups, demoralized by one fishbone analysis after another? What would happen if we augmented variance analysis with depth studies that help people to dream and define the very visions of quality standards? How about a star stories program to generate a narrative rich environment—where customers are asked to share stories of encounters with exceptional employees? How about a gathering with senior executives so we can celebrate our learning's with them, share with them how seeing the positive has changed our work and family lives, and even recruit them to join the PCN?

> The pilot now had a momentum all its own. The immediate response—an avalanche of requests for participation—confirmed that there were large numbers at GTE ready to be called to the task of positive change. To grow the network by the 100s, even thousands, it was decided to do a ten region training session, all linked and downloaded by satellite conferencing. A successful pilot of three sites—Seattle, Indianapolis, and Dallas—confirmed the same kind of energy and response could happen through distance technologies. Quite suddenly the power of a 1000 person network caught people's attention. Just imagine the 1000 "students" of organization life coming together in a year at an AI Summit to share learning from 10,000 innovations discovered at GTE. Very rapidly, by connecting and consistently noticing breakthroughs, new patterns of organizing would become commonplace knowledge. Changes would happen

*not by organized confrontation, diagnosis, burning platforms, or piecemeal reform but through irresistibly vibrant and real visions. And when everyone's awareness grows at the same time—that basic change is taking place in this area and that area, it is easier to coalesce a new consensus that fundamental change is possible. PCN was becoming a lightning rod for energy and enthusiasm we all greatly underestimated. **Then the unions raised questions. There were serious concerns, including the fact that they were not consulted in the early stages. We were told the initiative was over. There was to be a meeting of the unions and GTE at the Federal Mediation Offices in Washington D.C. to put the whole thing to rest.***

But at the meeting with the IBEW and the CWA leaders from both groups said they saw something fresh and unique about AI. They agreed to bring 200 union leaders together for a 2-day introduction. Their purpose: "to evaluate AI...to see if it should have any place in the future at GTE". A month later, the session takes place. It looks like it is going pretty well and then the moment of decision. Tables of eight were instructed to evaluate the ideas and cast a vote as a group: "yes, we endorse moving forward with AI" or "No, we withhold endorsement". For thirty minutes the 30 groups deliberated. Dan Young calls the vote. Tensions are felt. "Table one, how do you vote?" The response was ready: "we vote 100% for moving forward with AI and feel this is a historic opportunity for the whole system". Then the next table: "We vote 100% with a caveat—that every person at GTE have the opportunity to get the AI training, and that all projects going forward be done in partnership, the unions and the company". On and on the vote goes. 30 tables speak. 30 tables vote. Every single one votes to move forward. It was stunning. Eight months later AI is combined with the "conflictive partnership" model of John Calhoun Wells (1996) of the Federal Mediation Services at the kickoff session and announcement of a new era of partnership. The historic statement of Partnership states: "The company and the Unions realize that traditional adversarial labor-management relations must change in order to adapt to the new global telecommunications marketplace. It is difficult to move to cooperation in one quantum leap. However the company and the Unions have agreed to move in a new direction. This new direction emphasizes partnership..."

AI accelerates the nonlinear interaction of organization breakthroughs, putting them together with historic, positive traditions and strengths to create a "convergence zone" facilitating the collective repatterning of human systems. At some point apparently minor positive discoveries connect in accelerating manner and quantum change, a jump from one state to the next that cannot be achieved through incremental change alone, becomes possible. What is needed, as the Destiny Phase of AI suggests, are the network-like structures that liberate not only the daily search into qualities and elements of an organization's positive core but the establishment of a convergence zone for people to empower one another—to connect, cooperate, and cocreate. Changes never thought possible are suddenly and democratically mobilized when people constructively appropriate the power of the positive core and simply... *let go* of accounts of the negative.

But then the question is always voiced: "What do we do with the *real* problems?"

Basic Principles of Appreciative Inquiry

To address this question in anything other than Pollyannaish terms we need to at least comment on the generative-theoretical work that has inspired and given strength too much of Ai in practice. Here are five principles and scholarly streams we consider as central to AI's theory-base of change.

> **The Constructionist Principle:** *Simply stated— human knowledge and organiza-tional destiny are interwoven. To be effective as executives, leaders, change agents, etc., we must be adept in the art of understanding, reading, and analyzing organiza-tions as living, human constructions. Knowing (organizations) stands at the center of any and virtually every attempt at change. Thus, the way we know is fateful.*

At first blush this statement appears simple and obvious enough. We are, as lead-ers and change agents, constantly involved in knowing/inquiring/reading the people and world around us—doing strategic planning analysis, environmental scans, needs analysis, assessments and audits, surveys, focus groups, performance appraisals, and on. Certainly success hinges on such modes of knowing. And this is precisely where things get more interesting *because throughout the academy a revolution is afoot, alive with tremendous ferment and implication, in regards to modernist views of knowledge.* In particu-lar, what is confronted is the Western conception of objective, individualistic, historic knowledge—"a conception that has insinuated itself into virtually all aspects of mod-ern institutional life" (Gergen, 1985, P. 272). At stake are questions that pertain to the deepest dimensions of our being and humanity: how we know what we know, whose voices and interpretations matter, whether the world is governed by external laws inde-pendent of human choices and consciousness, and where is knowledge to be located (in the individual "mind", or out there "externally" in nature or impersonal structures)? At stake are issues that are profoundly fundamental, not just for the future of social science but for the trajectory of all our lives.

In our view the finest work in this area, indeed a huge extension of the most radi-cal ideas in Lewinian thought, can be found in Ken Gergen's *Toward Transformation in Social Knowledge* (1982) and *Realities and Relationships: Soundings In Social Construction* (1994). What Gergen does, in both of these, is synthesize the essential whole of the post modern ferment and crucially takes it beyond disenchantment with the old and offers alternative conceptions of knowledge, fresh discourses on human functioning, new vis-tas for human science, and exciting directions for approaching change. Constuctionism is an approach to human science and practice which replaces the individual with the *relationship* as the locus of knowledge, and thus is built around a keen appreciation of the power of language and discourse of all types (from words to metaphors to narrative forms, etc.) to create our sense of reality—our sense of the true, the good, the possible.

Philosophically it involves a decisive shift in western intellectual tradition from *cogito ergo sum,* **to** *communicamus ergo sum* and in practice constructionism replaces abso-lutist claims or the final word with the never ending collaborative quest to understand and construct options for better living. The purpose of inquiry, which is talked about as totally inseparable and intertwined with action, is the creation of "generative theo-ry", not so much mappings or explanations of yesterday's world but anticipatory artic-ulations of tomorrow's possibilities. Constructionism, because of its emphasis on the communal basis of knowledge and its radical questioning of everything that is taken-for-granted as "objective" or seemingly immutable, invites us to find ways to increase the generative capacity of knowledge. However there are warnings: "Few are pre-pared", says Gergen (1985, p. 271) "for such a wrenching, conceptual dislocation. How-ever, for the innovative, adventurous and resilient, the horizons are exciting indeed." This is precisely the call AI has responded to. Principle number two takes it deeper.

The Principle of Simultaneity: Here it is recognized that inquiry and change are not truly separate moments, but are simultaneous. Inquiry is intervention. The seeds of change—that is, the things people think and talk about, the things people discover and learn, and the things that inform dialogue and inspire images of the future—are implicit in the very first questions we ask. The questions we ask set the stage for what we "find", and what we "discover" (the data) becomes the linguistic material, the stories, out of which the future is conceived, conversed about, and constructed.

One of the most impactful things a change agent or practitioner does is to articulate questions. Instinctively, intuitively and tacitly we all know that research of any kind can, in a flash, profoundly alter the way we see ourselves, view reality, and conduct our lives. Consider the economic poll, or the questions that led to the discovery of the atom bomb, or the surveys that, once leaked, created a riot at a unionized automobile plant in London (see Cooperrider and Srivastva, 1987). If we accept the proposition that patterns of social-organizational action are not fixed by nature in any direct biological or physical way, that human systems are made and imagined in relational settings by human beings (socially constructed), then attention turns to the source of our ideas, our discourses, our researches—that is our questions. Alterations in linguistic practices—including the linguistic practice of crafting questions—hold profound implications for changes in social practice.

One great myth that continues to dampen the potential here is the understanding that first we do an analysis, and then we decide on change. Not so says the constructionist view. Even the most innocent question evokes change—even if reactions are simply changes in awareness, dialogue, feelings of boredom, or even laughter. When we consider the possibilities in these terms, that inquiry and change are a simultaneous moment, we begin reflecting anew. It is not so much "Is my question leading to right or wrong answers?" but rather "What impact is my question having on our lives together…is it helping to generate conversations about the good, the better, the possible… is it strengthening our relationships?"

The Poetic Principle: A metaphor here is that human organizations are a lot more like and open book than, say, a machine. An organization's story is constantly being co-authored. Moreover, pasts, presents, or futures are endless sources of learning, inspiration, or interpretation—precisely like, for example, the endless interpretive possibilities in a good piece of poetry or a biblical text. The important implication is that we can study virtually any topic related to human experience in any human system or organization. We can inquire into the nature of alienation or joy, enthusiasm or low morale, efficiency or excess, in any human organization. There is not a single topic related to organization life that we could not study in any organization.

What constuctionism does is remind us that it is not the "world our there" dictating or driving our topics of inquiry but again the topics are themselves social artifacts, products of social processes (cultural habits, typifying discourses, rhetoric, professional ways, power relations). It is in this vein that AI says lets make sure we are not just reproducing the same worlds over and over again because of the simple and boring repetition of our questions (not "one more" morale survey which everybody can predict the results ahead of time). AI also says, with a sense of excitement and potential, that there can be great gains to be made in a better linking of the means and ends of inquiry. Options now begin to multiply. For example, informally, in many talks with great leaders in the NGO world (Save the Children, World Vision) we have begun to appreciate the profound *joy* that CEO's feel as "servant leaders"— and the role this *positive affect* potentially plays in creating healthy organizations. But then one questions: is there a book on the Harvard Business book-list, or anywhere for that matter, on *Executive Joy*? And even if there isn't… does this mean that joy has nothing to do with good leadership, or healthy human systems? Why aren't we including this topic in our change efforts? What might happen if we did?

The poetic principle invites is re-consideration of aims and focus of any inquiry in the domain of change management. For it is becoming clearer that our topics, like wind-socks, continue to blow steadily onward in the direction of our conventional gaze. As we shall soon explore, seeing the world as a problem has become "very much a way of organizational life".

The Anticipatory Principle: The infinite human resource we have for generating constructive organizational change is our collective imagination and discourse about the future. One of the basic theorems of the anticipatory view of organizational life is that it is the image of the future, which in fact guides what might be called the current behavior of any organism or organization. Much like a movie projector on a screen, human systems are forever projecting ahead of themselves a horizon of expectation (in their talk in the hallways, in the metaphors and language they use) that brings the future powerfully into the present as a mobilizing agent. To inquire in ways that serves to refashion anticipatory reality—especially the artful creation of positive imagery on a collective basis—may be the most prolific thing any inquiry can do.

Our positive images of the future lead our positive actions—this is the increasingly energizing basis and presupposition of Appreciative Inquiry.

Whether we are talking about placebo studies in medicine (Ornstein and Sobel, 1987); reviews of a myriad of studies of the Pygmalion dynamic in the classroom (Jussim, 1986); studies of the rise and fall of cultures (Boulding,1966; Polak, 1973); research into the relationships between optimism and health (Seligman, 1998); studies of positive self-monitoring and ways for accelerating learning (Kirschenbaum, 1984); analysis of the importance of imbalanced, positive inner dialogue to personal and relational well-being (Schwartz, 1986); research on positive mood states and effective decision making Isen, 1983; studies from the domain of "conscious evolution" (Hubbard, 1998); or theories on how positive noticing of even "small wins" can reverberate throughout a system and change the world (Weick, 1990)—the conclusions are converging on something Aristotle said many years ago. "A vivid imagination", he said " compels the whole body to obey it". In the context of more popular writing, Dan Goleman (1987), in a well-written *New York Times* headline-article declares "Research Affirms the Power of Positive Thinking".

The Positive Principle. This last principle is not so abstract. It grows out of years of experience with appreciative inquiry. Put most simply, it has been our experience that building and sustaining momentum for change requires large amounts of positive affect and social bonding—things like hope, excitement, inspiration, caring, camaraderie, sense of urgent purpose, and sheer joy in creating something meaningful together. What we have found is that the more positive the question we ask in our work the more long lasting and successful the change effort. It does not help, we have found, to begin our inquiries from the standpoint of the world as a problem to be solved. We are more effective the longer we can retain the spirit of inquiry of the everlasting beginner. The major thing we do that makes the difference is to craft and seed, in better and more catalytic ways, the unconditional positive question.

Although the positive has not been paraded as a central concept in most approaches to organization analysis and change, it is clear we need no longer be shy about bringing this language more carefully and prominently into our work. And personally speaking it is it is so much healthier. We *love* letting go of "fixing" the world. We *love* doing interviews, hundreds of them, into moments of organization "alive". And we are, quite frankly, more effective the more we are able to learn, to admire, to be surprised, to be inspired alongside the people we are working with. Perhaps it is not just organizations—we too become what we study. So suggested, over and again, is the life-promoting impact of inquiry into the good, the better, and the possible. A theory of affirmative basis of human action and organizing is emerging from many quarters—social contructionism, image theory, conscious evolution and the like. And the whole thing is beginning, we believe, to make a number of our change-management traditions start to look obsolete.

Appreciative Inquiry and Power in Organizations

We could have easily called this section "Eulogy for Problem Solving". In our view the problem solving paradigm, while once perhaps quite effective, is simply out of sync with the realities of today's virtual worlds (Cooperrider, 1996). Problem solving approaches to change are painfully slow (always asking people to look backward to yesterday's causes); they rarely result in new vision (by definition we can describe something as a problem because we already, perhaps implicitly, assume an ideal, so we are not searching to expansive new knowledge of better ideals but searching how to close "gaps"); and in human terms problem approaches are notorious for generating defensiveness (it is not my problem but yours). But our real concern, from a social constructionist perspective, has to do with relations of power and control. It is the most speculative part of this chapter; and hopefully, it better illuminates the potentials advocated by AI. In particular is the more conscious linking of language, including the language of our own profession, to change. Words do create worlds—even in unintended ways.

> It was an unforgettable moment in a conference on AI for inner city change agents, mostly community mobilizers from the Saul Alinsky school of thought (**Rules for Radicals**), in Chicago. After two days a participant challenges: "This is naïve...have you ever worked in the depths of the inner city, like the Cabrini Green public housing projects?. You're asking me to go in and "appreciate" it...just yesterday I'm there and the impoverished children are playing soccer, not with a ball, no money for that, but with a dead rat. Tell me about appreciative inquiry in the housing projects!

A powerful question. It was one that made us go deeper theoretically. At one level we were arguing typical approaches to problem diagnosis, including the Alinsky confrontation methods, would work, but at about half the speed of AI. But then as we explored the subject of the *cultural consequences of deficit discourse* we began seeing a disconcerting relationship between the society-wide escalation of deficit-based change methods and the *erosion of people power*. The analysis, from here, could proceed from virtually any "professional" discipline—the diagnostic vocabularies of social work, medicine, organization development, management, law, accounting, community development, editing—but lets begin with psychology and the social sciences (ample linkage will be made to our own field). Ken Gergen's (1994) work, again, is at the forefront for anyone wanting something more than a suggestive summary.

Consider the following characterizations of the self: *impulsive personality, narcissism, anti-social personality, reactive depressive, codependent, self-alienated, type-A, paranoid, stressed, repressed, authoritarian, midlife crisis.* These are all terms commonly used by the mental-health professions and are now common among people in the culture itself. But importantly these terms, and several thousand others (see the 1996) have come into conventional usage only within the present century, many in only the last decade. But something else is noteworthy: the terminology's discredit, draw attention to problems, shortcomings, and incapacity's. Interestingly, the trajectory of the "professional" development of *vocabularies of human deficit* is rising at geometric rates, correlated as might be expected with the sheer growth in numbers of the profession. In 1892 when the American Psychological association was founded there were 31 members. By 1906 there were 181. The next thirty-one years witnessed an expansion of almost a hundredfold, to over 3000. In the next twenty-two years the figure grew again by twenty times, over 63,000. Add to this similar growth figures in social work, psychiatry, community development, and organization development and one realizes that the spiraling production of languages of deficit have become quite a growth industry. By 1980 mental illness was the third most expensive category of health disorder in the United States at more then $20 billion annually. By 1983, the costs for mental illness, exclusive of alcoholism and drug abuse, were estimated to be almost $73 billion. We have no figures for the consulting industry, but we can guess. While intentions are good, argues Gergen, some of the unintended consequences may not be.

From a constructionist perspective one realizes that words do not so much innocently "mirror" a world out there as they become vehicles for coordinating our actions with one another. Words in any profession function a bit like tools of the trade. When I used to give my son Matt a hammer, inevitably everything in the house soon became a nail.What happens when the "scientifically" legitimated vocabularies of human deficit become the common and explicit tool kit of all? Gergen suggests not everything about it is healthy. Such deficit discourse, when chronically used, "generates a network of increasing entanglements for the culture at large. Such entanglements are not only self serving for the professions, they also add exponentially to the sense of human misery" (1994 p. 142).

In particular deficit based change approaches have an unfortunate propensity to *reinforce hierarchy,* wherein "less than ideal" individuals, who learn to accept what sometimes becomes a lifelong label, are encouraged to enter "treatment programs" under expert supervision; to *erode community,* wherein the the mental health professions appropriate the process of interpersonal realignment that might otherwise (in other eras) have happened in a nonprofessional contexts like the family or community; to instill a sense of *self-enfeeblement,*wherein deficit terms essentialize the person and like a birthmark or fingerprint, the deficit is expected to inevitably manifest itself into many aspects of their lives (it is a "thing"); *to stimulate endless vocabulary expansion* wherein people increasingly construct their problems in the professional languages (diagnosing each other) and seek more help which in turn increased the numbers in the profession who are rewarded when they expand the vocabulary—"to explore a new disorder within the mental health sciences is not unlike discovering a new star in astronomy (p.159)". Gergen sums up: "As I am proposing, when the culture is furnished with a professionally rationalized language of mental deficit and people are increasingly understood according to this language, the population of "patients" expands. This population, in turn, forces the profession to extend its vocabulary, and thus the array of mental deficit terms available for cultural use (p.161). Is there no exit from such progressive infirmity?

After talking this over with the people in the inner city Chicago conference—and tracing the vocabularies of human deficit not only to the rise of the professions but also to the rise of bureaucracy, skeptical science, original sin theological accounts, the cynical media—the Alinsky trained activist sat down in a gasp. He said: "in the name of entertainment my people are being fed negative views of human violence—and they are surrounded by endless description of their negative "needs" their "problem lives". Even in my methods, the same. And what do I see? I see people asleep in front of their TVs. Unable to move, like sleeping dogs. Yes they have voice in the housing project assessments. But it is a certain kind of voice…it is visionless voice. They get to confirm the deficit analysis; all the reports are the same. "Yes" they say, "The reports are true". What is hitting me right now is how radical the AI message might be. Marx could have said it better: perhaps the vocabularies of human deficit are the opiates of the masses. People have voice in the analyses—this involvement is what we fought for. But people are not mobilized by it anymore. No, they are asleep. Visionless voice is probably worse than no voice.

Elsewhere we have cautioned, in our own discipline, that it is not so much the problem solving *methodologies* per se that are of central concern but the growing sense that we all, throughout the culture, have taken the tools a step further. It is not so much that organizations *have* problems, they *are problems* (see **figure two**). Somewhere a shift of this kind has taken place. Once accepted as fundamental truth about organizations, virtually everything in change-management becomes infused with a deficit consciousness. For example as French and Bell (1995) define it, "Action-research is both an approach to *problem solving*—a model or paradigm, and a *problem solving process*—a series of activities and events" (p. 88). Levinson, in the classic on *Organizational Diagnosis* (1972) likens it to therapy—"like a therapeutic or teaching relationship it should be an alliance of both parties to discover and resolve these problems…*looking for experiences which appear stressful to people. What kinds of occurrences disrupt or disorganize people?* (p. 37).

Figure 2: Two Paradigms for Organizational Change

Paradigm 1: Problem Solving	Paradigm 2: Appreciative Inquiry
"Felt Need" Identification of Problem	Appreciating and Valuing The Best of "What Is"
⇓	⇓
Analysis of Causes	Envisioning "What Might Be"
⇓	⇓
Analysis and Possible Solutions	Dialoguing "What Should Be"
⇓	⇓
Action Planning (Treatment)	
⇓	
Basic Assumption: An Organization is a Problem to be Solved.	*Basic Assumption: An Organization is a Mystery to be Embraced.*

Chris Argyris, again in another classic, asserts: One condition that seems so basic as to be defined as axiomatic is the generation of *valid information*...Valid information is that which describes the factors, plus their interrelationships, that *create the problem (1970, pp.16-17).*

Tough questions remain about power and deficit discourse. And of course there are an array of new innovations in the field, many in this volume, that are signaling significant departures. So at this point all we want to do is make a call for reflection and caution, taking a lesson from the wisdom of anthropology—*beware of the solid truths of one's own culture.*

Conclusion

To be sure *Appreciative Inquiry (AI)* begins an adventure. The urge and call to adventure has been sounded by many people and many organizations, and it will take many more to fully explore the vast vistas that are now appearing on the horizon.

As said at the outset we believe we are infants when it comes to our understanding of appreciative processes of knowing and social construction. Yet we are increasingly clear the world is ready to leap beyond methodologies of deficit based changes and enter a domain that is life-centric. Organizations, says AI theory, are centers of human relatedness, first and foremost, and relationships thrive where there is an appreciative eye—when people see the best in one another, when they share their dreams and ultimate concerns in affirming ways, and when they are connected in full voice to create not just new worlds but better worlds. The velocity and largely informal spread of the appreciative learnings suggests, we believe, a growing sense of disenchantment with exhausted theories of change, especially those wedded to vocabularies of human deficit, and a corresponding urge to work with people, groups, and organizations in more constructive, positive, life-affirming, even spiritual ways. AI, we hope it is being said, is more than a simple 4-D cycle of discovery, dream, design, and destiny; what is being introduced is something deeper at the core.

Perhaps our inquiry must become the positive revolution we want to see in the world? Albert Einstein's words clearly compel: *"There are only two ways to live your life. One is as though nothing is a miracle. The other is as though everything is a miracle".*

Appreciative Inquiry in Organizational Life

David L. Cooperrider and Suresh Srivastva
Case Western Reserve University

Abstract

This chapter presents a conceptual refiguration of action-research based on a "sociorationalist" view of science. The position that is developed can be summarized as follows: For action-research to reach its potential as a vehicle for social innovation it needs to begin advancing theoretical knowledge of consequence; that good theory may be one of the best means human beings have for affecting change in a postindustrial world; that the discipline's steadfast commitment to a problem solving view of the world acts as a primary constraint on its imagination and contribution to knowledge; that *appreciative inquiry* represents a viable complement to conventional forms of action-research; and finally, that through our assumptions and choice of method we largely create the world we later discover.

> *We are sometime truly to see our life as positive, not negative, as made up of continuous willing, not of constraints and prohibition.*
>
> *–Mary Parker Follett*

> *We are steadily forgetting how to dream; in historical terms, the mathematicist and technicist dimensions of Platonism have conquered the poetical, mythical, and rhetorical context of analysis. We are forgetting how to be reasonable in nonmathematical dialects.*
>
> *—Stanley Rosen*

Introduction

This chapter presents a conceptual reconfiguration of action research. In it we shall argue for a multidimensional view of action-research which seeks to both generate theory and develop organizations. The chapter begins with the observation that action-research has become increasingly rationalized and enculturated to the point where it risks becoming little more than a crude empiricism imprisoned in a deficiency mode of thought. In its conventional *unidimensional* form action research has largely failed as an instrument for advancing social knowledge of consequence and has not, therefore, achieved its potential as a vehicle for human development and social-organizational transformation. While the literature consistently signals the worth of action-research as a managerial tool for problem solving ("first-order" incremental change), it is conspicuously quiet concerning reports of discontinuous change of the "second order" where organizational paradigms, norms, ideologies, or values are transformed in fundamental ways (Watzlawick, et al., 1974).

Cooperrider, D.L., Srivastva, S. (1999). *Appreciative Inquiry in Organizational Life. Appreciative Management and Leadership.* Euclid, OH, Lakeshore Communications: 401-441.

In the course of this chapter we shall touch broadly upon a number of interrelated concerns—scientific, metaphysical, normative, and pragmatic. Linking these streams is an underlying conviction that action-research has the potential to be to the postindustrial era what "scientific management" was to the industrial. Just as scientific management provided the philosophical and methodological legitimacy required to support the bureaucratic organizational form (Clegg and Dunkerly, 1980; Braverman, 1974), action-research may yet provide the intellectual rationale and reflexive methodology required to support the emergence of a more egalitarian "postbureaucratic" form of organization. Unlike scientific management however, which provided the means for a technorational science of administration, action-research holds unique and essential promise in the sociorational realm of human affairs. It has the potential to become the paradigmatic basis of a truly significant—a humanly significant—generative science of administration.

In the first part of the essay it is suggested that the primary barrier limiting the potential of action-research has been its romance with "action" at the expense of "theory." This tendency has led many in the discipline to seriously underestimate the power of theory as a means for social-organizational reconstruction. Drawing largely on the work of Kenneth Gergen (1978, 1982), we re-examine the character of theoretical knowledge and its role in social transformation, and then appeal for a redefinition of the scientific aims of action-research that will dynamically reunite theory and practice. The aim of science is not the detached discovery and verification of social laws allowing for prediction and control. Highlighted here instead, is an alternative understanding that defines social and behavioral science in terms of its "generative capacity," that is, its "capacity to challenge the guiding assumptions of the culture, to raise fundamental questions regarding contemporary social life, to foster reconsideration of that which is 'taken for granted' and thereby furnish new alternatives for social actions" (Gergen, 1978, p. 1346).

Assuming that generative theory is a legitimate product of scientific work and is, in fact, capable of provoking debate, stimulating normative dialogue, and furnishing conceptual alternatives needed for social transformation, then why has action-research till now so largely downplayed creative theorizing in its work with organizations? Here we will move to the heart of the chapter and argue that the generative incapacity of contemporary action-research derives from the discipline's unquestioned commitment to a secularized problem-oriented view of the world and thus to the subsequent loss of our capacity as researchers and participants to marvel, and in marveling to embrace, the miracle and mystery of social organization. If we acknowledge Abraham Maslow's (1968) admonition that true science begins and ends in wonder, then we immediately shed light on why action-research has failed to produce innovative theory capable of inspiring the imagination, commitment, and passionate dialogue required for the consensual re-ordering of social conduct.

Appreciative inquiry is presented here as a mode of action-research that meets the criteria of science as spelled out in generative-theoretical terms. Going beyond questions of epistemology, appreciative inquiry has as its basis a metaphysical concern: it posits that social existence as such is a miracle that can never be fully comprehended (Quinney, 1982; Marcel, 1963). Proceeding from this level of understanding we begin to explore the uniqueness of the appreciative mode. More than a method or technique, the appreciative mode of inquiry is a way of living with, being with, and directly participating in the varieties of social organization we are compelled to study. Serious consideration and reflection on the ultimate mystery of being engenders a reverence for life that draws the researcher to inquire beyond superficial appearances to deeper levels of the life generating essentials and potentials of social existence. That is, the action researcher is drawn to affirm, and thereby illuminate, the factors and forces involved in organizing that serve to nourish the human spirit. Thus, this chapter seeks to enrich our conception of administrative behavior by introducing a "second dimension" of action-research that goes beyond merely a secularized problem-solving frame.

The proposal that appreciative inquiry represents a distinctive complement to traditional action-research will be unfolded in the following way: First, the role of theory as an enabling agent of social transformation will be considered; such consideration can help to eliminate the artificial dualism separating theory from practice. Second, we will challenge the problem-oriented view of organizing inherent in traditional definitions of action-research, and describe an affirmative form of inquiry uniquely suited for discovering generative theory. Finally, these insights will be brought together in a general model of the conceptual underpinnings of appreciative inquiry.

Toward Generative Theory in Action-Research

The current decade has witnessed a confluence of thinking concerning the paradigmatic refiguration of social thought. As Geertz (1980) notes, there is now even a "blurring of genres" as many social scientists have abandoned—without apology—the misdirected quest to mimic the "more mature" physical sciences. Turning away from a Newtonian laws-and-instances-type explanation rooted in logical empiricist philosophy, many social theorists have instead opted for an interpretive form of inquiry that connects organized action to its contextually embedded set of meanings, "looking less for the sorts of things that connect planets and pendulums and more for the sorts that connect chrysanthemums and swords" (Geertz, 1980, p. 165).

In the administrative sciences, in particular, this recent development has been translated into observable movement away from mechanistic research designs intended objectively to establish universal causal linkages between variables, such as organizational size and level of centralization, or between technology, environment, and organizational structure. Indeed, prominent researchers in the field have publicly given up the logical positivist idea of "certainly through science" and are now embarking on approaches to research that grant preeminence to the historically situated and ever-changing "interpretive schemes" used by members of a given group to give life and meaning to their actions and decisions (Bartunek, 1984). Indicative of the shift away from the logical positivist frame, researchers are converging around what has been termed the "sociorationalist" metatheory of science (Gergen, 1982). Recognizing the symbolic nature of the human universe, we now find a flurry of innovative work supporting the thesis that there is little about human development or organizational behavior that is "preprogrammed" or stimulus-bound in any direct physical or biological way. In this sense, the social universe is open to indefinite revision, change, and self-propelled development. And, this recognition is crucial because to the extent to which social existence is situated in a symbolic realm, beyond deterministic forces, then to that extent the logical positivist foundation of social science is negated and its concept of knowledge rendered illusionary.

Nowhere is this better evidenced than in the variety of works concerned with such topics as organizational paradigms (Brown, 1978; McHugh, 1970); beliefs and master scripts (Sproull, 1981; Beyer, 1981); idea management and the executive mind (Srivastva, 1983; 1985); theories of action and presumptions of logic (Argyris and Schon, 1980; Weick, 1983); consciousness and awareness (Harrison, 1982; Lukes, 1974); and, of course, an array of work associated with the concept of organizational or corporate culture (Ouchi and Johnson, 1978; Schein, 1983; Van Maanen, 1982; Deal and Kennedy, 1982; Sathe, 1983; Hofstede, 1980). As Ellwood prophetically suggested almost half a century ago, "This is the cultural view of human society that is [or will be] revolutionizing the social sciences" (Ellwood, 1938, p. 561).

This developing consensus on the importance of the symbolic realm—on the power of ideas—by such independent sources embracing such diverse objectives reflects the reality of organized life in the modern world. However reluctantly, even the most traditional social thinkers are now recognizing the distinctiveness of the postindustrial world for what truly is—an unfolding drama of human interaction whose potential seems limited or enhanced primarily by our symbolic capacities for constructing meaningful agreements that allow for the committed enactment of collective life.

Never before in history have ideas, information, and beliefs—or theory—been so central in the formulation of reality itself. Social existence, of course, has always depended on some kind of idea system for its meaningful sustenance. The difference now, however, is that what was once background has become foreground. Today, the very fact that society continues to exist at all is experienced not so much mechanistically (an extension of machines) or even naturalistically (a by-product of fateful nature) but more and more humanistically as a social construction of interacting minds—"a game between persons" (Bell, 1973). And under these conditions—as a part of the change from an agrarian society to a goods-producing society at first and then to an information society—ideas and meaning systems take on a whole new life and character. Ideas are thrust center stage as the prime unit of relational exchange governing the creation or obliteration of social existence.

This line of argument applies no less potently to current conceptions of social science. To the extent that the primary product of science is systematically refined idea systems—or theory—science too must be recognized as a powerful agent in the enhancement or destruction of human life. And while this presents an unresolvable dilemma for a logical empiricist conception of science, it spells real opportunity (and responsibility) for a social science that wishes to be of creative significance to society. Put most simply, the theoretical contributions of science may be among the most powerful resources human beings have for contributing to change and development in the groups and organizations in which they live. This is precisely the meaning of Kurt Lewin's early view of action-science when he proposed: "There is nothing so practical as good theory" (1951, p. 169).

Ironically, the discipline of action-research continues to insist on a sharp separation of theory and practice, and to underrate the role of theory in social reconstruction. The irony is that it does so precisely at a time when the cultural view of organizing is reaching toward paradigmatic status. The sad and perhaps tragic commentary on action-research is that it is becoming increasingly inconsequential just as its opportunity to contribute is on the rise (Argyris, 1983).

Observers such as Rappaport (1970) and Bartunek (1983) have lamented the fact that action-researchers have come to subordinate research aims to action interests. Levinson (1972) has gone even further by branding the discipline "atheoretical." And, Friedlander and Brown (1974) have noted that the definition of action-research in classic texts give virtually no mention to theory-building as an integral and necessary component of the research/diagnostic process, or the process of organizational change. Whenever theory is mentioned, it is almost always referred to as a springboard for research or diagnosis, not the other way around. Bartunek (1983, pp. 34) concludes that "even the most recent papers that describe action-research strategies tend to focus primarily on the process of action-research and only secondarily on the specific theoretical contributions of the outcomes of such research" (e.g., Frohman, Sashkin, and Kavanaugh, 1976; Shani and Pasmore, 1982; Susman and Evered, 1978; see Pasmore and Friedlander, 1982, for an exception). For those of us trained in the field this conclusion is not surprising. Indeed, few educational programs in organizational behavior even consider theory-building as a formal part of their curriculum, and even fewer place a real premium on the development of the theoretical mind and imagination of their students.

According to Argyris (1983), this lack of useful theorizing is attributable to two major factors. On the one hand practice-oriented scholars have tended to become so client-centered that they fail to question their clients' own definition of a problem and thereby to build testable propositions and theories that are embedded in everyday life. Academics, on the other hand, who are trained to be more scientific in their bent, also undercut the development of useful theory by their very insistence on the criteria of "normal" science and research—detachment, rigor, unilateral control, and operational precision. In a word, creative theorizing has literally been assaulted on all fronts by practitioners and academic scientists alike. It must also be noted that implicit in this critique by Argyris (1983), and others (e.g., Friedlander and Brown, 1974), is an underlying assumption that action-research has built into it certain natural conflicts that are likely to lead either to "action" (consulting) or "research" (diagnosis or the development of organizational theory), but not to both.

The situation is summed up by Friedlander and Brown (1974) in their comprehensive review of the field:

> We believe that research will either play a far more crucial role in the advancement of this field, or become an increasingly irrelevant appendage to it.... We have generally failed to produce a theory of change, which emerges from the change process itself. We need a way of enriching our understanding and action synergistically rather than at one or the other's expense—to become a science in which knowledge-getting and knowledge-giving are an integrated process, and one that is valuable to all parties involved (p. 319).

Friedlander and Brown concluded with a plea for a metatheoretical revision of science that will integrate theory and practice. But in another review over a decade later, Friedlander (1984) observed little progress coming from top scholars in the discipline. He then put words to a mounting frustration over what appears as a recurring problem:

> They pointed to the shortcomings of traditional research and called for emancipation from it, but they did not indicate a destination. There is as yet no new paradigm that integrates research and practice, or even optimizes useful knowledge for organizations.... I'm impatient. Let's get on with it. Let's not talk it, write it, analyze it, conceptualize it, or research it. Instead let's actively engage and experiment with new designs for producing knowledge that is, in fact, used by organizations (p. 647).

This recurrent problem is the price we pay for continuing to talk about theory and practice in dualistic terms. In a later section in this chapter another hypothesis will be advanced on why there is this lack of creative theorizing, specifically as it relates to action-research. But first we need to look more closely at the claim that social theory and social practice are, indeed, part of a synthetic whole. We need to elaborate on the idea that scientific theory is a means for both understanding and improving social practice. We need to examine exactly what it means to merge the idea and the act, the symbolic and the sociobehavioral, into a powerful and integral unity.

The Sociorationalist Alternative

As the end of the twentieth century nears, thinkers in organizational behavior are beginning to see, without hesitation, why an administrative science based on a physical science model is simply not adequate as a means for understanding or contributing in relevant ways to the workings of complex, organized human systems (see, for example, Susman and Evered, 1978; Beyer and Trice, 1982). Kurt Lewin had understood this almost half a century earlier but his progressive vision of an action science fell short of offering a clear metatheoretical alternative to conventional conceptions of science (Peters and Robinson, 1984). Indeed, the epistemological ambiguity inherent in Lewin's writing has been cited as perhaps the critical shortcoming of all his work. And yet, in hindsight, it can be argued that the ambiguity was intentional and perhaps part of Lewin's social sensitivity and genius. As Gergen (1982) suggests, the metatheoretical ambiguity in Lewin's work might well have been a protective measure, an attempt to shield his fresh vision of an action science from the fully dominant logical positivist temper of his time. In any event, whether planned or not, Lewin walked a tightrope between two fundamentally opposed views of science and never did make clear how theory could be used as both an interpretive and a creative element. This achievement, as we might guess, would have to wait for a change in the intellectual ethos of social science.

That change, as we earlier indicated, is now taking place. Increasingly the literature signals a disenchantment with theories of science that grants priority to the external world in the generation of human knowledge. Instead there is growing movement toward granting preeminence to the cognitive processes of mind and the symbolic processes of social construction. In *Toward Transformation in Social Knowledge* (1982), Kenneth Gergen synthesizes the essential whole of this movement and takes it one crucial step beyond disenchantment to a bold, yet workable conception of science that firmly unites theory with practice—and thereby elevates the status of theoretical-scientific work. From a historical perspective there is no question that this is a major achievement; it brings to completion the work abruptly halted by Lewin's untimely death. But more than that, what Gergen offers, albeit indirectly, is a desperately needed clue to how we can revitalize an action-research discipline that has never reached its potential. While a complete statement of the emerging sociorationalist metatheory is beyond the scope of this chapter, it is important at least to outline the general logic of the perspective, including its basic assumptions.

At the heart of sociorationalism is the assumption of impermanence—the fundamental instability of social order. No matter what the durability to date, virtually any pattern of social action is open to infinite revision. Accepting for a moment the argument of the social constructionists that social reality, at any given point, is a product of broad social agreement (shared meanings), and further granting a linkage between the conceptual schemes of a culture and its other patterns of action, we must seriously consider the idea that alterations in conceptual practices, in ways of symbolizing the world, hold tremendous potential for guiding changes in the social order. To understand the importance of these assumptions and their meaning for social science, let us quote Gergen (1982) at length:

> Is not the range of cognitive heuristics that may be employed in solving problems of adaptation limited only by the human imagination?
>
> One must finally consider the possibility that human biology not only presents to the scientist an organism whose actions may vary in an infinity of ways, but it may ensure as well that novel patterns are continuously emerging... variations in human activity may importantly be traced to the capacities of the organism for symbolic restruc-

turing. As it is commonly said, one's actions appear to be vitally linked to the manner in which one understands or construes the world of experience. The stimulus world does not elicit behavior in an automatic, reflex-like fashion. Rather, the symbolic translation of one's experiences virtually transforms their implications and thereby alters the range of one's potential reactions. Interestingly, while formulations of this variety are widely shared within the scientific community, very little attention has been paid to their ramifications for a theory of science. As is clear, without such regularities the prediction of behavior is largely obviated... to the extent that the individual is capable of transforming the meaning of stimulus conditions in an indeterminate number of ways, existing regularities must be considered historically contingent—dependent on the prevailing meaning systems of conceptual structure of the times. In effect, from this perspective the scientist's capacity to locate predictable patterns of interaction depends importantly on the extent to which the population is both homogeneous and stable in its conceptual constructions (pp. 1617).

While this type of reasoning is consistent with the thinking of many social scientists, the ramifications are rarely taken to their logical conclusion: "Virtually unexamined by the field is the potential of science to shape the meaning systems of the society and thus the common activities of the culture" (Gergen, 1978, p. 1349). Virtually unexamined is the important role that science can—and does—play in the scientific construction of social reality.

One implication of this line of thought is that to the extent the social science conceives its role in the logical positivist sense, with its goals being prediction and control, it not only serves the interests of the status quo (you can't have "good science" without stable replication and verification of hypotheses) but it also seriously underestimates the power and usefulness of its most important product, namely theory; it underestimates the constructive role science can have in the development of the groups and organizations that make up our cultural world. According to Gergen, realization of this fact furnishes the opportunity to refashion a social science of vital significance to society. To do this, we need a bold shift in attention whereby theoretical accounts are no longer judged in terms of their predictive capacity, but instead are judged in terms of their generative capacity—their ability to foster dialogue about that which is taken for granted and their capacity for generating fresh alternatives for social action. Instead of asking, "Does this theory correspond with the observable facts?" the emphasis for evaluating good theory becomes, "To what extent does this theory present provocative new possibilities for social action, and to what extent does it stimulate normative dialogue about how we can and should organize ourselves?" The complete logic for such a proposal may be summarized in the following ten points:

1. The social order at any given point is viewed as the product of broad social agreement, whether tacit or explicit.

2. Patterns of social-organizational action are not fixed by nature in any direct biological or physical way; the vast share of social conduct is potentially stimulus-free, capable of infinite conceptual variation.

3. From an observational point of view, all social action is open to multiple interpretations, no one of which is superior in any objective sense. The interpretations (for example, "whites are superior to blacks") favored in one historical setting may be replaced in the next.

4 Historically embedded conventions govern what is taken to be true or valid, and to a large extent govern what we, as scientists and lay persons, are able to see. All observation, therefore, is theory-laden and filtered through conventional belief sys-

tems and theoretical lenses.2

5. To the extent that action is predicated on ideas, beliefs, meanings, intentions, or theory, people are free to seek transformations in conventional conduct by changing conventional codes (idea systems).

6. The most powerful vehicle communities have for transforming their conventions—their agreements on norms, values, policies, purposes, and ideologies—is through the act of dialogue made possible by language. Alterations in linguistic practices, therefore, hold profound implications for changes in social practice.

7. Social theory can be viewed as a highly refined language with a specialized grammar all its own. As a powerful linguistic tool created by trained linguistic experts (scientists), theory may enter the conceptual meaning system of culture and in doing so alter patterns of social action.

8. Whether intended or not, all theory is normative and has the potential to influence the social order—even if reactions to it are simply boredom, rebellion, laughter, or full acceptance.

9. Because of this, all social theory is morally relevant; it has the potential to affect the way people live their ordinary lives in relation to one another. This point is a critical one because there is no such thing as a detached/technical/scientific mode for judging the ultimate worth of value claims.

10.   Valid knowledge or social theory is therefore a communal creation. Social knowledge is not "out there" in nature to be discovered through detached, value-free, observational methods (logical empiricism); nor can it be relegated to the subjective minds of isolated individuals (solipsism). Social knowledge resides in the interactive collectivity; it is created, maintained, and put to use by the human group. Dialogue, free from constraint or distortion, is necessary to determine the "nature of things" (sociorationalism).

In **Table 3.1** the metatheory of sociorationalism is both summarized and contrasted to the commonly held assumptions of the logical empiricist view of science. Especially important to note is the transformed role of the scientist when social inquiry is viewed from the perspective of sociorationalism. Instead of attempting to present oneself as an impartial bystander or dispassionate spectator of the inevitable, the social scientist conceives of himself or herself as an active agent, an invested participant whose work might well become a powerful source of change in the way people see and enact their worlds. Driven by a desire to "break the hammerlock" of what appears as given in human nature, the scientist attempts to build theories that can expand the realm of what is conventionally understood as possible. In this sense the core impact of sociorationalist metatheory is that it invites, encourages, and requires that students of social life rigorously exercise their theoretical imagination in the service of their vision of the good. Instead of denial it is an invitation to fully accept and exercise those qualities of mind and action that make us uniquely human.

Now we turn to a question raised earlier: How does theory achieve its capacity to affect social practice, and what are some of the specific characteristics of generative theory?

The Power of Theory in Understanding Organizational Life

The sociorationalist vision of science is of such far-reaching importance that no student, organizational scientist, manager, educator, or action-researcher can afford to ignore it. Good theory, as we have suggested, is one of the most powerful means we have for

Table 3.1: Comparison of Logical Empiricist and Socio-Rationalist Conceptions of Social Science

Dimension for Comparison	Logical Empiricism	Socio-Rationalism
01. Primary Function of Science	Enhance goals of understanding, prediction, and control by discerning general laws or principles governing the relationship among units of observable phenomena.	Enhance understanding in the sense of assigning meaning to something, thus creating its status through the use of concepts. Science is a means for expanding flexibility and choice in cultural evolution.
02. Theory of Knowledge and Mind	Exogenic—grants priority to the external world in the generation of human knowledge (i.e., the preeminence of objective fact). Mind is a mirror.	Endogenic—holds the processes of mind and symbolic interaction as preeminent source of human knowledge. Mind is both a mirror and a lamp.
03. Perspective on Time	Assumption of temporal irrelevance: searches for transhistorical principles.	Assumption of hstorically and contextually relevant meanings; existing regularities in social order are contingent on prevailing meaning systems.
04. Assuming Stability of Social Patterns	Social phenomena are sufficiently stable, enduring, reliable and replicable to allow for lawful principles.	Social order is fundamentally unstable. Social phenomena are guided by cognitive heuristics, limited only by the human imagination: the social order is a subject matter capable of infinite variation through the linkage ofideas and action.
05. Value Stance	Separation of fact and values. Possibility of objective knowledge through behavioral observation.	Social sciences are fundamentally nonobjective. Any behavioral event is open to virtually any interpretative explanation. All interpretation is filtered through prevailing values of a culture. "There is no description without prescription."
06. Features of "Good" Theory	Discovery of transhistorically valid principles; a theory's correspondence with face.	Degree to which theory furnishes alternatives for social innovation and thereby opens vistas for action; expansion of "the realm of the possible."
07. Criteria for Confirmation or Verification (Life of a Theory)	Logical consistency and empirical prediction; subject to falsification.	Persuasive appeal, impace, and overall generative capacity; subject to community agreement; truth is a product of a community of truth makers.
08. Role of Scientist	Impartial bystander and dispassionate spectator of the inevitable; content to accept that which seems given.	Active agent and coparticipant who is primarily a source of linguistic activity (theoretical language) which serves as input into common meaning systems. Interested in "breaking the hammerlock" of what appears as given in human nature.
09. Chief Product of Research	Cumulation of objective knowledge through the production of empirically disconfirmable hypothesis.	Continued improvement in theory building capacity; improvement in the capacity to create generative-theoretical language.
10. Emphasis in the Education of Future Social Science Professionals	Rigorous experimental methods and statistical analysis; a premium is placed on method (training in theory construction is a rarity).	Hermenuetic interpretation and catalytic theorizing; a premium is placed on the theoretical imagination. Sociorationalism invites the student toward intellectual expression in the service of his or her vision of the good.

helping social systems evolve, adapt, and creatively alter their patterns over time. Building further on this metatheoretical perspective we can talk about five ways by which theory achieves its exceptional potency:

1. Establishing a conceptual and contextual frame;
2. Providing presumptions of logic;
3. Transmitting a system of values;
4. Creating a group-building language;
5. Extending visions of possibility or constraint.

Establishing a Perceptual and Contextual Frame

To the extent that theory is the conceptual imposition of order upon an otherwise "booming, bustling, confusion that is the realm of experience" (Dubin, 1978), the theorist's first order of business is to specify what is there to be seen, to provide an "ontological education" (Gergen, 1982). The very act of theoretical articulation, therefore, highlights not only the parameters of the topic or subject matter, but becomes an active agent as a cueing device, a device that subtly focuses attention on particular phenomena or meanings while obscuring others. In the manner of a telescope or lens, a new theory allows one to see the world in a way perhaps never before imagined.

For example, when American eugenicists used the lens of biological determinism to attribute diseases of poverty to the inferior genetic construction of poor people, they literally could see no systematic remedy other than sterilization of the poor. In contrast, when Joseph Goldberg theorized that pellagra was not genetically determined but culturally caused (as a result of vitamin deficiency and the eating habits of the poor), he could discover a way to cure it (Gould, 1981). Similarly, theories about the "survival of the fittest" might well help executives locate "predators," "hostile environments," and a world where self interest reigns, where it is a case of "eat or be eaten." Likewise, theories of leadership have been known quickly to facilitate the discovery of Theory X and Theory Y interaction. Whatever the theory, it provides a potential means for members of a culture to navigate in an otherwise neutral, meaningless, or chaotic sea of people, interactions and events. By providing an "ontological education" with respect to what is there, a theory furnishes an important cultural input that affects people's cognitive set. In this sense "the world is not so constituted until the lens is employed. With each new distinction the groundwork is laid for alterations in existing patterns of conduct" (Gergen, 1982, p. 23).

As the reader may already surmise, an important moral issue begins to emerge here. Part of the reason that theory is, in fact, powerful is that it shapes perceptions, cognition's, and preferences often at a preconscious level, much like subliminal communications or even hypnosis. Haley (1973) talks about how Milton Erickson has made this a central feature of this psychotherapeutic work. But Lukes (1974) cautions that such thought control may be "the supreme and most insidious exercise of power," especially when it prevents people from challenging their role in the existing order of things and when it operates contrary to their real interests.

Providing Presumptions of Logic

Theories are also powerful to the extent to which they help shape common expectations of causality, sequence, and relational importance of phenomena within a theoretical equation. Consider, for example, the simple logic underlying almost every formal performance-appraisal system. Stripped to essentials, the theoretical underpinnings run something like this: "If you want to evaluate performance (P), then you must evaluate the individual employee (E); in other words, 'P = E'." Armed with this theory, many managers have entered the performance-appraisal meeting shaking with the thought of having to pass godlike judgment on some employee. Similarly, the employee arrives at the meeting with an arsenal of defenses, designed to protect his or her hard-won self-esteem. Little genuine communication occurs during the meeting and virtually no problem-solving takes place. The paperwork is mechanically completed, then filed away in the personnel office until the next year. So powerful is this subtle P = E equation that any alternative goes virtually unnoticed, for example the Lewinian theory that behavior (performance) is a function of the person and the environment (in this case the organizational situation, the "OS" in which the employee works). Following this Lewinian line, the theory underlying performance appraisal would now have to be expanded to read P = E ´ OS. That is, P ? E. To adequately assess performance there must be an assessment of the individual in relation to the organizational setting in which he or she works and vice-versa. What would happen to the performance-appraisal process if this more complete theory were used as a basis for re-designing appraisal systems in organizations throughout the corporate world? Isn't it possible that such a theory could help shift the attribution process away from the person-blame to systems analysis?3 By attributing causality, theories have the potential to create the very phenomena they propose to explain. Karl Weick, in a recent article examining managerial thought in the context of action, contends that thought and action are part and parcel of one another; thinking is best viewed as a kind of activity, and activity as the ground of thought. For him, managerial theories gain their power by helping people overlook disorder and presume orderliness. Theory *energizes* action by providing a *presumption of logic* that enables people to act with certainty, attention, care, and control. Even where it is originally inadequate as a description of current reality, a forceful theory may provoke action that brings into the world a new reality that then confirms the original theory. Weick (1983) explains:

Once the action is linked with an explanation, it becomes more forceful, and the situation is thereby transformed into something that supports the presumed underlying pattern. Presumptions [theories] enable actions to be tied to specific explanations that consolidate those actions into deterministic events…

The underlying explanation need *not* be objectively "correct." In a crude sense any old explanation will do. This is so because explanation serves mostly to organize and focus the action. The focused action then modifies the situation in ways that confirm the explanation, whatever it is.

Thus, the adequacy of any explanation is determined by the intensity and structure it adds to potentially self-validating actions. More forcefulness leads to more validation and more perceived adequacy. Accuracy is subordinate to intensity. Since situations can support a variety of meanings, their actual content and meaning are dependent on the degree to which they are arranged in sensible, coherent configurations. More forcefulness imposes more coherence. Thus, those explanations that induce greater forcefulness become more valid, not because they are more accurate, but because they have a higher potential for self-validation…the underlying explanations they unfold (for example, "This is war") have great potential to intensify whatever action is underway (1983, pp. 230-232).

Thus, theories are generative to the extent that they are forceful (e.g., Marx), logically coherent (e.g., Piaget), and bold in their assertions and consistency (e.g., Freud, Weber). By providing a basis for focused action, a logic for attributing causality, and a sequence specification that grounds expectations for action and reaction, a theory goes a long way toward forming the common expectations for the future. "And with the alteration of expectation, the stage is set for modification of action" (Gergen, 1982, p. 24).

Transmitting a System of Values

Beyond abstract logic, it is often the affective core of social theory that provides its true force and appeal, allowing it to direct perception and guide behavior. From the tradition of logical positivism, good "objective" theory is to be value-free, yet upon closer inspection we find that social theory is infused with values and domain assumptions throughout. As Gouldner (1970) so aptly put it, "Every social theory facilitates the pursuit of some, but not all, courses of action and thus, encourages us to change or accept the world as it is, to say yea or nay to it. In a way, every theory is a discrete obituary or celebration of some social system."

Nowhere is this better exemplified—negatively—than in the role scientific theory played in the arguments for slavery, colonialism, and belief in the genetic superiority of certain races. The scientific theory in this case was, again, the theory of biological determinism, the belief that social and economic differences between human beings and groups—differences in rank, status, political privilege, education privilege—arise from inherited natural endowments, and that existing social arrangements accurately reflect biological limits. So powerful was this theory during the 1800s that it led a number of America's highest-ranking scientific researchers unconsciously to miscalculate "objective" data in what has been brilliantly described by naturalist Steven Jay Gould (1981, p. 54) as a "patchwork of fudging and finagling in the clear interest of controlling a priori convictions". Before dismissing this harsh judgment as simple rhetoric, we need to look closely at how it was determined. One example will suffice.

When Samual Morton, a scientist with two medical degrees, died in 1851, the *New York Tribune* paid tribute saying, "Probably no scientific man in America enjoyed a higher reputation among scholars throughout the world than Dr. Morton" (in Gould, 1981, p. 51). Morton gained this reputation as a scientist who set out to rank racial groups by "objectively" measuring the size of the cranial cavity of the human skull, which he regarded as a measure of brain size. He had a beautiful collection of skulls from races throughout the world, probably the largest such collection in existence. His hypothesis was a simple one: The mental and moral worth of human races can be arrived at objectively by measuring physical characteristics of the brain; by filling skull cavities with mustard seed or lead shot, accurate measurement of brain size is possible. Morton published three major works, which were reprinted repeatedly as providing objective, "hard" data on the mental worth of races. Gould comments:

Needless to say, they matched every good Yankee's prejudices—whites on top, Indians in the middle, and blacks on the bottom; and among whites, Teutons and Anglo-Saxons on top, Jews in the middle, and Hindus on the bottom.... Status and access to power in Morton's America faithfully reflected biological merit (p. 54).

Morton's work was undoubtedly influential. When he died, the South's leading medical journal proclaimed: "We of the South should consider him as our benefactor, for aiding most materially in giving the Negro his true position as an inferior race" (in Gould, 1981, p. 69). Indeed Morton did much more than only give "the Negro his true position," as the following remarks by Morton himself convey:

Negroes were numerous in Egypt, but their social position in ancient time, was the same as it is now, that of servants and slaves. The benevolent mind may regret the inaptitude of the Indian civilization... [but values must not yield to fact]. The struc-

ture of his mind appears to be different from that of the white man, or can the two har-monize in social relations except on the most limited scale. [Indians] are not only averse to restraints of education, but for the most part are incapable of a continued process of reasoning on abstract subjects (in Gould, 1981, p. 53).

The problem with these conclusions—as well as the numerical data, which supported them—was that they were based not on "fact" but purely and simply on cultural fiction, on Morton's belief in biological determinism. As Gould meticulously shows, all of Morton's data was wrong. Having reworked it completely, Gould concludes:

Morton's summaries are a patchwork of fudging and finagling in the clear interest of controlling a priori convictions. Yet—and this is the most intriguing aspect of the case—I find no evidence of conscious fraud; indeed, had Morton been a conscious fudger, he would not have published his data so openly.

Conscious fraud is probably rare in science…The prevalence of unconscious finagling, on the other hand, suggests the general conclusion about the social context of science…prior prejudice may be found anywhere, even in the basics of measuring bones and totaling sums (pp. 5556).

Morton represents a telling example of the power of theory. Theory is not only a shaper of expectations and perceptions. Under the guise of "dispassionate inquiry" it can also be a peddler of values, typecasting arbitrary value as scientific "fact." Along with Gould, we believe that we would be better off to abandon the myth of "value-free" science and that theoretical work "must be understood as a social phenomenon, a gutsy, human enterprise, not the work of robots programmed to collect pure information" (Gould, 1981, p. 21). Even if Morton's data were correct, his work still could not be counted as value-free. His data and theories were not only shaped by the setting in which he worked; they were also used to support broad social policy. This is akin to making nature the source of cultural values, which of course it never can be ("What is" does not equal "what should be").

Creating a Group-Building Language

The sociorationalist perspective is more than a pessimistic epitaph for a strictly logical positivist philosophy. It is an invitation to inquiry that raises the status of theory from mere appendage of scientific method to an actual shaper of society. Once we acknowledge that a primary product of science—theory—is a key resource for the creation of groups, the stage is set for theory-building activity intended for the use and development of human society, for the creation of human options.

Students of human behavior have been aware of the group as the foundation of society since the earliest periods of classical thought. Aristotle, for example, discussed the importance of bands and families. But it was not until the middle of the present century that scientific interest in the subject exploded in a flurry of general inquiry and systematic interdisciplinary research (for a sample review of this literature see Hare, 1976). Among the conclusions of this recent work is the crucial insight that:

The face-to-face group working on a problem is the meeting ground of individual per-sonality and society. It is in the group that personality is modified and socialized and it is through the workings of groups that society is changed and adapted to its times (Thelen, 1954, p. vi).

Similarly, in the field of organization development, Srivastva, Obert, and Neilsen (1977) have shown that the historical development of the discipline has paralleled advances in group theory. And this, they contend, is no accident because:

Emphasis on the small group is responsive to the realities of social change in large

complex organizations. It is through group life that individuals learn, practice, devel-
op, and modify their roles in the larger organization. To enter programmatically at the
group level is both to confront and potentially co-opt an important natural source of
change and development in these systems (p. 83).

It is well established that groups are formed around common ideas that are
expressed in and through some kind of shared language which makes communicative
interaction possible. What is less clear, though, is the exact role that science plays in
shaping group life through the medium of language. However, the fact that science
frequently does have an impact is rarely questioned. Andre Gorz (1973) offers an explo-
sive example of this point.

In the early 1960s a British professor of sociology by the name of Goldthorpe was
brought in from a nearby university to make a study of the Vauxhall automobile workers in Luton, England. At the time, management at the factory was worried because
workers in other organizations throughout the United Kingdom were showing great
unrest over working conditions, pay, and management. Many strikes were being waged;
most of them wildcat strikes called by the factory stewards, not by the unions themselves. Goldthorpe was called in to study the situation at Vauxhall, to find out for management if there was anything to worry about at their factory. At the time of the study
there were at Vauxhall no strikes, no disruptions, and no challenges by workers. Management wanted to know why. What were the chances that acute conflict would break
out in the "well-managed" and "advanced" big factory?

After two full years of research, the professor drew his conclusions. Management,
he said, had little to worry about. According to the study, the workers were completely socialized into the system, they were satisfied with their wages and neither liked or
disliked their work—in fact, they were indifferent to it, viewing it as boring but
inevitable. Because their job was not intrinsically rewarding, most people did it just to
be done with it—so they could go home and work on other more worthwhile projects
and be with their family. Work was marginal and instrumental. It was a means to support other interests outside the factory, where "real life" began. Based then on his observations, Goldthorpe theorized that management had nothing to worry about: Workers
were passively apathetic and well integrated into the system. They behaved according
to middle-class patterns and showed no signs of strength as a group (no class-consciousness). Furthermore, most conflict with management belonged to the past.

The sociologist's report was still at the printer's when some employees got hold
of a summary of his findings. They had the conclusions copied and distributed reports
to hundreds of co-workers. Also at around this time, a report of Vauxhall's profits was
being circulated, profits that were not shared with the employees. The next day something happened. It was reported by the London Times in detail:

Wild rioting has broken out at the Vauxhall car factories in Luton. Thousands of work-
ers streamed out of the shops and gathered in the factory yard. They besieged the man-
agement offices, calling for managers to come out, singing the 'Red Flag,' and shouting.
'String them up!' Groups attempted to storm the offices and battled police which had
been called to protect them (quoted in Gorz, 1973).

The rioting lasted for two days. All of this happened, then, in an advanced factory where systematic research showed workers to be apathetic, weak as a group, and
resigned to accept the system. What does it all mean? Had the researchers simply mis-
read the data?

To the contrary. Goldthorpe knew his data well. He articulated the conclusions
accurately, concisely, and with force. In fact, what happened was that the report gave

the workers a *language* with which to begin talking to one another about their plight. It brought them into interaction and, as they discussed things, they discovered that Goldthorpe was right. They felt alike, apathetic but frustrated; and they were apathetic because they felt as individuals working in isolated jobs, that no one could do anything to change things. But the report gave them a way to discuss the situation. As they talked, things changed. People were no longer alone in their feelings, and they did not want things to continue as they were. As an emergent group, they now had a means to convert apathy into action, noninvolvement into involvement, and individual powerlessness into collective strength. "In other words," analyzes Gorz, "the very investigation of Mr. Goldthorpe about the lack of class-consciousness helped tear down the barriers of silence and isolation that rendered the workers apathetic" (p. 334).

The Vauxhall case is an important one for a number of reasons. At a general level it demonstrates that knowledge in the social sciences differs in quality and kind from knowledge generated in the physical sciences. For instance, our knowledge of the periodic chart does not change the elements, and our knowledge of the moon's orbit does not change its path. But our knowledge of a social system is different. It can be used by the system to change itself, thus invalidating or disconfirming the findings immediately or at some later time. Thus the human group differs from objects in an important way: Human beings have the capacity for symbolic interaction and, through language, they have the ability to collaborate in the investigation of their own world. Because of our human capacity for symbolic interaction, the introduction of new knowledge concerning aspects of our world carries with it the strong likelihood of changing that world itself.

Gergen (1982) refers to this as the "enlightenment effect" of scientific work, meaning that once the formulations of scientific work are made public, human beings may act autonomously either to disconfirm or to validate the propositions. According to logical positivist philosophy, potential enlightenment effects must be reduced or—ideally—eliminated through experimental controls. In social psychology, for example, deception plays a crucial role in doing research; enlightenment effects are viewed as contaminants to good scientific work. Yet there is an alternative way to look at the reactive nature of social research: it is precisely because of the enlightenment effect that theory can and does play an important role in the positive construction of society. In this sense, the enlightenment effect—which is made possible through language—is an essential ingredient making scientific work worthwhile, meaningful, and applicable. It constitutes an invitation to each and every theorist to actively participate in the creation of his or her world by generating compelling theories of what is good, and just, and desirable in social existence.

Extending Visions of Possibility

The position taken by the sociorationalist philosophy of science is that the conduct of inquiry cannot be separated from the everyday negotiation of reality. Social-organizational research is, therefore, a continuing moral concern, a concern of social reconstruction and direction. The choice of what to study, how to study it, and what to report each implies some degree of responsibility. Science, therefore, instead of being considered an endpoint, is viewed as one means of helping humanity create itself. Science in this sense exists for one singular overarching purpose. As Albion Small (1905) proposed almost a century ago, a generative science must aim at "the most thorough, intense, persistent, and systematic effort to make human life all that it is capable of becoming" (pp. 3637).

Theories gain their generative capacity by extending visions that expand to the realm of the possible. As a general proposition it might be said that theories designed to empower organized social systems will tend to have a greater enlightenment effect than theories of human constraint. This proposition is grounded in a simple but important consideration which we should like to raise as it relates to the unity of theory and practice: Is it not possible that scientific theory gains its capacity to affect cultural practices in very much the same way that powerful leaders inspire people to new heights? Recent research on the functioning of the executive mind (Srivastva, 1983; 1985) raises a set of intriguing parallels between the possibilities of a generative science and the workings of the executive mind.

The essential parallel is seen in the primary role that ideas or ideals play in the mobilization of diverse groups in the common construction of a desired future. Three major themes from the research stand out in this regard:

1. **Vision:** The executive mind works largely from the present and extends itself out to the longer-term future. It is powerful to the extent that it is able to envision a desired future state which challenges perceptions of what is possible and what can be realized. The executive mind operates beyond the frontier of conventional practice without losing sight of either necessity or possibility.

2. **Passion:** The executive mind is simultaneously rational and intuitive, which allows it to tap into the sentiments, values, and dreams of the social collectivity. Executive vision becomes "common vision" to the extent that it ignites the imaginations, hopes, and passions of others-and it does so through the articulation of self-transcending ideals which lend meaning and significance to everyday life.

3. **Integrity:** The executive mind is the mental muscle that moves a system from the present state to a new and different future. As such, this muscle gains strength to the extent that it is founded upon an integrity able to withstand contrary pressures. There are three dimensions to executive integrity. The first, system integrity, refers to the fact that the executive mind perceives the world (the organization, group, or society) as a unified whole, not as a collection of individual parts. The second type of integrity is *moral integrity*. Common-vision leadership is largely an act of caring. It follows the "path of the heart," which is the source of moral and ethical standards. Finally, integrity of vision refers to consistency, coherence, and focus. Executive vision—to the extent to which it is compelling—is focused and unwavering, even in the midst of obstacles, critics, and conflicting alternatives.

Interestingly, these thematic dimensions of the executive mind have their counterparts in recent observations concerning the utilization of organizational research. According to Beyer and Trice (1982), the "affective bonding" that takes place during the research largely determines the attractiveness of its results and generates commitment to utilize their implications. For example, Henshel (1975) suggests that research containing predictions of an appealing future will be utilized and preferred over research that points to a negative or repelling future: "People will work for predicted states they approve of and against those they detest" (p. 103). Similarly, Weiss and Bucavalas (1980) report that results which challenge the status quo are most attractive to high-level executives because they are the persons expected to make new things happen, at least on the level of policy. And, with respect to passion and integrity, Mitroff (1980) urges social scientists to become caring advocates of their ideas, not only to diffuse their theories but also to challenge others to prove them wrong and thus pursue those ideas which have integrity in action.

This section has explored a number of ways in which social theory becomes a powerful resource for change and development in social practice. The argument is simple.

Theory is agential in character and has unbounded potential to affect patterns of social action—whether desired or not. As we have seen, theories are not mere explanations of an external world lying "out there" waiting to be objectively recorded. Theories, like powerful ideas, are formative. By establishing perceptual cues and frames, by providing presumptions of logic, by transmitting subtle values, by creating new language, and by extending compelling visions of possibility or constraint—in all these ways social theory becomes a powerful means whereby norms, beliefs, and cultural practices may be altered.

Reawakening the Spirit of Action-Research

The key point is this: Instinctively, intuitively, and tacitly we all know that important ideas can, in a flash, profoundly alter the way we see ourselves, view reality, and conduct our lives. Experience shows that a simple economic forecast, political poll, or technical discovery (like the atomic bomb) can forever change the course of human history. Thus one cannot help but be disturbed and puzzled by the discipline of action-research in its wide-ranging indifference to theory. Not only does it continue to underrate the role of theory as a means for organizational development (Friedlander and Brown, 1974; Bartunek, 1983; Argyris, 1983) but it appears also to have become locked within an assumptive base that systematically distorts our view of organizational reality and inadvertently helps reinforce and perfect the status quo (Brimm, 1972).

Why is there this lack of generative theorizing in action-research? And, more importantly, what can be done to rekindle the spirit, excitement and passion required of a science that wishes to be of vital significance to organizations? Earlier we talked about a philosophy of science congenial to the task. Sociorationalism, it was argued, represents an epistemological point of view conducive to catalytic theorizing. Ironically though, it can be argued that most action researchers already do subscribe to this or a similar view of science (Susman and Evered, 1978). Assuming this to be the case, it becomes an even greater puzzle why contemporary action-research continues to disregard theory-building as an integral and necessary component of the craft. In this section we shall broaden our discussion by taking a look at some of the metaphysical assumptions embedded in our conventional definitions of action-research—assumptions that can be shown to govern our thought and work in ways inimical to present interests.

Paradigm 1: Organizing As A Problem to be Solved

The intellectual and spiritual origins of action-research can be traced to Kurt Lewin, a social psychologist of German origin who coined the term *action-research* in 1944. The thrust of Lewin's work centered on the need to bridge the gap between science and the realm of practical affairs. Science, he said, should be used to inform and educate social practice, and subsequent action would then inform science: "We should consider action, research, and training as a triangle that should be kept together" (Lewin, 1948, p. 211). The twofold promise of an action science, according to Lewin, was to simultaneously contribute to the development of scientific knowledge (propositions of an if/then variety) and use such knowledge for bettering the human condition.

The immense influence of Lewin is a complete puzzle if we look only to his writings. The fact of the matter is that Lewin published only 2 papers—a mere 22 pages—concerned directly with the idea of action-research (Peters and Robinson, 1984). Indeed, it has been argued that his enduring influence is attributable not to these writings but to the sheer force and presence of the man himself. According to biographer Alfred

Marrow (1968), Lewin was a passionate and creative thinker, continuously knocking at the door of the unknown, studying "topics that had been believed to be psychologically unapproachable." Lewin's character was marked by a spirit of inquiry that burned incessantly and affected all who came in contact with him, especially his students. The intensity of his presence was fueled further by the belief that inquiry itself could be used to construct a more democratic and dignified future. At least this was his hope and dream, for Lewin had not forgotten his experience as a refugee from fascism in the late 1930s. Understanding this background, then, it is clear why he revolted so strongly against a detached ivory-tower view of science, a science that is immersed in trivial matters, tranquilized by its standardized methods, and limited in its field of inquiry. Thus, the picture we have of Lewin shows him to have been a committed social scientist pioneering uncharted territory for the purpose of creating new knowledge about groups and societies that might advance the democratic ideal (see, for example, Lewin, 1952). It was this spirit—a relentless curiosity coupled with a conviction of the need for knowledge-guided societal development—that marked Lewin's creative impact on both his students and the field.

Much of this spirit is now gone from action-research. What is left is a series of assumptions about the world which exhibits little, if any, resemblance to the process of inquiry as Lewin lived it. While many of the words are the same, they have been taken too literally and in their translation over the years have been bloated into a set of metaphysical principles—assumptions about the essence of social existence-that directly undermine the intellectual and speculative spirit. Put bluntly, under current norms, action-research has largely failed as an instrument for advancing social knowledge of consequence and now risks being (mis)understood as little more than a crude empiricism imprisoned in a deficiency mode of thought. A quick sketch of six sets of assumptions embedded in the conventional view of action-research will show exactly what we are talking about while also answering our question about the discipline's lack of contribution to generative theory:

Research equals problem-solving; to do good research is to solve "real problems." So ingrained is this assumption that it scarcely needs documentation. Virtually every definition found in leading texts and articles equates action research with problem solving—as if "real" problem solving is virtually the essence of the discipline. For example, as French and Bell (1978) define it, "Action-research is both *an approach to problem solving—a model or paradigm, and a problem-solving process—a series of activities and events.*" (p. 88)4 Or in terms of the Bradford, Gibb, and Benne (1964) definition, "It is an application of scientific methodology in the clarification and solution of practical problems" (p. 33). *Similarly, Frohman, Sashkin, and Kavanaugh (1976) state: "Action research describes a particular process model whereby behavioral science knowledge is applied to help a client (usually a group or social system) solve real problems and not incidentally learn the process involved in problem solving" (p. 203). Echoing this theme, that research equals problem solving, researchers at the University of Michigan's Institute in Social Research state,*

Three factors need to be taken into account in an organization development [action-research] effort: The behaviors that are problematic, the conditions that create those behaviors, and the interventions or activities that will correct the conditions creating the problems. What is it that people are doing or not doing, that is a problem? Why are they doing or not doing these particular things? Which of a large number of possible interventions or activities would be most likely to solve the problems by focusing on why problems exist? (Hausser, Pecorella and Wissler, 1977, p. 2).

Here it is unmistakably clear that the primary focus of the action-research approach to organizational analysis is the ongoing array of concrete problems an organization faces. Of course, there are a number of differences in the discipline as to the overall definition and meaning of the emerging action-research paradigm. But this basic assumption—that research equals problem solving—is not one of them. In a recent review intended to discover elements of metatheoretical agreement within the discipline, Peters and Robinson (1984) discovered that out of 15 different dimensions of action-research studied, only 2 had unanimous support among leaders in the field. What were these two elements of agreement? Exactly as the definitions above suggest: Social science should be "action oriented" and "problem focused."

Inquiry, in action-research terms, is a matter of following the standardized rules of problem solving; knowledge is the result of good method. "In essence," write Blake and Mouton (1976), "it is a method of empirical data gathering that is *comprised of a set of rather standardized steps:* diagnosis, information gathering, feedback, and action planning" (pp. 101102). By following this ritual list, they contend that virtually any organization can be studied in a manner that will lead to usable knowledge. As Chiles (1983) puts it, "The virtue of the model lies in the sequential process…. Any other sequence renders the model meaningless" (p. 318). The basic idea behind the model is that "in management, events proceed as planned unless some force, not provided against by the plan, acts upon events to produce an outcome not contemplated in the plan" (Kepner and Tregoe, 1973, p. 3). Thus, a problem is a deviation from some standard, and without precise diagnosis (step one) any attempt to resolve the problem will likely fail as a result of not penetrating the surface symptoms to discover the true causes. Hence, like a liturgical refrain which is seldom questioned or thought about, Cohen, Fink et al. (1984) tell the new student that *knowledge is the offspring of processing information through a distinct series of problem-solving stages:*

Action-research begins with an identified problem. Data are then gathered in a way that allows a diagnosis which can produce a tentative solution, which is then implemented with the assumption that it is likely to cause new or unforeseen problems that will, in turn, need to be evaluated, diagnosed, and so forth. *This action-research method assumes a constantly evolving interplay between solutions, results, and new solutions…This model is a general one applicable to solving any kind of problem in an ongoing organization* (pp. 359-360).

Action-research is utilitarian or technical; that is, it should be initiated and designed to meet a need in an area specified by the organization, usually by "top management." The search is controlled by the "felt need" or object of inquiry; everything that is not related to this object should be dismissed as irrelevant.

As we are beginning to see, action-research conventionally understood does not really refer to research per se but rather to a highly focused and defined type of research called problem solving. Taken almost directly from the medical model, the disease orientation guides the process of inquiry in a highly programmed way. According to Levinson (1972), diagnostic action-research, "like a therapeutic or teaching relationship should be an alliance of both parties to discover and resolve these problems…. [The researcher] *should look for experiences which appear stressful to people. What kinds of occurrences disrupt or disorganize people"* (p. 37). Hence in a systematically limiting fashion, the general topic of research is largely prescribed—before inquiry even begins. As we would guess:

Typical questions in [action-research] data gathering or "problem sensing" would include: *What problems* do you see in your group, including problems between people that are interfering with getting the job done the way you would like to see it done? And *what problems* do you see in the broader organization? Such open-ended questions provide latitude on the part of respondents and encourage a *reporting of problems* as the individual sees them (French, 1969, pp. 183-185).

In problem solving it is assumed that something is broken, fragmented, not whole, and that it needs to be fixed. Thus the function of problem solving is to integrate, stabilize, and help raise to its full potential the workings of the status quo. By definition, a problem implies that one already has knowledge of what "should be"; thus one's research is guided by an instrumental purpose tied to what is already known. In this sense, problem solving tends to be inherently conservative; as a form of research it tends to produce and reproduce a universe of knowledge that remains sealed. As Staw (1984) points out in his review of the field, most organizational research is biased to serve managerial interests rather than exploring broader human and/or social purposes. But even more important, he argues, the field has not even served managerial interests well since research has taken a short-term problem focus rather than having formulated logic's of new forms of organization that do not exist. It is as if the discipline's *concept of social system development* means only clearing up distortions in current functioning (horizontal development) and does not include any conception of a stage-based movement toward an altogether new or transformed reality (vertical development or second-order change).

Action-research should not inquire into phenomena that transcend the competence of human reason. Questions that cannot be answered should not be asked and issues that cannot be acted upon should not be explored (i.e., action-research is not a branch of political philosophy, poetry, or theology). This proposition is a "smuggled-in" corollary to the preceding assumptions. It would appear that once one agrees with the ground rules of a pragmatic problem-solving science, the universe for inquiry is largely predetermined, defined, and delimited in scope. Specifically, what one agrees to a secularized view of a human universe that is predictable, controllable, and rational, one that is sequentially ordered into a series of causes and effects. As both a credit and a weakness, the problem-solving mode narrows our gaze in much the same manner that a blinder over one eye narrows the field of vision and distorts one's perception of depth. As a part of a long-term movement evidenced in social sciences, contemporary action-research embodies the trend toward metaphysical skepticism and denial (Quinney, 1982). That is, it operates out of a sacred void that cuts off virtually any inquiry into the vital forces of life. Indeed, the whole promise of modern science was that it would finally banish illusion, mystery, and uncertainty from the world. An inquiry process of immediate utility (problem solving), therefore, requires an anti-religious, secular spirit that will limit the realm of study to the sphere of the known. And because of the recognition that the formulation of a problem depends largely on one's views of what constitutes a solution, it is not surprising to find that *research on the utilization of research* shows a propensity for social scientists and organizations to agree on studying only those variables that can be manipulated (Beyer and Trice, 1982). As one might imagine, such a view has crippling implications for generative theorizing. For example, as typically practiced, action-research does little in the way of theorizing about or bringing beauty into organizational life. Does this mean that there is no beauty in organizing'? Does this mean that the realm of the esthetic has little or nothing to do with organizational dynamics'?

The tidy imagery of the problem-solving view is related to what Sigmund Koch (1981) has called, in his presidential address to the APA, the syndrome of "ameaningful thinking." One element of this syndrome is the perpetuation of the scientistic myth which uses the rhetoric of prediction and control to reassure people that their lives are not that complex, their situations not all that uncertain—and that their problems are indeed manageable through causal analysis. In the process, however, science tends to trivialize, and even evade, a whole class of issues that "transcend the competence of human reason" yet are clearly meaningful in the course of human experience. One way in which the field of inquiry is restricted, according to Koch, has to do with one's choice of methodology:

There are times and circumstances in which able individuals, committed to inquiry, tend almost obsessively to frustrate the objectives of inquiry. It is as if uncertainty, mootness, ambiguity, cognitive infinitude were the most unbearable of the existential anguishes…. *Ameaningful* thought or inquiry regards knowledge as the result of "processing" rather than discovery. It presumes that knowledge is an almost automatic result of a gimmickry, an assembly line, a "methology"… So strongly does it see knowledge under such aspects that it sometimes seems to suppose the object of inquiry to be an ungainly and annoying irrelevance (1981, p. 259).

To be sure, this is not to argue that all action-research is "ameaningful" or automatically tied to a standardized problem-solving method. Likewise, much of the success achieved by action-research until now may be attributed to its restricted focus on that which is "solvable. " However, it is important to recognize that the problem-solving method of organizational inquiry quite systematically paints a picture of organizational life in which a whole series of colors are considered untouchable. In this way the totality of being is obviously obscured, leading to a narrowed conception of human nature and cultural possibility.

Problems are "out there" to be studied and solved. The ideal product of action-research is a mirror-like reflection of the organization's problems and causes. As "objective third party " there is little role for passion and speculation. The action-researcher should be neither a passionate advocate nor an inspired dreamer (utopian thinker). One of the laudable and indeed significant values associated with action-research has been its insistence upon a collaborative form of inquiry. But unfortunately, from a generative-theory perspective, the term *collaboration* has become virtually synonymous with an idealized image of the researcher as a facilitator and mirror, rather than an active and fully engaged social participant. As facilitator of the problem-solving process, the action-researcher has three generally agreed-upon "primary intervention tasks": to help generate valid organizational data; to enable others to make free and informed choices on the basis of the data, and to help the organization generate internal commitment to their choices. Elaborating further, Argyris (1970) states:

One condition that seems so basic as to be defined as axiomatic is the generation of valid information… *Valid information is that which describes the factors, plus their interrelationships that create the problem* (pp. 1617).

Furthermore, it is also assumed that for data to be useful there must be a claim to neutrality. The data should represent an accurate reflection of the observed facts. As French and Bell (1978) describe it, it is important for the action-researcher to stress the objective, fact-finding features: "A key value inculcated in organizational members is a belief in the validity, desirability, and usefulness of the data" (p. 79). Then through feedback that "refers to activities and processes that 'reflect' or 'mirror' an objective picture of the real world" (p. 111), the action-researcher facilitates the process of prioritizing problems and helps others make choices for action. And because the overarching objective is to help the organization develop its own internal resources, the action-researcher should not play an active role or take an advocate stance that might in the long run foster an unhealthy dependency. As French and Bell (1978) again explain, an active role "tends to negate a collaborative, developmental approach to improving organizational processes" (p. 203).

As must be evident, every one of these injunctions associated with the problem-solving view of action-research serves directly to diminish the likelihood of imaginative, passionate, creative theory. To the extent that generative theory represents an inspired theoretical articulation of a new and different future, it appears that action-research would have nothing to do with it. According to French and Bell (1978) "Even the presenting of options can be overdone. If the [action-researcher's] ideas become the focal point for prolonged discussion and debate, the consultant has clearly shifted away from the facilitator role" (p. 206).

At issue here is something even more important. The fundamental attitude embodied in the problem-solving view is separationist. It views the world as something external to our consciousness of it, something "out there." As such it tends to identify problems not here but "over there": Problems are not ours, but yours; not a condition common to all, but a condition belonging to this person, their group, or that nation (witness the acid-rain issue). Thus, the action-researcher is content to facilitate *their problem solving* because he or she is not part of that world. To this extent, the problem-solving view dissects reality and parcels it out into fragmented groups, families, tribes, or countries. In both form and substance it denies the wholeness of a dynamic and interconnected social universe. And once the unity of the world is broken, passionless, mindless, mirror-like inquiry comes to make logical sense precisely because the inquirer has no ownership or stake in a world that is not his or hers to begin with.

Organizational life is problematic. Organizing is best understood as a historically situated sequence of problems, causes, and solutions among people, events, and things. Thus, the ultimate aim and product of action-research is the production of institutions that have a high capacity to perceive, formulate, and solve an endless stream of problems.

The way we conceive of the social world is of consequence to the kind of world we discover and even, through our reconstructions, helps to create it. Action-researchers, like scientists in other areas, approach their work from a framework based on taken-for-granted assumptions. To the extent that these assumptions are found useful, and are affirmed by colleagues, they remain unquestioned as a habitual springboard for one's work. In time the conventional view becomes so solidly embedded that it assumes the status of being "real," without alternative (Morgan, 1980; Mennhiem, 1936). As human beings we are constantly in symbolic interaction, attempting to develop conceptions that will allow us to make sense of and give meaning to experience through the use of language, ideas, signs, theories, and names. As many have recently shown, the use of metaphor is a basic mode under which symbolism works and exerts an influence on the development of language, science, and cognitive growth (Morgan, 1980; Ortony, 1979; Black, 1962; Keely, 1980). Metaphor works by asserting that A equals B or is very much like B. We use metaphors constantly to open our eyes and sensitize us to phenomenal realities that otherwise might go unnoticed. Pepper (1942) argues that all science proceeds from specifiable "world hypotheses" and behind every world hypothesis rests the boldest of "root metaphors."

Within what we are calling Paradigm I action-research, there lies a guiding metaphor which has a power impact on the theory-building activity of the discipline. When organizations are approached from the deficiency perspective of Paradigm I, all the properties and modes of organizing are scrutinized for their dysfunctional but potentially solvable problems. It is all too clear then that the root metaphor of the conventional view is that *organizing is a problem*. This image focuses the researcher's eye on a visible but narrow realm of reality that resides "out there" and is causally determined, deficient by some preexisting standard—on problems that are probably both understandable and solvable. Through analysis, diagnosis, treatment, and follow-up evaluation the sequential world of organizing can be kept on its steady and productive course. And because social existence is at its base a problem to be solved, real living equals problem solving, and living better is an adaptive learning process whereby we acquire new and more effective means for tackling tough problems. The good life, this image informs, depends on solving problems in such a way that problems of utility are identified and solutions of high quality are found and carried out with full commitment. As one leading theorist describes:

For many scholars who study organizations and management, the central characteristic of organizations is that they are problem-solving systems whose success is measured by how efficiently they solve problems associated with accomplishing their primary mission and how effectively they respond to emergent problems. Kilmann's approach (1979, pp. 214215) is representative of this perspective: "One might even define the essence of management as problem defining and problem solving, whether the problems are well-structured, ill-structured, technical, human, or environmental… In this view, the core task of the executive is problem management. Although experience, personality, and specific technical expertise are important, the primary skill of the successful executive is the ability to manage the problem-solving process in such a way that important problems are identified and solutions of high quality are found and carried out with the full commitment of organizational members (Kolb, 1983, pp. 109110).

From here it is just a short conceptual jump to the idealized aim of Paradigm 1 research:

Action-research tends to build into the client system an institutionalized pattern for continuously collecting data and examining the system's processes, as well as for the continuous review of *known* problem areas. *Problem solving becomes very much a way of organizational life* (Marguiles and Raia, 1972, p. 29).

I have tried in these few pages to highlight the almost obvious point that the deficiency/problem orientation is pervasive and holds a subtle but powerful grasp on the discipline's imagination and focus. It can be argued that the generative incapacity of contemporary action-research is securely linked with the discipline's guiding metaphor of social-organizational existence. As noted by many scholars, the theoretical output of the discipline is virtually nonexistent, and what theory there is, is largely problem-focused (theories of turnover, intergroup conflict, processes of dehumanization. See Staw, 1984 for an excellent review). Thus, our theories, like windsocks, continue to blow steadily onward in the direction of our conventional gaze. Seeing the world as a problem has become "very much a way of organizational life."

It is our feeling that the discipline has reached a level of fatigue arising from repetitious use of its standardized model. Fatigue, as Whitehead (1929) so aptly surmised, arises from an act of excluding the impulse toward novelty, which is the antithesis of the life of the mind and of speculative reason. To be sure, there can be great adventure in the process of inquiry. Yet not many action-researchers today return from their explorations refreshed and revitalized, like pioneers returning home, with news of lands unknown but most certainly there. Perhaps there is a different root metaphor from which to work.

Proposal for a Second Dimension

Our effort here is but one in a small yet growing attempt to generate new perspectives on the conduct of organizational research, perspectives that can yield the kind of knowledge necessary for both understanding and transforming complex social-organizational systems (Torbert, 1983; Van Maanen et al., 1982; Mitroff and Kilmann, 1978; Smirchich, 1983; Forester, 1983; Argyris, 1970; Friedlander, 1977). It is apparent that among the diverse views currently emerging there is frequently great tension. Often the differences become the battleground for fierce debate about theories of truth, the meaning of "facts," political agendas, and personal assertions of will. But, more fruitfully, what can be seen emerging is a heightened sensitivity to and interdisciplinary recognition of the fact that, based on "the structure of knowledge" (Kolb, 1984), there may be multiple ways of knowing, each of them valid in its own realm when judged according to its own set of essential assumptions and purposes. In this sense there are many different ways of studying the same phenomenon, and the insights generated by one approach are, at best, partial and incomplete. According to Jurgen Habermas (1971) different perspectives can be evaluated only in terms of their specified "human interests," which can broadly be differentiated into the realm of practical rationality and the realm of technical rationality. In more straightforward language Morgan (1983) states:

The selection of method implies some view of the situation being studied, for any decision on *how* to study a phenomenon carries with it certain assumptions or explicit answers to the question, "What is being studied?" Just as we select a tennis racquet rather than a golf club to play tennis because we have a prior conception as to what the game of tennis involves, so too, in relation to the process of social research, we select or favor particular kinds of methodology because we have implicit or explicit conceptions as to what we are trying to do with our research (p. 19).

Thus, in adopting one mode over another the researcher directly influences what he or she will finally discover and accomplish.

It is the contention of this chapter that advances in generative theorizing will come about for action-research when the discipline decides to expand its universe of exploration, seeks to discover new questions, and rekindles a fresh perception of the extra ordinary in everyday organizational life. In this final section we now describe the assumptions and philosophy of an applied administrative science that seeks to embody these suggestions in a form of organization study we call appreciative inquiry. In distinction to conventional action-research, the knowledge-interest of appreciative inquiry lies not so much in problem solving as in social innovation. Appreciative inquiry refers to a research perspective that is uniquely intended for discovering, understanding, and fostering innovations in social-organizational arrangements and processes.5 Its purpose is to contribute to the generative-theoretical aims of social science and to use such knowledge to promote egalitarian dialogue leading to social-system effectiveness and integrity. Whatever else it may be, social-system effectiveness is defined here quite specifically as a congruence between social-organizational values (the ever-changing non-native set of values, ideas, or interests that system members hold concerning the question, "How should we organize ourselves?") and everyday social- organizational practices (cf. Torbert, 1983). Thus, appreciative inquiry refers to both a search for knowledge and a theory of intentional collective action which are designed to help evolve the normative vision and will of a group, organization, or society as a whole. It is an inquiry process that affirms our symbolic capacities of imagination and mind as well as our social capacity for conscious choice and cultural evolution. As a holistic form of inquiry, it asks a series of questions not found in either a logical-positivist conception

Figure 3.1

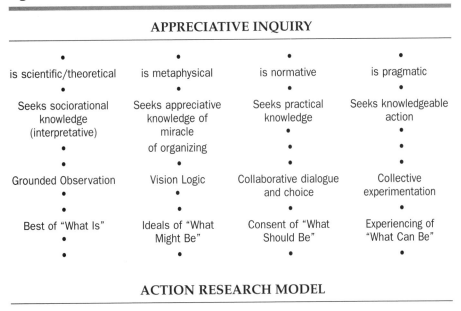

APPRECIATIVE INQUIRY

is scientific/theoretical	is metaphysical	is normative	is pragmatic
Seeks sociorational knowledge (interpretative)	Seeks appreciative knowledge of miracle of organizing	Seeks practical knowledge	Seeks knowledgeable action
Grounded Observation	Vision Logic	Collaborative dialogue and choice	Collective experimentation
Best of "What Is"	Ideals of "What Might Be"	Consent of "What Should Be"	Experiencing of "What Can Be"

ACTION RESEARCH MODEL

FOR A HUMANLY SIGNIFICANT
GENERATIVE SCIENCE OF ADMINISTRATION

of science or a strictly pragmatic, problem-solving mode of action-research. Yet as shown in **Figure 3.1**, its aims are both scientific (in a sociorationalist sense) and pragmatic (in a social-innovation sense) as well as metaphysical and normative (in the sense of attempting ethically to affirm all that social existence really is and should become). As a way of talking about the framework as it is actually practiced, we shall first examine four guiding principles that have directed our work in the area to date:

Principle 1: *Research into the social (innovation) potential of organizational, life should begin with appreciation.* This basic principle assumes that every social system "works" to some degree—that it is not in a complete state of entropy—and that a primary task of research is to discover, describe, and explain those social innovations, however small, which serve to give "life" to the system and activate members' competencies and energies as more fully functioning participants in the formation and transformation of organizational realities. That is, the appreciative approach takes its inspiration from the current state of "what is" and seeks a comprehensive understanding of the factors and forces of organizing (ideological, techno-structural, cultural) that serve to heighten the total potential of an organization in ideal-type human and social terms.

Principle 2: *Research into the social potential of organizational life should be applicable.* To be significant in a human sense, an applied science of administration should lead to the generation of theoretical knowledge that can be used, applied, and thereby validated in action. Thus, an applicable inquiry process is neither utopian in the sense of generating knowledge about "no place" (Sargent, 1982) nor should it be confined to academic circles and presented in ways that have little relevance to the everyday language and symbolism of those for whom the findings might be applicable.

Principle 3: *Research into the social potential of organizational life should be provocative.* Here it is considered axiomatic that an organization is, in fact, an open-ended indeterminate system capable of (1) becoming more than it is at any given moment, and (2) learning how to actively take part in guiding its own evolution. Hence, appreciative knowledge of what is (in terms of "peak" social innovations in organizing) is suggestive of what *might be* and such knowledge can be used to generate images of realistic developmental opportunities that can be experimented with on a wider scale. In this sense, appreciative inquiry can be both pragmatic and visionary. It becomes provocative to the extent that the abstracted findings of a study take on normative value for members of an organization, and this can happen only through their own critical deliberation and choice ("We feel that this particular finding is [or not] important for us to envision as an ideal to be striving for in practice on a wider scale"). It is in this way then, that appreciative inquiry allows us to put intuitive, visionary logic on a firm empirical footing and to use systematic research to help the organization's members shape the social world according to their own imaginative and moral purposes.

Principle 4: *Research into the social potential of organizational life should be collaborative.* This overarching principle points to the assumed existence of an inseparable relationship between the process of inquiry and its content. A collaborative relationship between the researcher and members of an organization is, therefore, deemed essential on the basis of both epistemological (Susman and Evered, 1978) and practical/ethical grounds (Habermas, 1971; Argyris, 1970). Simply put, a unilateral approach to the study of social innovation (bringing something new into the social world) is a direct negation of the phenomenon itself.

The spirit behind each of these four principles of appreciative inquiry is to be found in one of the most ancient archetypes or metaphorical symbols of hope and inspiration that humankind has ever known—the miracle and mystery of being. Throughout history, people have recognized the intimate relationship between being seized by the unfathomable and the process of appreciative knowing or thought (Marcel, 1963; Quinney, 1982; Jung, 1933; Maslow, 1968; Ghandi, 1958). According to Albert Schweitzer (1969), for example, it is recognition of the ultimate mystery that elevates our perception beyond the world of ordinary objects, igniting the life of the mind and a "reverence for life":

In all respects the universe remains mysterious to man… As soon as man does not take his existence for granted, but beholds it as something unfathomably mysterious, thought begins. This phenomenon has been repeated time and time again in the history of the human race. Ethical affirmation of life is the intellectual act by which man ceases simply to live at random… [Such] thought has a dual task to accomplish: to lead us out of a naive and into a profounder affirmation of life and the universe; and to help us progress from ethical impulses to a rational system of ethics (p. 33).

For those of us breastfed by an industrial giant that stripped the world of its wonder and awe, it feels, to put it bluntly, like an irrelevant, absurd, and even distracting interruption to pause, reflect deeply, and then humbly accept the depth of what we can never know—and to consider the ultimate reality of living for which there are no coordinates or certainties, only questions. Medicine cannot tell me, for example, what it means that my newborn son has life and motion and soul, anymore than the modern physicist can tell me what "nothingness" is, which, they say, makes up over 99 percent of the universe. In fact, if there is anything we have learned from a great physicist of our time is that the promise of certainty is a lie (Hiesenberg, 1958), and by living this lie as scientist doctrine, we short-circuit the gift of complementarity—the capacity for dialectically opposed modes of knowing, which adds richness, depth, and beauty to our lives (Bohr, 1958). Drugged by the products of our industrial machine we lose sight of and connection with the invisible mystery at the heart of creation, an ultimate power beyond rational understanding.

In the same way that birth of a living, breathing, loving, thinking human being is an inexplicable mystery, so too it can be said in no uncertain terms that *organizing is a miracle* of cooperative human interaction, of which there can never be final explanation. In fact, to the extent that organizations are indeed born and re-created through dialogue, they truly are unknowable as long as such creative dialogue remains. At this point in time there simply are no organizational theories that can account for the life-giving essence of cooperative existence, especially if one delves deeply enough. But, somehow we forget all this. We become lulled by our simplistic diagnostic boxes. The dilemma faced by our discipline in terms of its creative contribution to knowledge is summed up perfectly in the title of a well known article by one of the major advocates of action-research. The title by Marv Wiesbord (1976), has proven prophetic: "Organizational diagnosis: six places to look for trouble, with or without a theory." Content to transfer our conceptual curiosity over to "experts" who finally must know, our creative instincts lie pitifully dormant. Instead of explorers we become mechanics.

This, according to Koch (1981), is the source of "ameaningful" thinking. As Kierkegaard (1954) suggests, it is the essence of a certain dull-minded routine called "philistinism:

Devoid of imagination, as the Philistine always is, he lives in a certain trivial province of experience as to how things go, what is possible... Philistinism tranquilizes itself in the trivial (pp. 174175).

As we know, a miracle is something that is beyond all possible verification, yet is experienced as real. As a symbol, the word *miracle* represents unification of the sacred and secular into a realm of totality that is at once terrifying and beautiful, inspiring and threatening. Quinney (1982) has suggested with respect to the rejuvenation of social theory, that such a unified viewpoint is altogether necessary, that it can have a powerful impact on the discipline precisely because in a world that is at once sacred and secular there is no place, knowledge, or phenomenon that is without mystery. The "miracle" then is pragmatic in its effect when sincerely apprehended by a mind that has chosen not to become "tranquilized in the trivial." In this sense, the metaphor "life is a miracle" is not so much an idea as it is—or can be—a central feature of experience enveloping (1) our perceptual consciousness; (2) our way of relation to others, the world, and our own research; and (3) our way of knowing. Each of these points can be highlighted by a diverse literature.

In terms of the first, scholars have suggested that the power of what we call the miracle lies in its capacity to advance one's perceptual capacity what Maslow (1968) has called a B-cognition or a growth-vs-deficiency orientation, or what Kolb (1984) has termed integrative consciousness. Kolb writes:

The transcendental quality of integrative consciousness is precisely that, a "climbing out of"... This state of consciousness is not reserved for the monastery, but it is a necessary ingredient for creativity in any field. Albert Einstein once said, "The most beautiful and profound emotion one can feel is a sense of the mystical... It is the dower of all true science" (p. 158).

Second, as Gabriel Marcel (1963) explained in his William James lectures at Harvard on *The Mystery of Being,* the central conviction of life as a mystery creates for us a distinctly different relationship to the world than the conviction of life as a problem to be solved:

A problem is something met which bars my passage. It is before me in its entirety. A mystery on the other hand is something I find *myself* caught up in, and whose essence is therefore not before me in its entirety. It is though in this province the distinction between "in me" and "before me" loses its meaning (p. 80).

Berman's (1981) recent analysis comes to a similar conclusion. The re-enchantment of the world gives rise to a "participatory consciousness" where there is a sense of personal stake, ownership, and partnership with the universe:

The view of nature which predominated the West down to the eve of the Scientific Revolution was that of an enchanted world. Rocks, trees, rivers, and clouds were all seen as wondrous, alive, and human beings felt at home in this environment. The cosmos, in short, was a place of *belonging*. A member of this cosmos was not an alienated observer of it but a direct participant in its drama. His personal destiny was bound up with its destiny, and this relationship gave meaning to his life.

Third, as so many artists and poets have shown, there is a relationship between what the Greeks called *thaumazein—an experience which lies on the borderline between wonderment and admiration—and a type of intuitive apprehension or knowing that we call appreciative. For Keats, the purpose of his work was:*

to accept things as I saw them, to enjoy the beauty I perceived for its own sake, without regard to ultimate truth or falsity, and to make a description of it the end and purpose of my appreciations.

Similarly for Shelley:

Poetry thus makes immortal all that is best and most beautiful in the world… it exalts the beauty of that which is most beautiful… it strips the veil of familiarity from the world, and lays bare the naked and sleeping beauty, which is in the spirit of its forms.

And in strikingly similar words, learning theorist David Kolb (1984) analyzes the structure of the knowing mind and reports:

Finally, appreciation is a process of affirmation. Unlike criticism, which is based on skepticism and doubt (compare Polanyi, 1968, pp. 269ff.), appreciation is based on belief, trust, and conviction. And from this affirmative embrace flows a deeper fullness and richness of experience. This act of affirmation forms the foundation from which vital comprehension can develop… Appreciative apprehension and critical comprehension are thus fundamentally different processes of knowing. Appreciation of immediate experience is an act of attention, valuing, and affirmation, whereas critical comprehension of symbols is based on objectivity (which involves a priori controls of attention, as in double-blind controlled experiments), dispassionate analysis, and skepticism (pp. 104105).

We have cited these various thinkers in detail for several reasons: first, to underscore the fact that the powerful images of problem and miracle (in)form qualitatively distinct modes of inquiry which then shape our awareness, relations, and knowledge; and second, to highlight the conviction that the renewal of generative theory requires that we enter into the realm of the metaphysical. The chief characteristic of the modern mind has been the banishment of mystery from the world, and along with it an ethical affirmation of life that has served history as a leading source of values, hope, and normative bonding among people. In historical terms, we have steadily forgotten how to dream.

In contrast to a type of research that is lived without a sense of mystery, the appreciative mode awakens the desire to create and discover new social possibilities that can enrich our existence and give it meaning. In this sense, appreciative inquiry seeks an imaginative and fresh perception of organizations as "ordinary magic," as if seen for the first time—or perhaps the last time (Hayward, 1984). The appreciative mode, in exploration of ordinary magic, is an inquiry process that takes nothing for granted, searching to apprehend the basis of organizational life and working to articulate those possibilities giving witness to a better existence.

The metaphysical dimension of appreciative inquiry is important not so much as a way of finding answers but is important insofar as it heightens the living experience of awe and wonder which leads us to the wellspring of new questions—much like a wide-eyed explorer without final destination. Only by raising innovative questions will innovations in theory and practice be found. As far as action-research is concerned, this appears to have been the source of Lewin's original and catalytic genius. We too can re-awaken this spirit. Because the questions we ask largely determine what we find, we should place a premium on that which informs our curiosity and thought. The metaphysical question of what makes social existence possible will never go away. The generative-theoretical question of compelling new possibilities will never go away. The normative question of what kind of social-organizational order is best, most dignified, and just, will never go away, nor will the pragmatic question of how to move closer to the ideal.

In its pragmatic form appreciative inquiry represents a data-based theory building methodology for evolving and putting into practice the collective will of a group or organization. It has one and only one aim—to provide a generative theoretical springboard for normative dialogue that is conducive to self-directed experimentation in social innovation. It must be noted, however, that the conceptual world which appreciative inquiry creates remains—despite its empirical content—an illusion. This is important to recognize because it is precisely because of its visionary content, placed in juxtaposition to grounded examples of the extraordinary, that appreciative inquiry opens the status quo to possible transformations in collective action. It appreciates the best of "what is" to ignite intuition of the possible and then firmly unites the two logically, caringly, and passionately into a theoretical hypothesis of an envisioned future. By raising ever new questions of an appreciative, applicable, and provocative nature, the researcher collaborates in the scientific construction of his or her world.6

Conclusion

What we have tried to do with this chapter is present conceptual refiguration of action-research; to present a proposal arguing for an enriched multidimensional view of action-research which seeks to be both theoretically generative and progressive in a broad human sense. In short, the argument is a simple one stating that there is a need to re-awaken the imaginative spirit of action-research and that to do this we need a fundamentally different perspective toward our organizational world, one that admits to its uncertainties, ambiguities, mysteries, and unexplicable, miraculous nature. But now we must admit, with a certain sense of limited capability and failure, that the viewpoint articulated here is simply not possible to define and is very difficult to speak of in technological, step-by-step terms. From the perspective of rational thought, the miraculous is impossible. From that of problem solving it is nonsense. And from that of empirical science, it is categorically denied (Reeves, 1984). Just as we cannot prove the proposition that organizing is a problem to be solved, so, too, we cannot prove in any rational, analytical, or empirical way that organizing is a miracle to be embraced. Each stance represents a commitment—a core conviction so to speak—which is given to each of us as a choice. We do, however, think that through discipline and training the appreciative eye can be developed to see the ordinary magic, beauty, and real possibility in organizational life; but we are not sure we can so easily transform our central convictions.

In sum, the position we have been developing here is that for action-research to reach its potential as a vehicle for social innovation, it needs to begin advancing theoretical knowledge of consequence—that good theory may be one of the most powerful means human beings have for producing change in a post-industrial world; that the discipline's steadfast commitment to a problem-solving view of the world is a primary restraint on its imagination, passion, and positive contribution; that appreciative inquiry represents a viable complement to conventional forms of action- research, one uniquely suited for social innovation instead of problem solving; and that through our assumptions and choice of method we largely create the world we later discover.

References

Argyris, C. (1973). Action science and intervention. *The Journal of Applied Behavioral Science,* 19, 115140.

Argyris, C. (1970). *Intervention theory and methods.* Reading, MA: Addison-Wesley.

Argyris, C. and Schon, D. (1978). *Organizational learning: A theory of action perspective.* Reading. MA: Addison-Wesley.

Bartunek, J. (1983). How organization development can develop organizational theory. *Group and Organizational Studies.* 8, 303318.

Bartunek, J. (1984). Changing interpretive schemes and organizational restructuring: The example of a religious order. *Administrative Science Quarterly,* 27, 355372.

Bell, D. (1973). *The coming of the Post-Industrial society.* New York: Basic Books.

Beyer, J. (1981). Ideologies, values and decision making in organizations. In P. C. Nystrom and W. H. Starbuck (Eds.), *Handbook of organizational design, Vol. 2.* Oxford University Press.

Beyer, J. and Trice, H. (1982). Utilization process: Conceptual framework and synthesis of findings. *Administrative Science Quarterly,* 22, 591622.

Blake. R. and Mouton. J. (1976). *Consultation.* Reading, MA: Addison Wesley.

Bohr, N. (1958). *Atomic theory and human knowledge.* New York: John Wiley.

Bradford, L. P., Gibb, J. R., and Benne, K. (1964). *T-group theory and laboratory method.* New York: John Wiley.

Braverman, H. (1974). *Labor and monopoly capital.* New York: Monthly Review Press.

Brimm, M. (1972). When is change not a change? *Journal of Applied Behavioral Science,* 1, 102107.

Brown, R. H. (1978). *Leadership.* New York: Harper and Row.

Chiles, C. (1983). Comments on "design guidelines for social problem solving interventions." *Journal of Applied Behavioral Science* 19, 189191.

Clegg, S. and Dunkerley. D. (1980). *Organization, class, and control.* Boston: Routledge and Kegan Paul.

Cohen, A. R., Fink, S. L., Gadon, H., and Willits, R. D. (1984). *Effective behavior in organizations.* Homewood, IL: Irwin.

Cooperrider, D. (I 986). *Appreciative Inquiry: Toward a methodology for understanding and enhancing organizational innovation.* Unpublished Ph.D. dissertation, Case Western Reserve University, Cleveland, OH.

Deal, T. E. and Kennedy, A. A. (1982). *Corporate cultures.* Reading, Mass.: Addison-Wesley.

Dubin, R. (1978). *Theory Building.* New York: The Free Press.

Ellwood, C. (1938). *A history of social philosophy.* New York: Prentice-Hall.

Forester, John (1983). Critical theory and organizational analysis. In G. Morgan (Ed.). *Beyond methods* Beverly Hills, CA: Sage Publications.

French, W. L. (1969). Organization development objectives, assumptions, and strategies. *Management Review,* 12(2), 2334.

French, W. L. and Bell, C. H. (1978). *Organization development.* New Jersey: Prentice-Hall.

Friedlander, F. (1984). Producing useful knowledge for organizations. *Administrative Science Quarterly,* 29, 646648.

Friedlander, F. (1977). Alternative methods of inquiry. Presented at APA Convention. San Francisco, Ca.

Friedlander, F. and Brown, L. D. (1974). Organization development, *Annual Review of Psychology,* 25, 313341.

Frohman, M., Sashkin, M., and Kavanaugh, M. (1976). Action-research as applied to organization development. *Organization and Administrative Sciences,* 1, 129161.

Geertz, C. (1980). Blurred genres: The refiguration of social thought. *American Scholar,* 49, 165179.

Gergen, K. (1982). *Toward transformation in social knowledge.* New York: Springer-Verlag.

Gergen, K. (1978). Toward generative theory. *Journal of Personality and Social Psychology,* 36, 13441360.

Ghandi, M. (1958). *All men are brothers.* New York: Columbia University Press.

Gorz, A. (1973). Workers' control is more than just that. In Hunnius, Garson. and Case (Eds.), *Workers control.* New York: Vintage Books.

Gould, S. J. (1981). *The mismeasure of man.* New York: Norton and Company.

Gouldner, A. (1970). *The coming crisis of Western sociology.* New York: Basic Books.

Habermas, J. (1971). *Knowledge and human interests.* Boston: Beacon Press.

Haley, J. *Uncommon therapy.* New York: W. W. Norton, 1973.

Hare, P. H. (1976). *Handbook of small group research.* New York: The Free Press.

Harrison, R. (1982). *Leadership and strategy for a new age: Lessons from "conscious evolution."* Menlo Park, CA: Values and Lifestyles Program.

Hausser, D., Pecorelia, P., and Wissler, A. (1977). *Survey-guided development 11.* LaJolla, Calif.: University Associates.

Hayward, J. (1984). *Perceiving ordinary magic.* Gouldner: New Science Library.

Hiesenberg, W. (I 958). *Physics and philosophy: The revolution in modern science.* London: Allen and Urwig.

Henshel, R. (1975). Effects of disciplinary prestige on predictive accuracy. *Futures,* 7, 92106.

Hofstede, G. (1980). *Culture's consequences.* Beverly Hills, CA: Sage.

Jung, C. (1933). *Modern man in search of a soul.* New York: Harcourt, Brace and Company.

Keeley, M. (1980). Organizational analogy: Comparison of orgasmic and social contract models, *Administrative Science Quarterly,* 25, 337362.

Kepner, C. and Trego, B. (1973). *Executive problem analysis and decision making.* Princeton, NJ.

Kierkegaard, S. (1954). *The sickness unto death.* New York: Anchor Books. Translated by Walter Lowrie.

Kilmann, R. (1979). Problem management: A behavioral science approach. In G. Zaltman (Ed.). *Management principles for non-profit agencies and organizations.* New York: American Management Association.

Koch, S. (1981). The nature and limits of psychological knowledge. *American Psychologist,* 36, 257269.

Kolb, D. A. (1984). *Experiential learning.* Englewood Cliffs, NJ: Prentice-Hall.

Kolb, D. A. (1983). Problem management: Learning from experience. In S. Srivastva (Ed.), *The executive mind.* San Francisco: Jossey-Bass.

Levinson, H. (1972) The clinical psychologist as organizational diagnostician. *Professional Psychology,* 10, 485502.

Levinson, H. (1972). *Organizational diagnosis.* Cambridge, MA: Harvard University Press.

Lewin, K. (1948). Action research and minority problems. In G. W. Lewin (Ed.), *Resolving social conflicts.* New York: Harper and Row.

Lewin, K. (1951). *Field theory in social science.* New York: Harper and Row.

Lukes, S. (1974). *Power: A radical view.* London: Macmillan.

Mannheim, K. (1936). *Ideology and utopia.* New York: Harcourt, Brace and World.

Marcel, G. (1963). *The existential background of human dignity.* Cambridge: Harvard University Press.

Margulies, N. and Raia, A. P. (1972). *Organization development: Values, process and technology.* New York: McGraw Hill.

Marrow, A. (1968). *The practical theorist.* New York: Basic Books.

Maslow, A. (1968). *Toward a psychology of being.* New York: Van Nostrand Reinhold Co.

McHugh, P. (1970). On the failure of positivism. In J. Douglas (Ed.), *Understanding everyday life.* Chicago: Aldine.

Mitroff, I. (1980). Reality as a scientific strategy: Revising our concepts of science. *Academy of Management Review,* 5, 513515.

Mitroff, I. and Kilmann, R. (1978). *Methodological approaches to social sciences.* San Francisco: Jossey-Bass.

Morgan, G. (1983). *Beyond method.* Beverly Hills: Sage Publications.

Morgan, G. (1980). Paradigms, metaphors, and puzzle solving in organization theory. *Administrative Science Quarterly,* 24, 605622.

Ortony, A. (Ed.) (1979). *Metaphor and thought.* Cambridge: Cambridge University Press.

Ouchi, W. G. and Johnson, J. B. (1978). Types of organizational control and their relationship to emotional well-being. *Administrative Science Quarterly,* 23, 293317.

Pasmore, W., Cooperrider, D., Kaplan, M. and Morris, B. (1983). Introducing managers to performance development. In *The ecology of work,.* Proceedings of the Sixth NTL Ecology of Work Conference, Cleveland, Ohio.

Pasmore, W. and Friedlander, F. (1982). An action-research program for increasing employee involvement in problem solving. *Administrative Science Quarterly,* 27, 343362.

Pepper, S. C. (1942). *World hypothesis.* Berkeley, CA: University of California Press.

Peters, M. and Robinson, V. (1984). The origins and status of action research. *Journal of Applied Behavioral Science,* 20, 113124.

Quinney, R. (1982). *Social existence: Metaphysics, Marxism, and the social sciences.* Beverly Hills, CA: Sage Publications.

Rappaport, R. W. (1970). Three dilemmas of action-research. *Human Relations,* 23, 499513.

Reeves, G. (1984). The idea of mystery in the philosophy of Gabriel Marcel. In J. Schlipp, and L. Hahn, (Eds.), *The philosophy of Gabriel Marcel.* LaSalle, IL: Open Court.

Sargent, L. T. (1982). Authority and utopia: Utopianisms in political thought. *Polity,* 4, 565584.

Sathe, V. J. (1983). Implications of corporate culture. *Organizational Dynamics,* Autumn, 523.

Schein, E. (1983). The role of the founder in creating organizational culture. *Organizational Dynamics,* Summer, 1228.

Schweitzer, A. (1969). *The teaching of reverence for life.* New York: Holt, Rinehart and Winston.

Small, A. (1905). *General sociology: An exposition of the main development in sociological theory from Spencer to Ratzenhofer.* Chicago: University of Chicago Press.

Smirchich, L. (1983). Studying organizations as cultures. In G. Morgan (Ed.), *Beyond method.* Beverly Hills, CA: Sage Publications.

Sproull, L. S. (1981). Beliefs in organizations. In P. C. Nystrom and W. H. Starbuck (Eds.), *Handbook of organizational design, Vol. 2.* New York: Oxford University Press.

Srivastva, S. (1985). *Executive power.* San Francisco: Jossey-Bass Publishers.

Srivastva, S. (1983). *The executive mind.* San Francisco: Jossey-Bass Publishers.

Srivastva, S. and Cooperrider, D. (1986). The emergence of the egalitarian organization. *Human Relations,* London: Tavistock.

Srivastva, S., Obert, S. and Neilsen, E. (1977). Organizational analysis through group process: A theoretical perspective for organization development. In C. Cooper (Ed.) *Organization development in the U.K. and U.S.A.* New York: The Macmillan Press.

Staw, B. (1984). Organizational behavior: A review and reformulation of the field's outcome variables. *Annual Review of Psychology,* 35, 626666.

Susman, G. and Evered, R. (1978). An assessment of the scientific merits of action-research. *Administrative Science Quarterly,* 23, 582603.

Thelen, H. (1954). *Dynamics of groups at work.* Chicago University of Chicago Press.

Torbert, W. (1983). Initiating collaborative inquiry. In G. Morgan (Ed.). *Beyond method.* Beverly Hills, CA: Sage Publications.

Van Maanen, J., Dabbs, J. M., and Faulkner, R. R. (I 982). *Varieties of qualitative research.* Beverly Hills, Calif.: Sage Publications.

Watzlawick, P., Weakland, J., and Fish, R. (1974). *Change: Principles of problem formation and problem resolution.* New York: Horton.

Weick, K. E. (1983). Managerial thought in the context of action. In S. Srivastva (Ed.), *The executive mind.* San Francisco: Jossey-Bass.

Wiesbord, M. (1976). Organization diagnosis: Six places to look for trouble with or without a theory. *Group and Organization Studies,* 1, 430447.

Weiss, C. H. and Bucuvalas, M. (1980). The challenge of social research to decision making. In C. H. Weiss (Ed.), *Using social research in public policy making.* Lexington, MA: Lexington Books.

Whitehead, A. N. (1929). *The function of reason.* Boston: Beacon Press.

Whyte, W. F. (1982). Social inventions for solving human problems. *American Sociological Review,* 47, 113.

Positive Image, Positive Action:
The Affirmative Basis of Organizing

David L. Cooperrider
Case Western Reserve University

Be not afraid of life. Believe that life is worth living, and your belief will help you create the fact.

—William James.

We can easily forgive a child who is afraid of the dark. The real tragedy of life is when men are afraid of the light.

—Plato

Modern management thought was born proclaiming that organizations are the triumph of the human imagination. As made and imaged, organizations are products of human imagination. As made and imagined, organizations are products of human interaction and mind rather than some blind expression of an underlying natural order (McGregor, 1960; Berger and Luckmann, 1967; Pfeffer, 1981; Gergen, 1982; Srivastva and Associates, 1983; Schein, 1985; Unger, 1987). Deceptively simple yet so entirely radical in implication, this insight is still shattering many beliefs—one of which is the long-standing conviction that bureaucracy, oligarchy, and other forms of hierarchical domination are inevitable. Today we know that this simply is not true.

Recognizing the symbolic and socially constructed nature of the human universe, we now find new legitimacy for the mounting wave of sociocognitive and sociocultural research, all of which is converging around one essential and empowering thesis: that there is little about collective action or organization development that is preprogrammed, unilaterally determined, or stimulus bound in any direct physical or material way. Seemingly immutable ideas about people and organizations are being directly challenged and transformed on an unprecedented scale. Indeed, as we move into a postmodern global society we are breaking out of our parochial perspectives and are recognizing that organizations in all societies exist in a wide array of types and species and function within a dynamic spectrum of beliefs and lifestyles. And according to the social constructionist viewpoint, the possibilities are infinite.

Interestingly, there is an important parallel to this whole area of thought that has grown out of the neurosciences and studies of cognition and mind–brain interaction. The "consciousness revolution" of the 1970s is well documented and represents, argues Nobel Laureate Roger Sperry (1988), more than a mere Zeitgeist phenomenon; it represents a profound conceptual shift to a different form of causal determinism. According to the mentalist paradigm, mind can no longer be considered the opposite of matter. Mental phenomena, this paradigm contends, must be recognized as being at the top of

Cooperrider, D.L. (1999). *Positive Action: The Affirmative Basis of Organizing. Appreciative Management and Leadership.* Euclid, OH, Lakeshore Communications: 91-125.

the brain's "causal control hierarchy" whereby, after millenniums of evolution, the mind has been given primacy over bioevolutionary (Darwinian) controls that determine what human systems are and can become. In direct contradiction to materialist and behaviorist doctrine, where everything is supposed to be governed from below upward through microdeterminist stimuli and physiochemical forces, the new mentalist view gives subjective mental phenomena a causal role in brain processing and thereby a new legitimacy in science as an autonomous explanatory construct. Future reality, in this view, is permeable, emergent, and open to the mind's causal influence; that is, reality is conditioned, reconstructed, and often profoundly created through our anticipatory images, values, plans, intentions, beliefs, and the like. Macrodeterminisim or the theory of downward causation is a scheme, asserts Sperry, that idealizes ideas and ideals over chemical interactions, nerve impulse traffic and DNA. It is a brain model in which conscious, mental, and psychic forces are recognized as the crowing achievement of some 500 million years or more of evolution.

The impetus for the present contribution grows from the exciting challenge that is implicitly if not explicitly posed by the social constructionist and mentalist paradigms: that to a far greater extent than is normally acknowledged, we human beings create our own realities through symbolic and mental processes and that because of this, consciousness evolution of the future is a human option. Taking this challenge—that of a future-creating mental activism—one step further, the thesis explored in this paper is that the artful creation of positive imagery on a collective basis may well be the most prolific activity that individuals and organizations can engage in if their aim is to help bring to fruition a positive and humanly significant future. Stated more boldly a New York Times headline recently apprised the public that "Research Affirms Power of Positive Thinking" (Goleman, 1987, p. 15). Implied in the popular news release and the scholarly research that we will soon sample is the intriguing suggestion that human systems are largely heliotropic in character, meaning that they exhibit an observable and largely automatic tendency to evolve in the direction of positive anticipatory images of the future. What I will argue is that just as plants of many varieties exhibit a tendency to grow in the direction of sunlight (symbolized by the Greek god Helios), there is an analogous process going on in all human systems.

As a whole this essay is intended to serve as an invitation to broadly consider a number of questions: What is the relationship between positive imagery and positive action? More specifically, what are the common processes, pathways, or global patterns whereby mental phenomena attract or even cause those actions that bring about movement toward an ideal? Where do positive images of some unknown and neutral future come from in the first place? Could it be that organizations are in fact affirmative systems, governed and maintained by positive projections about what the organization is, how it will function, and what it might become? If so, what are the implications for management? Is it true that the central executive task in a postbureaucratic society is to nourish the appreciative soil from which affirmative projections grow, branch off, evolve, and become collective projections?

To set the stage for our discourse, the first section will begin with a general introduction to the concept of imagery. The second will look specifically at the relationship between positive imagery and positive action by reviewing recent works from diverse areas of study—medicine, cognitive psychology, cultural sociology, and athletics. While I am careful not to suggest that the studies sampled make anything close to an exhaustive case, I do submit, nevertheless, that the convergence of insight, across disciples, represent an exciting step forward in our understandings of the intricate pathways that link mind and practice. Finally, in the third section, I will discuss how such knowledge from diverse quarters holds a thread of continuity that has broad relevance for understanding organizations. In particular, I will offer a set of eight propositions about the affirmative basis of organizing. These propositions are provided for discussion, elaboration, and active experimentation and converge around three basic conclusions: (1) Organizations are products of the affirmative mind; (2) when beset with repetitive difficulties or problems, organizations need less fixing, less problem solving, and more reaffirmation—or more precisely, more appreciation; (3) the primary executive vocation in a postbureaucratic era is to nourish the appreciative soil from which new and better guiding images grow on a collective and dynamic basis.

Imagery: An Introduction

Throughout the ages and from a diversity of perspectives, the image has been considered a powerful agent in the guidance and determination of action:

A vivid imagination compels the whole body to obey it.
—*Aristotle (in Sheikh, 1984, p. 5)*

One of the basic theorems of the theory of image is that it is the image which in fact determines what might be called the current behavior of any organism or organization. The image acts as a field. The behavior consists in gravitating toward the most highly valued part of the world.
—*Kenneth Boulding (1966, p. 155)*

Mental anticipation now pulls the future into the present and reverses the direction of causality.
—*Erich Jantsch (1980, p. 14)*

Man is a being who, being in the world, is ever ahead of himself, caught up in bringing things alive with his projection.... Whatever comes to light owes its presence to the fact that man has provided the overall imaginative sunlight for viewing.
—*Edward Murray (1986, p. 64)*

To the empowering principle that people can withhold legitimacy, and thus change the world, we now add another. By deliberately changing the internal image of reality, people can change the world.
—*Willis Harman (1988, p. 1)*

Imagination is more important than knowledge.
—*Albert Einstein (in Sheikh, 1984, p. 5)*

It is clear that images are operative virtually everywhere: Soviet and U.S. diplomats create strategies on the basis of images; Theory X managers construct management structures that reflect the pictures they hold of subordinates; days or minutes before a public speech we all feel the tension or anxiety that accompanies our anticipatory viewing of the audience; we all hold self-images, images of our race, profession, nation, and cultural belief systems; and we have images of our own potential as well as the potential of others. Fundamentally, too, it can be argued that every organization, product, or innovative service first started as a wild but not idle dream and that anticipatory realities are what make collectivities click. (This is why we still experience King, Jr's "I Have a Dream" and sometimes find ourselves enlivened through the images associated with the mere mention of such figures as John F. Kennedy, Gandhi, Winston Churchill, Buddha, or Christ.)

Given the central and pervasive role of the image in relation to action, it is not surprising that research on the workings of the image has risen to be "one of the hottest topics in cognitive science" (Block, 1981, p. 1). Theorists disagree over definitions and argue whether images are direct encoding of perceptual experience (Pavid, 1971), are an artifact of the propositional structuring of reality (Pylyshyn, 1973), represent the sensory system par excellence that undergirds and constitutes virtually every area of cognitive processing, are primarily eidetic or visual (Ashen, 1977), or represent constructive or reconstructive process (Kosslyn, 1980). But in spite of the largely technical differences, Richardson (1969, pp. 2–3) seems to have provided adequate synthesis of a number of competing views in his often-quoted definition of the image as quasi-sensory, stimulus-independent representative experience: "Mental imagery refers to (1) all those quasi-sensory or quasi-perceptual experiences of which (2) we are self consciously aware and which (3) exist for us in the absence of those stimulus conditions that are know to reproduce their sensory or perceptual counterparts, and which (4) may be expected to have different consequences."

In subsequent work, Richardson (1983) retracts the fourth criterion; between 1969 and 1983 there was simply too much new evidence showing that self-initiated imagery can and often does have consequences, many of them physiological, that are indistinguishable from their genuine sensory counterparts. Merely an anticipatory image, for example, of a hostile encounter can raise one's blood pressure as much as the encounter itself. Similarly, numerous new studies now show that consciously constructed images can lead directly to such things as blood glucose increases, increased gastric acid secretion, blister formation, and changes in skin temperature and pupillary size. In an example closer to home, Richardson (1983, p. 15) suggests that "it suffices to remind the reader of what every schoolboy (or girl) knows. Clear and unmistakable physiological consequences follow from absorption in a favorite sexual fantasy." Mind and body are indeed a unified interdependent system.

Perhaps most important, as the above begins to make clear, it is the time dimension of the future—what Harry Stack Sullivan (1947) referred to as "anticipatory reality"—that acts as a prepotent force in the dynamic of all images (for a decision theory counterpart to this view, see Mitchell, Rediker, and Beach, 1986; Polak, 1973). The recognition that every social action somehow involves anticipation of the future, in the sense that it involves a reflexive look-forward-to and backward-from, has been analyzed by Alfred Schultz (1967) and Karl Weick (1976). Similarly, in Heidegger's brilliant formulation it is our nature not only to be thrown into existence (Geworfenheil) but to always be ahead of ourselves in the world, to be engaged in the unfolding of projected realities; all action, according to Heidegger, has the nature of a project (Heidegger refers to this as Entwurf, the continuous projecting ahead of a design or a blueprint). Much like a movie projection on a screen, human systems are forever projecting ahead of themselves a horizon of expectation that brings the future powerfully into the present as a causal agent.

Recent Works on the Positive Image–Positive Action Relationship

What all this suggests, of course, is that the power of positive imagery is not just some popular illusion or wish but is arguably a key factor in every action. To illustrate the heliotropic propensity in human systems at several levels of functioning I will now turn to six areas of research as example—placebo, Pygmalion, positive emotion, internal dialogue, cultural vitality, and metacognitive competence.

Positive Imagery, Medicine, and the Placebo

The placebo response is a fascinating and complex process in which projected images, as reflected in positive belief in the efficacy of a remedy, ignite a healing response that can be every bit as powerful as conventional therapy. Though the placebo phenomenon has been controversial for some twenty years, most of the medical profession now accepts as genuine, the fact that anywhere from one-third to two-thirds of all patients will show marked physiological and emotional improvement in symptoms simply by believing they are given an effective treatment, even when that treatment is just a sugar pill or some other inert substance (Beecher, 1955; White, Tursky, and Schwartz, 1985). Numerous carefully controlled studies indicate that the placebo can provide relief of symptoms in postoperative-wound pain, seasickness, headaches, angina, asthma, obesity, blood pressure, ulcers, and many other problems. In fact, researchers are now convinced that no system of the body is exempt from the placebo effect and that it is operative in virtually every healing encounter. Even more intriguing, the placebo is sometimes even more potent than typically expected drug effects: "Consider a series of experiments with a woman suffering from severe nausea and vomiting. Nothing the doctors gave her seemed to help. Objective measurement of her gastric contractions showed a disrupted pattern consistent with the severe nausea she reported. The doctors then offered her a 'new extremely powerful wonder drug' which would, they said, unquestionably cure her nausea. Within twenty minutes of taking this new drug, her nausea disappeared, and the same objective gastric tests now read normal. The drug which was given was not, of course, a new drug designed to relieve nausea. It was syrup of ipecac, which is generally used to induce vomiting, In this case, the placebo effect associated with the suggestion that the drug would relieve vomiting was powerful enough to counteract and direct an opposite pharmacological action of the drug itself" (Ornstein and Sobel, 1987, p. 79).

   According to Norman Cousins, now a faculty member at the UCLA School of Medicine, and understanding of the way the placebo works may be one of the most significant developments in medicine in the twentieth century. Writing in Human Options (1981), Cousins suggests that beyond the central nervous system, the hormonal system, and the immune system, there are two other systems that have conventionally been overlooked but that need to be recognized as essential to the proper functioning of the human being: the healing and the belief system. Cousins (1983, p. 203) argues that the two work together: "The healing system is the way the body mobilizes all its resources to combat disease. The belief system is often the activator of the healing system."

   Using himself as a living laboratory, Cousins (1983, p. 44) has movingly described how the management of his own anticipatory reality allowed him to overcome a life-threatening illness that specialists did not believe to be reversible and then, some years later, to again apply the same mental processes in his recovery from an acute heart attack: "What were the basic ideas involved in that recovery? The newspaper accounts had made it appear that I had laughed my way out of a serious illness. Careful readers of my book, however, knew that laughter was just a metaphor.… Hope, faith, love, will to live, cheerfulness, humor, creativity, playfulness, confidence, great expectations—all these, I believed, had therapeutic value."

   In the end, argues Cousins, the greatest value of the placebo is that it tells us that indeed positive imagery can and often does awaken the body to its own self-healing powers. Research in many areas now confirms this view and shows that the placebo responses are neither mystical nor inconsequential and that ultimately mental and psychophysiological responses may be mediated through more than fifty different neuropeptide molecular messengers linking the endocrine, autonomic, and central nervous systems (White, Tursky, and Schwartz, 1985). While the complex mind-body pathways are far from being resolved, there is one area of clear agreement: Positive changes in anticipatory reality through suggestion and belief play a central role in all placebo responses. As Jaffe and Bresler (1980, pp. 260–261) note, the placebo "Illustrates another important therapeutic use of imagery, namely, the use of positive future images to activate positive physical changes. Imagining a positive future outcome is an important technique for countering initial negative images, beliefs, and expectations a patient may have. In essence it transforms a negative placebo effect into a positive one.... The power of positive suggestion plants a seed which redirects the mind—and through the mind, the body—toward a positive goal."

Before moving on, there is one other perhaps surprising factor that adds significantly to the patient's placebo response—the expectancy or anticipatory reality of the physician. Placebo effects are strongest, it appears, when belief in the efficacy of the treatment is shared among a group (O'Regan, 1983). This then raises a whole new set of questions concerning not only the individual but the interpersonal nature of the positive image-positive action relationship.

Pygmalion and the Positive Construction of the Other

In effect, the positive image may well be the sine qua non of human development, as we now explore in the Pygmalion dynamic. As a special case of the self-fulfilling prophesy, Pygmalion reminds us that from the moment of birth we each exist within a complex and dynamic field of images and expectations, a vast share of which are projected onto us through an omnipresent environment of others.

In the classic Pygmalion study, teachers are led to believe on the basis of "credible" information that some of their students possess exceptionally high potential while others do not. In other words, the teachers are led, on the basis of some expert opinion, to hold a positive image (PI) or expectancy of some students and a negative image (NI) or expectancy of others. Unknown to the teachers, however, is the fact that the so-called high-potential students were selected at random; in objective terms, all student groupings were equivalent in potential and are merely dubbed as high, regular, or low potential. Then, as the experiment unfolds, differences quickly emerge, not on the basis of any innate intelligence factor or some other predisposition but solely on the basis of the manipulated expectancy of the teacher. Over time, subtle changes among students evolve into clear differences as the high-PI students begin to significantly overshadow all others in actual achievement. Over the last twenty years there have been literally hundreds of empirical studies conducted on this phenomenon, attesting both to its continuing theoretical and to its practical importance (Jussim, 1986; see Rosenthal and Rubin, 1978, for an analysis of over 300 studies).

One of the remarkable things about Pygmalion is that it shows us how essentially modifiable the human self is in relation to the mental projections of others. Indeed, not only do performance levels change, but so do more deeply rooted "stable" self-conceptions (Parsons and others, 1982). Furthermore, significant Pygmalion effects have been experimentally generated in as little time as fifteen minutes (King, 1971) and have the apparent capacity to transform the course of a lifetime (Cooper and Good, 1983). (I wonder how many researchers on this subject would volunteer their own children to be part of a negatively induced expectancy grouping?) Specific to the classroom, the correlation between teacher expectation and student achievement is higher than almost any predictive IQ or achievement measure, ranging in numerous studies from correlations of .5 all the way to an almost perfect (Brophy and Good, 1974; Crano and Mellon, 1978; Hymphreys and Stubbs, 1977). Likewise, in one of the earliest organizational examinations of this phenomenon, Eden and Shani (1982) reported that some 75 percent of the variance in achievement among military trainees could be explained completely on the basis of induced positive expectation on the part of those in positions of authority.

Obviously the promise of Pygmalion as a source of human development depends more on the enactment of positive rather than negative interpersonal expectancy. But how does the positive dynamic work and why?

A summary of the three stages of the positive Pygmalion dynamic is presented in **Figure 2.1.** In the first phase of the model, positive images of the other are formed through any number of means—for example, stereotypes, reputation, hearsay, objective measures, early performances, and naive prediction processes. As interactions occur over time, positive images begin to take shape and consist not only of prophesies but also tend to become elaborated by one's sense of its other possibilities as well as one's sense of "what should be," or normative valuations. Taken together the prophesies, possibilities, and normative valuations combine to create a broad brushstroke picture of interpersonal expectancy that has its pervasive effect through two primary mediators—expectancy-consistent cognition and expectancy-consistent treatment.

Figure 2.1: The Positive Pygmalion Dynamic (adapted from Jussim, 1986)

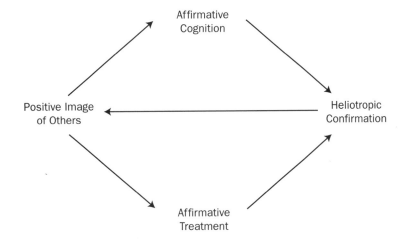

Considerable evidence, for example, indicates that a positive image of another serves as a powerful cognitive tuning device that appears to trigger in the perceiver an increased capacity to (1) perceive the successes of another (Deaux and Ernswiller, 1974), (2) access from memory the positive rather than negative aspects of the other (Hastie and Kumar, 1979), and (3) perceive ambiguous situations for their positive rather than negative possibilities (Darley and Gross, 1983).

While often spoken about in pejorative ways as cognitive bias or distortion ("vital lies," to use Goleman's popular term), it is quite possible that this affirmative capacity to cognitively tune into the most positive aspects of another human being is in fact a remarkable human gift; it is not merely an aberration distorting some "given" reality but is a creative agent in the construction of reality. We see what our images make us capable of seeing. And affirmative cognition, as we will later highlight in our discussion of positive self-monitoring, is a unique and powerful competency that owes its existence to the dynamic workings of the positive image.

The key point is that all of our cognitive capacities—perception, memory, learning—are cued and shaped by the images projected through our expectancies. We see what our imaginative horizon allows us to see. And because "seeing is believing," our acts often take on a whole new tone and character depending on the strength, vitality, and force of a given image. The second consequence of the positive image of the other, therefore, is that it supports differential behavioral treatment in a number of systematic ways.

For example, it has been shown, both in the field and the laboratory, that teachers who hold extremely positive images of their students tend to provide those students with (1) increased emotional support in comparison to others (Rist, 1970; Rubovitz and Maeher, 1973); (2) clearer, more immediate, and more positive feedback around effect and performance (Weinstein, 1976; Cooper, 1979); and (3) better opportunities to perform and learn more challenging materials (Brophy and Good, 1974; Swann and Snyder, 1980).

Finally, in the third stage of the model, people begin to respond to the positive images that others have of them. When mediated by cognitive, affective, and motivational factors, according to Jussim (1986), heliotropic acts are initiated on the basis of increased effort, persistence, attention, participation, and cooperation, so that ultimately, high PIs often perform at levels superior to those projected with low-expectancy images. Research also shows that such effects tend to be long lasting, especially when the Pygmalion dynamic becomes institutionalized. High-PI students, for example, when assigned to the higher academic tracks, are virtually never moved to a lower track (the same is also true for negative-expectancy students, according to Brophy and Good's 1974 review of the "near permanence" of tracking).

The greatest value of the Pygmalion research is that it begins to provide empirical understanding of the relational pathways of the positive image-positive action dynamic and of the transactional basis of the human self. To understand the self as a symbolic social creation is to recognize—as George Herbert Mead, John Dewey, George Simmel, Lev Vygotsky, Martin Buber, and many others have argued—that human beings are essentially modifiable, are open to new development, and are products of the human imagination and mind. We are each made and imagined in the eyes of one another. There is an utter inseparability of the individual from the social context and history of the projective process. And positive interpersonal imagery, the research now shows, accomplishes its work very concretely. Like the placebo response discussed earlier, it appears that the positive image plants a seed that redirects the mind of the perceiver to think about and see the other with affirmative eyes.

Positive Affect and Learned Helpfulness

While often talked about in cognitive terms, one of the core features of imagery is that it integrates cognition and affect becomes a catalytic force through its sentiment-evoking quality. In many therapies, for example, it is well established that focusing on images often elicits strong emotional reactions; whereas verbal mental processes are linear, the image provides simultaneous representation, making it possible to vicariously experience that which is held in the imagination (Sheikh and Panagiotou, 1975).

So what about the relation between positive emotion—delight, compassion, joy, love, happiness, passion, and so on—and positive action? To what extent is it the affective side of the positive image that generates and sustains heliotropic movement so often seen in human systems? While still in the formative stages, early results on this issue are making clear that there is indeed a unique psychophysiology of positive emotion (as Norman Cousins has argued) and that individually as well as collectively, positive emotion may well be the pivotal factor determining the heliotropic potential of images of the future.

This line of research is partly predicated on knowledge growing out of studies of negative affectivity. In one of the most hotly pursued lines of research of the last decade, investigators are now convinced of the reciprocal connections between high negative affectivity and (1) experiences of life stress; (2) deficiency cognition; (3) the phenomenon of "learned helplessness"; (4) the development of depression; (5) the breakdown of social bonds; and (6) the triggering of possible physiological responses like the depletion of brain catecholamine, the release of corticosteroids, the suppression of immune functioning, and ultimately the development of disease (Watson and Clark, 1984; Seligman, 1975; Brewin, 1985; Peterson and Seligman, 1984; Beck, 1967; Schultz, 1984; Ley and Freeman, 1984). **Table 2.1**, for example, illustrates the linkage between negative affect and disease. In spite of diversity of subjects, methods, and measures, a salient pattern emerges: A host

Table 2.1: The Relationship Between Negative Affect and Disease: Conclusions from 28 Papers on Affect and Disease

(adapted from Ley and Freeman, 1984, p. 57)

Disease	Affective State
Cancer	Depression
Cancer	Loss of hope
Leukemia	Depression, anxiety
Leukemia	Loss of significant other
Neoplasm	Hopelessness, despair
Cancer	Self-directed aggression
Cancer	Depression
Cancer	Hopelessness
Cancer	Hopelessness
Cancer	Depression, hostility
Lung cancer	Rigidity, repression, hostility, despair
Cancer	Decreased depression
Cancer	Lethargy, depression
Cancer	Affective disorder
Cancer	Affective disorder
Cancer	Affective disorder
Cancer	Repression of anger
'Physical illness'	Depression
Pernicious anemia	Depression
Hay fever	Helplessness
Asthma	Helplessness
Tuberculosis	Poor coping with stress
Coronary heart disease	High and frustrated aspiration
Coronary bypass, mortality	Hopelessness, depression
Psychosomatic illness	Hostility, depression, frustration, anxiety, helplessness
Various illnesses	Helplessness, hopelessness

of diseases, especially various forms of cancer, are associated with chronic and persistent negative images, expressed and embodied in feelings of helplessness and hopelessness. As one physician from Yale concludes, "cancer is despair experienced at the cellular level" (Siegel, 1986).

Probably the one finding that emerges most conclusively on the other side of the ledger is that while negative affectivity is notably linked to the phenomenon of learned helplessness, positive affect is intimately connected with social helpfulness. Somehow positive affect draws us out of ourselves, pulls us away from self-oriented preoccupation, enlarges our focus on the potential good in the world, increases feelings of solidarity with others, and propels us to act in more altruistic and prosocial ways (see Brief and Motowildo, 1986, for a review of altruism and its implications for management).

According to the work of Alice Isen and her colleagues, mood, cognition, and action form an inseparable triad and tend to create feedback loops of amplifying intensity. Positive affect, the evidence indicates, generates superior recall or access to pleasant memories (Isen, Shalker, Clark, and Karp, 1978); helps create a heightened sense of optimism toward the future (Isen and Shalker, 1982); cues a person to think about positive things (Rosenhan, Salovey, and Hargis, 1981); and, as a result, predisposes people toward acts that would likely support continued positive affect, like the prosocial action of helping others (Cunningham, Steinberg, and Grev, 1980; Isen and Levin, 1972; Isen, Shalker, Clark and Karp, 1978). In addition, positive affect has been associated with (1) increased capacity for creative problems solving (Isen, 1984); (2) more effective decision making and judgment (Isen and Means, 1983); (3) optimism and increased learning capacity—in particular, a sharpened capacity for perceiving and understanding mood-congruent or positive things (Bower, 1981; Clark and Isen, 1982).

In perhaps the most intriguing extension of this line of thought, Harvard's David McClelland has hypothesized a reinforcing set of dynamics between positive imagery, positive affect, prosocial action, and improved immune functioning. McClelland has even gone so far as to argue that merely watching an altruistic act would be good for the observer. He may be right.

For example, in one of McClelland's experiments, students were shown a film of Mother Theresa, a Nobel Peace Prize recipient, attending to the sick and dying poor in Calcutta. During the film, measures were taken of the student's immune functioning as defined by increases in salivary immunogobulin A (IgA—a measure of defense against respiratory infection and viral disease). In all cases, it was found that IgA concentrations immediately increased during the film and for some observers remained elevated for a period of up to one hour afterward.

It should be emphasized that these findings are controversial and that we are clearly in our infancy when it comes to really understanding the role of positive emotion as it relates to individual and collective well-being. The most important fact, however, is that studies like these are even being done at all. They represent a vital shift in research attention across a whole series of disciplines and reflect a change in the mood and spirit of our times. For example, as Brendan O'Regan (1983, p. 3) observes in relation to the field of psychoneuroimmunology, "We will no longer be focused on only the reduction of symptoms or the removal of something negative, and instead begin to understand health and well-being as the presence of something positive. It [the focus on the psychophysiology of positive emotion] may well be the first step in the development of what might be called an affirmative science... a science for humankind."

The Off-Balance Internal Dialogue

One of the more fascinating refinements of the notion of positive imagery comes from Robert Schwart's development of a cognitive ethology: the study within human systems of the content, function, and structure of the internal dialogue. Here the image is conceptualized as self-talk. Traced back to Plato and Socrates, cognition is seen as discourse that the mind carries on with itself. As in James's stream of consciousness, it is argued that all human systems exhibit a continuing "cinematographic-show of visual imagery" (Ryle, 1949) or an ongoing "inner newsreel" (Becker, 1971) that is best understood in the notion of inner dialogue.

The inner dialogue of any system—individual, group, organization, society—can be understood, argues Schwartz (1986), by categorizing its contents at the highest level of abstraction with respect to its functional role in achieving a specified aim. It is illustrated, for example, from a study of stressful medical procedure, that people may have thoughts that either impede the aim of the clinical intervention ("the catheter might break and stick in my heart"—negative image) or conversely may facilitate the goals of the care ("this procedure may save my life"—positive image). Hence, the inner dialogue functions as an inner dialectic between positive and negative adaptive statements, and one's guiding imagery is presumably an outcome of such an inner dialectic.

A whole series of recent studies have looked at this process, and results suggest a clear and definitive pattern of difference in the cognitive ecology of "functional" (healthy) versus "dysfunctional" (unhealthy) groups. **Table 2.2** presents data showing the ratios of positive to negative image statements for functional and dysfunctional groups across a series of seven independent studies. In all cases, there is a definite imbalance in the direction of positive imagery for those identified as more psychologically or socially functional. As can be seen, the functional groups are characterized by approximately a 1.7 : 1 ratio of positive to negative images. Mildly dysfunctional groups ("high" dysfunction was not studied) demonstrate equal frequencies, a balanced 1 : 1 internal dialogue.

Obviously, the sheer quantification of cognition has certain weaknesses. For one thing, it is clear that just one idea or image can transform the entire gestalt of a thousand others. But the findings do have meaning, especially when linked to other studies showing that images of hope or hopelessness can affect the body's innate healing system, its immune functioning, and other neurochemical processes. Especially disturbing are reports indicating that many of our children today are growing up in family settings where as much as 90 percent of the home's internal dialogue is negative, that is, what not to do, how bad things are, what was done wrong, who is to blame (Fritz, 1984).

But it is not just our children. In his powerful *Critique of Cynical Reason*, Peter Sloterdijk (1987) observes that the whole of postmodern society is living within an internal dialogue or cognitive environment of a universal, diffuse cynicism. As a predominant mindset of the post-1960s era, Sloterdijk takes the cynic not as an exception but rather as the average social character. It is argued that at both the personal and institutional levels, throughout our society there is a widespread disturbance of vitality, a bleakening of the life feeling, a farewell to defeated idealisms, and a sense of paralyzing resentment. Sociologically, Sloterdijk contends, today's cynicism is bureaucratic and it has become the predominant way of seeing things; psychologically, the modernist character is said to be a borderline melancholic, one who is able to keep the symptoms of depression under control and keep up appearances at both home and work. Our internal dialogue, as a society, Sloterdijk laments, has become more and more

Table 2.2: Ratios of Positive and Negative Thoughts for Functional and Dysfunctional Groups Across Seven Independent Studies

(reported in Schwartz, 1986)

Focus of Study	Cognitive Assessment	Functional M Positive	Negative	Ratio	Dysfunctional M Positive	Negative	Ratio
Assertiveness							
1. High vs. low	Inventory/ASST[a]	57.0	33.0	1.7:1	48.0	51.0	1:1.1
2. High vs. low	Inventory/ASST	59.0	35.0	1.7:1	48.0	51.0	1:1.1
3. High vs. low	Inventory/ASST-R[b]	41.8	35.8	1.8:1	38.0	33.2	1.1:1
Social Anxiety							
4. High vs. low Sample 2: Females & males combines	Inventory/SISST[c]	54.9	33.0	1.7:1	42.7	47.3	1:1.1
5. High vs. low socially anxious	Production/thought stening[d]	1.6	1.2	1.3:1	1.5	2.0	1:1.3
Test Anxiety							
6. High vs. low test anxious	Production/talking aloud	67.3	32.0	2.1	45.0	61.3	1:1.4
Self-esteem							
7. High vs. low self-esteem	Production/though sampling mean ratio	2.4	1.5 1.70:1	1.6:1	2.3 1:1.14	2.0	1.2:1

[a]Assertiveness Self-Statement Test.
[b]ASST-Revised generalizes to a broader range of assertive situations.
[c]Social Interaction Self-Statement Test.
[d]Scores averaged across high and low anonymity conditions.

morose, and nowhere, he argues (1987, p. 12), is this better exemplified than in the halls of academia: "The scenery of the critical intelligensia is… populated by aggressive and depressive moralists, problematists, 'problemholics,' and soft rigorists whose existential stimulus is no."

Whether one agrees with Sloterdijk or not, it is important to recognize that all human systems are conditioned by their internal dialogue. Our minds are bathed within any number of cognitive environments—family, school, church, play, and even the environments created by our research methods and problem-solving technologies—that provide cues to the ways we perceive, experience, and imagine reality.

So the question must therefore be asked, What kinds of cognitive environments maximize the "human possible"? What kinds of cognitive ecologies are we generating, and why? Can cognitive ecologies be developed, transformed, or enhanced? And what kinds of cognitive ecologies do we want?

The Positive Image as a Dynamic Force in Culture

As various scholars (for instance, Markley, 1976; Morgan, 1987) have noted, the underlying images held by a civilization or culture have an enormous influence on its fate. Ethical values such as "good" or "bad" have little force, except on an abstract level, but if those values emerge in the form of an image (for example, good = St. George, or bad = the Dragon), they suddenly become a power shaping the consciousness of masses of people (Broms and Gahmberg, 1983). Behind every culture there is a nucleus of images—the "Golden Age," "child of God," "Enlightenment," "Thousand-Year Reign of Christ," or "New Zion"—and this nucleus is able to produce countless variations around the same theme.

In his sweeping study of Western civilization, the Dutch sociologist Fred Polak (1973) argues essentially the same point concerning the heliotropic propensity of the positive image. For him (1973, p. 19), the positive image of the future is the single most important dynamic and explanatory variable for understanding cultural evolution: "Any student of the rise and fall of cultures cannot fail to be impressed by the role played in this historical succession of the future. The rise and fall of images of the future precedes or accompanies the rise and fall of cultures. As long as a society's image is positive and flourishing, the flower of culture is in full bloom. Once the image begins to decay and lose its vitality, however, the culture does not long survive."

For Polak, the primary question then is not how to explain the growth and decay of cultures, but how to explain the successful emergence or decay of positive images. Furthermore, he asks, how do the successive waves of optimism and pessimism or cynicism and trust regarding the images fit into the cultural framework and its accompanying dynamics? His conclusions, among others, include:

1. Positive images emerge in contexts of "influence-optimism" (belief in an open and influenceable future) and an atmosphere that values creative imagination mixed with philosophical questioning, a rich emotional life, and freedom of speech and fantasy.

2. The force that drives the image is only part cognitive or intellectual; a much greater part is emotional, esthetic, and spiritual.

3. The potential strength of a culture could actually be measured by the intensity, energy, and belief in its images of the future.

4. The image of the future not only acts as a barometer but actively promotes cognition and choice and in effect becomes self-fulfilling because it is self-propelling.

5. When a culture's utopian aspirations die out, the culture dies: "where there is no vision, the people perish" (Proverbs 29:18). Of special note here, anthropologists have shown that certain tribes have actually given up and allowed themselves to die when their images of the future have become too bleak. Ernest Becker (1971) notes the depopulation of Melanasia earlier in this century as well as the loss of interest by the Marquesan Islanders in having children. In the second case it appears that the islanders simply gave up when, in the face of inroads from white traders and missionaries, everything that gave them hope and a sense of value was eroded.

On this final point, Polak was intrigued with the following conclusion: Almost without exception, everything society has considered a social advance has been prefigured first in some utopian writing. For example Plato's Politeia opened the way, shows Polak, for a series of projections that then, via Thomas More's Utopia, had an impact on England's domestic and foreign policy. Similarly, Harrington's Oceana had immediate impact on France through the work of Abbé Sieyès, who used Harrington's model as a framework for his Constitution de l'An VII (about 1789). Later, these themes were "eagerly absorbed" by John Adams and Thomas Jefferson and emerged in a variety of American political institutions, not to mention the Declaration of Independence. While the word utopia has, in our society, often been a derogatory term, the historical analysis shows utopia to be, in Polak's words (1973, p. 138) "a powerhouse": "Scientific management, full employment, and social security were all once figments of a utopia-writer's imagination. So were parliamentary democracy, universal suffrage, planning, and the trade union movement. The tremendous concern for child-rearing and universal education, for eugenics, and for garden cities all emanated from the utopia. The utopia stood for the emancipation of women long before the existence of the feminist movement. All the concepts concerning labor, from the length of the work week to profit sharing (and sociotechnical systems design and QWL), are found in utopia. Thanks to the utopists, the twentieth century did not catch humanity totally unprepared."

Metacognition and Conscious Evolution of Positive Images

To the extent that the heliotropic hypothesis has some validity—that human systems have an observable tendency to macrodeterministically evolve in the direction of those "positive" images that are the brightest and boldest, most illuminating and promising—questions of volition and free agency come to the fore. Is it possible to create our own future-determining imagery? Is it possible to develop our metacognitive capacity and thereby choose between positive and negative ways of construing the world? If so, with what result? Is the quest for affirmative competence—the capacity to project and affirm an ideal image as if it is already so—a realistic aim or merely a romantic distraction? More important, is it possible to develop the affirmative competence of a large collectives, that is, of groups, organizations, or whole societies affirming a positive future together?

With the exception of the last question (there just has not been enough research here), most of the available evidence suggests quite clearly that affirmative competence can be learned, developed, and honed through experience, disciplined practice, and formal training.

Reviews on this topic, for example, are available in the areas of athletics and imagery, psychotherapy and imagery, imagery and healing, hypnosis and imagery, imagery and sexual functioning, and others related to overall metacognitive capacity (see Sheikh, 1983, for ten excellent reviews on these subjects).

In the case of athletics, as just one example, imagery techniques are fast becoming an important part of all successful training. In Superlearning, Ostrander (1979) discusses the mental methods used by Soviet and Eastern European athletes who have had such success in the Olympics in recent decades. Similarly, Jack Nicklaus's book Golf My Way (1974) offers a compendium of mental exercises to sharpen the affirmative function. For Nicklaus there is an important distinction to be made between a negative affirmation (for example, an image that says "don't hit it into the trees") and a positive affirmation (for instance, "I'm going to hit it right down the middle of the fairway"). Here again we find that the whole body, just like a whole culture, responds to what the mind imagines as possible. The important lesson, according to Nicklaus, is that affirmative competence can be acquired through discipline and practice and that such competence may be every bit as important to one's game as sheer physical capability.

Recent experimental evidence confirms this view and suggests something more: It is quite possible that the best athletes are as successful as they are because of a highly developed metacognitive capacity of differential self-monitoring. In brief, this involves being able to systematically observe and analyze successful performances (positive self-monitoring) or unsuccessful performances (negative self-monitoring) and to be able to choose between the two cognitive processes when desired. Paradoxically, while most in our culture seem to operate on the assumption that elimination of failures (negative self-monitoring) will improve performance, exactly the opposite appears to hold true, at least when it comes to learning new tasks. In one experiment, for example, Kirschenbaum (1984) compared a set of bowlers who received lessons on the components of effective bowling to those who did not receive the lessons (controls) and to groups who followed the lessons with several weeks of positive self-monitoring or negative self-monitoring (that is, they videotaped performances, edited out the positive or negative, and then selectively reviewed the corresponding tapes with the appropriate groups). As predicted, the positive self-monitors improved significantly more than all the others, and the unskilled bowlers (average of 125 pins) who practiced positive self-monitoring improved substantially (more than 100 percent) more than all other groups. Since then, these results have been replicated with other athletic activities such as golf, and evidence repeatedly indicates that positive self-monitoring significantly enhances learning on any task and is especially potent in the context of novel or poorly mastered tasks.

Some Implications for Management: Toward a Theory of the Affirmative Organization

> *We are some time truly going to see our life as positive, not negative, as made up of continuous willing, not of constraints and prohibition.*
>
> —*Mary Parker Follett*

That was a judgment of one of the great management prophets of the early 1940s who, in moving out of step with her time, prefigured virtually every new development in organizational thought and practice. Today, her ideas do not seem quite as strange as they once must have been. As we have seen in our overview of the placebo effect, Pygmalion dynamic, positive emotion, imbalanced inner dialogue, and positive self-monitoring, as well as the role of utopian imagery in the rise and fall of cultures, scholars are recognizing that the power of positive imagery is not just some popular illusion or wish but an expression of the mind's capacity for shaping reality. A theory of affirmation is emerging from many quarters. Admittedly its findings are still limited; unifying frameworks are lacking, and generalization across levels of analysis and disciplines makes for unintelligible and often confusing logic.

Nevertheless that knowledge—limited though it is—has important practical implications for organizations and management. In the rest of this discussion, I hope to push the current perspective onward by offering an exploratory set of propositions concerning what might be called the affirmative basis of organizing. When translated from the various disciplines into organizationally relevant terms, the emerging "theory of affirmation" looks something like this:

1. Organizations as made and imagined are artifacts of the affirmative mind. As understanding of organizational life requires an understanding of the dynamic of the positive image as well as the process through which isolated images become interlocked images and of how nascent affirmations become guiding affirmations. The starting point for a theory of affirmation is simply this: When it comes to understanding organizational existence from the perspective of human action, there is no better clue to a system's overall well-being than its guiding image of the future. In the last analysis, organizations exist because stakeholders who govern and maintain them carry in their minds some sort of shared positive projection about what the organization is, how it will function, and what it might become. Although pos-

itive imagery (in the form of positive thinking, utopian visions, affirmation, and the like) has not been paraded as a central concept in organizational and management thought, it can be usefully argued that virtually every organizational act is based on some positive projection on the part of the individual or group. Organizational birth itself, to take just one example, is impossible in the absence of some affirmative projection. But positive or negative, enabling or limiting, conscious or unconscious — all action is conditioned by the fact that we live in an anticipatory world of images. These guiding images are not detailed objectives but are paintings created with a larger brush stroke. They encompass many aspects of organizational life that mission statements, corporate strategies, or plans alone do not reveal. Just as it has been observed that the rise and fall of images of the future precede or accompany the rise and fall of societies, it can be argued that as long as an organization's image is positive and flourishing, the flower of organizational life will be in full bloom.

2. No matter what its previous history is, virtually any pattern of organizational action is open to alteration and reconfiguration. Patterns of organizational action are not automatically fixed by nature in any blind microdeterminist way—whether biological, behavioral, technological, or environmental. There is no such thing as an inevitable form of organization. There are no "iron laws." While affected by microdeterminist factors, existing regularities that are perceived are controlled by mentalist or "macro" factors exerting downward control. Just as in the Pygmalion dynamic reviewed earlier, organizations are genetically constituted socially in and through the images born in transaction among all participants. In this sense, existing regularities that are observed depend not on some dictate of nature but on the historically and contextually embedded continuities in what we might call (1) the prophetic image—expectancies and beliefs about the future; (2) the poetic image—imagined possibilities or alternatives of what might be; (3) the normative image—ideological or value-based images of what should be. When organizations continue to hold the same expectations and beliefs; when they continue to envision the same possibilities or alternatives; or when they continue to project the same conventional values, norms, or ideologies—it is under these macrodeterminist conditions that continuities in structures and practices will in fact be found.

3. To the extent that organizations' imaginative projections are the key to their current conduct, organizations are free to seek transformations in conventional practice by replacing conventional images with images of a new and better future. To a far greater extent than is normally assumed, organizational evolution is isomorphic with the mental evolution of images. In many respects, it can usefully be argued that organizations are limited primarily or even only by (1) their affirmative capacities of mind, imagination, and reason, and (2) their collective or coaffirmative capacity for developing a commanding set of shared projections among a critical segment of stakeholders.

In regard to the latter point, it can be argued further that the guiding image of the future exists deep within the internal dialogue of the organization. The image is not, therefore, either a person-centered or a position-centered phenomenon; it is a situational and interactional tapestry that is a public "property" of the whole rather than of any single element or part. While such things as executive vision and charismatic leadership may be understood as parallels to what I am talking about, their emphasis on the "Great Man" leads them to seriously understate and miscast the complex cooperative aspect of an organization's guiding image of the future. When it comes to collective entities like groups, organizations, or even whole societies, we must emphatically argue that the guiding image of the future does not, even metaphorically, exist within some individual or collective mass of brain. It exists in a very observable and tangible way in the living dialogue that flows through every institution, expressing itself anew at every moment.

4. Organizations are heliotropic in character in the sense that organizational actions have an observable and largely automatic tendency to evolve in the direction of positive imagery. Positive imagery and hence heliotropic movement is endemic to organizational life, which means that organizations create their own realities to a far greater extent than is normally assumed. As we have seen in the placebo, Pygmalion, and self-monitoring studies, the positive image carries out its heliotropic task by generating and provoking image-consistent affirmative cognition, image-consistent emotion, and self-validating action. Hence, it can be argued that positive images of the future generate in organizations (1) an affirmative cognitive ecology that strengthens peoples' readiness and capacity to recall the positive aspects of the past, to selectively see the positive in the present, and to envision new potentials in the future; (2) it catalyzes an affirmative emotional climate, for example, of heightened optimism, hope, care, joy, altruism, and passion; and (3) it provokes confident and energized action (see Weick, 1983, on this third point).

   Another aspect of the heliotropic hypothesis is that it predicts the following: When presented with the option, organizations will move more rapidly and effectively in the direction of affirmative imagery (moving toward the light) than in the opposite direction of negative imagery (moving against the light or toward "overpowering darkness"). Existing in a dynamic field of images, it can be argued that organizations move along the path of least resistance (Fritz, 1984) toward those images that are judged to represent the organization's highest possibilities — those images that are the brightest, most purposeful, or most highly valued. Positive images whose prophetic, poetic, and normative aspects are congruent will show the greatest self-fulfilling potential.

5. Conscious evolution of positive imagery is a viable option for organized systems as large as global society or as small as the dyad or group. Also, the more an organization experiments with the conscious evolution of positive imagery the better it will become; there is an observable self-reinforcing, educative effect of affirmation. Affirmative competence is the key to the self-organizing system. Through both formal and informal learning processes, organizations, like individuals, can develop their metacognitive competence—the capacity to rise above the present and assess their own imaginative processes as they are operating. This enhances their ability to distinguish between the affirmative and negative ways of construing the world. The healthiest organizations will exhibit a 2 : 1 or better ratio of positive-to-negative imagery (as measured through inner dialogue), while less healthy systems will tend toward a 1 : 1 balanced ratio. Similarly, it can usefully be argued that positively biased organizational monitoring (with selective monitoring and feedback of the positive) will contribute more to heliotropic movement than either neutral (characterized by inattention) or negative organizational monitoring (with a focus on problems or deficiencies). This effect, we would expect based on studies in athletics, will be more pronounced in situations where the affirmative projection is of a novel or complex future and where the tasks or actions required to enact the images are not yet fully tested or mastered.

The more an organization experiments with the affirmative mode, the more its affirmative and heliotropic competence will grow. This is why, in many organizations that have experimented with it, people have come to believe that organizationwide affirmation of the positive future is the single most important act that a system can engage in if its real aim is to bring to fruitation a new and better future. An image that asserts that the future is worth living for will, as William James ([1895] 1956) argued, provoke those actions that help create the fact. While not every future can be created as locally envisioned, there is always a margin within which the future can be affected by positive affirmation. The size of this margin can never be known a priori. Put another way, an organization will rarely rise above the dominant images of its members and stakeholders; or as Willis Harman (1988, p. 1) hypothesizes, "perhaps the only limits to the human mind are those we believe in."

6. To understand organizations in affirmative terms is also to understand that the greatest obstacle in the way of group and organizational well-being is the positive image, the affirmative projection that guides the group or the organization. Theorist Henry Wieman (1926, p. 286) gave a clear description of the seeming paradox involved here many years ago in his comparative analysis of Religious Experience and Scientific Method: "We are very sure that the greatest obstacle in the way of individual growth and social progress is the ideal [affirmative projection] which dominates the individual or group. The greatest instrument of achievement and improvement is the ideal, and therefore our constant failures, miseries, and wickedness are precisely due to the inadequacy of our highest ideals. Our ideals have in them all the error, all the impracticability, all the perversity and confusion that human beings that themselves erring, impractical, perverse and confused, can put into them. Our ideals are no doubt the best we have in the way of our constructions. But the best we have is pitifully inadequate. Our hope and full assurance…[are] that we can improve our ideals. If we could not be saved from our ideals, we would be lost indeed."

One of the ironies of affirmation is that it partially cripples itself in order to function. By definition, to affirm means to "hold firm." As we have seen, it is precisely the strength of affirmation, the degree of belief or faith invested, that allows the image to carry out its heliotropic task. So when our institutions are confronted with repetitive failure and amplifying cycles of distress; when time and energies are expended on such issues as compliance, discipline, obedience, motivation, and the like; or when almost every "new" surefire problem-solving technique does little but add a plethora of new problems—in every one of these cases the system is being given a clear signal of the inadequacy of its "firm" affirmative projections. To repeat, our positive images are no doubt the best we have, but the best is often not responsive to changing needs and opportunities. The real challenge, therefore, is to discover the processes through which a system's best affirmations can be left behind and better ones developed. For if we could not be saved from our best affirmative projections, "we would be lost indeed."

7. Organizations do not need to be fixed. They need constant reaffirmation. More precisely, organizations as heliotropic systems need to be appreciated. Every new affirmative projection of the future is a consequence of an appreciative understanding of the past or the present. Up to this point we have examined the nature of the positive image-positive action relationship but have said nothing about the mental artistry by which guiding images—prophesies, possibilities, and normative values—are in fact generated. We seem to have become preoccupied with the question

of "how to translate intention into reality and sustain it" (see for example Bennis and Nanus, 1985) and have ignored what is perhaps the more essential question.

An earlier set of writings (Cooperrider and Srivastva, 1987; Cooperrider, 1986) described a process of knowing that was preeminently suited to the task of providing both the data and mental inspiration through which human systems can fashion new affirmative projections on a dynamic and continuous basis. It was argued that appreciative inquiry is based on a "reverence for life" and is essentially biocentric in character: It is an inquiry process that tries to apprehend the factors that give life to a living system and seeks to articulate those possibilities that can lead to a better future. More than a method or technique, the appreciative mode of inquiry was described as a means of living with, being with, and directly participating in the life of a human system in a way that compels one to inquire into the deeper life-generating essentials and potentials of organizational existence.

As this concept relates specifically to leadership, an important clue to the meaning of executive appreciation is found in Isaiah Berlin's (1980, pp. 14–15) account of Winston Churchill's leadership during England's darkest hour:

> In 1940 he [Churchill] assumed an indomitable stoutness, an unsurrendering quality on the part of his people.... He idealized them with such intensity that in the end they approached his ideal and began to see themselves as he saw them: "the buoyant and inperturbable temper of Britain which I had the honour to express"—it was indeed, but he had the lion's share in creating it. So hypnotic was the force of his words, so strong his faith, that by the sheer intensity of his eloquence he bound his spell upon them until it seemed to them that he was indeed speaking what was in their hearts and minds. Doubtless it was there; but largely dormant until he had awoken it within them.

> After he had spoken to them in the summer of 1940 as no one else has ever before or since, they conceived a new idea of themselves.... They went forward into battle transformed by his words... He created a heroic mood and turned the fortunes of the Battle of Britain not by catching the [life-diminishing] mood of his surroundings but by being impervious to it, as he had been to so many of the passing shades and tones of which the life around him had been composed.

Churchill's impact and the guiding images he helped create were the result of his towering ability to cognitively dissociate all seeming impossibilities, deficiencies, and imperfections from a given situation and to see in his people and country that which had fundamental value and strength. His optimism, even in Britain's darkest moment, came not from a Pollyanna-like sense that "everything is just fine" but from a conviction that was born from what he, like few others, could actually see in his country: "Doubtless it was there; but largely dormant until he had awoken it."

In almost every respect the cognitive and perceptual process employed by Churchill, like many great executives, was that of the artist. The appreciative eye we are beginning to understand apprehends "what is" rather than "what is not" and in this represents a rigorous cognitive ability to bracket out all seeming imperfections from that which has fundamental value. For as the poet Shelly suggests, appreciation "makes immortal all that is best and most beautiful in the world.... It exalts the beauty of that which is most beautiful.... It strips the veil of familiarity from the world, and lays bare and naked sleeping beauty, which is in the spirit of its forms" (in Cooperrider and Srivastva, 1987, p. 164).

But this is only part of the story: Appreciation not only draws our eye toward life, but stirs our feelings, excites our curiosity, and provides inspiration to the envisioning mind. In this sense, the ultimate generative power for the construction of new values and images is the apprehension of that which has value. Nietzsche once asked of appreciation, "Does it not praise? Does it not glorify? Does it not select? Does it not bring 'that which is appreciated' to prominence? In all this, does it not strengthen or weaken certain valuations?" (in Rader, 1973, p. 12).

No one has expressed this more effectively than the artist Vincent van Gogh, who, in a letter to his brother (in Rader, 1973, p. 10), spelled out what could actually be an entire leadership course on the relationship between appreciation and the emergence of new values:

> I should like to paint a portrait of an artist friend, a man who dreams great dreams, who works as the nightingale sings, because it is in his nature. He'll be a fine man. I want to put into my picture of appreciation, the love I have for him. So I paint him as he is, as faithfully as I can. But the picture is not finished yet. To finish it, I am now the arbitrary colorist. I exaggerate the fairness of the hair; I come even to use orange tones, chromes, and pale lemon-yellow. Behind the head, instead of painting the ordinary wall of the mean room, I paint infinity, a plain background of the richest, intensest blue that I can contrive—and by this simple combination of the bright head against the rich blue background, I get a mysterious effect, like a star in the depths of an azure sky.

Like Churchill, van Gogh began with a stance of appreciative cognition. He viewed his friend through a loving and caring lens and focused on those qualities that "excited his preference" and kindled his imagination. The key point is that van Gogh did not merely articulate admiration for his friend: He created new values and new ways of seeing the world through the very act of valuing. And again, as Nietzsche (in Rader, 1973, p. 12) has elaborated: "valuing is creating: hear it, ye creating ones! Valuation is itself the treasure and jewel of valuating things."

In contrast to the affirmative projection that seeks certainty and control over events, the appreciative eye actually seeks uncertainty as it is thrown into the elusive and emergent nature of organizational life itself. Appreciation is creative rather than conservative precisely because it allows itself to be energized and inspired by the voice of mystery. As an active process of valuing the factors that give rise to the life-enhancing organization, appreciation has room for the vital uncertainty, the indeterminancy that is the trademark of something alive. In this sense, too, it differs from affirmation in that it is not instrumental. It does not have the capability of shaping the world closer to preexisting wants because it tends, in the end, to transform those wants into something very different from that which was originally affirmed. Executive appreciation, then, represents the capacity to rediscover in organizations what Bruner refers to as the "immensity of the commonplace" or what James Joyce terms the "epiphanies of the ordinary" (see Bruner, 1986, p. 198). Appreciation, as Churchill must have understood, is the mental strength that allows a leader to consciously peer into the life-giving present, only to find the future brilliantly interwoven into the texture of the actual.

8. The executive vocation in a postbureaucratic society is to nourish the appreciation soil from which affirmative projections grow, branch off, evolve, and become collective projections. Creating the conditions for organizationwide appreciation is the single most important measure that can be taken to ensure the conscious evolution of a valued and positive future. The "how" of appreciative inquiry is beyond

the scope of this discussion. But a number of final thoughts can be offered on the organizational prerequisites of appreciation. These comments stem from the experiences with a number of systems that have actually experimented with appreciative inquiry on a collective and organizationwide basis.

First, it is clear that the appreciative process has been most spontaneous and genuine in relatively egalitarian systems—organizations committed to an ideology of inclusion, consent, and coevolution (Srivastva and Cooperrider, 1986). Put more strongly, experience suggests that the creative power of appreciation will never be realized in a world that continues to place arbitrary restrictions or constraints on speech and action. It is the realm of action, not mind, that is the preeminent basis of those creative images that have the power to guide us into a positive future.

Second, experience indicates that if pursued deeply enough, appreciative inquiry arrives at a dynamic interpersonal ideal. It arrives at knowledge that enlarges our sense of solidarity with other human beings and provides an ever-expanding universe of examples and images concerning the possibilities for a more egalitarian future.

We are infants when it comes to our understanding of appreciative processes of knowing and social construction. Yet we are beginning to see that the power of appreciation rests with its self-reinforcing and self-generative capacity. Through appreciation of organizational life, members of an organization learn to value not only the life-enhancing organization but also learn to affirm themselves. As new potentials for inquiry are revealed and experienced within the "student," new insights are made available and shared with others in the organization. As sharing occurs, the inquiry becomes a joint process of knowing—others are invited to explore and question their own ideals or affirmative projections. Through dialogue, new knowledge and new images of possibility are constantly being made available. And while such knowledge is always felt as an interruption in the status quo, it is valued and turned into a heliotropic project because it represents a joint creation of a world that corresponds to the jointly imagined projection of human and social possibility.

Resources for Getting Appreciative Inquiry Started

An Example OD Proposal

David L. Cooperrider

"Appreciative Inquiry involves a paradigm shift, that will vitally transform, for example, how mergers or diversity intiatives are approached. The key, early on, is to prioritize several areas where there will be a high value-added contribution and, in those areas, take the appreciative approach to the hilt."

OVER THE PAST several years people have been asking more and more for practical tools that will help them transform their OD consulting practice away from the diagnostic problem-solving approaches toward more appreciative inquiry methods. One of the most common requests (when I do workshops on Appreciative Inquiry) is for examples of proposals – proposals that set the stage for OD contracting. This article presents a "composite picture" of several actual proposals that have led to major OD work. The "AMX" proposal represents the best of several projects that combine Appreciative Inquiry and Future Search. The corporate names used in this composite proposal are fictitious.

What I like most about the "whole system" change process spelled out here is that it completely lets go of problem solving. In my view, the problem solving paradigm, while once incredibly effective, is simply out of sync with the realities of today's virtual worlds. Problem solving is painfully slow (always asking people to look backwards historically to yesterday's causes); it rarely results in new vision (by definition we say something is a problem because we already implicitly assume some idea, so we are not searching to create new knowledge of better ideals, we are searching how to close gaps); and, in human terms, problem solving approaches are notorious for generating defensiveness (it is not my problem but yours).

Organizations are centers of human relatedness, first and foremost, and relationships thrive where there is an appreciative eye – when people see the best in one another, when they can share their dreams and ultimate concerns in affirming ways, and when they are connected in full voice to create not just new worlds but better worlds. Douglas McGregor was convinced of the power of positive assumptions about human beings. The AMX proposal is an example of an OD proposal that, in practical ways, mobilizes the appreciative process to the fullest extent I know how The proposal was written the week Congress passed legislation that would deregulate the telecommunications industry, changing the rules that guided the industry for over 60 years. AMX, one of the organizational giants, was literally in chaos with thousands being laid off. Facing the largest whole system transformation in their corporate history, the CEO asked, "How can we connect everyone to the adventure of creating the new century telecommunication organization?

Cooperrider, D. L. (1996). Resources for getting appreciative inquiry started: An example OD proposal. *Organization Development Practitioner* ,Vol. 28. 23-33.

THE AMX CONNECTS! PROPOSAL

Accelerating Organizational Learning For Winning the New Century

Background

During the past several years, AMX has positioned itself to take advantage of what may prove to be the greatest single business opportunity in history: the creation and management of the Information Superhighway Part of this positioning has been the clear articulation of the new strategic "ABC" vision and reaffirmation of the goal of being the most customer responsive business in the industry Along with the vision has come action. There are literally hundreds of successful new initiatives – reengineering, product innovations, new alliances, public relations campaigns, employee empowerment strategies, etc. – all combining to give birth to the new AMX. The entire system is in the thick of fundamental organizational transformation, and exists in a world where the economic, technological, and regulatory foundations of the business have radically changed. It simply is not the same business it used to be.

Important questions, therefore, are many: How can leaders accelerate positive transformation where the proof corporate change is revolutionary in result and evolutionary in execution? How can people reduce the time lag between exciting organizational innovations (initiatives, large and small, that illustrate what the new-century AMX organization can and should look like) and organizational storytelling, sharing, advocacy and mass learning from those innovations? How will employees sustain, over a period of years, corporate confidence and faith in AMX's abilities to make fundamental change even in the midst of inevitable setbacks? How can AMX complement its problemsolving culture with an appreciative mind set that selectively sees, studies, and learns from every positive new development? Can AMX develop and reclaim an oral tradition of storytelling that connects people across corporate generations and that propels the speed and spread of good news? How can AMX leaders decisively connect people throughout the system to the Future Search, and engage everyone in a "can do" way as social architects of the new century organization – a transformed organizational entity that lives its vision in all its structures, systems, strategies, management behaviors, job designs, partnerships; everything that the company does.[1]

Purpose

- The mission of AMX Connects! is to accelerate positive whole system transformation by actively connecting people to the "ABC" vision through the practice of Appreciative Inquiry.

Objectives

- To bring the "ABC" vision alive for 67,000 people at AMX by engaging a critical mass of people in an Appreciative Inquiry into the most positive and compelling

---

1. According to recent surveys by Yankelovich, 85% of Americans have lost confidence in the future. People report little confidence that current institutions and leaders will do the job. They see the gap between promised rhetoric about a better future and the continued breakdown, in the present, of many systems. Likewise the negative discourse and storytelling which dominates the media, politics, and the popular culture at large, is associated with increased levels of apathy among young and old, cynicism, fear, discrimination, and other damaging behavior. What is happening throughout society obviously has a spill-over effect in our corporations. Especially during times of major transition, ways are needed to rebuild essential connections, to renew hope, and to reinvigorate human creativity and leadership at all levels.

organizational innovations, practices, and traditions that (1) best illustrate the translation of the "ABC" vision into transformational action and (2) provide an anticipatory glimpse into the kind of organization AMX should and might become in the new century.

- To deliver tangible follow-up to the 1995 Leadership Workshop (which builds on the momentum of the Aspen, Colorado success where 140 regional and corporate executives were introduced to the theory of Appreciative Inquiry), and tie together executive education with real-time organization transformation. By co-leading the Appreciative Inquiry/Future Search process at the regional and corporate levels, the "action learning" design will contribute as much to leadership development as it does to organization development.

- To augment AMX's problem solving culture with an appreciative mind set that provides a paradigm shift in ways of looking at managerial analysis of all kinds – e.g., new options for approaching organization analysis, customer focus groups, strategic planning methods, reengineering studies, employee surveys, performance appraisal processes, public affairs methodologies, diversity initiatives, benchmarking approaches, merger integration methods, and many others.

- To build an affirmative atmosphere of hope and confidence necessary to sustain, over the next several years, the largest whole-system transformation in the company's history

- To discover and pioneer connections between Appreciative Inquiry/Future Search Conference methodologies (often involving hundreds of people interactively) and the voice, video, and data capabilities of AMX's advanced teleconferencing technologies. The potential for building connection and commitment to the future directions of the company are enormous: corporate visioning, advocacy, and good news telling will not be isolated to a few technical gurus, senior visionaries, or communication messengers, but will engage potentially thousands. When it comes to bringing vision alive, process is just as important as product. People want to be listened to and to be heard. The large group conference methodologies discussed below are truly impressive in their ability to cultivate the thrill of being a valued member in the creation of new and exciting futures.

Leadership

- AMX Connects! will be led by President Sheldon Abrahms; Susan Taft, Vice President Public Affairs; John Williams, Vice President of Organization Development, and the 140 individuals involved with the recent Leadership Conference. David L. Cooperrider and Associates from Case Western Re- Resources for Getting Appreciative Inquiry Started: An Example OD Proposal serve University's Weatherhead School of Management will provide outside guidance.

Timing

- The appreciative organizational inquiry and learning process will be formally inaugurated in 1996 with a workshop on Appreciative Inquiry Participants will be the leadership group of 140 through 1996 and 1997. Appreciative Inquiry will be introduced and Future Search Conferences completed in every region of Operations. Results from each of these will form the basis of a synthesizing corporate-wide Future Search in the spring of 1998 and will culminate with a future report – Images of The New Century AMX Organization – to be issued by the '1think tank" group of 140.

THE ABC'S OF APPRECIATIVE INQUIRY

In a typical Appreciative Inquiry, the process will lead up to a major Future Search Conference, two or three days in length, where a whole organization or representatives of the whole (anywhere from 100 to 1,000 people) will come together to both construct images of the system's most desired future and to formulate creative strategies to bring that future about. Often, an organizational model like the 7-S framework will serve as a template for building "possibility propositions" in each of the key organizational design areas - for example, what will the ideal organizational structures or systems look like in the future (the conference organizers will specify how far into the future to think... usually 3-5 years out). The stages for bringing the whole thing off productively typically follow the ABC sequence:

A – Appreciative understanding of your organization (from the past to present);

B – Benchmarked understanding of other organizations (exemplary models to learn from); and

C – Creative construction of the future (sometimes called the Future Search Conference).

One possible design would be to launch, in each of the regions, a broad-based set of Appreciative Inquiry interviews leading to a regional Future Search conference. The design of the interviews would stress storytelling and study into the "ABC" vision in action – examples of being "the easiest company to do business with"; times when people feel truly "empowered", examples of new forms of "servant leadership"; illustrations of how AMX is "winning in the new world"; etc. All of these interviews would be done face-to-face by AMX managers and employees within the region. All the best quotes, stories, and illustrations would be compiled into a regional report and used to inspire a regionally based Future Search Conference into "AMX In the New Century: Images of Organizational Possibility". At the Future Search Conference, with 100 to 2,000 people, participants meet for two or three days to design the organization's most desired future and formulate creative strategies to bring that future about. The key product is a planning document made up of "possibility propositions" describing the collective hopes and dreams people feel inspired to bring about. In the search conference mode, people learn to think of the future as a condition that can be impacted and created intentionally out of values, visions, and what's technically and socially feasible. Such purposeful planning greatly increases the probability of making the desired future come alive. What is unique about the Future Search Conference method as described here is (1) its Appreciative Inquiry Foundation (often experienced as a liberating personal paradigm shift for people); and (2) the broad base of authentic participation that is demanded.

We live in a world of relentless economic and social change, based on 21st century technologies. Now we struggle to discover management methods equal to the complexity The power of Appreciative Inquiry and the whole system focus of Future Search combine, our experience shows, to both accelerate and sustain change. Transformation happens faster, at lower cost, and with more inspired collective follow-up than older, more piecemeal or fragmented approaches. Studies show that one well facilitated Future Search with "everybody" – a metaphor for a broad cross-section of stakeholders – will produce more whole systems learning, empowerment, and feelings of connection around business vision than hundreds of fragmenting small group meetings.

The Future Search Conferences, held in each of the regions, would then be capped off with a corporate-wide Future Search of the top 140, the leadership group and key stakeholders representing the whole. If held concurrently in each of the ten regions, the potential for linking up via teleconference for positive story-telling across regions might add a creative and powerful integrative dimension. Literally thousands could be involved in real-time inquiry and transformational planning around the "ABC" vision. Each Future Search would involve something like the following:

1. A conference coordinating committee at the regional level of 4-6 people would meet to plan dates, time, location, meals, group meeting tasks, and who should attend. The goal is to get ""the whole system"" in the room, or at least strong representation of all those that have a clear stake in the future of the organization. Often then, this includes people "outside" of the community members, partner rule is organization like customers, organizations, etc. The ground that whomever comes to the Future Search must be there for the whole meeting and has the opportunity for full voice in the deliberations.

2. Participants (from 100 to 1000 people) sit in groups of eight to ten, with flip chart paper or a chalkboard available. Depending on the focus and assigned tasks, groupings may vary during the conference. All output from small group discussion is recorded, all ideas are valid, and agreement is not required to get ideas recorded.

3. The conference has four or five segments, each lasting up to a half day Each segment requires that people (a) look at or build a data base; (b) interpret it together; (c) draw conclusions for action.

4. The first major activity focuses on macro-trends likely to affect the organization in the future. Each group is asked to make notes on significant events, changes, and trends they see merging by looking at each of the past three decades from three perspectives: significant changes and events that happened at the world, personal, and institutional/industry levels over each of the past three decades. Each table reports to the total group, and a facilitator notes trends. The total conference then interprets the most positive macro-trends – those trends that indicate opportunities for building a better organization, society, or industry Even the macro trends that appear negative or threatening often generate creative thinking on hidden opportunities or possibilities for creating the future people want.

5. The second major activity focuses on the appreciative analysis of the organization. Each group has a copy of the Appreciative Inquiry report that was compiled earlier, with quotes, stories, and comments from all the appreciative interviews. Three questions are then posed to each group: (a) What are the most outstanding moments/stories from this organization's past that make you most proud to be a member of this organization? (b) What are the things that give life to the organization when it is most alive, most effective, most in tune with it"s over-arching vision, etc. (make a list of up to ten factors)? and (c) Continuity: What should we try to preserve about our organization – values, traditions, best practices – even as we change into the future? Again, consensus is not needed as the results are displayed and discussed by the whole conference.

6. The third major activity focuses on the benchmark understanding of the best practices of other organizations. Each group is given the report from benchmarking studies and is asked to make a list of the most interesting or novel things being done in other organizations. The list should include things that are interesting, novel, or even controversial and provocative. The list is not an endorsement of any of the practices – it is simply a compilation of interesting or new ideas and practices. There is to be no discussion of whether or not to adopt the practices in the present organization. If benchmark studies have not been done as part of the

preconference Appreciative Inquiry process then group members should generate the list from things they have seen in other organizations have heard or read about. Reports are made to the whole conference and people are asked to comment on the most interesting or novel ideas.

7. The fourth major activity focuses on the future, especially it"s creative construction. New groups are formed and are given a half day to develop a draft of a preferred, possible future. The focus is on translating the business vision into inspired organizational vision. The focus is on the organizational dimensions of the future. Using a model like the 7-S model or a homegrown model of organizational design elements, groups develop a set of ""possibility propositions"" of the ideal or preferred future organization (3-5 years into the future).

8. The fifth major activity focuses on the next action steps. Groups are then asked to reflect on what has surfaced and, depending on the nature of the groupings, to make three lists of suggested action steps: commitments they want to make as individuals to move the vision forward; action steps their region, and work unit, might take; and things the organization as a whole might do. Action proposals are shared in a total group session and a steering committee is formed to discuss proposals for the total organization, prioritize themes, and prepare a report to be presented at the capstone Future Search.

WHOLE SYSTEM INVOLVEMENT

In a comprehensive study of successful habits of visionary companies, Stanford University researchers Jerry Porras and James Collins put it simply:

It's become fashionable in recent decades for companies to spend countless hours and sums of money drafting elegant vision statements, values statements, purpose statements, aspiration statements, mission statements, purpose statements, objective statements, and so on. Such pronouncements are all fine and good – indeed, they can be quite useful – but they are not the essence of a visionary company Just because a company has a ""vision statement"" (or something like it) in no way guarantees that it will become a visionary company! If you walk away from this book thinking that the most essential step in building a visionary company is to write such a statement, then you will have missed the whole point. A statement might be a good first step, but it is only a first step.

—Taken from *Built to Last*, 1994

Translating core vision into everything the company does requires ways of connecting everyone – evoking ownership, commitment, under-standing, involvement, and confidence in the vision"s promise. This proposal provides a do-able way to proceed: it is logistically possible and financially feasible to design a process where all of operations (67,000 people) are involved. Everyone, at a minimum, would be a participant in the Appreciative Inquiry as an interviewer, interviewee, or both. And up to 10,000 would participate in at least three other engaging activities of learning and doing: workshops on Appreciative Inquiry (one day long); conducting the interviews (doing 5-10 interviews); and one or more Future Search Conferences (three days in length). The working assumption, at the regional level, is that approximately 1,000 people would participate in a day long introduction to Appreciative Inquiry They would subsequently be charged with completing 5-10 interviews apiece, and then would serve as delegates to the regional Future Search Conference.

MEASURING FOR RESULTS

AMX Connects! will measure its results by asking how each step, and the whole process, achieves discrete, agreed upon objectives. This is a demanding approach that will force everyone involved to focus on how the method of Appreciative Inquiry actually affects the way people think, communicate, and act in relation to the process of whole system transformation. Some of the areas of expected impact include:

- Reduction in the time lag between organization innovations (innovations that are consistent with the "ABC" vision) and their spread throughout the corporation.
- The strengthening of a ""can do"" climate of hope and confidence in the corporation"s ability to manage the transition and realize its transformational goals.
- Significant increase in the corporation"s positive internal dialogue about the future (e.g.,less cynical and deficit oriented discourse; less fear; less negativity; more vocabularies of positive possibility; more rapid spread of good news developments).
- Development of a more appreciative leadership mindset and culture which provides managers with new options for dealing with corporate and customer surveys, re-engineering, strategic planning analysis, team-building, merger integration, performance appraisal and others.
- Significant increase in the feeling of connection to the corporation's "ABC" vision at all levels and regions of AMX Operations.

SUSTAINABILITY

The telecommunications industry is going through a profound change that involves reassessment of economic foundations, technological infrastructures, organizational forms and processes, and managerial mindsets. The whole-system transformation being called for is both comprehensive in scope and fundamental in nature. There are a number of things, therefore, that must not be overlooked. First, we must not overlook the reality of people"s resistance to such profound change – to even thinking about it – since it involves challenge to the inner assumptions which have become an inherent part of the culture and individual ways of constructing the "way things ought to be". Nor should we fail to note that the coming changes will bring about a great deal of fear and uncertainty; in fact, keeping down the fear is probably the greatest challenge of all, since only with low levels of fear can people see clearly and take the right actions. But perhaps most important is the need to address questions of sustainability What will make the appreciative inquiry/future search methodologies as outlined earlier more than just a one-time high? What will be done to sustain learnings at regional, corporate, and individual levels? Our own evaluations of Appreciative Inquiry and the evaluation studies of large group Future Search Conferences suggest the following five strategies for long term sustainability.[3]

---

3. See Wilmot, Tim (1995) "The Global Excellence in Management Program: A Two Year Evaluation of 25 Organizations Using Appreciative Inquiry" Case Western Reserve University For detailed analysis of large group methods and outcomes – from Ford Motor Company, First Nationwide Bank, SAS, Marriott, and Borning – see Jacobs, R. (1994) *Real Time Strategic Change: How to Involve an Entire Organization In Fast and Far Reaching Change*, San Francisco: BerrettKoeliler Publishers. For ten case studies of the Future Search methods see Weisbord, M. (1992) *Discovering Common Ground: How Future Search Methods Bring People Together To Achieve Breakthrough Innovation, Empowerment, Shared Vision, and Collaborative Action*, San Francisco: Berrett- Koehler

(1) **Skillbuilding: The Process of Organizational Transformation is a School for Leadership Development.** In many respects, there is really no such thing as organizational transformation, there is only individual transformation. Because of this, especially with the leadership group of 140, every major session will involve both organizational analysis and personal planning as well as skillbuilding modules around all the phases of appreciative inquiry and the methods of facilitating interactive, large group meetings. In GE"s recent whole system ""Workout Program"", for example, it was found that the most important outcome of the initial large group Workouts was managerial skill development – the Workout conference methodologies have become a way of life for almost two-thirds of the work units. Of course, Chairman and CEO John F Welch played a major role in making the new participatory methods a priority He was notorious in his surprise appearances at local Workout sessions and was consistent in his message: 'building a revitalized "human engine" to animate GE"s formidable 'business engine' "

(2) **Extending Appreciative Inquiry Into Change Efforts Where There Will Be High Value-Added.** Already there are plans being made by various AMX staff to use the appreciative methodologies to re-think and revitalize organization development practices like corporate surveys, customer focus groups, public affairs projects, etc. These efforts at extending Appreciative Inquiry should be made more systematic and priority driven. Our suggestions is that we should prioritize no more than five major extensions of Appreciative Inquiry – for example AI's contributions to merger integration methods, organizational surveys, process re-engineering, and diversity initiatives. Each of these efforts should be carefully documented and written up later in the form of a practitioner manual (e g, a merger integration manual, or a customer focus group manual). Appreciative Inquiry involves a paradigm shift that will vitally transform, for example, how mergers or diversity initiatives are approached. The key, early on, is to prioritize several areas where there will be a high value-added contribution and, in those areas, take the appreciative approach to the hilt.

(3) **Customized Regional Follow-up Consultation.** In preparation for the Future Search Conferences, and in response to needed follow-up at the regional level, there will be a consultant/facilitator team made up of internal AMX professionals (e.g., OD, HR, PA) and a specialist from Cooperrider and Associates. This consultant team will commit, up front, to ten days of consulting follow-up at the regional level to tailor-make a response to the initiatives generated at the Future Search Conferences. By definition, the customized response is unknown at this time, but our experience shows that the commitment to ten days of follow-up consultation is the single most important thing that can be done to ensure sustainability In a recent study of Appreciative Inquiry with 25 organizations, it has been found that ninety percent of the organizations are continuing with the appreciative methodologies, some two years after the start (see Wilmot, 1995). An essential attribute of the sustainability was that in each case, all ten days of promised follow-up consultations were in fact used. Likewise, the follow-up was completely at the initiative and request of the organizations themselves. Each organization had to "apply" in writing for the follow-up: what were the goals, what kind of support did they need facilitation, training, outside evaluation, retreat design, organization analysis, one-on-one personal counseling). The lesson is simple we must plan for sustainability from the beginning, and the commitment to the customized follow-up opportunity is critical.

(4) **Advanced "Internal Consultant " Learning Partnership.** Each year there will be two special sessions among all internal AMX change agents that are involved with Appreciative Inquiry and the Future Search Conferences. The learning partnership will deal with advanced theoretical and practice issues, and will use clinical/field-based modes of learning. The purpose will be to build internal skills and competencies, to build a support network among AMX units and regions, and to make good use of the program's evaluation studies for advanced professional development.

(5) **Appreciative Inquiry "On-line".** Already there have been discussions with specialists at AMX about how to accelerate the spread of innovations and good news storytelling by adding an Appreciative Inquiry protocol to the new AMX on-line suggestion program. An analogy here is useful: an ongoing Appreciative Inquiry will be to the "whole system transformation" what time-lapse photography is to the visible blossoming of an otherwise imperceptible flower. Putting Appreciative Inquiry on-line is a very exciting venture that has yet to be done anywhere. There is no question the time is ripe for this to happen; and it makes sense that it would be inaugurated at AMX, where leadership in the positive human impact of advanced technology lies at the forefront of the corporate mission. One way to introduce the on-line approach would be to conceive of the 67,000 interviews as mini-training sessions in Appreciative Inquiry After each interview, people would be given a short booklet with simple instructions on how to use the internal online "web page". Stories and new images would be made available on a continuous basis. An award could even be established for the stories that best anticipate and give a glimpse of the new AMX, living its vision today The implications of Appreciative Inquiry on-line are far reaching and exciting indeed. We are infants A when it comes to our understanding of the power of this kind of non-hierarchical information sharing and whole system dialogue. The results could be revolutionary.

In the course of developing the ideas described above, it has become clear that people at AMX have this hope that there's a little window of opportunity for really responding to a radically changed business environment. That window of opportunity, and the current season of hope being expressed, is going to last about as long as Sheldon Abrahms, in the early days of his new presidency, uses this occasion to boldly enroll everyone in the positive transformation. To make it all work we (as an internal/external team) will not only need to work collaboratively, responsively, and flexibly as a "learning organization," but we also will need to be united around a shared revolutionary intent.

CONCLUSION

The relational, large group, participatory methods outlined here fly in the face of old hierarchical, piecemeal problem-analytic approaches to change. Likewise the appreciative paradigm, for many, is culturally at odds with the popular negativism and professional vocabularies of deficit that permeate our corporations and society at large. Most important, however, there are people, many people throughout AMX, that feel the time has come to make the "positive revolution" happen. These are the individuals that are just waiting to step forward and lead. The constructive, creative, and indispensable voices of the new AMX already exist. But their critical mass has yet to be legitimized. AMX Connects is about mass mobilization, it is about the is in full voice. It is internal about systematic creation of an organization that is in full voice. It is about transformation of the corporation's dialogue. It is about creating, over the next several years of discovery and transition, a center stage for the positive revolutionaries.

Appreciative Inquiry Bibliography
(includes references cited within the handbook)

Aram, J. D. (1990). Appreciative Interchange: The Force that Makes Cooperation Possible. *Appreciative Management and Leadership: Revised Edition.* S. Srivastva and D. L. Cooperrider. Euclid, OH, Lakeshore Communications: 175-204.

Ashcraft, M (1998). *Fundamentals of Cognition.* Addison-Wesley-Longman. Reading, Massachusetts.

Assistance, V. T. (1996). *Appreciative Inquiry: An Approach to Organizational Analysis and Learning.* Rosslyn, VA, Volunteers in Technical Assistance.

Banaga, G. (1998). A Spiritual Path to Organizational Renewal. *Lessons from the Field: Applying Appreciative Inquiry.* S. Hammond and C. Royal. Plano, TX, Practical Press, Inc.: 260-271.

Barrett, F. J. and D. L. Cooperrider (1990). Generative metaphor intervention: A new approach for working with systems divided by conflict and caught in defensive perception. *Journal of Applied Behavioral Science* 26(2): 219-239.

Barrett, F., G. F. Thomas, et al. (1995). The central role of discourse in large-scale change: A social construction perspective. *Journal of Applied Behavioral Science* 31(3): 352-372.

Barrett, F. (1995). Creating appreciative learning cultures. *Organizational Dynamics* 24(2): 36-49.

Barrett, F. J. (1998). Creativity and improvisation in jazz and organizations: Implications for organizational learning. *Organization Science* 9(5): 605-622.

Barrett, F. (1999). Knowledge Creating as Dialogical Accomplishment: A Constructionist Perspective. *Social Creativity.* A. Montuori and R. Purser. Cresskill, NJ, Hampton Press. Vol. 1: 133-151.

Barrett, F. (2000). Cultivating an Aesthetic of Unfolding: Jazz Improvisation as a Self-organizing System. *The Aesthetics of Organization.* S. Linstead and H. Hopfl. London, Sage Publications: 228-245.

Barrett, F. (2000). Learning to appreciate the sublime: Don't knock the rock. *Between fathers and sons: Pivotal narratives in mens' lives.* R. Pellegrini and T. R. Sarbin. London, Sage Press.

Barrett, F. and R. Peterson (2000). Appreciative learning cultures: Developing competencies for global organizing. *Organization Development Journal* 18(2): 10-21.

Barros, I. and D. L. Cooperrider (2000). A story of Nutrimental in Brazil: How Wholeness, Appreciation, and Inquiry Bring out the Best in Human Organization. *Organization Development Journal* 18(pt. 2): 22-28.

Bergquist, W., K. Merritt, et al. (1999). *Executive Coaching; An Appreciative Approach.* Sacramento, CA, Pacific Soundings Press.

Bilimoria, D., D. L. Cooperrider, et al. (1995). A Call to Organizational Scholarship: The Organization Dimensions of Global Change: No Limits To Cooperation. *Journal of Management Inquiry* 4(1): 71-90.

Bilimoria, D., T. B. Wilmot, et al. (1996). Multi-Organizational Collaboration for Global Change: New Opportunities for Organizational Change and Development. *Research in Organizational Change and Development.* R. W. Woodman and W. A. Pasmore. Greenwich, CT, JAI Press. 9: 201-236.

Blair, M. (1998). Lessons From Using Appreciative Inquiry in a Planning Exercise. *Lessons from the Field: Applying Appreciative Inquiry.* S. Hammond and C. Royal. Plano, TX, Practical Press, Inc.: 186-214.

Booy, D. and S. Sena (2000). "Capacity Building using the Appreciative inquiry approach: The experience of world vision Tanzania." *Global Social Innovations, Journal of the GEM Initiative* 3(1): 4-11.

Bosch, L. (1998). Exit Interviews With an "Appreciative Eye". *Lessons from the Field: Applying Appreciative Inquiry.* S. Hammond and C. Royal. Plano, TX, Practical Press, Inc.: 230-243.

Bowling, C., J. Ludema, et al. (1997). Vision twin cities appreciative inquiry report. Cleveland, OH, Case Western Reserve University.

Bowling, C. J. (2000). Human cooperation: Appreciative processes for creating images of governance. *Department of Organizational Behavior.* Cleveland, Ohio, Case Western Reserve University.

Brittain, J. (1998). Do We Really Mean It? How We Change Behavior After the Provocative Propositions are Written. *Lessons from the Field: Applying Appreciative Inquiry.* S. Hammond and C. Royal. Plano, TX, Practical Press, Inc.: 216-229.

Browne, B. (1998). Imagine Chicago: A Study in Intergenerational Appreciative Inquiry. *Lessons from the Field: Applying Appreciative Inquiry.* S. Hammond and C. Royal. Plano, TX, Practical Press, Inc.: p. 76-89.

Buckingham, S. T. (1999). Leadership Skills in Public Health Nursing: An Appreciative Inquiry. Victoria, British Columbia, Royal Roads University: 67.

Bunker, B. B. (1990). Appreciating Diversity and Modifying Organizational Cultures: Men and Women at Work. *Appreciative Management and Leadership: The Power of Positive Thought and Action in Organizations.* S. Srivastva and D. L. Cooperrider. Euclid, OH, Lakeshore Communications: 126-149.

Bunker, B. B. and B. T. Alban (1997). *Large Group Interventions: Engaging the Whole System for Rapid Change.* San Francisco, CA, Jossey-Bass, Inc.

Burgoyne, E. and N. Lofaro (1999). Appreciative inquiry, Head Start Information & Publication Center; www.hskids-msc.org/infocenter/guides/ai_intro.htm.

Bushe, G. R. and T. Pitman (1991). Appreciative Process: A Method for Transformational Change. *OD Practitioner* 23(3): 1-4.

Bushe, G. R. (1995). Advances in Appreciative Inquiry as an Organization Development Intervention. *Organization Development Journal* 13(3): 14-22.

Bushe, G. R. and G. Coetzer (1995). Appreciative inquiry as a team-development intervention: A controlled experiment. *Journal of Applied Behavioral Science* 31(1): 13-30.

Bushe, G. R. (1997). Attending to others: Interviewing appreciatively. *Discovery and Design Inc.* Vancouver, B.C.

Bushe, G. R. (1998). Appreciative inquiry with teams. *Organization Development Journal* 16(3): 41-50.

Bushe, G. R. (2000). The appreciative self: Inspiring the best in others. *Clear Leadership: How outstanding leaders make themselves undertook, cut through organizational mush, and help everyone get real at work,* Davies-Black.

Bushe, G. R. (2001). Meaning making in teams: Appreciative inquiry with pre-Identity and post-identity groups. *Appreciative Inquiry: Applications in the Field.* F. Barrett, R. Fry, and D. Whitney.

Carter, L., A. Mische, et al. (1993). *Aspects of Hope: The Proceedings of a Seminar on Hope*. New York, NY, ICIS Center for a Science of Hope.

Chaffee, P. (1997). Unafraid of the light: Appreciative inquiry and faith communities. *Interfaith Center at the Presidio*. San Francisco, CA.

Chaffee, P. (1997). Ring of breath around the world: A report of the United Religions Initiative Global Conference. *United Religions, A Journal of the United Religions Initiative*. San Francisco. 4.

Chandler, D. (2001). AI Improves For-Profit Companies: Quantifiable Financial Results of Using AI. *AI Newsletter*. London: 7.

Coffey, A. and P. Atkinson, (1996). *Making Sense of Qualitative Data*, Newbury Park, CA: Sage Publications.

Collins, J. and J. Porras (1994). *Built to Last: Successful Habits of Visionary Companies*, New York, NY: Harper Business.

Cooperrider, D. L. (1986). Appreciative Inquiry: Toward a Methodology for Understanding and Enhancing Organizational Innovation. Department of Organizational Behavior. Cleveland, OH, Case Western Reserve University: 353.

Cooperrider, D. L. and S. Srivastva (1987). Appreciative inquiry in organizational life. *Research in organization change and development*. W. P. R. Woodman. Greenwich, CT, JAI Press. 1: 129-169.

Cooperrider, D. and S. Srivastva (1999). Appreciative inquiry in organizational life. *Appreciative management and leadership: Revised Edition*. S. Srivastva and D. L. Cooperrider. Euclid, OH, Lakeshore Communications: 401-442.

Cooperrider, D. and S. Srivastva (1999). The emergence of the egalitarian organization. *Appreciative management and leadership: Revised Edition*. S. Srivastva and D. L. Cooperrider. Euclid, OH, Lakeshore Communications: 443-484.

Cooperrider, D. L. and W. A. Pasmore (1991). "Global Social Change: A New Agenda for Social Science?" *Human Relations* 44(10): 1037-1055.

Cooperrider, D. L. (1999). Positive Image, Positive Action: The Affirmative Basis of Organizing. *Appreciative Management and Leadership: The Power of Positive Thought and Action in Organizations*. S. Srivastva and D. L. Cooperrider. Revised, Euclid, Ohio: Lakeshore Communications.

Cooperrider, D. L. and D. Bilimoria (1993). "The Challenge of Global Change for Strategic Management: Opportunities for Charting a New Course." *Advances in Strategic Management* 9: 99-141.

Cooperrider, D. L. (1995). Introduction to appreciative inquiry. *Organization Development*. W. French and C. Bell. Englewood Cliffs, NJ, Prentice Hall International.

Cooperrider, D. L. and T. Thachenkery (1995). Building the Global Civic Culture: Making Our Lives Count. *Global and International Organization Development*. P. Sorenson, T. C. Head, N. J. Mathys, J. Preston and D. Cooperrider. Champaign, IL, Stipes Publishing: 282-306.

Cooperrider, D. L., F. Barrett, et al. (1995). Social Construction and Appreciative Inquiry: A Journey in Organizational Theory. *Management and Organization: Relational Alternatives to Individualism*. D. Hosking, P. Dachler and K. Gergen. Aldershot, UK, Avebury Press: 157-200.

Cooperrider, D. L. (1996). The "Child" as Agent of Inquiry. *OD Practitioner* 28(1 & 2): 5-11.

Cooperrider, D. L. (1996). Resources for Getting Appreciative Inquiry Started: An Example OD Proposal. *OD Practitioner* 28(1 & 2): 23-33.

Cooperrider, D. L. (1996). Special Issue: OD and the global agenda. *The Organization Development Journal* 14(4).

Cooperrider, D. L. and G. S. Khalsa (1997). The Organization Dimensions of Global Environmental Change. *Organization and Environment* 10(4): 331-341.

Cooperrider, D. L. and S. Srivastva (1998). An Invitation to Organizational Wisdom and Executive Courage. *Organizational Wisdom and Executive Courage*. S. Srivastva and D. L. Cooperrider. San Francisco, CA, New Lexington Press.: 1-24.

Cooperrider, D. L. and D. Whitney (1999). When Stories have Wings: How "Relational Responsibility" Opens New Options for Action. *Relational Responsibility: Resources for Sustainable Dialogue*. S. McNamee and K. Gergen. Thousand Oaks, CA, Sage Publications: 57-64.

Cooperrider, D. L. and D. Whitney (1999). *Collaborating for Change: Appreciative Inquiry*. San Francisco, CA, Berrett-Koehler Communications, Inc.

Cooperrider, D. L. and D. Whitney (1999). Appreciative Inquiry: A Positive Revolution in Change. *The Change Handbook: Group Methods for Shaping the Future*. P. Holman and T. Devane. San Francisco, CA, Berrett-Koehler Publishers, Inc.: 245-261.

Cooperrider, D. L. and J. Dutton (1999). *The Organizational Dimensions of Global Change: No Limits to Cooperation*. Thousand Oaks, CA, Sage Publications.

Cooperrider, D. L., P. F. Sorensen, et al. (2000). *Appreciative Inquiry: Rethinking Human Organization Toward a Positive Theory of Change*. Champaign, IL, Stipes Publishing.

Cooperrider, D. (2000). Appreciative Inquiry in Action. *Global Social Innovations: Journal of the GEM Initiative* 1(3): entire issue. Entire issue dedicated to AI.

Cooperrider, D. (2000). An Appreciative Inquiry Conversation Guide: Creating a Small Forum in Which Leaders of the World Religions Can Gather in Mutual Respect and Dialogue. *Global Social Innovations, Journal of the GEM Initiative* 1(3): 23-26.

Covey, S., (1990). *The 7 Habits of Highly Effective People*, Simon & Schuster.

Cummings, T. G. (1990). The Role of Executive Appreciation in Creating Transorganizational Alliances. *Appreciative Management and Leadership: The Power of Positive Thought and Action in Organizations, Revised Edition*. S. Srivastva and D. L. Cooperrider. Euclid, OH, Lakeshore Communications: 205-227.

Cummings, L. L. and R. J. Anton (1990). The Logical and Appreciative Dimensions of Accountability. *Appreciative Management and Leadership: The Power of Positive Thought and Action in Organizations, Revised Edition*. S. Srivastva and D. L. Cooperrider. Euclid, OH, Lakeshore Communications: 257-286.

Curran, M. (1991). Appreciative inquiry: A third wave approach to OD. *Vision/Action*(December): 12-14.

Curran, M. and G. Work (1998). Creating Opportunities for Learning AI. *Lessons from the Field: Applying Appreciative Inquiry*. S. Hammond and C. Royal. Plano, TX, Practical Press, Inc.: 244-257.

DeKluyver, C. (2000). *Strategic Thinking: An Executive Perspective*, New York City, NY: Prentice Hall.

Elliott, C. (1999). *Locating the Energy for Change: An Introduction to Appreciative Inquiry*. Winnipeg, International Institute for Sustainable Development, University of Cambridge Publishers.

Foster, M. (1998). Imagine Dallas: Appreciative Inquiry for a Community. *Lessons from the Field: Applying Appreciative Inquiry*. S. Hammond and C. Royal. Plano, TX, Practical Press, Inc.: 90-100.

Frost, P. J. and C. P. Egri (1990). Appreciating Executive Action. *Appreciative Management and Leadership: The Power of Positive Thought and Action in Organizations, Revised Edition*. S. Srivastva and D. L. Cooperrider. Euclid, OH, Lakeshore Communications: 289-322.

Fry, R. E., F. Barrett, et al. (2001). *Appreciative Inquiry and Organizational Transformation: Reports from the Field*. Westport, CT, Quorum Books.

Fuller, C., T. Griffin, et al. (2000). "Appreciative Future Search: Involving the Whole System in Positive Organization Change." *Organization Development Journal* 18(2): 29-41.

Gergen, K. J. (1990). Affect and Organization in Postmodern Society. *Appreciative Management and Leadership: The Power of Positive Thought and Action in Organizations, Revised Edition*. S. Srivastva and D. L. Cooperrider. Euclid, OH, Lakeshore Communications: 153-174.

Gergen, K.J. (1991). *The Saturated Self*, Basic Books.

Gergen, K. J. (1994). *Realities and Relationships: Soundings in Social Construction*. Cambridge, MA, Harvard University Press.

Gergen, K. J. (1999). *An Invitation to Social Construction*. Thousand Oaks, CA, Sage.

Gergen, K. J., S. McNamee, et al. (2001). Toward Transformative Dialogue. *International Journal of Public Administration* 24(7): 679-709.

Gibbs, C. and S. Ackerly (1997). *United Religions Initiative global summit summary report*. United Religions Initiative Global Summit, San Francisco, CA.

Gibbs, C. (2002). The United Religions Initiative at Work: Interfaith Dialogue through Appreciative Inquiry, Sowing Seeds of Transformation, *Interfaith Dialogue and Peacebuilding*, Washington, D.C.: United States Institute of Peace.

Golembiewski, R. T. (1998). Appreciating Appreciative Inquiry: Diagnosis and Perspectives on How to Do Better. *Research in Organizational Change and Development*. R. W. Woodman and W. A. Pasmore. Greenwich, CT, JAI Press. 11: 1-45.

Golembiewski, R. T. (1999). Fine-Tuning Appreciative Inquiry: Two Ways of Circumscribing the Concept's Value-Added. *Organization Development Journal* 17(3): 21-28.

Golembiewski, B. (2000). Three Perspectives on Appreciative Inquiry. *OD Practitioner* 32(1): 54-58.

Gotches, G. and J. Ludema (1995). Appreciative Inquiry and the Future of OD. *Organization Development Journal* 13(3): 5-13.

GTE (1997). GTE Asks Employees to Start a Grassroots Movement to Make GET Unbeatable in the Marketplace. Dallas, TX, GTE: 15-19.

Hagevik, S. (2000). Appreciative Inquiry and Your Career. *Journal of Environmental Health* 63(1): 39, 44.

Hall, J. (1998). The Banana Kelly Experience: Strength-based Youth Development:. *Lessons from the Field: Applying Appreciative Inquiry*. S. Hammond and C. Royal. Plano, TX, Practical Press, Inc.: 114-125.

Hammonds, K., (July 2001). Leaders for the Long Haul, *Fast Company,* 56-58.

Hammond, S. (1998). What is appreciative inquiry? *The Inner Edge* 1(2): 36-27.

Hammond, S. A. (1998). *The Thin Book of Appreciative Inquiry.* Plano, TX, Thin Book Publishing Co.

Hammond, S. and C. Royal (1998). A follow-up to the thin book: Frequently asked questions. *Lessons from the field: Applying appreciative inquiry.* S. S.Hammond and C. Royal. Plano, TX, Practical Press, Inc.: Chapter 13.

Harman, W. W. (1990). Shifting Context for Executive Behavior: Signs of Change and Revaluation. *Appreciative Management and Leadership: The Power of Positive Thought and Action in Organizations.* S. Srivastva and D. L. Cooperrider. San Francisco, CA, Jossey-Bass Inc.: 37-54.

Head, R. L. and M. M. Young (1998). Initiating Culture Change in Higher Education through Appreciative Inquiry. *Organization Development Journal* 16(2): 65-72.

Head, R. (1999). School of Management. Cleveland, OH, Case Western Reserve University: 18-19.

Head, R. L. (1999). Appreciative Inquiry as a Team-Development Intervention for Newly Formed Heterogeneous Groups. *Organization Development.* Lisle, IL, Benedictine University: 131.

Head, T. C., P. F. Sorensen, et al. (2000). Is Appreciative Inquiry OD's Philosopher's Stone? *Appreciative Inquiry: Rethinking Human Organization Toward a Positive Theory of Change.* D. L. Cooperrider, P. F. J. Sorensen, D. Whitney and T. F. Yaeger. Champaign, IL, Stipes Publishing L.L.C.: 217-232.

Head, T. C. (2000). Appreciative Inquiry: Debunking the Mythology Behind Resistance to Change. *OD Practitioner: Journal of the Organization Development Network* 32(1): 27-32.

Hock, D. (1999). *Birth of the Chaordic Age.* San Francisco; Barrett and Koehler.

Holman, P., A. Paulson, et al. (1998). Creating a Healthy Hilltop Community: Coordinating Hospital Planning with the Needs of a Community. *Lessons from the Field: Applying Appreciative Inquiry.* S. Hammond and C. Royal. Plano, TX, Practical Press, Inc.: 62-73.

Hopper, V. L. (1991). An Appreciative Study of Highest Human Values in a Major Health Care Organization. *Department of Organizational Behavior.* Cleveland, Ohio, Case Western Reserve University: 186.

Hubbard, B. M. (1998). *Conscious Evolution: Awakening the Power of Our Social Potential.* Novato, CA, New World Library.

Johnson, P. C. and D. L. Cooperrider (1991). Finding a Path with Heart: Global Social Change Organizations and Their Challenge for the Field of Organizational Development. *Research in Organizational Change and Development.* R. W. Woodman and W. A. Pasmore. Greenwich, CT, JAI Press. 5: 223-284.

Johnson, P. and D. L. Cooperrider (1991). Global Integrity: Beyond Instrumental Rationality in Transnational Organizing. *Journal of Transnational Associations.*

Johnson, P. C. (1992). Organizing for Global Social Change: Toward a Global Integrity Ethic. *Department of Organizational Behavior.* Cleveland, OH, Case Western Reserve University: 478.

Johnson, S. and J. Ludema (1997). Partnering to Build and Measure Organizational Capacity: Lessons from NGOs Around the World. Grand Rapids, MI, Christian Reformed World Relief Committee (CRC): 190.

Jonas, H., R. Fry, and S. Srivastva (1989). The Office of the CEO: Understanding the Executive Experience, *Academy of Management Executive*, 3 (4).

Jones, D. A. (1998). A Field Experiment in Appreciative Inquiry. *Organization Development Journal* 16(4): 69-78.

Kaczmarski, K. and D. L. Cooperrider (1997). Constructionist leadership in the global relational age. *Organization and Environment* 10(3): 235-258.

Kaczmarski, K. M. and D. L. Cooperrider (1998). Constructionist Leadership in the Global Relational Age: The Case of the Mountain Forum. *The Organizational Dimensions of Global Change: No Limits to Cooperation:*. D. L. Cooperrider and J. E. Dutton. Thousand Oaks, CA, Sage Publications: 57-87.

Kanungo, R. N. and J. A. Conger (1990). The Quest for Altruism in Organizations. *Appreciative Management and Leadership: The Power of Positive Thought and Action in Organizations*. S. Srivastva and D. L. Cooperrider. Euclid, OH, Lakeshore Communications: 228-256.

Kaye, B. and B. Jacobson (1999). True Tales and Tall Tales: The Power of Organizational Storytelling. *Training & Development* 53(3): 44-50.

Kelm, J. (1998). Introducing the Appreciative Inquiry Philosophy. *Lessons from the Field: Applying Appreciative Inquiry*. S. Hammond and C. Royal. Plano, TX, Practical Press, Inc.: 160-172.

Khalsa, G. S. and K. M. Kaczmarski (1996). *The United Religions Initiative summit conference summary*. United Religions Initiative Summit Conference, San Francisco, CA.

Khalsa, G. S. and K. M. Kaczmarski (1997). Chartering and Appreciative Future Search. *Global Social Innovations: Journal of the GEM Initiative* 1(2): 45-52.

Khalsa, G. S. and D. S. Steingard (1999). The Relational Healing Dimension of Organizational Development: Transformative Stories and Dialogue in Life-Cycle Transitions. *Research in Organizational Change and Development*. W. A. Pasmore and R. W. Woodman. Stamford, CT, JAI Press, Inc. 12: 269-318.

Khalsa, G. S. (2000). The Pilgrimage Toward Global Dialogue: A Practical Visionary Approach. *Breakthrough News*: 8-10.

Khalsa, G. S. (2000). The appreciative summit conference: A case story of the United Religions initiative first global summit. Cleveland, OH.

Liebler, C. J. (1997). Getting Comfortable with Appreciative Inquiry: Questions and answers. *Global Social Innovations: Journal of the GEM Initiative* 1(2): 30-40.

Liebling, A., D. Price, et al. (1999). Appreciative Inquiry and Relationships in Prison. *Punishment & Society* 1(1): 71-98.

Livingston, J. (1999). The Human and Organizational Dimensions of Global Change. An Appreciative Inquiry Interview with Robert Golembiewski. *Organization Development Journal* 17(1): 109-115.

Lord, J. G. (1995). The Philanthropic Quest: A Generative Approach for Professionals Engaged in the Development Process. Cleveland, Ohio, Philanthropic Quest International.

Lord, J. G. (1998). The practice of the quest: Evolving a new paradigm for philanthropy and social innovation—A casebook for advancement professionals grounded in the quest. Cleveland, OH, Philanthropic Quest International.

Ludema, J., T. Wilmot, et al. (1997). Organizational hope: Reaffirming the constructive task of social and organizational inquiry. *Human Relations* 50(8): 1015-1052.

Ludema, J. (1997). Narrative inquiry: Collective storytelling as a source of hope, knowledge, and action in organizational life. *Department of Organizational Behavior.* Cleveland, OH, Case Western Reserve University.

Ludema, J. D. (2000). From deficit discourse to vocabularies of hope: The power of appreciation. *Appreciative inquiry: Rethinking human organization toward a positive theory of change.* D. L. Cooperrider, P. F. Sorensen, D. Whitney and T. F. Yaeger. Champaign, IL, Stipes Publishing L.L.C.: 265-287.

Ludema, J. D. (2000). *Leadership symposium 2000: Global staffing and retention - Appreciative inquiry report on global staffing and retention.* McDonald's worldwide convention, Orlando, FL.

Ludema, J. D., D. L. Cooperrider, et al. (2001). Appreciative Inquiry: The Power of the Unconditional Positive Question. *Handbook of Action Research: Participative Inquiry and Practice.* P. Reason and H. Bradbury. London, England, Sage Publications: 189-199.

Ludema, J.D., B. Mohr, D. Whitney, and T. Griffin (available Summer 2003). *The Appreciative Inquiry Summit: A Practitioner's Guide for Leading Positive Large-Group Change,* SanFrancisco, CA: Berrett-Koehler.

Luechauer, D. L. (1999). Applying Appreciative Inquiry Instead of Problem-Solving Techniques to Facilitate Change. *Management Development Forum* 2(1).

Mahé, S. and C. Gibbs. (2003) *Birth of a Global Community: Appreciative Inquiry as Midwife to the United Religions Initiative.* Euclid, OH: Lakeshore Communications.

Mann, A. J. (1997). An Appreciative Inquiry Model for Building Partnerships. *Global Social Innovations: Journal of the GEM Initiative* 1(2): 41-44.

Mann, A. J. (2000). Variations on a Theme: The Flexibility of the 4-D model. *Global Social Innovations: Journal of the GEM Initiative* 1(3): 12-15.

Mantel, M. J. and J. D. Ludema (2000). From Local Conversations to Global Change: Experiencing the Worldwide Web Effect of Appreciative Inquiry. *Organization Development Journal* 18(Part 2): 42-53.

McGehee, T. (200x). *WHOOSH: Business in the Fast Lane: Unleashing the Power of a Creation Company.* Cambridge, MA, Perseus Pub.

Mead, Margaret and her work on intergenerational learning, visit the Mead Centennial 2001, The Institute for Intercultural Studies at *www.mead2001.org.*

Mellish, L. (1998). Strategic Planning: Appreciative Inquiry in a Large-scale Change at an Australian University. *Lessons from the Field: Applying Appreciative Inquiry.* S. Hammond and C. Royal. Plano, TX, Practical Press, Inc.: 48-61.

Mellish, L. (2001). Appreciative Inquiry at Work. *AI Newsletter*(12): 8.

Mirvis, P. H. (1988). Organization Development: Part I - An Evolutionary Perspective. *Research in Organizational Change and Development.* W. A. Pasmore and R. W. Woodman. Greenwich, CT, JAI Press, Inc. 2: 1-57.

Mirvis, P. H. (1990). Merging of Executive Heart and Mind in Crisis Management. *Appreciative Management and Leadership: The Power of Positive Thought and Action in*

Organizations. S. Srivastva and D. L. Cooperrider. San Francisco, CA, Jossey-Bass Inc.: 55-90.

Mirvis, P. H. (1997). Soul work" in organizations. *Organization Science* 8(2): 193-206.

Mohr, B. J., E. Smith, et al. (2000). Appreciative Inquiry and Learning Assessment. *OD Practitioner* 32(1): 33-53.

Mohr, B. J. (2001). Appreciative Inquiry: Igniting Transformative Action. *The Systems Thinker* 12(1): 1-5.

Mohr, B. (2001). A Guide to Appreciative Inquiry. Waltham, MA, Pegasus.

Murrell, K. (1998). A Personal Cross Cultural Exile into Appreciative Inquiry. *Lessons from the Field: Applying Appreciative Inquiry*. S. Hammond and C. Royal. Plano, TX, Practical Press, Inc.: 272-281.

Muscat, M. (1998). The federal quality consulting group: Using the vision story process to rebuild an organization. *The Inner Edge* 1(2): 18-19.

Muscat, M. (1998). Imagine Chicago: Dreams and visions for a 'second city' of the future. *The Inner Edge* 1(2): 23-24.

Odell, M. (1998). Appreciative Planning and Action: Experience from the Field. *Lessons from the Field: Applying Appreciative Inquiry*. S. Hammond and C. Royal. Plano, TX, Practical Press, Inc.: 126-143.

Odell, M. (2000). "From Conflict to Cooperation: Approaches to Building Rural Partnerships." *Global Social Innovations, Journal of the GEM Initiative* 1(3): 16-22.

Olson, E. E. and G. H. Eoyang (2001). *Facilitating Organization Change: Lessons from Complexity Science*. San Francisco, Jossey-Bass/Pfeiffer.

Pages, M. (1990). The Illusion and Disillusion of Appreciative Management. *Appreciative Management and Leadership: The Power of Positive Thought and Action in Organizations*. S. Srivastva and D. L. Cooperrider. Euclid, OH, Lakeshore Communications: 353-380.

Pepitone, J. S. (1995). Appreciative Inquiry. *Future Training: A Roadmap for Restructuring the Training Function*. Dallas, TX, AddVantage Learning Press: 211-214.

Peterson, R. (1993). Design aid (TM): A Multimedia Tool for Appreciative Organization Design. *Organizational Development and Transformation*, California Institute of Integral Studies: 87.

Pinto, M. and M. Curran (1998). The Laguna Beach Education Foundation, Schoolpower: Using AI and Philanthropy to Improve Public Education. *Lessons from the Field: Applying Appreciative Inquiry*. S. Hammond and C. Royal. Plano, TX, Practical Press, Inc.: 16-30.

Polak, F. (1973). *The Image of the Future* (abridged by E. Boulding from the Dutch *Die Toekomst Is Verleden Tijd*). SanFrancisco, CA; Jossey-Bass.

Quinn, R. E. (2000). Appreciative Inquiry as a Method of Support. *Change the World: How Ordinary People Can Achieve Extraordinary Results*. San Fransico, CA, Jossey-Bass: 219-223, 245-246.

Quintanilla, G. L. (1999). An Appreciative Inquiry Evaluation of a Science Enrichment Program for Children and Youth: Preliminary Findings. *Department of Social Work*. San Diego, CA, San Diego State University.: 104.

Radford, A. (1998-2002). *Appreciative Inquiry Newsletter*.

Rafferty, T. M. (1999). Whose Children Are These? An Appreciative Inquiry, The Union Institute: 204.

Raimy, E. (1998). Precious Moments. *Human Resource Executive* 12(11): 1, 26-29.

Rainey, M. A. (1996). An Appreciative Inquiry into the Factors of Culture Continuity During Leadership Transition. *Organization Development Practitioner* 28(1 & 2): 34-41.

Robinson-Easley, C. A. (1999). The Role of Appreciative Inquiry in the Fight to Save Our Youth. Unpublished Doctoral Dissertation, Naperville, IL, Benedictine University.

Rosenthal, R. (1969). *Pygmalion in the Classroom.* Holt, Rinehart and Winston: New York.

Royal, C. (1994). The NTL diversity study: The use of appreciative inquiry to discover best experiences around diversity in a professional OD organization. Alexandra, VA, NTL Institute for Applied Behavioral Science.

Royal, C. (1996). Appreciative inquiry, Occasional Paper for the MacArthur Foundation.

Royal, C. (1996). Appreciative inquiry, community development, and sustainability, Occasional Paper for the MacArthur Foundation.

Royal, C. and S. Hammond (1998). Frequently Asked Questions: What Consultants Want to Know Most about AI. *Lessons From the Field: Applying Appreciative Inquiry.* S. Hammond and C. Royal. Plano, TX, Practical Press Inc.: 174-185.

Ryan, F. J., M. Soven, et al. (1999). Appreciative Inquiry: Using Personal Narratives for Initiating School Reform. *Clearing House* 72(3): 164-167.

Salter, C. (2000). We're Trying to Change World History. *Fastcompany.* November: 230.

Schiller, M. (1998). A Dialogue About Leadership & Appreciative Inquiry. *Organization Development Journal* 16(4): 79-84.

Schiller, M., B. M. Holland, et al. (2001). *Appreciative Leaders: In the Eye of the Beholder.* Taos, Taos Institute Publications.

Sekerka, L. and D. Cooperrider, (2001), The Appreciative Inquiry Conversation and its Impact on Affect, View of Self, and Creativity. Paper presented at the Academy of Management Annual Meeting, August 2001, Washington, DC.

Sekerka, L., D. Cooperrider, and J. Wilken, (2001) *An Appreciative Organizational Development Intervention: Positive Emotions Set the Stage for Change.* Poster session presented at the Positive Psychology Summit, October, 2001, Washington, DC.

Seligman, M. (1992). *Helplessness: On Development, Depression and Death.* W.H. Freeman: New York.

Sorensen, P. F. (1996). About This Issue: Appreciative Inquiry—A Contemporary Approach. OD Practitioner 28(1/2): 34.

Sorensen, P. F., L. A. Gironda, et al. (1996). Global organization development: Lessons from Scandinavia. *Organization Development Journal* 14(4): 46-52.

Sorensen, P. F. and T. F. Yaeger (1997). Exploring organizational possibilities: Appreciative inquiry. *Training Today*: 7-8.

Sorensen, P. F. and T. F. Yaeger (1998). A universal approach to change: Appreciative inquiry. *Training Today*: 7-8.

Sorensen, P. F., T. F. Yaeger, et al. (2000). Appreciative Inquiry 2000: Fad or Important New Focus for OD? *OD Practitioner* 32(1): 3-5.

Srivastva, S. and D. L. Cooperrider (1986). The emergence of the egalitarian organization. *Human Relations* 39(8): 683-724.

Srivastva, S. and F. J. Barrett (1986). Functions of Executive Power: Exploring New Approaches. *Executive Power*. S. Associates. San Francisco, CA, Jossey-Bass: 312-329.

Srivastva, S. and F. J. Barrett (1988). Foundations For Executive Integrity: Dialogue, Diversity, Development. *Executive Integrity: The Search for High Human Values in Organizational Life*. S. Srivastva. San Francisco, CA, Jossey-Bass: 290-319.

Srivastva, S. and F. J. Barrett (1990). Appreciative Organizing: Implications for Executive Functioning. *Appreciative Management and Leadership: The Power of Positive Thought and Action in Organizations*. S. Srivastva and D. L. Cooperrider. San Francisco, CA, Jossey-Bass, Inc.: 381-400.

Srivastva, S. and D. L. Cooperrider, Eds. (1999). *Appreciative Management and Leadership: The Power of Positive Thought and Action in Organizations*. Euclid, OH, Lakeshore Communications.

Srivastva, S., R. E. Fry, et al. (1999). Introduction: The Call for Executive Appreciation. *Appreciative Management and Leadership: The Power of Positive Thought and Action in Organizations*. S. Srivastva and D. L. Cooperrider. Euclid, OH, Lakeshore Communications: 1-33.

Srivastva, S., D. Bilimoria, et al. (1995). Management and organization learning for positive global change. *Management Learning* 26(1): 37-54.

Srivastva, S. and D. L. Cooperrider, Eds. (1998). *Organizational wisdom and executive courage*. San Francisco, CA, New Lexington Press.

Srivastva, S. and D. L. Cooperrider, Eds. (1999). *Appreciative Management and Leadership: The Power of Positive Thought and Action in Organizations, Revised Edition*. Euclid, OH, Lakeshore Communications.

Stavros, J. M. (1998). Capacity Building Using An Appreciative Approach: A Relational Process of Building Your Organization's Future. *Department of Organizational Behavior*. Cleveland, OH, Case Western Reserve University.

Stavros, J.M. (2000). *Northern and Southern Perspectives of Capacity Building Using an Appreciative Inquiry Approach*, Winter 2000, *Journal of Global Social Innovations*, Washington, DC.

Stavros, J.M. and A.K. Meda (2003). An Assisted Living Center: Cultivating the Positive Core Through Appreciative Inquiry, Paper presentation at the Southwest Academy of Management Annual Meeting in Houston, TX and Organization Development Institute Annual Conference in Williamsburg, VA.

Stewart, A. and C. Royal (1998). Imagine South Carolina: A Citizen's Summit and Public Dialogue. *Lessons from the Field: Applying Appreciative Inquiry*. S. Hammond and C. Royal. Plano, TX, Practical Press, Inc.: 102-113.

Strauss, A. and J. Corbin (1990). *Basics of Qualitative Research: Grounded Theory Procedures and Techniques*, Newbury Park, CA: Sage Publications.

Tenkasi, R. (2000). The Dynamics of Cultural Knowledge and Learning in Creating Viable Theories of Global Change and Action. *Organization Development Journal* 18(2): 74-90.

Thatchenkery, T. J. (1996). Affirmation as Facilitation: A Postmodernist Paradigm in Change Management. *OD Practitioner* 28(1/2): 12-22.

Vaill, P. B. (1990). Executive Development as Spiritual Development. *Appreciative Management and Leadership: The Power of Positive Thought and Action in Organizations.* S. Srivastva and D. L. Cooperrider. Euclid, OH, Lakeshore Communications: 323-352.

Watkins, J. M. and D. L. Cooperrider (1996). Organizational inquiry model for global social change organizations. *Organization Development Journal* 14(4): 97-112.

Watkins, J. M. and D. L. Cooperrider (2000). Appreciative Inquiry: A Transformative Paradigm. *OD Practitioner* 32(1): 6-12.

Watkins, J. M. and B. J. Mohr (2001). *Appreciative Inquiry: Change At the Speed of Imagination.* San Francisco, Jossey-Bass/Pfeiffer.

Webb, L. D. (1999). Appreciative Inquiry As a Way to Jump Start Change. *At Work: Creating a More Enlightened World of Business & Work* 8(2): 16-18.

Weisbord, M. (1994). *Discovering Common Ground,* San Francisco, CA: Berrett-Koehler.

Weisbord, M. and S. Janoff (2000). *Future Search: An Action Guide to Finding Common Ground in Organizations and Communities,* Second Edition, SanFrancisco, CA: Berrett-Kohler.

Whalley, C. (1998). Using Appreciative Inquiry to Overcome Post-OFSTED Syndrome. *Management in Education* 12(3): 6-7.

White, T. H. (1996). Working in interesting times. *Vital Speeches of the Day* 62(15): 472-474.

Whitney, D. (1996). Postmodern principles and practices for large scale organization change and global cooperation. *Organization Development Journal* 14(4): 53-68.

Whitney, D. and C. Schau (1998). Appreciative Inquiry: An Innovative Process for Organization Change. *Employment Relations Today* 25(1): 11-21.

Whitney, D. (1998). Let's change the Subject and Change Our Organization: An Appreciative Inquiry Approach to Organization Change. *Career Development International* 3(7): 314-319.

Whitney, D. and D. L. Cooperrider (1998). The appreciative inquiry summit: Overview and applications. *Employment Relations Today* 25(2): 17-28.

Whitney, D. and D. L. Cooperrider (2000). The appreciative inquiry summit: An emerging methodology for whole system positive change. *OD Practitioner* 32(1): 13-26.

Whitney, D. (2001). Postmodern challenges to organization development. *HRD Strategies for 2000 AD.*

Whitney, D., D.L. Cooperrider, M. Garrison and J. Moore, (2001). Appreciative Inquiry and Culture Change at GET: Launching a Positive Revolution, *Appreciative Inquiry and Organization Transformation,* Westport, CT: Quorum Books.

Whitney, D., D. L. Cooperrider, B. Kaplin and A. Trosten-Bloom. (2001). *Encyclopedia of positive questions, Volume I: Using AI to Bring Out the Best in Your Organization.* Cleveland, Lakeshore Communications.

Whitney D. and A. Trosten-Bloom, (2003). *The Power of Appreciative Inquiry: A Practical Guide to Positive Change,* SanFrancisco, CA: Barrett Kohler.

Williams, R. F. (1996). Survey Guided Appreciative Inquiry: A Case Study. *OD Practitioner* 28(1/2): 43-51.

Wilmot, T. B. and J. D. Ludema (1995). Odyssey into Organizational Hope. *Organizational Behavior: Experiences and Cases*. D. Marcic. Minneapolis/St. Paul, West Publishing Company: 109-112.

Wilmot, T. B. (1996). Inquiry & innovation in the private voluntary sector/Global Social Innovations. *Global Social Innovations: Journal of the GEM Initiative* 1(1): 5-12.

Wilson, T. (1995). "Imagine Shaping a Better Chicago". *Chicago Tribune*. Chicago, IL: 2.

Wishart, C. G. (1998). Toward a Language of Human Abundance: The Holistic Human Logic of Culturally Sustainable Development. *Department of Organizational Behavior*. Cleveland, OH, Case Western Reserve University: 278.

Woodman, R. W. and W. A. Pasmore, Eds. (1987). *Research in organizational change and development: An annual series featuring advances in theory, methodology and research*. Greenwich, CT, JAI Press.

Yaeger, T. (1999). Responses from Russia: An Appreciative Inquiry Interview with Konstantin Korotov, RODP. *Organization Development Journal* 17(3): 85-87.

Yballe, L. and D. O'Connor (2000). Appreciative Pedagogy: Constructing Positive Models for Learning. *Journal of Management Education* 24(4): 474-483.

Zemke, R. (1999). Don't fix that company! *Training* 36(6): 26-33.

Zemke, R. (2000). David Cooperrider: Man on a mission. *Training* 37(11): 52-53.

For more information on Appreciative Inquiry, please visit the following websites:

www.aiconsulting.org

www.aipractitioner.com – Ai Practitioner

www.avikus.net – Lifescapes

www.lakeshorepublishers.com/AI:bookstore

www.taosinstitute.net

www.thinbook.com

http://appreciativeinquiry.cwru.edu

Glossary

A

Affirmative competence—The organization draws on the human capacity to appreciate positive possibilities by selectively focusing on current and past strengths, successes and potentials.

Affirmative topic choice—The topics identified in the Discovery phase that guide the formation of the interview guide. It is a positive descriptive phase representing the organization's focus for change.

Anticipatory learning—A type of learning that creates positive images of the future

Anticipatory principle—A fundamental principle that says our positive images of the future lead our positive actions. This is the increasingly energizing basis and presumption of Appreciative Inquiry.

Appreciate—A verb that means, "to value something." It's the act of recognizing the best in the people or the world around us; affirming the past and present strengths, successes and potentials; to perceive those things that give life (health, vitality and excellence) to living systems. It also means to increase in value, e.g. the economy has appreciated in value. Synonyms: valuing, prizing, esteeming and honoring.

Appreciative Inquiry—The cooperative search for the best in people, their organizations, and the world around them. It involves systematic discovery of what gives a system "life" when it is most effective and capable in economic, ecological, and human terms.

Appreciative Inquiry Summit—A three-to-four-day Appreciative Inquiry intervention that seeks to gather the whole system in one room to collectively go through all phases of the 4-D cycle. This process can include hundreds to thousands of participants.

Appreciative interview—An interview that uncovers what gives life to an organization, department, or community when at its best.

Appreciative learning culture—An organizational culture that fosters and develops the following competencies to create an appreciative learning system: affirmative, expansive, generative and collaborative competencies.

Appreciative paradigm—A unique perspective of the organizational world that views organizations as mysteries to be embraced.

C

Capacity building—A relational process that builds an organization's future to pursue its vision, mission and goals and sustain its existence. This process pushes boundaries to develop and strengthen an organization and its people.

Chaordic organization—An organizational structure (such as Appreciative Inquiry Consulting, LLC) that allows its owners to be autonomous while at the same time connecting all of them around a compelling shared identity and meaningful purpose.

Co-construct—(co-create)—A term used to describe a collaborative construction of the organization's future state. It is developed out of social construction theory, which states human systems create their social reality by the words they speak.

Core competencies—These are the value capabilities that assist the organization in creating strength bases relative to key competition.

Change agent—This is a person adept in the art of reading, understanding and analyzing organizations as living, human constructions.

Collaborative competence—The organization creates forums in which members engage in ongoing dialogue and exchange unique perspectives.

Constructionist principle—A fundamental principle and belief in Appreciative Inquiry that says human knowledge and organizational destiny are interwoven. To be effective, organizations must be understood as human constructs.

Continuity—This is associated with the part of the Appreciative Inquiry process that seeks to maintain the best of the organization's history, image, and culture during the time of the organization's transformation into the future state envisioned by its stakeholders.

Continuity search—A search that seeks out and then preserves what the organization does best.

D

Deficit-based approach to problem solving—It begins with seeking out the problem, the weak link in the system. Then, diagnosis and alternative solutions are recommended. Appreciative inquiry challenges this traditional paradigm with an "affirmative" approach to embrace an organization's challenges in a positive light.

Design—This is phase three of the 4-D model in which participants create the provocative proposition by determining the ideal, "how can it be?" The organization's future is co-constructed. This is where the stakeholders work together to transfer the dreams.

Design elements—Those elements that are considered in the social architecture of the organization's future.

Destiny—This is phase four of the 4-D model in which participants continue to co-construct their preferred future by defining, "what will be?" Stakeholders begin the planning and implementation process to bring the dreams that have been designed to life. Stakeholders create action plans and assign responsibility commitments.

Discovery—This is phase one of the 4-D model, where participants inquire into the life-giving forces of the organization to begin to understand and build their positive core. Participants uncover and value the best of "what is?" This information is generated through the engaging appreciative interviews.

Distinctive competencies—A strength that gives an organization a superior advantage in the marketplace.

Discover, Dream, Design, Destiny—4-D cycle—This model displays the Appreciative Inquiry approach in four phases that is designed to meet the unique challenges of the organization and its industry.

- Discovery—Appreciating, "What gives life?"
- Dream—Envisioning Results, "What might be?"
- Design—Co-Constructing, "How can it be?"
- Destiny—Sustaining, "What will be?"

Dream—This is phase two of the 4-D model where participants dialogue and create the dream for the organization. A collective vision is defined as to "What might be?"

E

Expansive competence—The organization challenges habits and conventional practices, provoking stakeholders to experiment in the margins, make expansive promises that challenges them to stretch in new directions, and evoke a set of higher values and ideals that inspire them to passionate engagement.

F

Fateful—The words we choose and the questions we ask determine the events and answers we find.

Future search—A methodology created by Marv Weisbord and Sandra Janoff that allows for the whole system (stakeholders) to co-create the organization's future.

G

Generative competence—The organization constructs integrative systems that allow stakeholders to see the results of their actions, to recognize that they are making a meaningful contribution, and to experience a sense of progress.

Generative learning—The type of organizational learning that emphasizes continuous experimentation, systematic thinking and a willingness to think outside the limits of an issue.

H

Habitus mentalis— These are habitual styles of thought.

Heliotropic—A term that implies that people have an observable and largely "automatic" tendency to move in the direction of affirming images of the future.

I

Improvisational capacity—This is capacity to allow for change to happen with endless variation. Appreciative inquiry is not just one way of change; there are infinite ways for destiny phase to occur.

Indra's Net—A web of relationships that sparkle, nourish, and amplify. It is an ancient image of oneness and diversity.

Inner dialogue—A term used to describe the conversation that goes on within the mind of a person and within the collective mind of the organization. An organization's inner dialogue can typically be ascertained by listening to the informal communication channels within the organization.

Inquiry—A verb that describes the act of exploration and discovery. It also refers to the act of asking questions and of being open to seeing new potentials and possibilities. Synonyms: discovery, search, study and systematic exploration.

Interview guide—The primary data collection tool used during the Discovery phase of Appreciative Inquiry. Interview questions are determined based on the affirmative topic choice. These questions are open-ended and designed to elicit rich storytelling from the interviewee. It is also called: interview protocol.

L

Life-giving forces—Those elements or experiences within the organization's past and/or present that represent the organization's strengths when it is operating at its very best. A life-giving force could be a single moment in time, such as a particular customer transaction, or it could be large in scope. It can be any aspect that contributes to the organization's highest points and most valued experiences or characteristics.

M

Metaphor—This is an element or a figure of speech in which an expression is used to refer to something that denotes a suggested similarity. In Appreciative Inquiry, metaphors are used because they have the power to facilitate "meaning making" and generate a better understanding within the mind of the receiver and listener.

O

Open space technology—A process created by Harrison Owen that allows the stakeholder to discuss what they can and will do to contribute to the realization of the organizational dream as articulated in the provocative propositions. This technique can be used during the Design phase and Appreciative Inquiry summit.

Organization Architecture—This is the model for designing the organization's future. This is where the design elements are selected to create the ideal organization.

P

Paradigm—The generally accepted perspective of a particular discipline, theory or mindset at a given time.

Placebo effect—A process created in the twentieth century in which projected images, as reflected in positive belief, ignite a healing process that can be as powerful as conventional therapy.

Poetic principle—A fundamental principle and belief in the Appreciative Inquiry approach that says human organizations are like open books. The story of the system is constantly being co-authored and it is open to infinite presentations.

Positive core—This is what makes up the best of an organization and its people.

Positive image—positive action—An Appreciative Inquiry theory that posits the more positive and hopeful the image of the future, the more positive the present day action.

Problem-solving paradigm—A fundamental perspective that views organizations as problems to be solved.

Provocative propositions—Statements that bridge the best of "what is" with the organization's vision of "what might be." It becomes a written articulation of the organization's desired future state that is written in the present tense to guide the planning and operations in the future. Also known as possibility proposition and possibility statements.

Pygmalion effect—An area of research that provides empirical understanding of the relational pathways of the positive image-positive action dynamic.

S

Sense-making—A term from action-research that represents the analytical process within Appreciative Inquiry where the organization defines and learns about the change.

Simultaneity—A fundamental principle and belief within Appreciative Inquiry thought that recognizes that inquiry and change are not separate moments, but are simultaneous.

Social architecture—It addresses the design elements critical to an organization to support the positive core. The first step in the Design phase is to identify this architecture.

Systematic management—A style of management that uses a fixed and organized plan.

T

Theme identification—Part of the Dream phase of the Appreciative Inquiry process where participants identify important threads from the interview data and summary sheets that pinpoint life-giving forces within the organization.

Transformative—Having the power or tendency to transform. To change a system in nature, disposition, heart, character, or the like; to convert. Appreciative inquiry is a transformative process for any organization.

W

Whole System Change—A term used to refer to the ultimate goal of Appreciative Inquiry to transform an entire organization at one time. Methodologies used include AI Summits, Future Search and Open Space Technologies.

Wonder—rapt attention or astonishment at something awesomely mysterious or new to one's experience.

Index

Statement of Appreciative Inquiry Consulting

During the summer of 2001, the doors were opened to an exciting new global organization, Appreciative Inquiry Consulting, LLC (AIC). Co-owners of AIC are committed to **creating a positive revolution in change** and to discovering the positive core in our clients' systems. AIC's **purpose and principles** describe a way of being and of doing business in the world that is having a deep and lasting impact on organizations in the business, public, and social sectors.

Since spring of 1999, a small design team has been convening to lay the foundation for AIC in preparation for opening the doors to others who share the purpose and principles. AIC represents a new organizational form—sometimes called "chaordic." In this organizational form, AI consultants and practitioners join as an "AI Centre." The network of all of the centres around the world constitutes a loose alliance of those working with AI. Appreciative Inquiry Consulting, LLC, has been created so co-owners can exchange knowledge and practices; collaborate on projects of mutual interest; meet for practice sharing and conferences; and benefit from a common identity in creating marketing materials, products, and services.

The AIC web site showcases the work of AIC co-owners. It provides an evolving resource pool of designs, templates, working papers, protocols, and other artifacts of their collective work in AI. A small central office is available to field phone calls from those looking for AI practitioners and to coordinate a referral system to link practitioners throughout the network.

Co-ownership of AIC is open to all who share its purpose and principles. The web site lists the purpose and principles at *www.aiconsulting.org* and includes a description of the process for joining the positive revolution in change AIC stands for.

Appreciative Inquiry Consulting, LLC
"A Positive Revolution in Change"
5411 41st Street NW
Washington, DC 20015
Phone: 202-363-9292
Fax: 202-363-0038

About the Authors

Dr. David L. Cooperrider is professor and chair of the SIGMA Program for Human Cooperation and Global Action at the Weatherhead School of Management at Case Western Reserve University. He has served as researcher and consultant to a wide variety of organizations, including Allstate, Cap Gemini Ernst & Young, GTE-Verizon, Roadway Express, Nutrimental, World Vision, Cleveland Clinic, Imagine Chicago, American Red Cross, and United Religions Initiative. These projects are inspired by the Appreciative Inquiry (AI) methodology for which he is co-originator. He has been recipient of *Best Paper of the Year Awards* at the Academy of Management. GTE was awarded the 1998 Best Organization Change Program by ASTD.

David has designed a series of dialogues using AI with 25 of the world's top religious leaders, started in 1998 by His Holiness the Dalai Lama, who said, "If only the world's religious leaders could just know each other . . . the world will be a better place." Using AI, the group has held meetings in Jerusalem and at the Carter Center in Atlanta. David was recognized in 2000 as among "the top ten visionaries" in the field by *Training Magazine* and has been named in *Five Hundred People of Influence*. He is past president of the National Academy of Management's Division of Organization Development and a cofounder of the Taos Institute. He has lectured and taught at Stanford University, MIT, the University of Chicago, Katholieke University in Belgium, Pepperdine University, and others. David has published 7 books and authored over 40 articles and book chapters.

His wife Nancy is an artist; and his daughter and two sons are in high school in Chagrin Falls, Ohio. The AI Commons web site he helped create is *http://appreciativeinquiry.cwru.edu*. David's e-mail is DLC6@cwru.edu.

Dr. Diana Whitney, President of Corporation for Positive Change and co-Founder of the Taos Institute, is an internationally recognized consultant, speaker, and thought leader on the subjects of Appreciative Inquiry, positive change, and spirituality at work. She is the author of four books and dozens of articles, and chapters including *Appreciative Inquiry* with David Cooperrider, and *The Power of Appreciative Inquiry* with Amanda Trosten-Bloom. In addition, she has edited three collections on Appreciative Inquiry including: *Appreciative Inquiry and Organization Transformation*, and *Appreciative Inquiry: Rethinking Human Organization Toward a Positive Theory of Change*. Diana teaches and consults in the Americas, Europe, and Asia. She has lectured and taught at Antioch University, Case Western Reserve University, Ashridge Management Institute in London, Eisher Institute in India and others. She is a

Distinguished Consulting Faculty at Saybrook Graduate School and Research Center.

The focus of Diana's consulting is strategic planning, mergers, large-scale transformation, and service excellence. Her clients include British Airways, Hunter Douglas, Cap Gemini Ernst & Young, Accenture, GTE-Verizon, GE Capitol, Johnson & Johnson, Sandia National Labs, NY Power Authority, PECO, Veterans Affairs and the Department of Labor. Her work with GTE led to the 1998 Best Organization Change Award by ASTD. Diana served as a consultant to the United Religions Initiative, a global interfaith organization dedicated to peace and cooperation among people of different religions, faiths, and spiritual traditions. She lives in Taos, New Mexico and can be reached at diana@positivechange.org.

Dr. Jacqueline M. Stavros is associate professor at the Graduate College of Management, Lawrence Technological University, and principal in the Corporation for Positive Change. She is a trainer and consultant specializing in Appreciative Inquiry, strategic change, leadership, international marketing, cross-cultural communications and e-learning. She has been using Appreciative Inquiry to help her students and clients identify their positive core and opportunities for profitable growth. She works in a wide variety of industries: automotive, banking, information technology, education, health care, government, NGOs, and professional services. She has served as a consultant to ERIM International, General Motors, FCI Automotive, Small Business Development Center Network, Global Marketing Insights, Tendercare, and Tuffy Mufflers.

Her most recent presentations and publications include "Global Capacity Building Using Appreciative Inquiry" and "Appreciative Inquiry in Total Quality Action for AQP." She is currently researching and co-authoring two other books, **New Horizons in Strategy to Teach Your Organization to SOAR!** and **Lifescapes: An Appreciative Journey to a Preferred Future**. She is a member of the Positive Change Corps for Appreciative Inquiry and Education, Taos Institute, American Marketing Association, Organization Development Network, and North American Association of International Trade Educators. She lives with her husband Paul and two children, Ally and Adam, in Michigan and can be reached at jstavros@comcast.net.

The Power of Appreciative Inquiry

Diana Whitney and Amanda Trosten-Bloom

The Power of Appreciative Inquiry is a comprehensive and practical guide to using Appreciative Inquiry for strategic large-scale change. Written by pioneers in the field, the book provides detailed examples along with practical guidance for using AI in an organizational setting.

Paperback, 264 pages • ISBN 1-57675-266-7
Item #52667 $27.95

The Appreciative Inquiry Summit
A Practitioner's Guide for Leading Large-Group Change

James D. Ludema, Diana Whitney, Bernard J. Mohr, Thomas J. Griffin

The first book to provide a comprehensive practitioner's guide to the AI Summit—the preferred method when applying whole-scale change to large groups—*The Appreciative Inquiry Summit* provides step-by-step guidance for planning and running an AI Summit.

Paperback, 300 pages • ISBN 1-57675-248-8
Item #52488 $29.95

Collaborating for Change
Appreciative Inquiry

David L. Cooperrider and Diana Whitney

This handy booklet provides an overview of Appreciative Inquiry—a change strategy which supports full-voiced appreciative participation in order to tap an organization's positive change core and inspire collaborative action that serves the whole system.

Booklet, 46 pages • ISBN 1-58376-044-X
Item #6044X $8.95

Berrett-Koehler Publishers
PO Box 565, Williston, VT 05495-9900
Call toll-free! **800-929-2929** 7 am-9 pm Eastern Standard Time

Or fax your order to 802-864-7627
For fastest service order online: **www.bkconnection.com**

Encyclopedia of Positive Questions, Vol. 1

Using AI to Bring Out the Best in Your Organization

Diana Whitney, David L. Cooperrider,
Amanda Trosten-Bloom, and Brian S. Kaplan

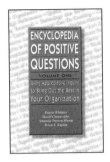

This timely book is composed of generic interview questions central to the "Discovery" phase of the Appreciative Inquiry process. This workbook on the power of positive questions has implications for every aspect of business—measurement systems, custom focus groups, quality management, team building, performance appraisal, surveys—indeed everywhere we ask questions or gather data related to positive change efforts.

ISBN: 1933403-055
212 pp
$18.95

Birth of a Global Community: Appreciative Inquiry in Action

The Story of the United Religions Initiative
Charles Gibbs and Sally Mahé

The birth of the United Religions Initiative (URI) is the story of how hundreds, then thousands of people across cultures, oceans, and faith traditions began to share a common call to make the world they live in more like the world they yearned for in their dreams. The book also tells the story of how an emergent processs of organizational change—the Appreciative Inquiry (AI) process—came along at just the right time to provide the engine for the new organization and its development.

ISBN: 1893435-423
384 pp
$24.95

Appreciative Management and Leadership Revised Edition

The Power of Positive Thought and Action in Organizations
Suresh Srivasta and David L. Cooperrider

"Based on the theory and practice of Appreciative Inquiry, Appreciative Management and Leadership offers a revolutionary alternative—a positive approach to organizing intended to unleash the entrepreneurial spirit of all organizational members and mobilize system-wide action in pursuit of a common purpose. This book is a "must read" for all thought leaders—chief executives, managers, change agents, scholars, and practitioners—who want to create and sustain vital organizations in a world of rapid change."

ISBN: 1893435-059
548 pp
$49.50

James D. Ludema
Professor of Organization Development
Benedictine University, Chicago, IL

Crown Custom Publishing, Inc.
Brunswick, OH

Appreciative Inquiry Handbook (w/CD)
Premium Edition

The First in a Series of AI Workbooks for Leaders of Change
David L. Cooperrider, Diana Whitney, and Jacqueline M. Stavros

The *AI Handbook* contains everything needed to launch any kind of AI initiative, from a one-hour introduction to AI to a complete two-day program. From abstract principles underlying AI to actual tools used in different settings, from detailed descriptions of AI interventions to practical tips to classic AI articles, the authors have amassed in one place, in workbook form, all of the introductory concepts, examples, and aids necessary to engage yourself and others in Appreciative Inquiry. The Premium Edition contains the illustrative CD-ROM.

ISBN:1893435-172
466 pp
$66.00 with CD

ISBN: 1933403-101
$45.00 (without CD)

Appreciative Inquiry Handbook
(Premium Edition) CD

PC Version
Windows 95/98/NT/2000 compatible

Contains a wealth of information to aid you in presenting this methodology to members of your own organization: the "4-D Diagram", Sample Interview Guides, Workshop agendas, AI PowerPoint slides, a set of original Classic articles, and more.

ISBN: 1893435-180
$30.00

Place your order by simply...

Calling toll free: **(877) 225-8820** from 8:30 a.m.–4:30 p.m., EST

Or by faxing at **(330) 225-9932**

Or email to **carl@crowncustompublishing.com**

Or visit us online at **www.crowncustompublishing.com**

Crown Custom Publishing, Inc.
Brunswick, OH